Creating Young Writers

Using the Six Traits to Enrich Writing Process in Primary Classrooms

SECOND EDITION

Vicki Spandel

WRITER IN RESIDENCE,
GREAT SOURCE EDUCATION GROUP

WITH A FOREWORD BY BARRY LANE

PEARSON

Boston ■ New York ■ San Francisco
Mexico City ■ Montreal ■ Toronto ■ London ■ Madrid ■ Munich ■ Paris
Hong Kong ■ Singapore ■ Tokyo ■ Cape Town ■ Sydney

This book is lovingly dedicated to all those teachers—primary students included—who are making magic happen in their classrooms.

EXECUTIVE EDITOR: Aurora Martínez Ramos
EDITORIAL ASSISTANT: Lynda Giles
MARKETING MANAGER: Danae April
PRODUCTION ADMINISTRATOR: Janet Domingo
EDITORIAL PRODUCTION SERVICE:
  Modern Graphics, Inc.

ELECTRONIC COMPOSITION: Modern Graphics, Inc.
COMPOSITION AND PREPRESS BUYER: Linda Cox
MANUFACTURING BUYER: Linda Morris
INTERIOR DESIGNER: The Davis Group
COVER DESIGNER: Joel Gendron

For related titles and support materials, visit our online catalog at www.ablongman.com.

ISBN 10: 0-205-53702-2
ISBN 13: 978-0-205-53702-0

Library of Congress Cataloging-in-Publication Data

Spandel, Vicki.
  Creating young writers : using the six traits to enrich writing process in primary classrooms / Vicki Spandel.—2nd ed.
      p. cm.
  Includes bibliographical references and index.
    ISBN 0-205-53702-2
    1. English language—Composition and exercises—Study and teaching (Primary) 2. Language arts (Primary) I. Title.
LB1528.S67 2008
372.62'3—dc22

2007017171

Printed in the United States of America

10 9 8 7 6 5 4 3 2 1   [CIN]   11 10 09 08 07

Contents

3 TEACHING TRAITS CONCEPTUALLY: INTRODUCTORY LESSONS   85

4 TRAIT BY TRAIT—MORE IDEAS FOR TEACHING   108

5 MAKING CHANGES: PORTFOLIOS, REVISING, REFLECTING, PUBLISHING   149

6 MODELING   181

7 LOVING BOOKS   195

Foreword

Years later, Louise wondered if she'd used the right rubric that night she decided to marry Neil.

The word *assessment* stems from the Latin verb *assidere*, to "sit beside." When we assess anything, we sit beside it and describe it. The best tools for assessing help us describe something with such insight that we come to share a common language and common understanding that drives both teaching and learning.

In our everyday life we assess things all the time. When I take my car to the auto mechanic to get the noisy muffler fixed, I listen for that pinging sound on the way home—and that's one way I assess the work. When my daughter insists she *did* in fact clean her room, I may offer a brief assessment based on the unmatched socks behind her door. Assessment can even help people reflect on how they managed to get themselves into their present situation. Consider Louise, for instance. . . .

When it comes to writing, the six traits offer us a sensible, thoughtful, helpful way to talk about words on the page. The forerunner to this book—*Creating Writers*—is not only the bible of six-trait writing, but reflects Vicki Spandel's unique ability to teach assessment in a way that drives and even inspires instruction. Her dozens of student samples and her close observations of master teachers light the way for other teachers to begin linking trait-based instruction to writing process and making the teaching of writing both joyful and effective.

With *Creating Young Writers*, Vicki's work now reaches primary classrooms—but why should we bother with assessment at primary levels? Isn't it enough that young students are writing? Must we rip their work off the refrigerator door and slice it apart? Well, the truth is that when it's done right, assessment celebrates writing, helping young writers value what they have done and repeat their success in later works. In *Creating Young Writers*, Vicki shows teachers how to look at any piece of writing and focus on the power and strengths within. The shared language of the craft she creates with terms like *organization*, *leads*, *fluency*, *detail*, and many others offers students and teachers both increased understanding of how writing works and a sense of control over that writing. Knowing the craft helps keep the ball in their court. It builds confidence—one of the best foundations for skill.

It's probably no surprise to those who know me that my favorite of the six traits is voice, the personal expression in a piece of writing, or—as a second grader once described it to me—"My tongue on the page!" Once a young writer recognizes the sound of his or her own voice, it's much easier to recognize the kind of impersonal voice that so often obscures meaning in a piece of writing. On a good day, a teacher may even overhear a student writer say, "You know, I like this story, but the first part doesn't sound like me. I don't hear my voice!" This kind of self-assessment (which applies to any of the six traits) will go much further than any grade or comment because it is fueled by the writer's own perception.

In my work teaching writing across the United States, I have seen first-hand the desire of young writers to be taken seriously, to be treated as young artists in the studio—not just students completing assignments. In *Creating Young Writers*, Vicki showcases the work of these young writers/artists, and encourages teachers to work alongside their students, in a writing workshop that features process, sharing, modeling, literature, writers' language, and positive feedback. The kind of atmosphere, in short, where assessment and instruction truly do sit side by side, each supporting the other.

In this book, you will find numerous samples of fiction and nonfiction books to help you and your students learn from master authors. In addition, you'll find practical writing lessons that combine traits with writing process, and numerous authentic student samples that show ideas, voice, fluency, and other features of strong writing emerging in the work of our very youngest writers. At a time in the United States where mandated testing has tempted too many of our veteran and first-year teachers to turn to formulaic writing instruction for quick answers, *Creating Young Writers* comes as a precious antidote: real writing instruction that can motivate students and boost test scores without deadening spirits.

Vicki Spandel is a writer who teaches writing. If you read her book carefully and follow its philosophy, you are likely to find yourself immersed in the world of writing, creating along with your students and going further as a writing teacher than you ever dreamed you could. As the title suggests, you will create a class of writers, and one important member of that class will be you.

Barry Lane

Preface

Almost as soon as *Creating Writers* (the parent text for this book) first made its debut in 1990, primary teachers began asking for a version specific to their needs—and no wonder. Beginning writers write and learn a bit differently. Their writing—especially that of our youngest writers, K and pre-K—may, at first, look like scribbles or collages of letters and letter-like shapes. It often incorporates art as well as text. But it has one thing in common with every piece of writing ever produced: It expresses the writer's voice and human spirit. It is the making of meaning.

From the first day that he or she picks up a pencil or crayon, the primary writer recognizes that writing has significance. It has power. Writing shapes lives, influences thought, changes laws, captures history, and takes readers into other worlds. Virtually nothing else we do can match what we achieve through writing. It should not surprise us that primary writers want to be a part of it all; what an opportunity for us! After all, most of the work, most of the effort, the insight, the recognition, and the achievement will come *from them*. We have only to provide a welcoming, safe environment in which they can work, strategies that support the writer's craft, modeling that lets them see how writing looks as it unfolds, and belief that they are indeed writers.

The truth is, they are writing in their heads from the very beginning. They are thinking of ideas and expressing them orally with remarkable voice and fluency. This is where writing begins—not with paper, but with something to say. As they recognize the power of capturing thoughts in written form, primary writers pay ever more attention to the world of print around them, writing at every opportunity, imitating with uncanny perception what they hear and see. We can help by sharing the literature that moves us, encouraging them to see that everything we need and hunger to know about writing well is right there, right in the very books that surround us. We just have to open them and look—and we can give them a language for thinking and speaking as writers. That's where the 6 traits—and this book—come in.

Six-trait-based writing began in 1984 as a model for assessment. It was developed by *teachers*—not a research organization, not a testing company, not a publishing house. By teachers. Teachers who wanted a way of assessing writing that would take them to the core of what makes writing work. More than 20 years ago, the teachers of Beaverton, Oregon (where the 6 traits originated) said that if they could get inside writing, figure out what makes writing effective and what creates roadblocks, they could teach it more effectively—at every grade level. The result was dramatic. Checklists, continuums, and rubrics exploded onto the writing scene, providing a bridge to writing success for students who suddenly had the tools to assess *themselves*. But perhaps the impact of the traits should not have surprised us so. Think about it. In what endeavor do we *not* need language to support us? We cannot learn anything from cooking to skiing to surgery without the aid of language. Language is empowering. Writer's language opens doors for students and changes their thinking forever. It gives them independence. Students who understand—and can talk about—such things as voice, strong verbs, fluency, free verse, imagery, sensory detail, leads, and conclusions see and hear literature differently. Their "sense" of good writing is awakened. They learn to "read" their own writing and develop an instinct for revision. And all this begins—*must begin*, in fact—at the primary level, where excitement for writing and capacity to learn and use language are at their peak. In case you think primary writers are not ready for trait-based writing, I hope that the examples within this book will persuade you to see it differently.

Because trait-based writing is based on the acquisition of language and a growing understanding of how writers work, it does not replace, but only enhances the writing process. The traits will enrich and expand your teaching without stepping on the toes of *any* of the good things you are already doing—such as reading aloud, conferring with students, modeling writing and revision, inviting students to share their writing, and so on. Every one of these strategies can benefit from the addition of a common language for talking and thinking about writing. This common vocabulary will enable your students to see strengths in their own or others' writing that previously went overlooked. When you tell them their voice is strong, their word choice makes sense, or their detail helps you picture what they are describing, they will know precisely what you mean—and they will know how to achieve it again.

Like the first edition, this text provides numerous student samples, K through grade 3, designed to help you recognize early signs of the traits as they might look in your own students' work. It also includes many lesson ideas and strategies for teaching the traits and trait language to even the youngest writers. New features of this edition include the following:

✔ *Many* new recommendations for books you can use as mentor texts with every trait
✔ Additional new samples from primary writers who continue to teach all of us
✔ Newly revised continuums that reflect what *young writers can do*—rather than focusing on what they cannot yet do in their writing
✔ Interactive activities and questions (at the close of *every chapter*) that will (I hope) encourage you to use this text within a study group or class
✔ New lessons for modeling and revision—and an even closer link to writing process

If the 6 traits of writing are new to you, skim through the book, and you are likely to feel right at home within a short time. These 6 traits—ideas, organization, voice, word choice, sentence fluency, and conventions—are familiar to anyone who writes or teaches writing. They are simply the basic qualities that make writing work. As a teacher, you can be sure you are working with these traits—or some of them—as you discuss writing with your students, write comments on their papers, read to them, or model writing for them. You cannot help it. You may call them by slightly different names, but you are using them all the same. So what I offer you in this book is *not* a new curriculum or program, but rather, a way of making your teaching—as *you* do it, with your voice, your style, your special technique—easier and more organized. Perhaps the writing samples I have included here will remind you of your own students' work, and you will hear echoes of the voice, the ideas, the words, and the rhythm of the students who write and learn with you. Welcome—and I hope you enjoy the journey as much as I have.

Acknowledgments

So many people have contributed to the making of this book that it is impossible to thank them all individually, but I wish to mention some whose work has most surely paved the way for me.

First of all, my deepest thanks to each of the student writers who contributed personal text and/or artwork to this project. Your work was magnificent, and gave me hours of pleasure. Just as with the first edition, it was impossible to include every piece—and just as with the first edition, every young writer whose work passed through my hands contributed to my understanding of writing, and of young writers. Thanks also to the many teachers and parents who granted me the extraordinary privilege of publishing their students' work. What a rare and special gift.

Very special thanks go to the highly talented Miss Olivia Perata, whose extraordinary art graces the cover of this edition. I am honored to share your work in this way, Olivia. Thank you for inspiring us all.

I also wish to thank Miss Noami Brautigam, whose remarkable collage art appeared on the cover of the first edition (where it garnered much attention). My deep apologies for the inadvertent spelling of Noami's name in that edition; it is my heartfelt wish that she receive full credit and recognition for her contribution. I also wish to thank Noami's mother, Beth Olshansky, for so generously sharing her daughter's artwork and writing, as well as numerous student samples and ideas based upon her research and innovative approach to using art in the teaching of writing. (Particular pieces inspired by Ms. Olshansky's work are cited at the conclusion of each chapter.) Beth Olshansky has developed two dynamic art-and-literature–based approaches to writing: *Picturing Writing: Fostering Literacy Through Art* and *Image-Making Within the Writing Process*, both designed to meet the needs of students with diverse learning styles (visual, verbal, and kinesthetic) through writing process, literature, and the use of hands-on art experiences. For more information on these programs, please visit www.picturingwriting.org.

I am infinitely grateful to Penny Clare (a former student of Beth's), who taught me so very much about the use of writing process and art in creating ideas, expanding thinking, and expressing thoughts. Because of you, Penny, I will never look at young writers' work the same way again.

In addition, thanks to *all* the teachers who allowed me to visit classrooms, to work with their students, and who shared their insights about the many ways there are to "make magic" within a primary writing environment. Special thanks to the incomparable Arlene Moore (my friend and colleague—and one of the best teachers I've ever had); the extraordinary Lois Burdett, whose wizardry with both Shakespeare and writing continues to amaze and entertain us all; Leila Naka and her talented daughter Allison Naka, through whose generous spirits I received both ideas and extraordinary samples from Allison's kindergarten writers; Judy Mazur, who has made 6-trait writing truly her own, and who consistently elicits phenomenal writing from her students; Julie Towne, who expects (and gets) wondrous writing from her kinder writers; and

Sammie Garnett, who (though she does not seem to appear in this book) is really behind every line. I also wish to acknowledge my appreciation to Ginnie Hoover, Linda Laws, Kim Gregory, Tommy Thomason and his wife Debby, Julie Ahrens, Jenny Wallace, Karen Ritchie, Barbara Kamrath, and the many other teachers who spent so much time helping me collect the samples of student writing and art without which this book would not have been possible. Special thanks to former Principal David Hanaike and the students of Pu'uhale Elementary School for so many wonderful writing samples.

Thank you also to Kathryn McCormick, video producer and photographer extraordinaire, who made possible the photographs that help show young student writers at work.

I would like to thank Rhea Vytlacil for reviewing this edition.

In addition, I wish to acknowledge my many colleagues and friends at Great Source Education Group, Wilmington, Massachusetts, who have been so supportive of my work and who will find this book, I hope, a wonderful complement to *Write Traits® Kindergarten: Bringing the Traits to Kinderwriters, The Write Traits Classroom Kits*, and their other valuable writing resources. I am lucky to work in an environment that nurtures imagination.

Special thanks to Ann Marland, who always helps me behind the scenes in too many ways to describe, and who makes sure I get enough caffeine to meet (most) deadlines—and to May Fan, M.D., who continues to be the best doctor around, and lets me share the writings of her creative and very witty children.

Finally, my deepest appreciation to the many people who have been my mentors since the whole 6-trait wild ride began: Carol Meyer, former Evaluation and Assessment Specialist for the Beaverton, Oregon, School District who remains to this day one of my best friends; the Analytical Writing Assessment Model Committee, whose genius launched it all in 1984; Rick (Richard) Stiggins, the guru of classroom assessment, who has taught me enough to fill many college textbooks; the brilliant Donna Flood, whose invaluable knowledge, friendship, and insight continue to shine a welcome light on my path; Barry Lane, whose humor has literally rescued me countless times and who dares to write the way he speaks; Ronda Woodruff, who allowed me to teach alongside her, and who can never be replaced; Margery Stricker Durham, who remains my favorite teacher—the toughest by far, the most interesting, and the best— and who may not escape this book, even though she's in Montana; Sneed B. Collard, who writes the best nonfiction books I've ever toted around; Tommy Thomason, who laughs when I tell him he writes skinny books, but who does a masterful job of condensing; Donald Graves, who said bravely and truthfully that writing without voice was merely writing "to whom it may concern," and whose words have helped me keep this vibrant trait of voice alive in teachers' hearts and minds; and Jeff Hicks and Fred Wolff (along with all the other remarkable trainers at Write Traits), who care enough about 6-trait writing to miss meals, sleep, and planes, and who make it all come alive for teachers.

Only families of other writers know how much they have to put up with, so I won't try to list all the wonderful, quiet, and important ways my family supports me. I'll just say thanks to Jerry, Nikki, Mike, Jack, and Chris. I am so very lucky to have you all. And don't forget, Jack, my dear heart (who will soon be old enough to read these lines), even if you never take *any other advice I give you*, take this: Be a writer.

Vicki Spandel

Face to Face with the Six Traits

We can start on the first day of school, establishing the expectation that youngsters will learn to read and write. We don't need to wait until children know all their letters, know their sound-to-symbol relationships, know how to spell all the words they want to use. We don't need to wait until children can read. Young children are writers as soon as they draw or put a symbol on paper and tell us what it says. We should call them writers and treat them as writers from that moment on.

—Marcia S. Freeman

Teaching the Youngest Writers, p. ix

My beliefs about children and writing are based on three assumptions: (1) young children can write, (2) young children want to write, and (3) young children possess the knowledge, interests, and experiences to write about.

—Carol Avery

And With a Light Touch, p. 65

We believe that when children first come to school, they have already started learning to write.

—Katie Wood Ray
—Lisa B. Cleaveland

About the Authors (2004, p. 49)

This book begins with the foundational belief that young children can and do write. The drive—the need to communicate with others—is a natural thing, so what we teach is not so much *doing it* as doing it *well*, doing it with *purpose*. How can we do this? By making time for writing, certainly. Time alone, however, will not do the trick—at least not the amount of time given to us. So we must teach our students to look within—within their own writing and within the writing of others. That's where the lessons lie. That's where the truth is.

Have you ever asked yourself what makes good writing work? If so, you are a critical reader—and probably a writer as well. Ever ask this question of your students? If so, you are already a six-trait writing teacher at heart. The six-trait model came about because teachers asked this question of their students and of themselves. This book can show you how to turn the answer to this question into powerful writing instruction.

Third-grade teacher Judy Mazur asked her students one day to complete this sentence: "Good writing has . . . ." According to Judy, her students had "immersed themselves in writing" for the past six months, and she wanted to get their perspectives as readers and critics. Here are their responses:

✔ Punctuation
✔ Voice
✔ A problem and a solution
✔ Interesting leads
✔ Good language
✔ Exciting characters
✔ Setting
✔ Author's name and other information
✔ Main idea
✔ Details
✔ Mysterious ending
✔ It's understandable
✔ Conclusion
✔ Title
✔ Sensory images

Judy's students are already thinking like writers. They may not have known it at the time, but they touched on virtually every one of the traits that teachers themselves have most often identified as vital to writing success: *ideas, organization, voice, word choice, sentence fluency,* and *conventions* (Spandel, 2005, p. 2). We shouldn't be surprised by this. In Judy's class, after all, students read and write all the time. It's natural for them to ask the question, "What makes writing work?" both from a reader's and a writer's point of view. Further, as we can see from this one activity, Judy herself encourages this sort of reflective thinking, which heightens students' awareness. This question about what makes for successful writing, along with the answers students, teachers, and writers have come up with, is the foundation for this book.

WHERE DO THE SIX TRAITS COME FROM?

Traits of good writing have been around as long as writing itself. No one *invented* them any more than Newton invented gravity. Strong writers—people such as Sandra Cisneros, Eve Bunting, Cynthia Rylant, Roald Dahl, Maurice Sendak, Mem Fox, and Faith Ringgold—all incorporate these traits (qualities) into their writing, even though they have not been to six-trait workshops and certainly do not (so far as anyone knows) write with rubrics in their hands. The point is, the traits are not a novelty; they're simply the essence of what makes writing *work* and so are an inherent part of every piece of writing ever generated and every piece to come. It is impossible to write well without compelling ideas, some sense of structure, strong voice, well-chosen words, fluent sentences, or conventions that give clarity to meaning.

Writers (and readers, for that matter) have long had a sense of what makes writing work; they just have not (for the most part) bothered to write it down.

So it is not the traits themselves that are new but the *rubrics that describe them*. It's a little like sketching a new map reflecting geographic features that have been around for ages.

The six traits that are the focus of this book were first described in detail and put into rubric form (see Appendix) by a group of seventeen teachers in the Beaverton, Oregon, school district in 1984. These teachers had done a little brainstorming of their own, but they wanted to make sure that what was in their heads matched the actual qualities they would find in student writing. To do this, they read hundreds of sample student papers and ranked them into three groups based on their effectiveness: strong, midlevel (or developing), and just beginning (in need of extensive revision). Then they documented their reasons for ranking the papers as they did. Because six prominent features influenced their rankings, their responses were translated into the first draft of what is now known as the *six-trait model of instruction and assessment*. They did not start out looking for six important writing features; it just turned out that way. If they had come up with four key qualities or eight, we would have had a different model.

The most recent version of their original six-trait rubric appears in the Appendix of this book. It is intended for use by students in *grades 3*

> *Coupled with pictures of animals, with human forms, with a starry night sky or other images that today we can only identify as abstract, we look at these men's and women's hands, along with smaller prints that perhaps belong to children, and cannot help but be deeply moved by the urge of our ancestors to leave some permanent imprint of themselves behind.*
>
> **—Steve Graham and Dolores Perin**
> Foreword
> *Writing Next*, 2007

Figure 1.1

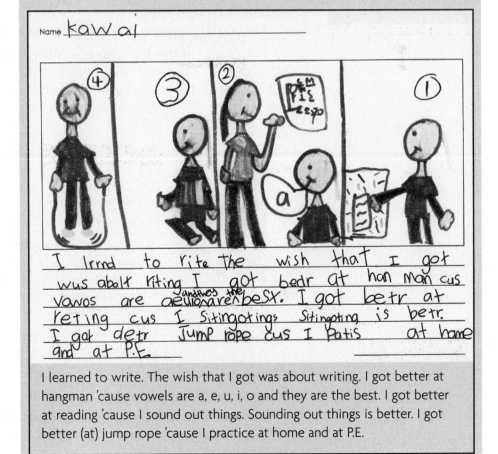

What I Accomplished in Kindergarten (K)

I learned to write. The wish that I got was about writing. I got better at hangman 'cause vowels are a, e, u, i, o and they are the best. I got better at reading 'cause I sound out things. Sounding out things is better. I got better (at) jump rope 'cause I practice at home and at P.E.

on up—right through college. The adapted version for primary writers (grades K through 3) appears in Chapter 8, Assessing Young Writers. It has been modified to incorporate aspects and nuances of each trait that are characteristic of younger writers' work.

IT'S MEANING—NOT TERMINOLOGY—
THAT COUNTS!

One interesting thing about writing traits is that no matter *who* identifies them (from students to professional writers and long-time teachers), common threads continue to emerge. In 1984–1985, for example, I also worked with teachers in the Portland, Oregon, public schools, who—quite independently of Beaverton—came up with their own rubric for assessing student writing. They used the same method Beaverton had used: reading, ranking, and recording. Their six traits were virtually identical.

Earlier, in the 1960s, a writer-researcher named Paul Diederich (1974) used this same reading-ranking method to answer the question "What makes writing work?" Diederich, in fact, had been the inspiration in both Beaverton and Portland. The teacher-writer team Diederich worked with identified five traits, ranked here in order of apparent influence on readers' thinking:

✔ Ideas
✔ Mechanics (usage, sentence structure, punctuation, and spelling)
✔ Organization and analysis
✔ Wording and phrasing
✔ Flavor (voice, tone and style, and personal qualities)

Notice that in this list sentence fluency appears as both sentence structure and style. Otherwise, the parallel to Beaverton's six-trait list is striking. In his work on the International Assessment, researcher Alan Purves (1992) and his team of educational reviewers also identified five traits (Spandel, 2005, pp. 3, 23):

✔ Content
✔ Organization
✔ Style and tone
✔ Surface features (primarily conventions)
✔ Personal response of the reader

In this set of traits, style encompasses voice, word choice, and fluency; personal response also touches on voice. Again, the match is very strong.

Within the past several years, the state of Texas revised its state rubric to incorporate these key features of writing:

✔ Focus and coherence
✔ Organization
✔ Development of ideas
✔ Voice
✔ Conventions

Again, the links are very strong, despite slight variations in wording. *Focus and coherence* is connected to the traits of *ideas* and *organization* (in the six-trait model). *Organization* connects not only to that trait specifically but also to *word choice* (because it addresses absence of wordiness) and *fluency* (how sentences link together to create a smooth flow of ideas). *Development of ideas*, similarly, connects to *ideas* directly but also to *voice* because it touches on risk taking to promote individual style. *Voice* is virtually the same in both rubrics, emphasizing individual approach and perspective as well as audience awareness. In the Texas rubric, however, *conventions* also encompasses phrasing and fluency—thus connecting that feature to the six-trait model's *sentence fluency* and *word choice*. I use Texas only as an example; *many* state rubrics contain language that strongly reflects the six traits.

In 1984, teacher and writer Donald Murray (pp. 66–67) identified his own list of six traits:

- ✔ Meaning
- ✔ Authority
- ✔ Voice
- ✔ Development
- ✔ Design
- ✔ Clarity

Murray's list is unique in that it is the only one not to include conventions in any form. *Meaning* and *development*, however, could be construed essentially as *ideas*; we could consider *clarity* part of *ideas*, too. *Design*, of course, is *organization*—by another name. And *authority* is a part of *voice*, but it also comes, certainly, from knowledge of the topic—again part of *ideas* in our rubric. *Voice* can be said, in its broadest sense, to encompass *word choice* and *sentence fluency* because it is closely connected to both.

The point is that terms are secondary. It's the concept that counts. No matter what we choose to call these key traits—and no matter whether there are six of them or five (or some other number)—*most* of us are moved by the same things in writing. So as adult readers, suppose that we were to read a piece about the history of mathematics from Charles Seife's *Zero: The Biography of a Dangerous Idea:*

> A key clue to the nature of Stone Age mathematics was unearthed in the late 1930s, when archaeologist Karl Absolom, sifting through Czechoslovakian dirt, uncovered a 30,000-year-old wolf bone with a series of notches carved in it. . . . A wolf bone was the Stone Age equivalent of a supercomputer. Gog's ancestors couldn't even count up to two, and they certainly didn't need zero. In the very beginning of mathematics, it seems that people could only distinguish between one and many. A caveman owned one spearhead or many spearheads; he had eaten one crushed lizard or many crushed lizards. There was no way to express any quantities other than one or many. (2000, pp. 6–7)

Do you like this piece? I find it very engaging, so I ask myself, "Why? Why do I like this so much?" Well, it's an intriguing idea, expressed clearly and with authority; it has voice; and it has fluency. Perhaps some people would say that it's skillfully punctuated. True. But—score one for Murray—it's the *voice* that really grabs me. It's voice that keeps people who do not normally read math books for pleasure reading *Zero*. This is the power of writing traits: They keep readers reading. But now, what does all this have to do with writing or with young writers?

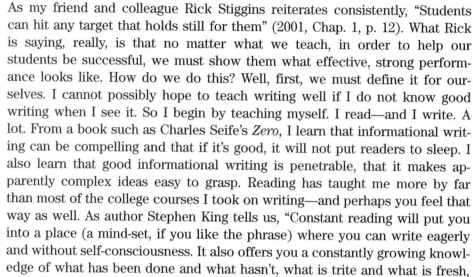

CREATING A VISION OF SUCCESS

As my friend and colleague Rick Stiggins reiterates consistently, "Students can hit any target that holds still for them" (2001, Chap. 1, p. 12). What Rick is saying, really, is that no matter what we teach, in order to help our students be successful, we must show them what effective, strong performance looks like. How do we do this? Well, first, we must define it for ourselves. I cannot possibly hope to teach writing well if I do not know good writing when I see it. So I begin by teaching myself. I read—and I write. A lot. From a book such as Charles Seife's *Zero*, I learn that informational writing can be compelling and that if it's good, it will not put readers to sleep. I also learn that good informational writing is penetrable, that it makes apparently complex ideas easy to grasp. Reading has taught me more by far than most of the college courses I took on writing—and perhaps you feel that way as well. As author Stephen King tells us, "Constant reading will put you into a place (a mind-set, if you like the phrase) where you can write eagerly and without self-consciousness. It also offers you a constantly growing knowledge of what has been done and what hasn't, what is trite and what is fresh,

what works and what just lies there dying (or dead) on the page" (2000, p. 150). In *What You Know By Heart*, Katie Wood Ray puts it this way: "Every single text we encounter presents a whole chunk of curriculum, a whole set of things to know about writing" (2002, p. 92).

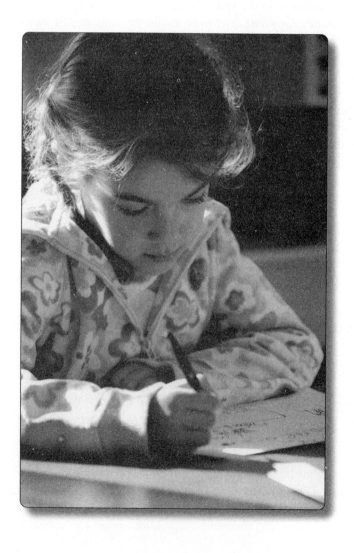

Next, I must share my vision with students. I have several ways to do this. One is to share with *them* samples of what good writing can look like. And of course, writing comes in many shapes and forms, so I will need numerous examples: picture books, chapter books, poems, recipes, newspaper clippings, some of my own work, and some by other students, too. In addition, I must model writing for them—let them see it in action. This is critical because in modeling I show students both process and product. Writing is not, after all, just about publishing. It's about getting there and making decisions along the way. And finally, I can share rubrics—rubrics that define in writing my vision of successful performance. If my students were eighth graders (or even fifth graders), I could hand rubrics out, and we could review them together. With primary students, I'll need to find some other methods. I will need to use the language of the rubrics when I talk about writing and when I share books. I also will need to use it when I talk about my own writing as I model. When I comment on students' work, I will weave in some trait language: "Alicia, your *voice* comes through loud and clear here" or "Sean, you have written a *full sentence*, and I can read every word!" or "Frances, you have used a *new word* here—*nerve-wracking*—it really helps me picture how you felt in that huge auditorium!"

This is a book about teaching writing traits to *very young writers*—writers who may not even be creating anything like conventional text yet, who are writing with scribbles and lines and pictures and imitations of print. So why share traits with them at this age? Are they even ready? Absolutely.

First, as Judy Mazur's student list shows, young writers are already thinking about writing anyway. Why not tap into that insight? Why not give form and language to what subconsciously, instinctively many already know? Children are inherently good evaluators. Some of the best. They know a good, chewy cookie from a dry imitation. They know a warm, friendly voice from one that's remote or cold. And they know a good piece of writing from one that is listless, voiceless, tired, or just plain confusing. Ask them, and you'll see. In teaching traits, we respect their skill as assessors and offer some guidance to make their senses even more acute.

Second, as Rick Stiggins has pointed out, we do it to create a vision of success for students. If we teach them what to look for in good writing, we increase—exponentially—the chances that they will write well, too. Think of these six elements not so much as traits for judging writing quality but rather as keys to writing well. If we had called them the *six keys to good writing*, people likely would have made the instructional connection immediately. This is where the *true* power of trait-based instruction lies—showing students the *keys* to writing well:

✔ Have a strong, clear idea.
✔ Use details and pictures to paint a picture in your reader's mind.
✔ Write with authority and voice.
✔ Organize your information so that a reader can follow it.
✔ Use words that make sense—and that are lively as well.
✔ Write with fluency and variety—the way good dancers dance.
✔ Make your conventions as strong as you can so that readers can figure out your message.

In short, teach your students to *look within*. Looking within is the essence of good assessment, which is not really about making judgments at all but about building understanding.

It's All About Language

At primary level, teaching traits is *mostly* about teaching language, giving students a writer's vocabulary for thinking, speaking, and working like writers. Remember, you do not need to be writing fluent sentences yourself to know what fluency is. Your ears will tell you. You do not need to write stories filled with voice to know voice when you hear it. The smile on your face, the tears in your eyes, or the chill up your back will tell you. And this knowledge will become a foundation for your own writing so that as you begin to generate stories, poems, essays, or explanations of your own, voice, fluency, and all the rest will slip in as easily as old friends slip into your house for a visit.

A QUICK REVIEW OF THE TRAITS—THROUGH THE EYES OF JUDY'S STUDENTS

If you have read *Creating Writers*, the six traits are already very familiar to you. If you haven't, this very quick review will get you started on forming some definitions in your own mind—definitions I'll help you to expand and refine in the chapters that follow through student examples and teaching ideas.

Take a closer look at the students' list at the beginning of this chapter. Let's see if we can connect that list to the six traits teachers and writers have identified. As we do so, ask yourself two things:

✔ Which of these traits is already evident in some way in *my own students' writing?*
✔ Which of these traits *would I like to teach to my students if I could?*

Connecting to Ideas

Judy's students listed *main idea, details, exciting characters*, and *setting*. What do these important elements of writing have in common? They are all part of a larger concept we have come to call *ideas*. Ideas are the heart and soul of good writing, the writer's main message or story line. The main ideas and details are critical to any piece of writing; characters and setting play an important role in a story—one form of writing.

Notice, too, the students' use of the word *understandable*. This is an insightful comment. Pick up any piece of writing, anywhere, written for any purpose at all, and the very first thing that is likely to strike you is whether the writing makes sense. As basic as an element such as *clarity* may sound, it is hardly a given. Just this morning my computer warned me that I had just committed a "sharing violation." A little clarity on that one would have helped.

Judy's students also recognize that good writing has a *main idea* and *details* that create images in a reader's mind. Here's a detailed snapshot from Beverly Cleary's autobiography (*A Girl from Yamhill*) in which Cleary describes an episode with her first grade teacher, Miss Falb:

> Once I was ordered, without being told why, to the cloakroom, where I huddled, sniffling, among rubbers and lunch bags. For weeks after that, the smell of peanut butter sandwiches made my stomach curl. Once a plump and cheerful girl named Claudine was punished by being sentenced to crouch in the dark cave under Miss Falb's desk with Miss Falb's feet in their ugly black oxfords. (1988, p. 78)

Feel yourself cringing just a little? Smell the rubbers and lunch bags? That's clarity—and detail.

Connecting to Organization

Organization is the design and structure of a piece of writing; it holds the information together and also presents it to the reader in a way that is both comprehensible and memorable. A mystery story and a recipe may be organized very differently, but both need structure (what Murray calls *design*).

Judy's students mentioned several essentials of strong organization: an *interesting lead, problem and solution* (a type of structure), and a *mysterious ending* (or other good conclusion).

A good lead (beginning) is vital. Once a writer has a message or story in mind, the big question is "How/where should I begin?" All readers know this well. If the lead is flat, readers get bored and go on to something else. *Jack on the Tracks* (by Jack Gantos) opens this way: "It was dark. Dad was driving and I was riding shotgun" (2001, p. 3). Suppose that Gantos had started his book like this: "In this book, I will explain to you, the reader, how it feels to move to another town." It's not likely that many readers would have gotten to page four. Leo Lionni's much-loved children's book, *Frederick*, opens with this line: "All along the meadow where the cows grazed and the horses ran, there was an old stone wall" (1967, p. 1). You want to know who lives under that wall, don't you? It doesn't take young readers/listeners long to learn that a good lead takes you by the hand.

Organization is also about internal structure, creating a pattern that showcases ideas effectively so that you are not just tossing them at a reader in some hodge-podge manner.

Certainly, as Judy's students noted, a good conclusion is critical. When you find a greeting card with a picture you like and then open it, what are you looking for? The punch line. It's the ending that makes any joke work. When we are disappointed in a book—or a TV show or film—what is it that lets us down? Often it's the ending. We feel our time's been wasted if the ending's not right. But when it works, we know that, too. It's sad when Charlotte (in *Charlotte's Web* by E. B. White) dies, but we don't want White to write, "Charlotte lived on and on—forever!" Not really. There is more comfort in his closing comment: "It is not often that someone comes along who is a true friend and a good writer. Charlotte was both" (1980, p. 184). That same sense of closure that goes with every just-right ending is found in the final line of *A Dog's Life* by Ann M. Martin (2005): "I open my eyes and tilt my head back to look at Susan's lined face. She smiles at me, and we sit pressed into each other, two old ladies" (p. 182).

Connecting to Voice

All readers respond to *voice*. Judy's students are no exception. Of all the thousands of definitions put forward for this elusive concept, I still like Donald Murray's best. "Voice," Murray says, "separates writing that is read from writing that is not read" (1984, p. 144). That cuts right to it. Voice is the quality that keeps us tuned in, that makes us feel as if we know the writer. It's a sharing of self. Voice also forms a bond between reader and writer; it creates a sense of trust. Very often I hear voice defined as personality: "It's the personality of the writer on the page." This is true, to an extent, but voice is so much more than personality. It is also confidence (that comes from knowing a topic well), enthusiasm, curiosity, and a passion for honesty that is uncompromising. As Anne LaMott reminds us, "Good writing is about telling the truth" (1995, p. 2).

Young reader-writers are among the greatest judges of voice because they have not learned to feign politeness or interest they do not feel. Read any piece of writing to a group of first graders, and you will know at once from their body language and facial expressions whether they think it has voice (or, sometimes, whether the way you are *reading* it allows the voice to come out). As we shall see from their examples, young writers virtually explode with voice. It is a natural part of who they are. In *Children's Letters to God: The New*

> *If I read a book [and] it makes my whole body so cold no fire can warm me, I know that is poetry.*
>
> —Emily Dickinson, American poet (1830–1886)

Collection, Nan comments on how difficult it must be for God to love everyone in the world because, as she confesses, "There are only 4 people in our family and I can never do it" (Hample and Marshall, 1991).

Connecting to Word Choice

Word choice is all about using the right word at the right moment. Good word choice contributes to clarity certainly, but it can also evoke feelings, moods, likes, and dislikes. Judy's students refer to *sensory images* and *good language.* For young writers, *good* language often means *new* language. As a first grader told me with some passion one day, "We're sick of words we already know. We want some new ones."

In his classic, *Amos and Boris,* William Steig tells the story of an unlikely but devoted friendship between the whale Boris and the courageous little mouse Amos. He might have written, "Boris loved how cute and sweet little Amos was. And Amos admired Boris for being so big and strong." Those words make sense, but they don't *sing.* Luckily for us, Steig wrote instead, "Boris admired the delicacy, the quivering daintiness, the light touch, the small voice, the gemlike radiance of the mouse. Amos admired the bulk, the grandeur, the power, the purpose, the rich voice, and the abounding friendliness of the whale" (1971). These words are likely to be "new ones" for many students who hear them, but they will hear and even *feel* the power when you read this magical tale aloud, and soon Steig's words will belong to them, too.

In *The Twits,* mischievous author Roald Dahl, always up for a bit of the grotesque, forces us to look closely at Mr. Twit's moustache, where we are dismayed to find "maggoty green cheese or a moldy old cornflake or even the slimy tail of a tinned sardine" (1980, p. 7). Then comes the killer line: "By sticking out his tongue and curling it sideways to explore the hairy jungle around his mouth, he was always able to find a tasty morsel here and there to nibble on." That's the power of verbs. Looking was bad enough, but Dahl's verbs force us, like it or not, to mentally probe through the moustache for the maggoty cheese.

Connecting to Sentence Fluency

Sentence fluency is the rhythm and flow of language—the way it plays to the ear. Poetry, like song lyrics, is the essence of fluency when it is well crafted. Prose, however, can mimic the qualities that make those two forms of writing so captivating. Less-fluent writing is sometimes choppy or repetitive: "We ate together. It was fun. We sat on a rock. It was by the lake." Or it may be a series of thoughts linked by endless connectives: "We ate together and so it was fun because we sat on a rock and it was by the lake." Fluent sentences are varied both in length and in structure. The variety is purposeful: "Helen laughed. *Perhaps* she found my outfit odd. *Small wonder*—since it had previously belonged to a professional rodeo clown." Skillful writers find ways to hook sentences together. They also read their own writing aloud to get the sound and rhythm. Fluency is readily measured by how easy it is to read text aloud and to weave in plenty of expression as you do so.

When Judy's students refer to *good language*, they may be dancing around the edges of *fluency*, as well as referring to words they like. After all, the two go together. Further, both *word choice* and *fluency* contribute to *voice*. When the little mouse Amos (of *Amos and Boris*) first sets sail, Steig describes the scene this way: "He was enjoying his trip immensely. It was beautiful weather. Day and night he moved up and down, up and down, on waves as big as mountains, and he was full of wonder, full of enterprise, and full of love for life" (1971). Notice the varied sentence beginnings, the purposeful use of repetition to create rhythm, and the masterful emphasis that goes with the parallel structure—"full of wonder, full of enterprise, and full of love for life." Sometimes we think that students do not notice these little differences on writing. They do, though. I *would* be surprised to hear second graders chatting about the effectiveness of parallel structure, but it would not surprise me at all to have one say (as second grader Marie said to me), "I like the sound of that" (meaning *Amos and Boris*).

"Yes," I said, "he writes with a lot of *fluency*." This simply gives Marie a word for describing what she has noticed anyway.

Connecting to Conventions

The trait of *conventions* includes anything a copy editor would deal with: spelling, punctuation, use of capitals, grammar and usage, and indenting or using other means to indicate paragraphing. These are textual conventions. This trait also can include manipulation of text features (for example, font size or type, bullets, illustrations, graphics) to create effective presentation on the page. These are *visual* conventions.

As the name implies, *conventions* signify what is currently acceptable. Whereas once wehadnospacesbetweenwordsforexample, we now consider such spacing essential to readability. It is all a matter of common usage, though, and conventions are ever changing. Further, conventions as I'll address them in this book begin with the simplest of traditions, such as writing from left to right on the page and making sure that the letter *E* always faces the same way. As students gain conventional skill, they can begin to concern themselves with correct spelling; proper use of capital letters, periods versus question marks; and so on.

While Judy's students do not cover the whole range of conventions, they certainly touch on this important trait with attention to punctuation and mention of a title, as well as the author's name and other critical information. Although they do not mention spelling, capitalization, and grammar specifically, my hunch is that they are aware of the need for these attention-to-detail features of writing.

Presentation (format, layout) on the page—or visual conventions, if you will—are highly significant to many young writers, especially once they are ready to publish and to think about title pages, book covers, and so on. We should not judge a book by its cover we are told, but we most surely do, as designers are well aware. I am skeptical of anyone who claims *never* to have bought a book solely on the basis of its cover—the illustration, the font, the color, the whole look of it. The covers of Chris Van Allsburg's books invariably hook me. Even if I did not know him to be ingenious, the covers would persuade me to give him a chance. Which book covers call to you?

WHERE SHOULD I BEGIN?

Begin with writing, providing opportunities for your students to write often and for many purposes—even if they write only a word, a phrase, or letter string at first. Opportunity is the key. Write with them, and model writing. Create stories and poems, and share them with your students. Do not collect or assess everything; the thought of doing this will inhibit you from encouraging writing. And if you want writing to feel as natural as breathing, you must do it. All the time, every day—to think, to reflect, to recall, to record, and to create.

Begin with talking. Don't be timid about using good writers' language. Talk about the voice you hear in the books you share. Listen together for fluency, and talk about what you find. Use terms such as *detail, lead, conclusion, making connections, audience, word choice,* and *conventions.* In writing, as in nearly anything we do, knowing the language of the territory is the first step to power.

Begin with reading, with sharing the books you love. In the case of primary students, the first experience with writing traits often comes from listening to language used well, from conversation, and from the wondrous experience of being read to by someone who truly believes that books are magical. If you can picture yourself, long ago, comfortably curled up somewhere—on a rug or favorite pillow, in a snug chair, or perhaps resting on your elbows at the foot of the bed—and listening to a voice that lifted meaning from the page, remembering how very good that felt, then you already know what it means to teach the traits. It all springs from that treasured time.

Here's the secret: Young students *hear* the traits long, *long* before those traits ever appear in their own writing. When you ask students to describe what they picture as you read and they can do that, you have taught them what details are. You have only to give it a name. When you see students hanging on your words, waiting for you to turn the page, and they ask you to please, *please* keep reading, you have taught the trait of voice. You have only to give it a name. Soon your students will be listening for favorite words and inviting leads and conclusions that ring true—and all the things that you and they teach one another to value in writing. When you name these things, you empower your students to think and to speak like writers. It is a fine gift.

Figure 1.2

Laura (K): The "joy" of writing

CHAPTER 1 IN A NUTSHELL

- The six traits of good writing are not an invention but simply a way of describing the qualities of good writing that have been with us as long as writing itself.
- What *is* new is the use of *rubrics*—written descriptions that capture what the key qualities of writing look like at various levels of performance.
- Rubrics may use slightly different terminology or language, but in the end, most tend to focus on similar key features, and these features of good writing should be the focus of our instruction.
- Good teaching means creating for students a vision of success. We do this by sharing samples of strong writing (often through literature) and by sharing the language of the rubrics through our comments and the way we talk about writing.
- Teach the traits through writing—simply providing time and opportunity to write—through talking—using the language of the traits yourself—and through reading—remembering that young students hear and recognize the traits in action even before those same traits show up in their personal writing.

STUDY GROUP: INTERACTIVE QUESTIONS AND ACTIVITIES

1. **Activity.** Brainstorm your own list of the qualities *you* think are most important to good writing. As you do this, (1) work with a group, and (2) have before you samples of writing: student samples, excerpts from books or journals. As you list the qualities, try to connect each of them to one of the six traits: **ideas** (content, main theme or message, details); **organization** (lead, design or order, transitions and connections, ending); **voice** (presence, individuality, tone and flavor, honesty, liveliness and energy); **word choice** (carefully selected words,

precision of meaning, phrasing, strong verbs, sensory connections); **sentence fluency** (rhythm, readability, smooth sentence flow, sentence-to-sentence continuity, authentic dialogue); **conventions** (spelling, punctuation, grammar and usage, paragraphing, capitalization, presentation on the page).

2. **Discussion.** Analyze the personal list you put together in Activity 1. Are there any traits you weighted somewhat more heavily than others? Are any traits omitted altogether from your list? Discuss how this might influence your teaching and whether you might make an adjustment.

3. **Activity and discussion.** Analyze a sample of your own writing using the six-trait rubric that appears in the appendix of this book. What traits are strongest in your own work? What traits do you think you—as a writer—need to work on most? How can you use this insight to strengthen the modeling you do for students? Discuss this with colleagues.

4. **Activity and discussion.** As a group, select two or more favorite books: adult or young adult literature, picture books, nonfiction—or your choice. Select two or more passages of 100 words or more to analyze using the six-trait rubric from the appendix. What strengths do you see within each sample? What does this tell you about why you are drawn to particular literature? Discuss this.

5. **Activity and discussion.** As you can see from the section called "It's Meaning—Not Terminology—That Counts!" people have come up with slightly different (though remarkably similar) lists of key writing traits. Further, each trait goes by different names. With your group, brainstorm as many associated terms and connections as you can for each of the six traits: for example, for *ideas*, you might think of *content*, *meaning*, *message*, and so on. Compare your list to a set of state standards and/or to the rubric used by your state for writing assessment. What similarities or differences do you see?

6. **Activity.** If you are currently teaching, brainstorm a list of important writing traits or characteristics with your students. You can do this by first sharing one or two favorite pieces of writing to get their mental wheels turning, and then asking students to complete this sentence (as Judy did with her students): *Good writing has . . . .* Once you create the list, keep it posted where you and your students can see it and add to it throughout the school year.

WHAT'S NEXT?

Chapter 2 offers numerous examples of students' writing, helping you identify the key features in young writers' text and art that show development of ideas, organization of information, expression of voice, thoughtful word choice, fluency, and emerging conventions.

SOURCES CITED

Avery, Carol. 2002. *And With a Light Touch*, 2d ed. Portsmouth, NH: Heinemann.

Cleary, Beverly. 1988. *A Girl from Yamhill*. New York: William Morrow.

Dahl, Roald. 1980. *The Twits*. New York: Penguin.

Dickinson, Emily. Quoted in *Largely Literary Designs*. Yellow Springs, OH: Antioch Publishing.

Diederich, Paul B. 1974. *Measuring Growth in English*. Urbana, IL: National Council of Teachers of English.

Gantos, Jack. 2001. *Jack on the Tracks*. New York: Farrar, Straus and Giroux.

Graham, Steve, and Dolores Perin. 2007. *Writing Next: Effective Strategies to Improve Writing of Adolescents in Middle and High Schools—A report to Carnegie Corporation of New York*. Washington, DC: Alliance for Excellent Education.

Hample, Stuart, and Eric Marshall, compilers. 1991. *Children's Letters to God: The New Collection*. New York: Workman.

King, Stephen. 2000. *On Writing: A Memoir of the Craft*. New York: Scribner.

Lamott, Anne. 1995. *Bird by Bird*. New York: Anchor Books.

Lionni, Leo. 1967. *Frederick*. New York: Knopf.

Martin, Ann M. 2005. *A Dog's Life*. New York: Scholastic.

Murray, Donald M. 1984. *Write to Learn*. New York: Holt, Rinehart and Winston.

Purves, Alan C. 1992. "Reflections on Research and Assessment in Written Composition," *Research in the Teaching of English 26* (February), pp. 108–122.

Ray, Katie Wood, with Lisa B. Cleaveland. 2004. *About the Authors: Writing Workshop with Our Youngest Writers*. Portsmouth, NH: Heinemann.

Ray, Katie Wood. 2002. *What You Know by Heart*. Portsmouth, NH: Heinemann.

Seife, Charles. 2000. *Zero: The Biography of a Dangerous Idea*. New York: Penguin Putnam.

Spandel, Vicki. 2005. *Creating Writers Through Six-Trait Writing Assessment and Instruction*, 4th ed. Boston: Allyn & Bacon.

Steig, William. 1971. *Amos and Boris*. New York: Farrar, Straus and Giroux.

Stiggins, Richard J. 2001. *Student-Involved Classroom Assessment*, 3d ed. Upper Saddle River, NJ: Prentice Hall.

White, E. B. 1980. *Charlotte's Web*. New York: HarperCollins.

2 Looking Within: Seeing Traits in Children's Writing

Children can write sooner than we ever dreamed possible.
Most children come to school knowing a handful of letters, and
with these they can write labels and calendars, letters and sto-
ries, poems and songs. They will learn to write by writing
and by living with a sense of "I am one who writes."

—Lucy McCormick Calkins
The Art of Teaching Writing (1994, p. 83)

Writing is actually a form of thinking. If
teachers who want to encourage students to be
good thinkers are not using creative writing,
they are missing out on the best way to get
students to process information, which
is especially valuable in learning.

—Bea Johnson
Never Too Early to Write (1999, p. 11)

Although we pay lip service to the
idea that a picture is worth a thousand
words, we don't really believe it. It's the
thousand words that really interest us.

—Tom Newkirk
More than Stories: The Range of Children's Writing
(1989, p. 65)

In order to support our student writers
we must know them; teaching writing can't
be learned by reading a book or attending
a summer course. Those are important tools . . .
but the truth is that our student writers teach
us how to be teachers of writing, and
assessment is the way we learn.

—Kathleen Strickland and James Strickland
Making Assessment Elementary (2000, p. 66)

Jodie, a September first grader, writes the following note:

Hlo! IUS TLVNSTL WEMVDNDNW IHV A DGNMDBN I HLPMYMOMCK

To the untrained eye (i.e., anyone not used to reading primary children's work), this may look like a jumble of letters without meaning. That's our assessment brain at work, of course. In truth, Jodie is rather an accomplished young writer. She is thinking and writing in full sentences, and combining several ideas into one note. She is even experimenting a bit with conventions, including an exclamation point for emphasis and putting spaces between sections of her note (although not as yet between individual words). To fully appreciate Jodie's accomplishments, we have only to translate her note into more conventional English:

> Hello! I used to live in Seattle. We moved, and now I have a dog named Ben. I help my mom cook.

Now we may look at the same passage and say, "Wow—how did I miss all that?" The traits of writing—the qualities that define good writing—sometimes look rather different in primary-level examples—especially those from very young students. This is why we must teach ourselves what to look for and then remind ourselves how important it is to comment on it. The commenting part is critical. It is unlikely, after all, that a primary student will sit down one day and say to herself, "Well, this is the day I put some real voice into my writing." Young writers usually do not know, unless we tell them, what qualities are exhibited in their work. Further, they trust us to see what is there and to tell the truth about it.

Look again at Jodie's original writing. What comments is she likely to receive from a teacher? How about this one:

> *Jodie, this is good. Now we need to work on your spelling and punctuation.*

This is a well-intentioned comment, but there are some problems. First, the teacher is missing what is *right*, what is *strong*, in Jodie's work. Because Jodie cannot see these things for herself, she goes on to the next piece no wiser about what she has to build on. Wait, you may be saying, the teacher specifically said, "This is good." True. *Good* is a broad, general term, though. This kind of language works between adults because we accept at face value the fact that much of what we say has no real content, explicit or implicit. Consider how we typically greet each other:

> *"How are you doing?"*
>
> *"Great—and you?"*

This common exchange really means nothing beyond "Hello." We speak to one another from habit. We must not speak to our young writers this way, however. They need detail. If something is good about their writing, we need to tell them what it is.

Second, the reference to spelling and punctuation is likely to suggest to Jodie that these are the two things she most urgently needs to work on. Were that not the case, why would the teacher focus on it? This kind of comment, repeated often enough, will eventually teach Jodie that conventions are the *most* significant element in any piece of writing. This is not to say that Jodie does not have some work to do on her conventions. Her spelling is in a phonemic stage, prephonetic, and most of the punctuation is missing. She is not, however, ready to make all these corrections—yet. Further, her writing shows thinking, and we do not want to overlook this essential part of writing in our zeal to make things "correct." So what *do* we do? Three things:

1. Let's tell Jodie explicitly what is *strong* in her writing.

   Jodie, you are writing in whole sentences! Good for you. Your writing has detail, and I can read it without your help. Want me to show you?

2. We can suggest *one* kind of addition—a writer's secret, if you will—that Jodie can incorporate into her writing.

Jodie, now that you are writing whole sentences, I think you are ready to use periods to show where a sentence ends. This little clue helps your reader. Would you like me to show you how it works?

3.   We can translate Jodie's work into conventional print so that she will be able to read it down the road. This step is optional, but I like it because it preserves text that will soon be "lost" to Jodie as her own reading/writing skills advance and the kind of writing she is doing right now becomes difficult for her to decode.

Jodie, I'm thinking that we could save your writing about the move and your dog Ben, and I could also give you a "book" version so that you'd be able to read this for as long as you want. Would you like to see what your writing—your ideas—look like in book language?

What have we done here? We taught Jodie to look at her writing in a different way—to see first what is strong, what is working. We have begun to add one new skill to her writing, the use of periods. She may get the hang of this on the first try; many young writers do. Or she may sprinkle her text liberally with random periods for some time to come; many young writers do this, too. Either way, it is a step forward. Third, we have honored Jodie in step 3 by suggesting that her text is worth preserving and by showing her a way of doing it that links reading and writing.

A LITTLE WARM-UP

For the sake of teaching ourselves how the six traits of writing look "in action," let's leave the primary world for a moment or two (a world in which the traits are sometimes a little trickier to recognize) and see how they play out in some examples from an older writer. You will look at two examples, A and B, and simply ask yourself the old critic's question: What's the difference? As you do so, here's a reminder list of what the six traits are all about that may help trigger some responses.

Ideas

Clarity, focus, and detail all working together to make the writer's message clear

Organization

The overall design or structure of a piece of writing, including the lead, the flow of ideas, use of transitional words or phrases, and the conclusion

Voice

The writer's *way* of expressing ideas—the general sound and tone of the piece, the link between writer and reader, the fingerprints of the writer on paper

Word Choice

The words and phrases the writer selects to get the message across

Sentence Fluency

The flow and rhythm of language, variety in sentences, natural sound, and degree to which text can be read with expression and interpretation

Conventions

A combination of spelling, punctuation, capitalization, paragraphing, grammar, and usage (and sometimes layout or presentation) working together to make text easy for the reader to process

Using this list of reminders, see what differences you spot between sample A and sample B.

Sample A

John felt hungry. He felt he needed something to eat soon. He was ready to eat just about anything. He was that hungry.

Sample B

John stumbled along a dusty North Dakota road headed for a town that in his mind had no name. He had not eaten in over four days, and though he had a little water left, it wasn't enough to fool his empty stomach for long. Biting his lower lip, he leaned against a fence post, turning his back to the hot wind. If he did not eat soon, he did not think he could keep walking. While he had heard of people eating grass, he was not sure whether it was really edible, or whether it could make a person sick. He thought he might have to find out for himself if something resembling lunch did not come along soon. That's when he saw the family, stopped by the road. Were they eating, or was he imagining it?

Note: Before you read the following list, write down (on a piece of scratch paper) what you notice as you compare sample A to sample B.

OK—now read the following list. Perhaps you noted several (or more) of these differences:

✔ Sample A relies on generalities, whereas sample B is highly detailed. (*Ideas*)
✔ Sample A has short, choppy sentences, whereas the sentences in sample B are graceful and varied. (*Fluency*)
✔ Sample B has more voice than sample A. (*Voice*)
✔ Sample B seems to be leading somewhere—it has a sense of growing tension and anticipation—whereas sample A seems more a collection of random thoughts. Sample B also has a stronger lead. (*Organization*)
✔ The words in sample B are more interesting and specific than those in sample A. (*Word Choice*)

Did you also notice other differences we missed?

THE PRIMARY CONNECTION

Now that you have had a chance to "look within" the text of an older writer, let's take it to another level—spotting signs of the traits in the writing of younger students, in which those traits are not always so obvious. Keep in mind that at the primary level, writing can take many forms: scribbling, playing with letter shapes, creating letter or word strings, drawing, combining text and art, labeling, listing, and writing sentences or paragraphs. We must learn to look for signs of the traits in all these various forms. A picture, for instance, may contain detail or voice even from a young writer who is not yet producing text. Gradually, as he or she relies more on text and less on pictures to express meaning, the voice and detail shift into the text also. So an important question to ask, always, is this: "How is this child expressing him- or herself?"

If the answer is "in pictures," look there first. If the answer is "orally," listen. Remember, too, that students *hear* traits before they express them. In other words, a student recognizes fluency in a poem or song before she writes with fluency—even before she has a name for what she hears. Molly, a kindergartner, loves music and poetry because "That's when we get to clap our hands and move around!" This is Molly's way of responding to fluency—she feels the rhythm, she hears the beat.

TRACKING DOWN IDEAS

Writers who include detail in their work are those who have learned to be good observers—to take a close look at the world. This is what author/teacher Barry Lane calls "fine tuning the binoculars" (2001, p. 17). As we bring the world into focus, the degree of detail sharpens, like this:

Level 1 (beginning—out of focus and fuzzy)

Look! A green thing!

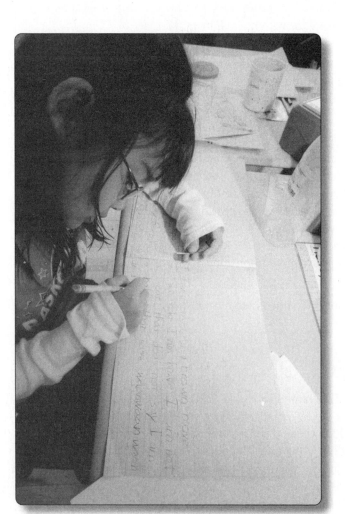

Level 3 (middle—coming into focus)

Hey! It's a ponderosa pine tree.

Level 5 (strong—totally focused, picking up detail)

Wow. There's a 100-foot ponderosa with a red-tailed hawk perched at the top, searching the forest floor for a mouse.

Young writers can learn to spot details and make a mental note of them long before they are ready to incorporate *all* those details into their writing. However, details often do find their way into children's drawings and into what they share orally. We must teach ourselves to look for the little details—and to listen for them—so that we can tell our young writers, "Hey! You were really paying attention. You noticed how the fins look on a goldfish (or the petals on a flower or the eyes on the face of a surprised person)."

What to Look for in Pictures

✔ *Interesting details*—facial expressions, fingers and toes, leaves on the trees, eyes that show emotion
✔ *Unusual details*—a different hair-do, things in the windows of a house, people or animals in motion, smoke rising from the chimney, waves on the water
✔ *Labels*—use of words to expand the meaning of a picture

What to Look for in Text

✔ A message that makes sense

✔ More than one statement on the same topic; for example, "I hate flies. They bite."

✔ Details; for example, "I love my dog because *she is brave* and *she can swim*. She is *pretty*. She has *two white paws*."

✔ New information; for example, "Some kinds of dogs do not bark at all."

✔ A strong main idea; for example, "I love picnics" *or* "I can cook."

What to Say in Your Comments

✔ I understood your message perfectly.

✔ You wrote more than one sentence on the same topic. That's what I call focused.

✔ I can picture your dog perfectly. You painted a picture for me with your details.

✔ Are there really dogs that do not bark? I did not know that! I learned something from your paper.

✔ I love this topic. Where did you get your idea?

Note: Although real-life writing sometimes does call for us to write on other people's topics (an assigned letter, report, evaluation, etc.), writers also need the skill of finding and defining their own topics. If you provide the topic routinely, you will encourage students to depend on you for this. Writers do not always get assignments, topics, or story starters. They have to think. And they have to learn to spot the moments or ideas within their experience that are worthy of writing time. Yes, it takes practice. Yes, sometimes it is hard—and frustrating. The best writing, however, comes from original thinking, not from 30 clone papers on "my best gift ever." As Marcia Freeman reminds us, "We must show young writers that we believe they have something to say. We must help them tap into their personal experiences, expertise, and interests. If we select topics for them and provide many story starters, we send young writers a message: You are not able to pick meaningful topics" (1998, p. 25).

Some Examples

Look carefully at the samples of student writing included here, noticing any details or other signs of ideas that strike you. Do not be too influenced by my comments because what leaps out at you may not be the same at all as what strikes me. Just remember, the student writer/artist does not know what's there—yet. You can unlock the door with your comments.

In Figure 2.1, Thomas creates a brief summary of *Peter Pan.* It's a bit tricky to read because, like many primary students, he is innovative about placing text, finishing the first line in the middle and then going to line two and popping back up to line one for the ending of the sentence. You have to be patient! Notice how many letter-sound connections he makes. He is also including spaces between words. His ideas are clear and complete, and much of the content is carried by the art. Notice his use of labels. Michael seems to bear a striking resemblance to Captain Hook.

Figure 2.1

"Peter Pan flies to Neverland. I know he laughs and he does everything." Thomas (K)

Lists are a wonderful way for young children to share ideas without the need for a lot of text. In Figure 2.2, Liam shares all the things he loves: snow, sun, pizza, sand, and ice cream. You can probably think of numerous innovative ways to use lists with your students: things done, remembered, wished for,

Figure 2.3 Dinosaurs By Patrick (K)

Figure 2.2

List of "Things I Love." Liam (K)

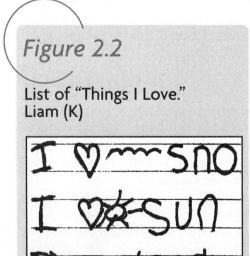

hoped for. Lists at this early age *are* the writing; later, they may become a basis for writing.

It is a breakthrough moment when young writers create text we can interpret without their help—or with just an interpretive hint. As soon as we know Patrick is hearing *th* as *d*, we can put picture and text together (Figure 2.3) to determine that dinosaurs are big, they eat meat and plants, they live in Jurassic Park, and they become extinct (in this version) thanks to their unfortunate habit of eating other (*udr*) dinosaurs. This piece is rich with detail.

When we think of detail, we long for extended explanations, imagery, sensory details, examples, and anecdotes. With beginning writers, though, we must be realistic. Any complexity of thought is welcome, especially when the writer's message clearly outstrips his spelling skills. In Figure 2.4, Ryan tells us that "Vipers are venomous and they are very fast." A deadly combination.

By grade 1, we usually see increased detail emerging both in pictures and in text. For example, in Figure 2.5, Andrew shows a very detailed picture of moving day. Start looking for the "little things" in this picture, and you will be amazed at this student's observational skills: bricks on the chimney, billows of smoke, bars on the windows, fruit on the tree and a nice hollow for nesting, a smiling sun with avant garde glasses, and of course, the use of text: "Move." Also notice the not-so-happy face on the driver. Moving is hard.

First grader Zachary has a flair for imagery. In Figure 2.6, Zachary creates a picture of his room that is vivid and anything but enticing.

In Figure 2.7, Devon goes for originality—a trait that never receives enough audience appreciation. How nice is his dad? Why, "as nice as some pudding." There's a simile you don't hear every day. Moreover, Devon expands his writing, giving reasons for his affection: Dad takes his children out for ice cream, takes them hunting, and has (apparently) bought them a bear and video camera, the perfect gifts!

Writing is strongest when it's real. In Figure 2.8, Kurt recounts the story of being injured by a boat propeller. He has no difficulty staying focused. Notice

Figure 2.4

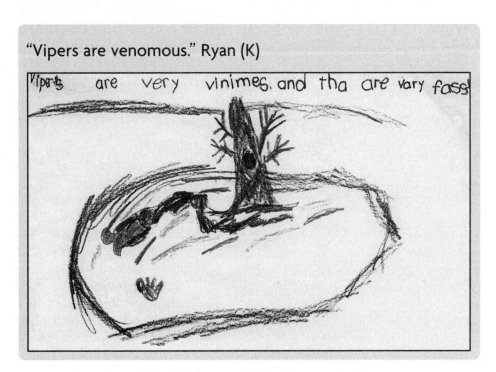

"Vipers are venomous." Ryan (K)

Figure 2.5

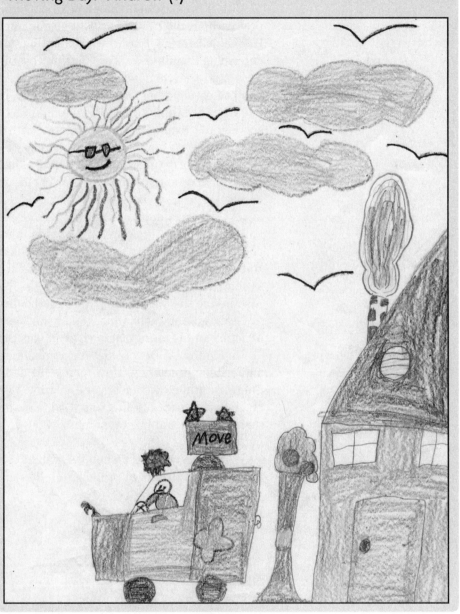

Figure 2.6   "My Room."

The gum hangs from my ceiling. My room looks like a Pigsty. There is a cupcake on my desk that is full of fuzz.

It was hard to clean up!

By Zachary (1)

the expanded details. Kurt manages to tell a lot without telling too much.

Prompts have their limitations, and for the most part, children do their best writing on their own topics. However, a wide-open prompt such as "The best gift I ever got" sometimes elicits remarkably personal, voice-filled writing because the writer can take it in any direction. Witness Sarah's response in Figure 2.9. Many children, of course, write about the "specialness" of a family, but Sarah gives very explicit reasons: Mom helps her find things, her brother never tattles on her, and it is easy to make Anna smile. This part of her writing is original and rings true. Dad has taken care to bury

Figure 2.7

"Nice Dad." Devon (1)

ThE Nice DaD.

You ahe as NicE as SomE
    PuDDiNG.
YoU Take us out For icecream,
aND you takeme with Grampa
        to go HuNtiNg For BiRDs!
a ND I likethe beah

        aND ViDEO camEra.

You are the Nice DaD.

☆☺☆ Love DeVon
        I Love you DaD

Figure 2.8

"The Time I Got Hurt." Kurt (2)

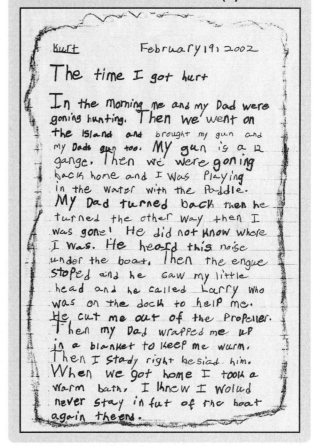

Kurt   February 19, 2002
The time I got hurt

In the morning me and my Dad were
goning hunting. Then we went on
the Island and brought my gun and
my Dads gun too. MY gun is a 12
gange. Then we were goning
back home and I was Playing
in the water with the Paddle.
MY Dad turned back then he
turned the other way then I
was gone! He did not know whore
I was. He heard this noise
under the boat. Then the engue
stoped and he saw my little
head and he called Larry who
was on the dock to help me.
He cut me out of the Propeller.
Then my Dad wrapped me up
in a blanket to keep me warm.
Then I stady right besiad him.
When we got home I took a
warm bath. I knew I wolud
never stay in fut of the boat
again the end.

Figure 2.9

"The best gift I ever got"

The best gift thet I ever got was love. Because my family is so speshel to me. My mom and dad help me find som thing when I lost it. My brother lets me play with him som times. He rilly never tattles on me. I all ways make Anna smile. She is my little sister. Molleghy all ways makes me lagh she is verey nice to me. She is just a toddler. I had a dog, but he dieyd I can visit him every day. My dad baryd him in the woods. he was verey verey old. He was back and white. My brother Sam nows wait he look like. He has a pickcher of him. But I keep it in my mined. Molleghy was verry little thin when Werthles was a round. Anna did not get to see Werthles. But we got lots of pickchers of him.

By Sarah (2)

Figure 2.10

Kristen's idea chart. (Based on Beth Olshansky's *Picturing Writing*)

Name Kristen Spring snow Picturing Writing			page #
Snow	sky	trees	sounds
Glittery ✓ fluffy ✓ Powdery sparckels ✓ cristels ✓	electric Black smooth ✓	swooshing ✓ blowing ✓	whimpering chrunchy ✓

The glittery snow sparckels like crystals onner the fluffy snow. the electric black sky is as smooth as a pond in the lsky. the swooshing thees are blowing agenst my face. The sound of whimppering mackes a shiver go from my head to my toes. the chrunchy snow soothes my hart. A chunck of snow fell down on me my dogy started shacking all his made snow fall on himthe Fcareyed him in and gave him a bath.

The End

the dog (Worthless? What a great name.) in a spot where Sarah can visit him every day. That's love.

The question of when and how to introduce the idea of true revision troubles every primary teacher (see Chapter 5 for more ideas on this). Writing/art

Figure 2.11

Kristen's picture. Kristen (2)

The glittery fluffy snow sparkles like crystals. The electric black sky is as smooth as a pond. The swishing trees and the cold wind blow against my face. The sound of my dog whimpering makes a shiver that goes from my head to my toes. The crunching snow soothes my heart. A chunk of snow fell down on me. Plop! My dog started barking. All his barking makes snow fall on him! Plop! Plop! I carried him inside my warm house and gave him a bath. Ahhh!

teacher Penny Clare uses a multistep approach (based on Beth Olshansky's *Picturing Writing*) that encourages students not so much to change their writing as to help it grow. In Figure 2.10 you can see Kristen's idea chart, in which she simply jotted some first thoughts. Based on this, she created a picture (Figure 2.11). This led to a rough draft, followed by the final that accompanies her picture. Art is based on detail—looking *at* and *inside* the world around us. Drawing and painting help us focus and shape our ideas. We often think of art as the frosting on the cake, but in terms of its role in guiding thinking, art is sometimes the recipe.

Justin's piece (Figure 2.12) is based on a wholly original idea, and has a kind of energy we often see when children write on personal topics. Notice how the range and clarity of details make the voice sparkle in this piece, particularly in the reference to the "terrific five food groups" and Justin's delightful description of his brain "bellowing" a warning when he's about to go off-track.

By grade 3, the ability of students to create striking imagery and sustained stories/essays is growing by leaps and bounds. Notice how Michael thoughtfully groups together images and impressions, creating a collage for us in "What I See Through My Eyes" (Figure 2.13). In an expository piece on alliga-

Figure 2.12

"My Faithful Brain." Justin (2)

My Faithful Brain

My brain is faithful. It is as smart as Tomas Edesen. It loves God Jesis and the holy speret. My brain leads me to apregheate the terrific five food groups. It adores school and Sunday school. It loves to do Science, math, geografy, playing, watching vidyos and tv. And when I'm about to do something wrong, my brain bellows out "No. My brain is brighter than the sun and more delishus than pumpken pie. My brain is me!

Justin

Figure 2.13

What I see through my eyes

The sun

glistening on a group of trees

A storm has just passed by

Millions of pinecones

laying on the ground

silent as can be.

Snow capped mountains

in the distance

Mount Rainier sitting alone

glittering in the sun

Birds chirping

As they look for their lunch.

By Michael (3)

tors (Figure 2.14), Annie is playing with the concept of metaphor after listening to Janell Cannon's enchanting book *Verdi*. In the first paragraph, Annie feels compelled to use as many metaphors as possible, practicing this new skill. By paragraph 2, however, she has fallen into a wonderfully relaxed rhythm, using metaphor to expand meaning and to help the reader picture the cunning and skill an alligator uses in hunting.

In her piece entitled "Black Widows" (Figure 2.15), Frances manages to juggle quite an extraordinary amount of factual information, yet she sustains a tone of interest and curiosity throughout. This is an excellent example of information presented clearly, but it also shows the impact of sheer enthusiasm on voice.

Sometimes very young writers startle us with their level of complexity, and their ability to sustain thinking through an extended

Figure 2.14

Alligators

Alligators look cool. Their color is almost as green as grass. Their tummy is like the tan desert floor. Teeth are very sharp like needles. The tail is long like the Mississippi River. It's skin is like mountains in a row. The jaws snap closed like a steel trap. Alligators are cool.

Alligators need good skills to survive. They need sharp eye sight. They have to be as still as a log when they are hunting. They are strong enough to drag their victim into the water and hold it there. Alligators have to be sly like a fox in order to know when to attack. They have to have a good sense of smelling like a dog because they rely on their smelling in the dark. Alligators are good hunters.

"Alligators." Annie (3)

Figure 2.15 "Black Widows." Frances (3)

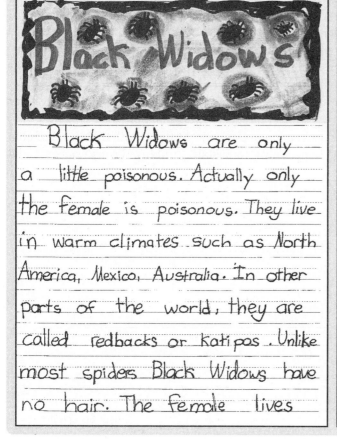

Black Widows are only a little poisonous. Actually only the female is poisonous. They live in warm climates such as North America, Mexico, Australia. In other parts of the world, they are called redbacks or katipos. Unlike most spiders Black Widows have no hair. The female lives up to 18 months and can have from 250 to 750 eggs. On the other hand males can only live for 25 to 40 days. There are 4 species of Black Widows. When they are ready they shed their skins. The Black Widow, Theridiidae, are only 1½ inches wide and also they have 8 eyes and legs. I used to think spiders were scary, but now I think they're cool.

by Frances

piece. When first grader Jaclyn (Figure 2.16) was given access to multiple blank pages, she simply kept the flow of ideas going, creating a book—*Winter*—with numerous illustrations. Though some pages contain just a *little text*, each contributes to the overall continuity of the whole. She never loses focus, and the power of her imagery pulls us right into her world. Who knows how many books our students—even kindergartners—would write if we *just gave them more paper.*

Figure 2.16 Winter By Jaclyn (1) (continued on next 3 pages)

Figure 2.16   Continued

In the morning you dress anxiously to go out into the shadows of the earth.

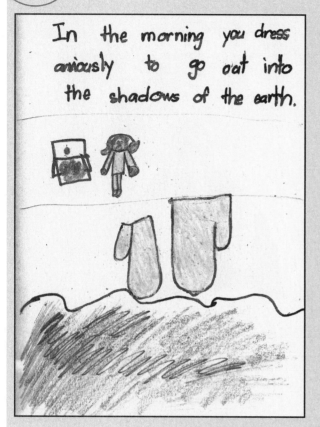

The snow does a silent ballet in your paradise place.

The snow whispers of silence the beauty of the earth.

Hey the earth is beautiful.

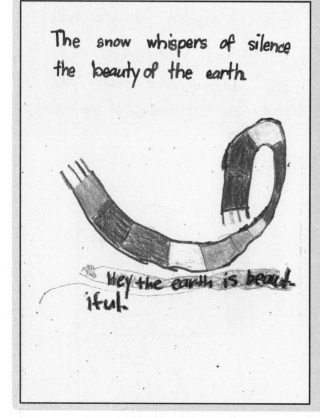

You find that Winter on the earth is grand

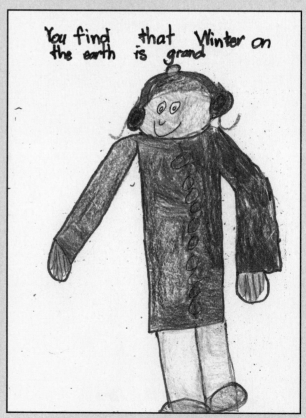

Figure 2.16 Continued

You have your shivering hands in your freezing pokets.

You sip your cocoa by a crackling fire and hear a wonderful story.

You have finished your cocoa and have beautiful fantasies ...

of

Figure 2.16   Continued

Full Text for *Winter* By Jaclyn (1)
Dedicated to Jack Frost.

Copyright May 28, 2003.

Every evening as you have visions of your destiny in the glazing white snow you make the full desires of your heart known. In the morning you dress anxiously to go out into the shadows of the earth. The snow does a silent ballet in your paradise place. The snow whispers of silence the beauty of the earth. *Hey the earth is beautiful.* You find that winter on the earth is grand. You have your shivering hands in your freezing pokets. You sip your cocoa by a crackling fire and hear a wonderful story. You have finished your cocoa and have beautiful fantasies . . . of your future.

CHECKLISTS AND RUBRICS/CONTINUUMS
Checklists

Figure 2.17 shows a primary checklist for ideas. You may find the difficulty level of this checklist about right for your students, or you may wish to simplify it—or even add a bit more information. The checklist should grow with you; change or expand it as your student writers gain a stronger sense of what a topic is, what a detail is, and what it means to make a message clear to a reader.

Figure 2.17 ☑

Primary Checklist for Ideas

☐ I thought of my own idea.

☐ My message makes sense.

☐ My writing has details.

☐ My picture has details.

☐ My writing makes a picture in your mind.

Rubrics/Continuums

In Chapter 8 you will find primary-level continuums (descriptors, no numbers) for *ideas* and the other five traits described here. Those continuums span five stages of performance from that of the most rudimentary writers who are just beginning to make marks on paper through a level at which young writers not only create meaning but also expand that meaning with imagery, insight, and detail. Rubrics (with numbers) for older students, or those who are writing at a higher level of skill than grade level might suggest, appear in the Appendix.

SPOTTING ORGANIZATION

Organization for young writers does not usually include a whiz-bang lead, logical sequencing of ideas, and a killer conclusion. It may be as simple as the linking of picture writing with text. Do the two go together? Does each enhance the other? For some young writers/artists, organization begins with the sequencing of pictures, using more than one visual to tell a story or write an all-about paper. Sometimes drawing first helps a student writer organize his or her thoughts. Remember that in its early stages, organization often takes one of three forms:

1. Grouping things that logically go together
2. Telling things in an order that makes sense
3. Coordinating verbal writing (text) with picture writing

The addition of a title and use of the words *The End* are helpful organizational devices for young writers. At grade 8 writing, we are dismayed to find students still finishing a piece with *The End*, but at primary level, we value the student's recognition that an ending is needed. First things first.

As students grow in their organizational skills, and as they begin to rely on text as much as or more so than on pictures, we find other signs: multiple sentences that stay on one topic, a progression of ideas from general to specific or from the beginning of a story to the end, the use of surprise at the close of a story or essay, the use of a striking statement or question to kick off the writing, and so on. Even at primary level, some

I discovered that not only could first graders select topics, but they could also present coherent and detailed information about those topics on paper.
—**Carol Avery**
And With a Light Touch (2002, p. 2)

students become quite adept at using transitional words such as *later, then, next, the next day, another reason, first, second,* and so on. These connecting words—or *transitional words*—build bridges between ideas and the need to be noticed.

For many students, listing is a comfortable method of organizing information. If you provide opportunities for creating lists—a grocery list, a to-do list, or a recipe, for example—you encourage this simple but effective way to keep track of ideas.

What to Look for in Pictures
✔ Pictures and text that enhance each other
✔ Pictures in sequence that tell a story or develop a concept
✔ Use of a title or label

What to Look for in Text
✔ Use of an introductory device such as a title
✔ Use of words that suggest a beginning: *once, one day, yesterday,* and so on
✔ Use of words that connect ideas: *meanwhile, however, then, next,* and so on
✔ Use of words that show a sense of conclusion: *at last, finally, when it was all over,* and so on
✔ More than one sentence about the same idea (focus)
✔ A progression of ideas or a pattern of some sort: comparison of two things, problem to solution, from first to last, from large idea to small, and so on
✔ A surprise ending
✔ Use of the words *The End*

What to Say in Your Comments
✔ I could follow this from beginning to end. I never felt lost!
✔ You started with one topic—*mosquitoes*—and you stayed with it through the whole paper. That's what I call being focused.
✔ This ending was a real surprise. Surprises make writing interesting.
✔ I noticed you used a word here—*meanwhile*—to connect ideas. Word bridges like this really help me as a reader.
✔ I like the way you started your paper, helping me picture the turtle. That was a good lead.
✔ You began with a problem—the short recess—and then you came up with a solution—having recess instead of lunch. That's a good way to organize information.

Comments, you may have noticed, provide a sneaky but nonetheless effective way of teaching the traits. You can work in the language of the traits (little things like *details, leads, conclusions, linking words, titles, surprise, ideas, focus,* and so on) in a gentle manner. Those words stick with your students, and each one provides one more step up in thinking about writing.

Some Examples

Kindergartner Brock (Figure 2.18) displays a wonderful sense of sequencing in a short piece on planting a rose. "Look what you've done!" this piece seems to say. "You planted a rose! Now all you need are water and sun—and soon you'll have flowers!"

Figure 2.18

"Planting a Rose." Brock (K)

YOU PlHd a Sed. It xl gro ni to a rozl. We
haf to givit som whrdr odd San.

You planted a seed. It will grow into a rose! We have to give
it some water and sun.

In its earliest stages, organization shows itself with such simple features as coordinated placement of text and picture on the page—a spatial organization, if you will. Cognitive organization is evident through the relationship between text and picture. They "go together," we say. If you think this is a small feat to be readily dismissed, I would ask you to consider this: Professional authors (see Chapter 7) are so deft in coordinating illustrations with text that they choreograph the whole relationship like a dance, deliberately determining, page to page, which will carry the force of the message. They guide our eyes from words to pictures and back again in a delicate balance that gives us information while holding our attention. Amanda's piece on playing with her dog and bunnies (Figure 2.19) effectively illustrates picture-text organization.

Text and pictures go together beautifully in Joely's book, "What Animals Don't Do" (Figure 2.20). In her book, Joely also illustrates another highly sophisticated organizational trait—deliberate patterning for effect. Many young writers follow patterns in crafting sentences because it is comfortable to do so; for example, "I love summer. I love the sun. I love frogs." This example is a little different. Joely is using the pattern deliberately to build to her conclusion: "But I do!" The climax page is everything, and it tells us that her use of patterning is purposeful and meant to keep us on the hook. Like many young writers, Joely uses art to stimulate her thoughts. The text is dictated but is totally hers. Sometimes we underestimate the value of dictation to capture longer or more complex messages from young writers.

Sometimes—whether we are noticing organization, word choice, voice, or whatever—moments within a piece stand out. This is the case with Justin's story (Figure 2.21 on page 41), entitled, "The vakshin [Vacation]." Justin has a growing sense of what a lead is and introduces his paper with a question. I particularly like the ending: "I will always remember when a fish hit me with his fin

Figure 2.19

"Dogs and Bunnies." Amanda (K)

I AM PLAYING WITH MY DOG AND BUNES.

Figure 2.20   "What Animals Don't Do" (14 pages). Joely (K)

Figure 2.20 Continued

Parrots don't get dressed.

Seals don't ride horses.

Tigers don't dance.

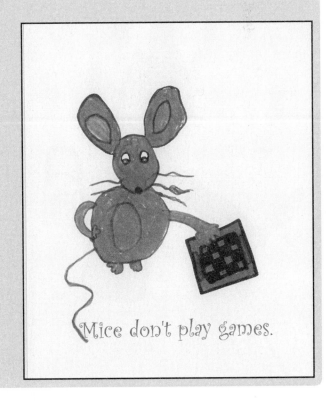

Mice don't play games.

Figure 2.20 Continued

Tortoises don't go shopping.

Giraffes don't roller skate.

Cats don't do projects.

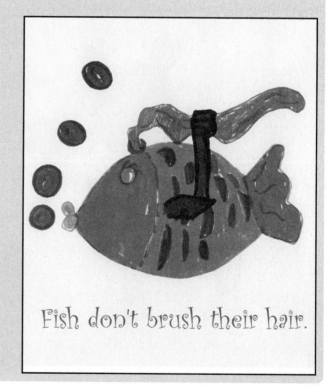

Fish don't brush their hair.

Figure 2.20 Continued

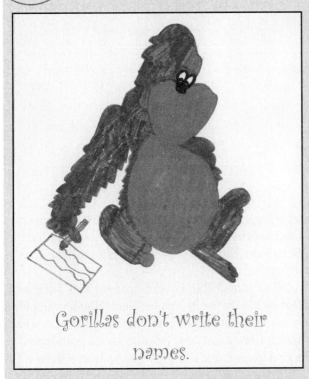

Gorillas don't write their names.

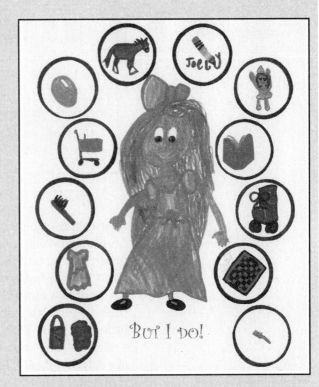

But I do!

and I thought it was a shark." What he is really saying is, "*This* is the moment I remember most." I was delighted that he dared to finish without a cliché wrap-up: "I hope we go back to Florida next year!"

How-to papers are naturals for teaching organization. Although step-by-step structure certainly is not the only organizational pattern writers need, it is

Figure 2.21 "The Vakshin" By Justin (1)

The vakshin

Have you benn on a vokshin be for. I went fodast in Florida it is like California. I went shrthing thair. And I wipt out. I frict out wine I jumpt of the shrth bord. I will aowas rentr wine a fish hit me with he's fin and I tho th it wse a shark.

The Vacation

Have you been on a vacation before? I went four days in Florida. It is like California. I went surfing there. And I wiped out. I freaked out when I jumped off the surfboard. I will always remember when a fish hit me with his fin and I thought it was a shark.

Figure 2.22

"How to Make a Snowman" Felicia (1)

First, I would make three snowballs. one small, one medium and one big. second, put the big snowball on the bottum, medium in the middle, and small snowball on the top. next, I would get a carrot for a nose. I would stick it in the middle of the small snowball. Then I would get small rocks for the eyes and mouth. then I will get a hat that doesn't fit me. or you can get any hat. do the same thing with the scarf. Then I would get small rocks again for the buttons. Next, I would get two sticks and stick it in the middle. do it side to side. That's it.

a refreshing change from chronological patterning, and it is a fairly simple one for most students to understand because it's easy to tell when steps are left out or are written out of order. Notice the thoroughness of Felicia's instructions in "How to Make a Snowman" (Figure 2.22).

Andrew's story "Honey Cat" (Figure 2.23), is well-ordered and filled with fresh details. For example, Honey has "wobbly stripes," and "She let me pull a little on her tail. That's not common about cats." I love the conclusion, in which Andrew lets us know that though Honey Cat now belongs to his grandparents, she was his first. Within his first paragraph lies a dynamite lead. Given a bit more experience, Andrew will likely "hear" this himself and will dare to pick

Figure 2.23

"Honey Cat"

Last Christmas, I was at my grandma and grandpa's house. Every Christmas we go there. They live on a farm. A cat was abandoned by their house. There was more than a foot of snow on the ground. The cat was lucky to find their horse barn.

I was doing chores with my grandparents when I first saw the cat. She had black, white, and brown wobbly stripes. When I saw her the next morning, I thought of a name for her. The name was, "Honey," because she is my little honey. I fed her every day I was there. She let me pull a little on her tail. That's not common about cats. She liked me petting her with strokes from her neck down to her tail. Honey followed me wherever I went but not inside the house.

Honey is now their cat, but at first she wasn't. She's sort of like my cat when I'm there. I kiss her sometimes, because I love her.

By Andrew (1)
Written by Andrew Hicks, May 26, 2001,
as a story assigned by Mrs. Giles, his first grade teacher.

Figure 2.24

Baby Bird By Ries (K)

I fand a babby berd. It cudit opin its iss.
It Had a Kut on its leg.
I cherid to fed It But that nit It Did.
the End

Bi Ries

I found a baby bird. It couldn't open its eyes.
It had a cut on its leg.
   I carried [it home] to feed it but that
night it died.

The language we use in our minilessons to talk about writing will become the language the students speak when they talk about writing.

—Katie Wood Ray

—Lisa B. Cleaveland

About the Authors (2004, p. 97)

right up on those last two sentences; for example, "With more than a foot of snow on the ground, the cat was lucky to find the horse barn." Would I suggest this lead to Andrew right now? No, not exactly. However, because he has so many strengths to comment and build on—fluency, voice, order, detail—it doesn't hurt to toss out one suggestion. I might say this: "The last two sentences in your first paragraph *really* caught my attention—wow. Like the start of a chilling mystery story. I was wondering what would happen if you started with these details—the snow and the cat hunting for the horse barn." Then what happens *happens*. But it will be his, not mine.

Ries (Figure 2.24) tells a multipart story of finding a baby bird. Notice how all the events in this piece work together to form a whole story: Ries finds the bird, notices two problems (it can't open its eyes, it has a cut on its leg) and carries it (home, presumably) to try to feed it. But . . . that night the bird dies. This tiny story has a lead, development, tension, turning point, and conclusion. By calling these elements what they are, we help Ries understand what has made this story so successful, and what to do next time.

Why do we not encourage students more often to collaborate as authors and illustrators? We should because when students get together, as Ashley and Shelby did (Figure 2.25), remarkable things happen. They talk, for one thing. And for young writers, talking is among the most effective prewriting (and writing) techniques. They share ideas, feed off each other's imaginations, and share responsibilities for writing and illustrating—just as published writers and illustrators do.

In his piece *At the Beach* (Figure 2.26), Noah illustrates two keys to good organization. Not only does he connect everything he says to his main idea (going to the beach), but he makes a "most important" point: He must remember the sunscreen. His creative punctuation also tells us just how to read this piece with maximum voice.

In *Luna the Shark* (Figure 2.27), Jamielyn gives us an excellent example of a very useful organizational structure: before and after (or, if you prefer, problem and solution). Luna starts out as a bully, but finds she cannot make friends without changing her attitude. We can point out the success of this design—"I enjoyed guessing whether Luna would ever behave differently"—and also encourage Jamielyn to listen for the same design in the literature she hears.

Alec cuts right to the heart of the matter with his introduction to the paper "Foxes" (Figure 2.28): "A fox appears in the moon's silvery shadows." This is enticing and masterful.

Pearson takes a bit longer to launch into his story "Fishing in Alaska" (the story really begins with the second paragraph), but once the action begins, it moves at high speed (Figure 2.29). Notice his skillful use of present tense, which gives this story a sense of immediacy. Everything is happening right now! Short sentences (and one fragment) build a kind of tension and energy that give this story wonderful voice.

Figure 2.25

"We Love Volcanoes" Ashley and Shelby (K)

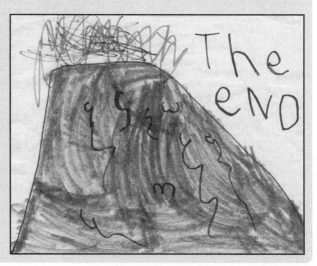

Figure 2.26   **At the Beach by Noah (K)**

This summer i am going to the beach. At the beach, i am going to climb up rocks and also if i am not ssick! i am going in the water. But! befor i go in the water this is the inpotint thing. I need some sunsscreen.

Figure 2.27   **Luna the Shark by Jamielyn (3)**

One morning on a sunny day, Luna went off to school with a bunch of other fishes glaring at her suspiciously. while she was swimming she thought, "Oh, I bully a lot of fishes and sharks." her sister Christine was having a party with her friends. her mother Elizabeth asked, "Luna, why don't you invite your friends over too?" but she is a bully. How will she make friends?

Luna wanted friends but she declared, "That's just who I am." After, she started seeing and hearing how everybody are together with their friends. So, she started feeling lonely. She has one little problem she needs to solve.

Luna is jealous of other fishes with friends, but as she thought, should I be kind or stay the same? She asked her mother, "what can I do?" She replied, "you cant get friends if you're acting like a bully!" So, Luna changed her attitude.

The next day, she saw the fishes she always bullied, they ran away. Luna proved that she changed by having the little fishes ask her mother to find the truth about her. One year passed, Luna wasn't the same Luna anymore. when she swims with the other fishes, they now laugh and talk.

Figure 2.28

"A Fox"

> A fox appears in the moon's silvery shadows. His orange bushy fur keeps him as steamy as an oven. Hail started to rapidly fall as the fox leaped off through the brisk night. He lunges on a squirrel and dashes to his den. He curls up in a ball as his tail fades away from the dim light and takes a rest from a long day.
>
> By Alec (3)

Figure 2.29

"Fishing in Alaska"

> Hi, my name is Pearson. You are about to hear about the most exciting day of my life.
>
> It's about 8:00 in the morning. I'm going halibut fishing with my dad, my uncle, and my grandpa. We're at the fishing spot. What's this? My dad has one! He's brought it onto the boat. Its tail is slapping frantically. It's a giant sixty-five pounder! It's as big as me!
>
> The waves are crashing over the boat. I'm up. It's raining ice cold rain. I'm freezing. I've got one! It's extremely hard to reel it in. Finally it's over. It's on the boat. Thirty pounds.
>
> My grandpa is seasick so he can't fish. My uncle catches one that weighs thirty pounds, too. My uncle and I catch two more thirty pounders. We go home and have some hot chocolate.
>
> By Pearson (3)

Figure 2.30

"The Day I Got My Dog"

> The day I got my dog we were really only supposed to be looking. My mom, my dad, and I got into our car and drove down to PetCo (where they sold rescued dogs on Saturdays) and went in to have a look. There were a lot of dogs to choose from.
>
> We were looking around when we saw an adorable puppy in one of the cages. We immediately knew that he wouldn't be there the next Saturday—so we got him.
>
> When we got home, we ended up calling him "Puppy" all day because we couldn't think of a name for him. Then, when I was about to go into my room to go to bed, my mom came down the hall and said that my dad had thought up a name for our dog.
>
> "How about Tucker?" she asked. I agreed and we still have him today.
>
> By Max (3)

Figure 2.31 ☑

Primary Checklist for Organization

☐ My writing and my picture go together.

☐ My paper has a beginning.

☐ My writing has ORDER.

☐ You will NOT feel lost!

☐ I make WORD BRIDGES.

☐ My paper has an ending.

Max begins his story "The Day I Got My Dog" (Figure 2.30) so gracefully that it's easy to overlook how effective his lead really is. When he tells us "We were really only supposed to be looking," we know at once what will happen. Notice the conclusion: It doesn't hang around on the back porch—it says a quick good-bye and exits. Max already has a good sense of what to leave out of a story as well as what to put in. Sometimes we do young writers a disservice with the old standard line: "Tell me more." More isn't always the answer, and it usually is not what we really want either. It's the "right" details that count—and this writer not only includes them but puts them in an order that is easy to follow.

See Figure 2.31 for a primary checklist for organization.

ON THE HUNT FOR VOICE

Voice is among the most rewarding traits to teach at primary level because, first of all, it shows up in both picture writing and text writing. Pictures have personality, appeal, individuality—all the attributes of voice. Furthermore, primary writers tend to be uninhibited in their expression, and lack of inhibition usually promotes voice. In short, this is an area in which you can often reward young writers who struggle in other areas—such as organizing writing or using conventions correctly.

Voice is expression personalized. Any time you look at a picture and say to yourself, "Oh, this *has* to be Kawai's work," you know it has voice. Of course, sometimes we recognize voice without knowing the artist/writer at all. A picture may make you laugh (or cry). It may be haunting—or may cause you to connect to a memory of your own you thought was buried. You may find yourself mentally characterizing it: It's whimsical, silly, honest, frightening, or stunning. If it creates an emotional response, it has voice. It speaks to us—somehow, in some way.

Because voice is personal, it tends to emerge more strongly in certain types of writing (although writers with powerful voice cannot be held down by form). Voice blossoms in personal narrative, persuasive writing, letters of all kinds, role modeling, journals, and memoirs. A set of directions is less likely to encourage voice, but this is not to say it cannot happen, as in this student's tip: "If the horse you're drawing looks more like a dog, make it a dog" (Lewis, 1994).

Voice also comes from caring about topic and audience. Bored writers have little or no voice because their hearts just aren't in it. Lucy Calkins says, "When writers learn to listen for the voice of a story, to look for language with a little luck in it, we approach writing with a

> The responsive teacher is an encourager, and there are two important reasons for that. One is that the student doesn't know what is good, what has potential, what is working any more than the inexperienced student [knows] what doesn't work. We learn to write primarily by building on our strengths, and it is important for the teacher to encourage the student to see what has potential, what has strength, and what can be developed
>
> **—Donald Murray**
>
> *A Writer Teaches Writing* (1985, p. 157)

Don Murray says the role of the teacher of writing is to laugh and cheer. I try to remember his advice as I listen to writers talk about their writing

—Carol Avery

And With a Light Touch (2002, p. 66)

different sort of expectation. Instead of expecting ourselves to write silly, short texts, we hold our subject in our hands and say, 'This is going to be huge.' We expect to layer our writing with the deepest, richest parts of our lives" (1994, p. 259).

My litmus test for voice is always the same, regardless of the piece or the age of the writer: *Would I share it?* If the answer is "yes," I know that the piece is strong in voice. Think of the writing you love to share aloud with your students, the books that are favorites (for them and for you). Those books are rich with voice. What works for professional writers works for your students as well.

What to Look for in Pictures

✔ A unique or distinctive style or approach
✔ Emotions, as expressed on the faces of characters, for example
✔ Humor
✔ Passion, as expressed through color or style
✔ A piece you would like to share with others

What to Look for in Text

✔ Strong expression of feeling
✔ Text that makes you feel like laughing or crying—or that gives you the chills
✔ Text that makes a connection to a personal memory
✔ Text you remember—and think about
✔ Text you would like to share with others
✔ Text that communicates directly with the audience—for example, a question: *Do you like vegetables? Have you ever been to California? Are you afraid of snakes?*

What to Say in Your Comments

✔ I loved reading this. I read it twice. That's voice.
✔ I could tell how you felt when your dog ran away.
✔ I had to read this aloud. Then I could *really* hear your voice.
✔ You write like you mean it. I like that.
  ✔ You write as if you care how the reader feels.
  ✔ I can tell you care about this topic and you want me to care, too.
  ✔ This sounded like you and no one else. That's a sign of voice.
  ✔ This moment right here [point it out] really caught my attention.

So often, children don't even realize they have done remarkable things in their writing. We must help them see this and then make room for celebration.

—Katie Wood Ray
—Lisa B. Cleaveland

About the Authors (2004, p. 138)

Voice is like springtime in March. One moment it's powerful; you feel the sun on your shoulders and smell change in the air. The next—whoosh, the March wind blows, and the moment is gone. That's OK. Moments of voice are indicators of good things to come—and the writer's voice, like the sun, will return. Nurture it. Make sure that you let students know which moments, specifically, have the most power. Writers rarely sustain voice every moment through an entire piece of writing; that takes about as much energy as doing aerobics all day long. It's hard to be on stage 24/7.

Some Examples

As readers, sometimes we feel we need a whole text, or at least a paragraph, to really hear voice. This is not always so. Sometimes, a line will do. Eduardo, the K-2 kid (Figure 2.32), simply cannot hold in his exhuberance. He has nailed the essence of voice.

Ries (Figure 2.33) gives us a lesson on injecting voice into informational writing. Joke around a bit—just to see if the reader is paying attention. We were paying attention, and now we're chuckling.

In Sarah's paper "Best Friends" (Figure 2.34), we hear strong emotions emerging. Notice the capital letters on "Sad Ending" and "Tears Dripped." Check out A. A. Milne's *Winnie the Pooh* and you'll find capital letters on most

Figure 2.32

By Eduardo (K)

I em so ixsitid BCUs I am K-2 Kid!!!!!

Figure 2.33

Lincoln By Ries (K)

Ries
Lihcoln
verey Was
Jost Ferst The Peisndt
keing! He wos Nmer 16.
HS Fas is oh The Pene.

Lincoln was the very first president. Just kidding! He was number 16. His face is on the penny.

Figure 2.34

"Best Friends"

Once when I lived in Dover I had a best friend named Kristen. She let me go to her Bday partys. We always got surprised. One time a storyteller came and gave us a lot of candy. We had a very good friendship togather until a Sad Ending came. Tear's Dripped from our eyes. I was moving after this day. Every one I new gave me going away presents. Even Mrs. B who was old and lived across the street from me. She really meant alought to me. I will always miss her so. I will always Remember her in my Life. and the day I met her. She was special because She always made my day special.

By Sarah (2)

significant words. Capitals signify importance. I love the line: "I will always miss her so." You don't just *hear* the voice there—you *feel* it.

Papers about best friends bring out voice with young writers because feelings are strong. It's even better when the writing includes some strikingly original comments, as is the case with Kris's piece (Figure 2.35). She tells us that a good friend "is someone who can defend you." Notice, too, that Kris thinks for herself: "A friend that make's me play with them all the time is a person I don't like." Writers with voice are writers with opinions.

Expressive language often contributes to voice. Wait a minute, though—isn't that word choice? Yes, but because the traits are closely linked, it is hard to change one without affecting the other. Lilly (Figure 2.36) increases the voice in her piece when she calls *Anne of Green Gables* "an old classic" or refers to "fire-burnt red hair" and "wide imaginations" and most especially in her closing line: "Her imagination inspires mine."

Joleen (Figure 2.37) is clearly fond of her father, and writing about what she loves, what amuses her, puts voice into her text—and into her illustration as well. *Go dad*, indeed! Cirque du Soleil, eat your heart out.

Voice is passion, certainly. It's spontaneity, too. Notice how the two combine in Jana Leigh's paper (Figure 2.38). It was the Friday before Mother's Day, and the

Figure 2.35

"A Good Friend"

I really miss my best friend Alyssa she moved to Philadolphea. I think a good friend is someone who can defend you. Alyssa and I meet in kindergarten. We are now pen pals. We had lots of play dates. We would play with my dog. A friend that make's me play with them all the time is a person I don't like. To have a best friend I think you need to know that person for a wyhill. Friends allways cheer me up when I'm in the dump's.

By Kris (2)

Figure 2.36

Review of *Anne of Green Gables*

Dear Mrs. R,
The book I am reading is an old classic and it is called Anne of Green Gables. Anne reminds me of Peppie long Stockings. Anne reminds me of her because they both have fire-burnt red hair and have wide imaginations.

I liked this book because it has a lot of excitement and Anne is sort of energetic and happy all of the time. Her imagination inspires mine.

Always,
Lilly

By Lilly (3)

Figure 2.37

My Dad Is Strog! By Joleen (K)

Name Joleen   Date 5-22

My dad is strogl! he can kere me in won hand. he is fne! Laf wn he crez me. my dad max me pix me up and go dAd!

My dad is strong! He can carry me in one hand. He is funny! My dad makes me laugh when he picks me up and carries me. Go dad!

Figure 2.38 "No Mom's Allowed" Jana Leigh (K)

NO MOM'S ALPLLD in tis CLAS NLAS you Dot HAV A DIALD in tis DLAS NOLK

kindergarten class was making Mother's Day cards. Jana Leigh was worried because her mother worked as a school secretary. What if she should burst in and see her card ahead of time? Her teacher, Debby, helped her come up with a solution: How do you keep unwanted people out of a room? A sign, of course. Jana Leigh's sign reads "No moms allowed in this class unless you don't have a child in this class. No. Knock." She doesn't add "This means you," but we can read between the lines. Her illustration shows a fist knocking on the door with sound waves emanating.

Alyssha's teacher just lost her mother and is feeling the pain of that loss. In a heartfelt letter (Figure 2.39), Alyssha assures her that all will be well because her students are so close to her, they are like her brothers and sisters. Who could fail to take comfort in such a message?

Nothing contributes more to voice than flat-out honesty, the kind of frank honesty expressed in Morgan's paper "What Hurts my Feelings Most" (Figure 2.40). You can sense the force of Morgan's feelings from the capital letters, the exclamation points, and the simple but to-the-point disclosure: "It makes me want to punch them in the face. . . ." This is a real-life paper, written from the heart. It is sad and angry at

Figure 2.39   "Dear Mrs. Choffnes" Alyssha (2)

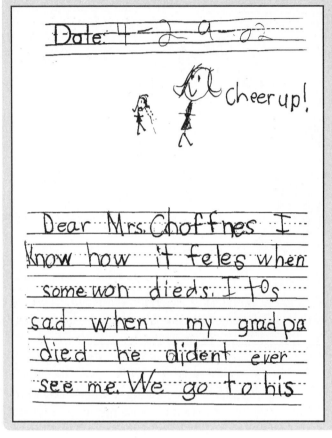

Date 4-2-9--02

Cheer up!

Dear Mrs. Choffnes I
know how it feles when
some won dieds. I tos
sad when my grad pa
died he dident ever
see me. We go to his

grave a lot and
bring him a bastest of
flowers. I am sorry
for you. But you have
us os you dont hafe
to cry. We are
your sisters and brothers
so you have lots
of brothers and sisters.
So you have friends and
family. --- Alyssha

Figure 2.40

"What Hurts My Feelings Most"

> What hurts my Feelings most is when
> people scream at me. I HATE IT!! It makes
> me want to punch them in the face but my
> dad said not to. Some times when people
> scream at me it makes me cry. My sister
> screams at me all the time but when my
> sister screams at me some times I have to
> punch her. I do not now why, just because. I
> just hope no one screams at me.
>
> By Morgan (2)

the same time. The voice bites. A paper like this can make a teacher uncomfortable because it is not a fluffy topic (What if you woke up one day and discovered you were the tooth fairy?), nor does it have a happy wrap-up. Yet it is just what Morgan needed to write at this time, and if we honor those feelings and provide an environment in which it is safe to be honest about anger or sadness, we encourage real writing with real voice. After all, it's better to *write* about bad feelings than express them physically.

In "The Bad Day" (Figure 2.41), writer Sujaytha expresses more anger, this time at the unfairness of life. Everything seems to go fine for the brother (Isn't that always the way?), while Sujaytha struggles with resentment, cut off from friends and TV. We have all experienced similar feelings, and if the line "It wusen't a dazzling day for me" found its way onto one of those filing cabinet magnets, a lot of us would buy it. When we identify and empathize, that's voice.

FIGURE 2.41 "The Bad Day"

The time when I had a bad day I setet a tantrum. I screming in pels erys. It wusen't a dazzling day for me. Puey I didn't get frens. No TV ether. Its not far that my druther gets good day. I don't like that. Not I sied n-o-t wich prte bo you not understad like that.

By Sujaytha (1)

The time when I had a bad day I started a tantrum. I [was] screaming in people's ears. It wasn't a dazzling day for me. Phooey. I didn't get friends. No TV either. It's not fair that my brother gets [a] good day. I don't like that. Not, *I said n-o-t which part do you not understand* <u>like</u> that.

Amity's poem "Only a Dad" (Figure 2.42) expresses voice in both text and art—neatly combined in her original lettering. The real secret to the voice in this one, though, lies in Amity's clear and deep sympathy for Dad, who is nearly too tired to read but does it anyway and manages to cook dinner—even if it's "without any perk."

Figure 2.42 "Only a Dad" Amity (1)

Only A Dad

Only a dad with a tired face,
can read me a book at any pace.
Only a dad who comes home from work,
can cook a dinner without any perk.
Only a dad who comes home from skiing,
can play with me all the time except when I'm peeing.

I LOVE YOU DAD!

Your daughter,
Amity

Figure 2.43

"Math Book"

> My math book is a source of learning. It is verdi. Verdi means green. My math book is made of paper. The paper is glossy. Its cover is dense. It's as hard as wood. The darn thing is thick and heavy! Math books are wonderful. Don't you think so, too? (The 2nd to last sentence isn't true.)
>
> By Tommy (3)

Following the reading of Janell Cannon's book *Verdi*, students in Cindy's class were invited to do some imitative writing, and Tommy chose his green math book (Figure 2.43) as his focus. Notice how the voice shifts in this piece, gaining momentum. At first, the book is a "source of learning." Very scholarly, very formal tone here. Later we learn that "the darn thing is thick and heavy!" just as we suspected. Tommy tells us that "math books are wonderful," but he can't live with this untruth and confesses at the end. My favorite part.

The theme of Amy's paper (Figure 2.44) seems to be "Why does everyone else get the spotlight—especially when I am the interesting one in the family?" This paper is not as angry as Sujaytha's (see Figure 2.41), but it has a definite strong undertone. Amy clearly appreciates the "funny moments" in her parents' videos but also questions why they have overlooked her; it's this attitude that makes her voice strong and individual. Notice also the abundance of details—the frosting-coated finger and Dad's big feet. When writers notice small but significant details, we say to ourselves, "Ah, I can really see *and* feel that," and the voice soars. Detail is part of ideas, but serves as a building block for voice as well.

Morgan, a second grader, is struggling a bit with conventions (Figure 2.45), and when this happens, there is always a risk that the voice will be buried. With a little decoding, we uncover a well-crafted story about a personally embarrassing moment—commenting on a scarecrow that turns out to be a live person. The story ends with a bit of philosophy, too; the writer thinks no one else has embarrassing moments then learns that this is not so. Here is a paper that needs a fair amount of work on conventions, but we can give this writer some real incentive by taking Donald Murray's advice and showing appreciation for

Figure 2.44

"Home Videos"

> When my sister was born she was funny. I know this because I wacthed Home Videos. These are some things she did: At Christmas she showed my mom her mad face. She grabbed her dress and waiked, for a second. When my mom asked her to show her her happy face she smiled. When my <u>brother</u> was one, when he just turned one that is, he stuck his finger in his cake and did nothing with the frosting on his finger. He also put on my dads shoes wicth were two times bigger than his own feet. Those were some funny moments. My mom and dad tape recorded them. But from what I saw there wasn't much about me when I was a baby. I didn't see my first birthday tape recorded.
>
> By Amy (3)

Figure 2.45 **An Embarrassing Moment.**

It's Halloween! can I have my costume. Im Dorth. Im going. I wint to the frst haes. Im at the the last haes. Tat haes hase a cut scar crol. You have a cut scar crol I saed to the latey. Thacs! Saed the scar crol. That wus the most endarsin momit. I Jupt 3! Fee! are wun was lafen. I awes have inbarsin momits. No wun haes inbarsin momits. Then I fown out its not truw. I dot fill so bad inney more. By Morgan (2)	It's Halloween! Can I have my costume? I'm Darth. I'm going. I went to the first house. [Now] I'm at the last house. That house has a cute scarecrow. "You have a cute scarecrow," I said to the lady. "Thanks!" said the scarecrow. That was the most embarrassing moment. I jumped three feet! Everyone was laughing. I always have embarrassing moments. No one [else] has embarrassing moments. Then I found out it's not true. I don't feel so bad anymore.

the strengths we see: insight and voice. Have someone read it aloud to you, and you may be startled (like the writer herself) by the detail, organizational flow, *and* voice.

As noted earlier, letters bring out voice. Carly (Figure 2.46) is writing to the school secretary on learning of her (the secretary's) mother's death. Carly puts her whole self into this piece. There is not one shred of artificiality. Not one line is routine or borrowed. She is completely, wholly herself. This is the epitome of voice. Notice the original and strong language, too: "glum for the rest of her sole breaking life."

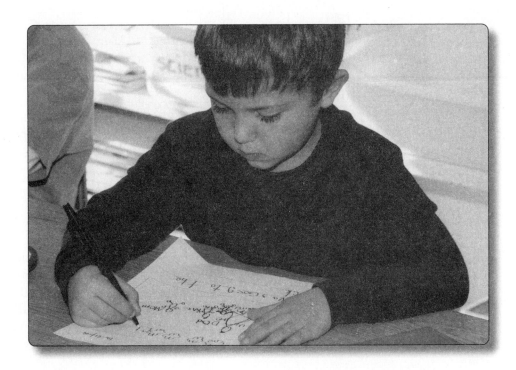

Figure 2.46

"Dear Mrs. Baker" Carly (2)

> Dear Mrs. Baker,
> I know how you feel! Once I was four and I went to visit my unbelievabl great great aunt and she died, two or three months later. When she died I felt like a once contented and proud swan who lost its feathers. Instead of swimming with the other beautiful swans she just stayed in the pussywillos and long green grass, glum for the rest of her sole breaking life. When my teacher Mrs. Burdett broke the news to us about your dear mom, it was heartache to hear. I know you will never forget your mom, I'm sure she meant the univurse to you!
> Love, Carly

Figure 2.47

Primary Checklist for Voice

- ☐ I like my writing.
- ☐ This sounds like ME!
- ☐ My paper shows feelings.
- ☐ You will like reading this OUT LOUD.
- ☐ I am writing this for _____.

Pieces with this level of voice deserve oral reading and deserve to be read with passion. Read slowly and put your heart and soul into it. That's what the writer did, and her work can only come alive with the best interpretive reading your skill and ear for language will allow. Don't be timid! Give back to Carly in the same generous spirit she has given to us.

See Figure 2.47 for a primary checklist on voice.

IN SEARCH OF WORD CHOICE

When I share books with children, they may describe them as "expressive," "delightful," "outrageous," "fantastic," or my favorite, "rememberable." Unfortunately, these words often do not make their way onto paper. On paper, the same books become "good," "fun," "sad," or "cool." There goes the air out of the balloon.

Very young students often are capable of striking, extraordinary word choice; it may show up primarily in their speech, however, not in their *writing*. Don't despair. Encourage what you *hear*, and do some team writing that allows children to express themselves orally and to use the full power of the vocabulary that lives in their minds. Create word walls and personal dictionaries that will put expressive words—the words young writers would prefer to use—right at their fingertips. Be a recorder for your students (so that they can use their oral vocabularies), or let older writers fill this role; they will learn from each other. And don't forget to comment on those early blossoming bits of word choice when you find them.

What to Look for in Pictures
✔ Striking labels or titles
✔ Speech (often enclosed in a bubble)
✔ Language woven into the picture—for example, via signs

What to Look for in Text
✔ Words of *any* kind!
✔ Words you can read and make sense of
✔ Words that replace old, tired standards—for example, something other than *nice, good, fun, cool, neat, really, very*
✔ Strong verbs—the heart of good writing
✔ Words that paint a picture
✔ Sensory words that help you hear, smell, feel, or touch the moment
✔ A stretch to use a new or unusual word
✔ The right word at the right moment—for example, "My socks were *soggy*" (compare *wet*)

What to Say in Your Comments
✔ This is the perfect word—*slimy*. I can feel that myself!
✔ Right here you said, "I raced home." *Raced* is a powerful verb. It has energy.
✔ Your word choice—*creepy, scary*—really gives your paper voice.
✔ I think this word—*delicate*—is a new one for you. I love it when you use a word you haven't used before.
✔ *Every word you used made sense to me and helped me understand your message.*
✔ *You write as if you love words.*
✔ I hope you put *zoom* in your personal dictionary. I like it.

Remember that spelling has nothing to do with word choice per se. Many young writers use powerful words they cannot spell yet. It is fine to share correct spelling as you comment on a word as long as you do not make spelling the focus of the comment. One good way to do this is to add the word to a student's personal dictionary. What you want the student to notice is that he or she is using words in a powerful way, words that have meaning, words that get a reader's attention. When students think spelling is the primary goal, they will fall back on words they know, and then everything will become *sad, fun,* and *nice* again.

Some Examples

Word choice does not have to be serious all the time. We can enjoy Abby's playfulness in "My Old Car" (Figure 2.48). "Cagu-bop tick-tick crack-crack." Ever have a car like that? You might sell it, but like Abby, you won't forget it.

Figure 2.48 "My Old Car."

This is my story. It's about my old car. It ues to go ccagubop titik crakcrak. Tase because it was vary old. We use to have it. Bet we sal it. Now we have a new one. I ♥ my new car.

By Abby (1)

My Old Car
This is my story. It's about my old car. It used to go cagu-bop tick-tick crack-crack. That's because it was very old. We used to have it. But we sold it. Now we have a new one. I ♥ my new car.

The action in sports papers encourages the use of strong verbs. We certainly can see this in Matthew's paper "Basketball" (Figure 2.49). After a fairly routine beginning, Matthew's paper springs to life: "I zoom down the cort. I nailed a three ponter. Swoosh." Go, Matthew!

Strong words are like hugs. You don't really need 50 to be happy. Usually, one or two will do. Consider Aly's poem *Pencil* (Figure 2.50). She invents a word, *yondering*, from two concepts—wandering and meandering—and somehow, it is just right. A writer, she confirmed "has the right" to invent.

Figure 2.49

"Basketball."

I like to play basketball. It is vary fun. I zoom down the cort. I nailed a three ponter. Swoosh. Yes! I can't whait till are next game.

By Matthew (1)

That burst of creativity (though satisfying to readers) wasn't enough for the writer. In her words: "I was going to leave it at 'around,' but then I thought, 'That's not a good ending. I need a better one.' So I said to myself, how about 'leaving a track of scattered letters'?" How *about* that. As Aly made her thinking visible, through her words and illustration, her own work prompted her, and the right words came.

Kate's swimming experience inspired Cameron (Figure 2.51) to write about the short life of bubbles: the "precious jewels of the water." That's a memorable bit of phrasing, but I particularly like "and in that same second/it disappears/and reappears. . . ." Anyone who has watched bubbles trace the path of a swimmer can

Figure 2.50

Pencil By Aly (3)

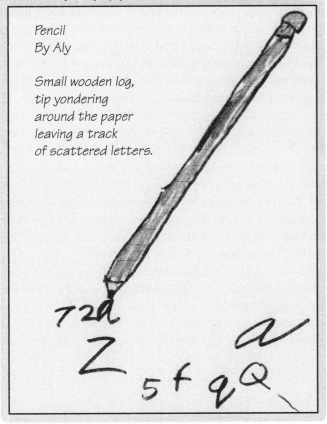

Pencil
By Aly

Small wooden log,
tip yondering
around the paper
leaving a track
of scattered letters.

Figure 2.51

Bubbles By Cameron (3)
Inspired by Kate's Swimming

Precious jewels
of the water
are created
In a second
and in that same second
it disappears
and reappears
again and again
until it's barren
This is the life
of a bubble

Figure 2.52

"Kangaroo News"

There was a kangaroo. He lived in australia. And it was very nosiey the poor kangaroo could not get any relacksashon. He tried to ask the other anmals to be quite but the preted to not hear him that made the kanaroo very mad but that didn't stop him no ser he ceped on trying he asked and he asked but the other animmales did not lishen to him they were to rud so see how he stops them in my other kangaroos' news.

By Andrew (1)

see this perfectly. Good word choice often causes us to pull up snapshots from the scrapbooks our own memories compile.

"Kangaroo News" (Figure 2.52) has several things going for it—one of them word choice. We learn, for instance, that the "poor kangaroo could not get any relaxation." Andrew hasn't quite got the spelling of this word down, but what is important is his use of it; it's just right. We wouldn't want him to say, "The poor kangaroo could not rest" just to get the spelling right. We also find out that the other animals would not listen because they were too "rud [rude]." Again, the perfect word. Did you notice the fluency in this piece? True, it is missing periods; Andrew will learn to put those in. For now, notice how smooth the phrasing is and how easily this writer glides from thought to thought [edited version]: "He tried to ask the other animals to be quiet, but they pretended to not hear him. That made the kangaroo very mad, but that didn't stop him. No sir! He kept on trying. He asked and he asked. . . ." This writer already has a good ear for how words should go together. When you get a paper like this, do not mourn the missing periods; read it aloud first so that the writer can hear the flow. *Then* you can say, "I'd like to give you one writer's tip [i.e., periods] to help show where these strong sentences begin and end." Also notice how Andrew's ending builds anticipation for the next installment; this is good organization!

In "Cat's" (Figure 2.53), Yong Jin, a first grader, uses repetitive language, not at all unusual at this age. We value variety but sometimes look for it too soon. Particularly in second-language students or in reluctant writers, certain words—because they are familiar—become "comfort words." It is natural to repeat them, and they can help build confidence, a vital stepping stone for any writer. Here is where a personal dictionary can be a huge help. Ask the student what he or she might like to say about cats—or any topic. Make a list of key words in large print. These can go on a large-sized Post-It® note right on the corner of the paper. This makes it easier for the writer to incorporate them with ease. Soon new words become comfort words, too. Notice the picture sequencing in this piece. The picture-text coordination is very sophisticated.

As readers, we value words for different reasons. In "Red Wolf" (Figure 2.54), Brandon makes an exceptional word choice—*respect*—to show how each wolf must respond to the pack. It is helpful to say, "I learned something important from this word." It is not just that we *like* the word; it is the *right* word. Precision is an important element of word choice. Notice that Brandon's teacher has written some text on the page—with Brandon's permission. She writes words as he reads his paper to her. These are not corrections. She is interjecting "book text" so that Brandon will be able to read his own writing down the road, and of course, he can use her words for reference, too.

Figure 2.55 shows the rough draft (and polished final) from the first two pages of Jamie's book *Someone Special.* This extraordinary example shows us so well why we must read beyond spelling to appreciate the nuances of word choice. In this case, words create energy but also vivid images: "seems to glow," "swishes through the trees," "slithers through the grass," "not the wind

Figure 2.53   "Cat's" Yong Jin (1)

Figure 2.54

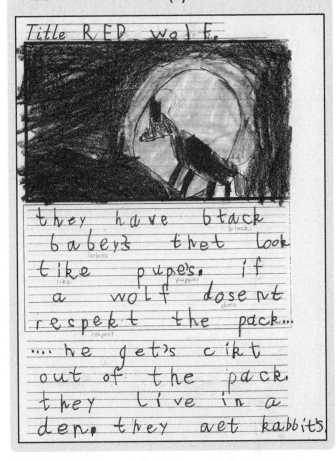

"Red Wolf" Brandon (2)

Title RED wolf.

they have black
babeys thet look
like pupes. if
a wolf dosent
respekt the pack...
....he get's cikt
out of the pack.
they live in a
den. they aet rabbits

Figure 2.55   "Someone Special"

I know someone speshul. Only I can see him. He comes out at night. He sems to gloow at me. He wishes throow the trees. He slivers throow the grass. And he maks rippels in the wataer. And he blose with the wind. He's not the swan who swims and drinks from the siver lake. He's not the wind snak who glads with the wind. He's not the grat bear paw that bealogs to the bear of the wild. He's not the butafull flower with one leav and the switist neckter. And He's not the sparkulling purple rock.

By Jamie (1)

I know someone special. Only I can see him. He comes out at night. He seems to glow at me. He swishes through the trees. He slithers through the grass. He makes ripples with the water and he blows in the wind. He's not the swan who swims and drinks from the silver lake. He's not the wind snake who glides with the wind. He's not the great bear paw that belongs to the bear of the wild. He's not the beautiful flower with one leaf and the sweetest of nectar. He's not the sparkling purple rock.

(Revised and edited version shared courtesy of Beth Olshansky, who holds copyright to Jamie's published book, *Someone Special*.)

snake," "not the great bear paw," and so on. Precise meaning is one reason to appreciate word choice; the beauty of the words themselves is another.

It is not often that a very young student can go for the rhyme and still come up with particularly strong word choice. Conor is the exception: "Lots of packing. Three circles tracking" (Figure 2.56). What an image this is. Then later: "Oh no, oh great—Warm weather here, a snowman's fate!" and just after that: "He's melting, he's dripping, His body is tipping." The rhymes do not seem forced because the words are just right to carry the meaning. They're playful, too, and add voice. Wouldn't you love to see a poem by this writer in about ten years?

In Figure 2.57, Miles, a third grader, illustrates a simple way to use a word collage to create a multi-image poem. His sister does not seem to have many redeeming qualities, but of course, he's joking (mostly), as we discover in the last line.

Students learn many new words from reading (and being read to), so it is not surprising that we hear some of them in a book review like Riley's (Figure 2.58). Riley is captivated by *skittering, scampered, lightning,* and *terrified*— and now that he has used them in his book review, perhaps they will show up in other writings. Asking students to tell you specifically which words they like is one way to encourage exploration.

Janica (Figure 2.59) starts right on a strong note with her onomatopoeia: "Swish, swish, swish. . . ." Other phrases capture our attention, too: "always wanted it perfect," "swift shoes," "mean as a bully," "like a hurricane buffeting at us," "meanest dolphin ever," "we got injured badly," "a fabulous thing." This

Figure 2.56

"The Last Snowman"

> Lots of packing.
> Three circles tracking.
> Two eyes and a carrot nose.
> Without any toes.
> A scarf, a pipe, and buttons of blue.
> Sticks for arms and a black hat too.
> Oh no, oh great—
> Warm weather here, a snowman's fate!
> He's melting, he's dripping,
> His body is tipping.
> Its hat falls down.
> Propping on the snowy wet ground.
> He melted. He's gone.
> A big puddle in our lawn.
>
> By Conor (3)

Figure 2.57 "Sister" Miles (3)

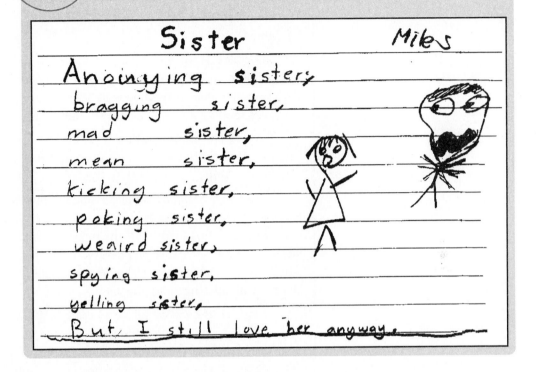

Sister   Miles

Anoinying sistery
bragging sister,
mad   sister,
mean   sister,
kicking sister,
poking sister,
weaird sister,
spying sister,
yelling sister,
But, I still love her anyway.

writer clearly enjoys expressive language. Janica's text and illustration work together beautifully; this is strong organization. Reading aloud will help this very imaginative writer catch those little things that plague us all: for example, "Our face[s] turned very dark ...," "... she look[ed] at us. ..." Such tiny changes will enhance already varied fluency.

Figure 2.58

Book Review

Dear Mrs. R,

I am reading The Witches. What I like about the book is it has vivid discriptions like scitering, scampered, lihting and terfied. And the boy almost got caught by the witches again. He already got turned into a mouse by the witches.

As always
Riley

By Riley (3)

Figure 2.59

The Meanest Dolphin By Janica (3)

The Meanest Dolphin
by Janica

"Swish, swish, swish, swish," a loud noise sounded from the house. Abegail and I looked out of the window and there was a sound of a broom. Tisha cleaned the house because there were seashells and pieces of food all around her house. Tisha always wanted it perfect.

She was the fastest dolphin because she practice and practice. She use her swift shoes that no one can beat, but Abegail and I knew it was cheating.

She was as mean as a bully. Also, she pushed us on the sand really hard like a hurricane buffiting at us. Our face turned very dark and red. We thought she was the meanest dolphin ever. We got injured badly by Tisha. The other dolphins were going some where else, so they didn't see us. Abegail and I thought we should give her a lesson. The lesson is a fabulous thing for her.

We talked to her. Abegail and I said, "stop working fast! you keep on pushing us on the road and we're worried that you might bully someone." At first, Tisha took a while for her to work slow, between she look at us she starts to feel sorrowful. Tisha learned her lesson and apologized to us. Abegail and I said, "Now your attitude toward us is better!"

Figure 2.60

"Champions"

Tension mounted as the kick-off drew near all was scilent exept for murmers from the crowd

Jacob (middle forward) passed to Trent (left fororward) who took it up-field, but a Cosmos player booted it down to our end, and I passed to Jacob who bolted to their goal, shot, and SCORED!

They penetrated our defences only once. How they got in the championship is beyond me.

We scored twice more then the ref blew his whistle in a shrill, sharp blast. The lightning croud went wild. WE HAD WON!

By Max (3)

Figure 2.61

Primary Checklist on Word Choice

- ☐ My words make sense.
- ☐ I like the words I chose.
- ☐ My favorite word in this paper is _____.
- ☐ I used a new word. It is _____.
- ☐ My words help you see, hear, feel, smell, or taste things.

Max (Figure 2.60) clearly loves strong words: "murmers from the crowd," "booted it down to our end," "bolted to their goal," and "penetrated our defences." He holds our attention from first to last. I particularly like "How they got in the championship is beyond me" because it rings with voice. This expression reminds us that everyday words can be used with style. Notice how much strong word choice adds to the lead: "Tension mounted as the kick-off drew near. . . ." What a contrast to the more common "Last Saturday we had a game."

See Figure 2.61 for a primary checklist on word choice.

STALKING SENTENCE FLUENCY

At the primary level, one of the first things to look for is *use of sentences*. Period. That's it! Students speak and think in sentences long before they write them, so getting a sentence—even *one*—on paper is a victorious moment and should be recognized. As students gain skill and confidence, they develop a kind of generative fluency. They just write a *lot*. This too is a victory. You may not feel celebrational when you are reading three pages of text that you do not find particularly interesting. Perhaps you should, though. Look at it this way. We want students to feel a certain comfort level with writing, as if writing were a natural part of everyday life, which it should be. This comfort comes, in part, from writing often and writing a lot. Never mind that not every phrase or

> *There is absolutely no substitute, nothing you can practice or simulate, that teaches you to do the thinking necessary to generate text other than trying your hand at it. When someone actually writes, he has to bring together layers and layers of many separate pieces of information to generate the text that helps him say what he wants to say.*
>
> **—Katie Wood Ray**
> **—Lisa B. Cleaveland**
> *About the Authors* (2004, p. 52)

sentence is profound. The writer is gaining a sense of balance, much the way a beginning biker does.

Early on, expect to see patterned writing from young students: "I like my dog. I like school. I like my house. I like math." Short, choppy, repetitive sentences would seem to be just the opposite of what we are looking for in fluent writing. This is so, but it is only a first step—like making your way across a river rock to rock. Remember: Look for the positive. The student is writing in multiple sentences and quite possibly imitating a pattern she has heard in oral reading. The student's repertoire of patterns will expand as her ear improves and as she is exposed to more sophisticated text. No wonder what we choose to share aloud with students matters so much.

As students gain greater skill, they usually break free of this repetition, saving it for emphasis and effect. Then the writing looks more like this: "Of all the things in my life, I love my dog the most. I also like school, especially math." This is breakthrough writing—combined ideas and varied rhythm. Some of this can be taught directly; some must rely on example.

What to Look for in Text*

✔ Appearance of sentences (whether written in conventional text or as letter strings or word strings)
✔ Use of multiple sentences, whether patterned or not
✔ Use of varied sentence beginnings
✔ A mix of statements and questions
✔ A mix of long and short sentences
✔ A complex or compound sentence mixed in with simple sentences
✔ Use of connecting words—*however, then*—that link sentences together (Yes, this is also part of organization.)
✔ Experimentation with poetry
✔ Experimentation with dialogue
✔ Dialogue that echoes the way people really speak

> *Powerful writers and powerful speakers have two wells they can draw on for that power: one is the well of rhythm; the other is the well of vocabulary. But vocabulary and a sense of rhythm are almost impossible to "teach" in the narrow sense of the word. So how are children expected to develop a sense of rhythm or a wide vocabulary? By being read to, alive, a lot!*
>
> **—Mem Fox**
> *Radical Reflections* (1993, p. 68)

What to Say in Your Comments

✔ You are using sentences in your writing. This is exciting!
✔ I notice that you are writing several sentences and not just one—terrific!
✔ Did you notice that you began this sentence in a different way? I love variety.
✔ I noticed you have some long sentences and some short sentences. This gives rhythm to your writing.

---

*Fluency is less likely than other traits to reveal itself in picture form (use of dialogue is an exception) because it is by definition an integral part of *text* structure.

✔ I love the sound of this when I read it aloud. Did you read it aloud?

✔ You used some dialogue here. It's fun to hear your characters speak.

✔ This dialogue sounds so real. It helped me get inside the characters' heads.

Fluent writers are experimenters. They try their hands as poets. They make characters speak. They dare to begin sentences in different ways and to try varied patterns, including fragments. They also break the rules sometimes and use repetition for effect. To test the fluency of any piece of writing, read it aloud and listen. *Really* listen. Read it more than once if you need to. Have someone read it to you so that you can focus on how it sounds, not how it looks on the page. If the fluency is there, you will hear it. Set the bar high, but do not expect it to happen all at once. Sentence fluency really must be acknowledged at different levels: level 1: appearance of sentences (or a first sentence); level 2: use of multiple sentences; and level 3: use of varied patterns, structures, and lengths to create a smooth rhythm and flow. Some primary students will achieve level 3 with ease; for others, more time may be needed.

Some Examples

Zhiquae, a kindergarten writer, is just beginning to get the idea of sentences on paper. "Flowers grow. Smell good," she writes (Figure 2.62). Not *quite* whole sentences, but very close—more than single words. We could say to her, "Tell me about the flowers." Zhiquae might answer, "They smell good." Then we can say, "You added an important word to this sentence, *they*. We could put that in your writing, if you like." I would write it for her and let her add it with a caret (ʌ).

Khalik, also a kindergartner, is writing just a single sentence—but it is a complete sentence (Figure 2.63). It is even punctuated with an exclamation point, so we have two achievements to celebrate. (One of the last Pluto fans!)

Figure 2.62

"Flowers" Zhiquae (K)

Figure 2.63

Single-sentence piece. Khalik (K)

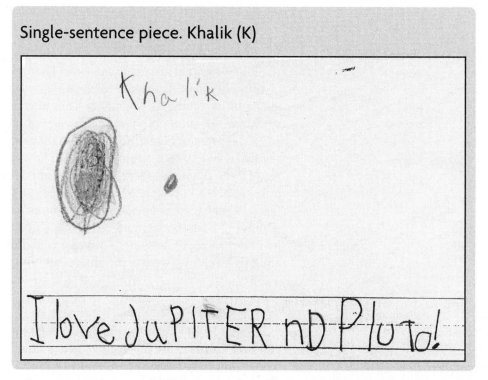

In his paper on fishing (Figure 2.64), kindergartner Alex has moved on to a whole new level: multiple sentences on the same topic. The sentences even begin in different ways. They end with periods, too. If we let Alex know how many things he is doing well, we are likely to launch him into a fluent tear that will have him writing half pages, full pages, and then whole books.

Figure 2.64

Multiple-sentence writing. Alex (K)

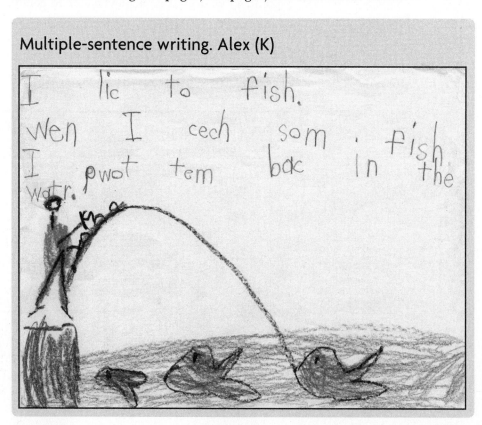

First grader Emily is not only writing multiple sentences on the same topic but is also beginning sentences in a variety of ways: "A long time ago . . . ," "These people . . . ," "They were . . . ," and "When it was late fall . . . ." (Figure 2.65). This amount of variety is quite sophisticated for so young a writer. Read this piece aloud to appreciate how smoothly it flows. Also notice the detail in both text and picture. That's a rather authoritarian king addressing the group of disgruntled pilgrims.

With just a bit of decoding, we discover that Olivia is using sentence structure to create tension and mystery—a highly advanced skill (Figure 2.66). Notice that her piece opens with a tranquil ocean scene, the crab scurrying about

Figure 2.65 "The Pilgrims" Emily (1)

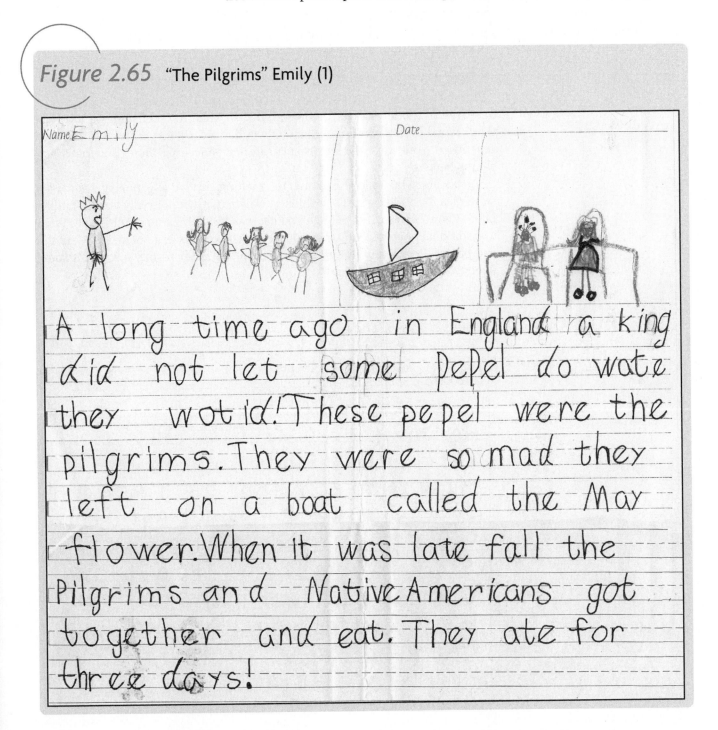

Name Emily   Date

A long time ago in England a king did not let some pepel do wate they wotid! These pepel were the pilgrims. They were so mad they left on a boat called the May flower. When it was late fall the Pilgrims and Native Americans got together and eat. They ate for three days!

Figure 2.66 "Life of a Crab"

Looking at the ocean rising idive the sand bneth the wotr, a Crab screy irond tring to find a Home. A sckhoul of fish Swam By. They wrey looking for foed to eat. Of cose they fowd baby plants to eat. But a shark fond something—a lot of somthing—a hole Sckhool of something! But thes how sharks hafe to leve.

By Olivia (2)

Looking at the ocean rising above the sand, beneath the water, a crab scurried around trying to find a home. A school of fish swam by. They were looking for food to eat. Of course, they found baby plants to eat. But a shark found something—a lot of something—a whole school of something! But that's how sharks have to live.

in search of a home. Enter the school of fish, then the menacing shark. Read that second-to-last sentence aloud. Olivia has an ear for drama and effective repetition. Note the reluctant realism in her stoic final line: "But that's how sharks have to live."

Students who enjoy listening to, reciting, or writing poetry have ideal strategies for building skills in fluency. Calvin quite impulsively wrote "Lucky's Life" (Figure 2.67) when his beloved cat was killed by a dog. This paper is not in traditional poetry format, but make no mistake, this *is* a poem. It has rhythm and power. Perhaps in poetry more than in any other form we see how much fluency contributes to voice.

Figure 2.67   "Lucky's Life" Calvin (2)

Lucky's Life
By: Calvin
He would play and play
until the sun went Down!
He was the King of the House
He wore the Crown! But then
came the Day stormy and
Black when Big Dog Cooper
came out for a snack!
He Chomped and chomped and
Chomped away! Lucky lay dead
nearly all day!

Figure 2.68　Extended text.

My first best friend was Alyssa now my best friend is Colleen now I will tell you what a friend is . . . to me. I think it is somebody who cares like if anything happned He/She would be there to help you out because if you fell or you were felling blue. They don't tell secrets about you like if they were with somebody that's a different friend and they wisper to that person and looked at you that it woulded [wouldn't] be a good way to show a friend you liked her. Have you ever hread someone say "look at that new girl she is so uncool well if I hread that I would go talk to the new girl and let her play with me cause I know how it feels to be new. So now you know what I think it is to be a friend.

By Rebecca (2)

Young writers often go through a phase in which written text mimics conversation and, in doing so, omits neat starts and stops. Consider Rebecca's paper, for instance (Figure 2.68). She is a fluent writer in the sense of generating a great deal of text and keeping the flow of ideas going. Now, if we can "disconnect" some of the individual thoughts by eliminating some *because* or *like* links, we can give this text a whole new sound. This is a case where modeling can be extremely helpful. Create a "superlinked" paragraph. Then read your own text aloud before and after eliminating connectives such as *so, because, and, like.* Do not expect students to grasp this difficult concept with one demonstration—or two. Keep doing it. Meanwhile, you can feel happy that students like Rebecca are (with ease!) generating extended text.

It is not only older students who generate extended text. Although the following two examples do not *yet* show quite the smooth transitional flow of older students' work, they do demonstrate remarkable comfort with the act of writing—and ability to keep text flowing. Julie (Figure 2.69) creates five full sentences—as does Andrew (Figure 2.70). Both have excellent text-picture coordination, indicating a strong sense of "having something to say," and might write even more, given a multipage book. Julie has not yet begun to experiment with

Figure 2.69

The Carnival By Julie (K)

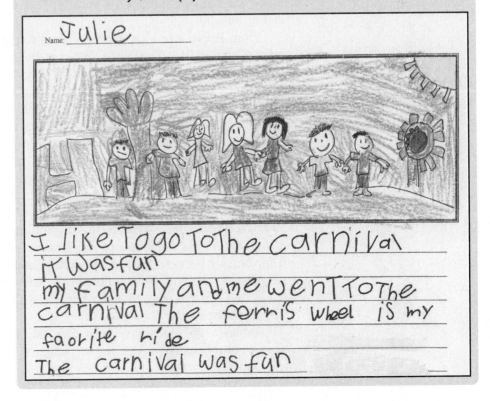

Name: Julie

I like To go To The carnival
IT was fun
my family and me wenT To The
carnival The ferris wheel is my
faorite ride
The carnival was fun

Figure 2.70

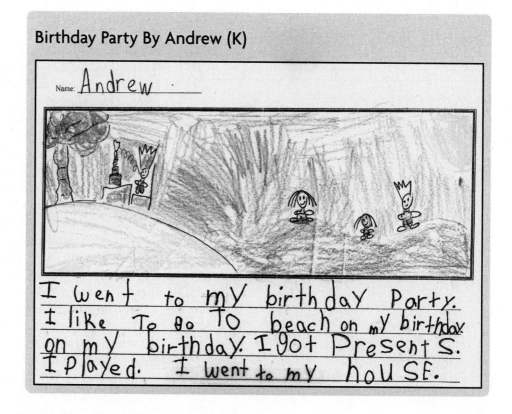

Birthday Party By Andrew (K)

Name: Andrew

I went to my birthday Party. I like To go To beach on my birthday on my birthday. I got Presents. I played. I went to my house.

periods, while Andrew uses them routinely (even in the *middle* of one sentence: *On my birthday I got presents.*). For both students, hearing text aloud will help strengthen the connection between the mark (.) and the idea: *end of thought.*

From Brian, a second grader, comes further proof that poetry builds fluency (Figure 2.71). Notice the different beginnings in this creative piece inspired by the work of Beth Olshansky. Wonderful word choice as well.

A quick glance at Raechel's piece "Spring" (Figure 2.72) might create the impression that several sentences begin with the pronoun "I." True. Actually though, variety abounds in this piece. Notice the different sentence lengths, as well as the unusual way Raechel puts her thoughts together: "Its colors are like a rainbow, so misty." It does not hurt to say, "That is a beautiful sentence. I love the way it sounds." Raechel also mixes short with long and has some varied beginnings: "As I dig . . ." and "In the sandy beach . . .".

The whimsical, onomatopoetic poems of Douglas Florian (*Mammabilia*, 2000; *Insectlopedia*, 1998) are the inspiration for Abby's "Tiger Cub" (Figure 2.73). This is a good example of playful word choice, too, of course, but I chose it for fluency because I loved the rhythm and the way Abby puts the word of emphasis at the end of each line. Some writers do this instinctively; perhaps she is one. It's still true, though, that when it comes to attention, last place in line wins first prize.

Although the fluency in Pearson's "My Favorite Game" (Figure 2.74) is somewhat inconsistent, this paper has particularly strong moments. It starts

Figure 2.71

Poem. Brian (2)

The blazing sun is blowing heat onto me.
My broken tip is suffering in the great heat.
But inside me I am dark, gloomy, and cold.
My old face is falling apart.
When it is dark I rest my ancient eyes.
I am a pyramid.

Brian

Figure 2.72

"Spring"

I can't wait for spring to come for in the spring I hunt for seaglass. In the sandy beach I dig for the smooth colorful seaglass. Its colors are like a rainbow, so misty. As I dig I see tiny pieces hidden beneath the sand. I love to dig for seaglass. I feel so free.

By Raechel (3)

Figure 2.73

"Tiger Cub"

We are cats hear us purrrr
We have stripes upon our furrrr
We run through the forest like a blurrrr
We are a baby tigerrrr

By Abby (3)

Figure 2.74

"My Favorite Game"

On a Saturday, I had a baseball game. For the first few games, I only hit singles. But last year, I always hit triples and doubles. So we've been having me take hitting lessons. It was Saturday and time for the game. Little did I know, the next 4 games, (skipping the 3rd,) would be big hitting streaks. I would be part of it. I play center field so I don't get the ball very much. Unless when I back up right or left fielder and they miss. Then we were up to bat. I was 6th. When I was up, the first pitch sailed in. It was low and in the middle. I swung. Contact! It flew past shortstop and landed. I rounded first and stopped at 2nd. The next kid hit a single but I went home. The next inning I hit a single and a double. We won the game. I got player of the game. The game Lucas hit a triple but the next game we lost. Then Conner my feand hit a grand slam 4 run homer. I love baseball.

By Pearson (3)

Figure 2.75

Primary Checklist for Fluency

- ☐ I wrote a sentence.
- ☐ I wrote MORE than one sentence!
- ☐ Some sentences are long and some are short.
- ☐ Some are telling sentences and some are questions.
- ☐ My sentences begin with different words.
- ☐ I like reading this OUT LOUD.

out strong, with notable variety in sentence beginnings and lengths. There is also nice use of a single fragment: "Contact!" This provides a good opportunity to point out to Pearson (because he is clearly ready) what a fragment is and how it can work—sometimes. If Pearson had written, "I swung. I made contact," much of the oomph would have been lost. Help a student like Pearson (a strong and fluent writer already) to see where the really effective moments are: "Little did I know, the next four games would be big hitting streaks." Then encourage him to read his writing aloud to sharpen an already good ear for language patterns.

See Figure 2.75 for a primary checklist for fluency.

NOTICING CONVENTIONS

At the primary level, conventions begin simply with such elements as text flowing from left to right on the page or use of spaces between words. Discovery of punctuation marks or capital letters is significant, regardless of whether these things are employed correctly. Correct use comes later. Very young writers who are still experimenting with letters and numbers may have trouble recalling which direction letter *F* or *B* is supposed to face. More experienced writers are trying to recall whether commas go inside or outside quotation marks.

The secret in assessing (and teaching) conventions is to notice what the student *does* know and to build on that. Remember that nothing is automatic—even writing from left to right. All must be learned.

Although the term *conventions* encompasses a wide range of concerns from spelling to paragraphing, it is spelling that usually gets the most attention. Maybe this is because it stands out. We notice it. Forget a comma, and only a few people get excited. Misspell *because*, however, and the whole world is in an uproar. In looking at beginners' writing, let me suggest that you base your response to conventions more on readability and adventurous borrowing than on correctness alone. Correct use of conventions is a fine goal, but it is not the only goal. Think about it. Do you want students who only write within the safe parameters of the few conventions they feel sure of? Or do you want them to reach and borrow? If you said "yes" to the latter question, then you must reward reaching and borrowing.

> . . . *I knew this would be a long night. The patient was riddled with embedded clauses and comma splices. Gerunds clung to his sides and participles dangled from his shoulders as he collapsed on the table.*
>
> **—Barry Lane**
> After THE END (1993, p. 205)

What to Look for in Text* (Beginning Level)

✔ Left-to-right orientation on the page
✔ Continuation of text onto the next line
✔ Correct directionality for letters and punctuation marks
✔ Experimentation with punctuation, whether correct or not

---

*Conventions, by definition, apply primarily to text. However, look for experimentation and new skills as text is incorporated into pictures through dialogue, signs, labels, and so on. Also look for visual conventions, such as use of bullets or numbers, or general layout and presentation in a poster, brochure, or greeting card.

✔ Readable spelling (you can tell what the words are)
✔ Use of capitals, whether placed correctly or not
✔ Application of "classroom" conventions—for example, name on paper, date on paper, use of a title

What to Look for in Text (Advanced Level)

✔ Phonetic spelling on more difficult words
✔ Correct spelling of simple words, high frequency words
✔ Terminal punctuation that is correct—or mostly correct
✔ Capital letters on names
✔ Capital letters to begin sentences
✔ Correct use of periods and question marks
✔ Experimentation with quotation marks
✔ Use of exclamation points
✔ Use of commas in a series
✔ Experimentation with more sophisticated punctuation marks—for example, parentheses, semicolons, colons, dashes, ellipses, and so on
✔ Indentation or double spacing to show a new paragraph
✔ Respect for margins

What to Say in Your Comments

✔ I see that you have discovered periods [or whatever]. Terrific!
✔ You knew this was a question—and used a question mark.
✔ It is so helpful when you put a title on your paper; then I have a clue about your topic.
✔ I'm glad you remembered to put your name on your paper.
✔ I see that you used parentheses here. Tell me why.
✔ How did you know to use a comma [or other punctuation] here?
✔ This is so close to the correct spelling. Would you like to see how close you came?
✔ You have spaces between all your words now. That really helps your reader.
✔ You left margins on the sides. That makes your piece easier to read. It looks good, too.
✔ You used this word five times and spelled it right every time. Is this in your personal dictionary?
✔ I see that you used an exclamation point to show some strong feelings here.

Young writers are borrowers. Therefore, the development of conventions goes in stages, something like this:

1. Noticing a convention
2. Borrowing a convention for use in personal text
3. Knowing the name of the convention
4. Knowing the correct use of the convention
5. Using the convention correctly
6. Teaching its correct use to others
7. Noticing misuse of the convention
8. Correcting misuse of the convention in someone else's text
9. Correcting a misuse of the convention in personal text
10. Using a convention creatively to bring out meaning or voice

We do our students a service by celebrating the discovery of conventions—then correct use and eventually correction of faulty text. Experimentation is the order of the day for very young writers, who will soon be avid editors if we don't set them to correcting too much too soon.

Some Examples

Consider as you look at conventions whether you are viewing the work of a beginner or a more advanced primary-level writer. Advanced primary writers tend to be those who can easily generate several sentences (or more) of text. Beginners may still be working on individual words.

Alyssa, a kindergartner, is exploring the world of writing. Her imitative writing moves from left to right on the page, although as yet we do not have recognizable letters (Figure 2.76). The octopus and lollipop are quite recognizable once we know her message. Alyssa dictates the text to accompany the picture. Fluency and strong word choice are evident in her dictation, although she is not yet ready to show these features in writing.

Brady, also a kindergartner, is creating some quite recognizable letter shapes (Figure 2.77) and may or may not be starting to connect letters with sounds (*B* for brother—could be coincidental). He is showing left-to-right orientation, and his letters not only are identifiable but also show correct directionality.

Karen (Figure 2.78) has created letter strings that are, in fact, quite readable with a little effort. She has made many letter-sound connections. Notice that her letter directionality is quite good, and she has discovered exclamation points. At first, we might think her picture and text have little to do with each other. Notice, however, the "hair" added to the snowman (reminiscent of Mom, perhaps?). It could also be that building snowmen is what Mom and Karen do when they "play." Sometimes we must dig a little to find the connection that does not leap out at us.

Brian, another kindergarten writer, creates text that is readable without his help: "Me and my penguins are friends" (Figure 2.79). He spells several sight words correctly and also manages the very difficult *penguins*. He also comes very close on *Frensd*, a word with which many older writers struggle. Brian has discovered periods, and they are prominent in his writing; like many beginning writers, however, he uses more than he needs. Notice his use of capital letters, too. Although they are not placed correctly yet, he is distinguishing between upper and lower case—a first step. He is also placing spaces between words.

First grader Andrew has the advantage of creating text on a word processor (Figure 2.80). He is beginning to develop some fluency with multiple sentences. Periods and capitals are placed correctly, and spacing is

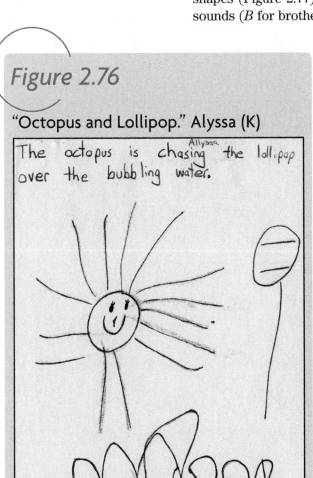

Figure 2.76

"Octopus and Lollipop." Alyssa (K)

Figure 2.77

Early conventions. Brady (K)

Figure 2.78

Snowman (and My Mom) By Karen (K)

I love my mom because she loves me! She makes me food. She plays with me!

Figure 2.79

"Me and My Penguins." Brian (K)

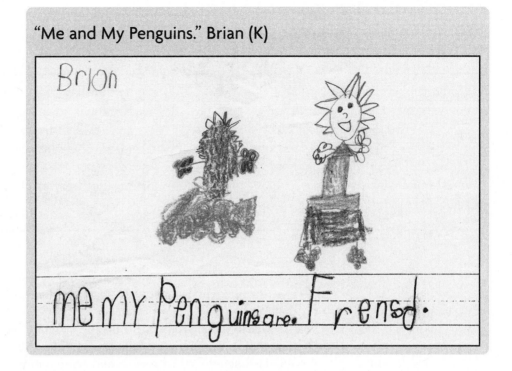

good. Numerous sight words are spelled correctly, and the entire text is readable (with just a bit of work). Some help with the words *magic pebble* and *arrowhead* has made Andrew's task easier. Notice sentence three; it is the only one that wanders from the assigned topic, and interestingly, it has the most voice: "I wish that Mrs. Keefer would let me go outside whenever I want." This is his real message.

Figure 2.80 Expanding skills with conventions. Andrew (1)

I got the magic pebble from the sky. It loks like a arrowhead. I wish that misiskefr wod let mw go awt sighd winevr I wont. I hae I nevr los my magic pebble.

In "My Brth" (Figure 2.81), Rebecca struggles with both spelling and punctuation, yet she manages to create a readable piece with quite a lot of voice. Again, resist the temptation to take on too much at once. Begin with what is done well, focusing on one to three strengths: She spells *brother* correctly in the text (although not in her title), along with *house* and *because*. These words could be added to a master spelling dictionary in her writing folder or notebook. She is using periods, but sometimes they come in the middle of a sentence. The question is: Does she hear the text this way? To find out, you could try reading it aloud to her (with plenty of inflection and long pauses), asking her to indicate where the periods should go (rapping on the desk, nodding, and so on). You may need to read more than once. You can also do this, pen in hand, if you read text that has no punctuation. Let your voice rise or fall to

Figure 2.81 "My Brth"

> My brother is a manyack. Because he is wlold. An he bothrs me a lot so wut I do is yel at he so I yel shut the dore an lock it. My brother is rille men so you wid not wot to cum to my house. Be-cause you wid get mad I wish me brother wiol be nis
>
> By Rebecca (1)

> My brother is a maniac because he is wild. And he bothers me a lot. So what I do is yell at him, so I yell, shut the door, and lock it. My brother is really mean so you would not want to come to my house because you would get mad. I wish my brother would be nice.

give the student a hint where each period should go. Then you can insert them together.

Ellie's paper "What Taylor Is Like" (Figure 2.82) is a very interesting mix. Although just a first grader, Ellie shows much control over conventions, creating standard sentences with ease and punctuating them correctly. She also uses parentheses correctly—and this needs to be pointed out to her because it's a major step. Her spelling is particularly interesting because she spells some chal-

Figure 2.82 "Taylor"

> Taylor is my friend. In my story I would like to tell you all about her because she is one of my bestest friends. She is very nice. She's a very, very, very good friend to have as a best friend. I love her. We read together. Were in the same class. Were in Older phonics and Older Math. We to go cocurr [soccer] together. If we go out to recess we play together. If we stay in we work together. On funtastic Friday if were aloud to we do the same thing together. We always sit by each other at phonics unless some one already is sitting on both sides of either of us. She loves me. (We don't love each other like we love our family.) Were funny. We do jokes. We stick together. We draw together. We do arts and crafts together. We make posters together. We make books together. We try to be on the same tubl [table] for math jornal [journal] so we can do something together. Her clothes are all ways pretty. Her socks are allways pretty. She has brown hair. She has brown eyes. She weares a bow or a braid in her hair when she comes to school.
>
> By Ellie (1)

Figure 2.83

The freedom of poetry.

Hamster in my lunch
Hamster on the floor
Hamster on the teachers head
I'm in class no more
Goblins
Goblins are scary
Goblins are crooks
Goblins are sneacky
With their menacing looks

By Will (3)

lenging words correctly: *funtastic, Friday, phonics, posters, together, something, school, because, recess, unless, crafts, either,* and so on. On the other hand, the paper has some curious errors: *tubl, jornal,* and *cocurr.* These are relatively simple errors to remedy, though; hand Ellie the words on a Post-It note, and she will (most likely) be off and running. One key thing to work on? With a first grader this strong in conventions, I would put the focus elsewhere: How about trying some varied sentence beginnings? Stir a little fluency into this mix, and you will have a powerhouse writer. Her excellent vocabulary is being buried inside patterned sentences.

One of the great things about poetry is that it's loosey-goosey enough to permit freedom with punctuation (and other conventions). Will gets by with virtually no punctuation whatsoever (Figure 2.83). His spelling is excellent (OK, *sneacky*). This writer is ready for something more challenging. Why not focus on end-of-line punctuation for poetry? Ask Will what he hears at the end of each line—a pause (comma), a long pause (dash), a stop (period), a strong stop with emphasis (exclamation point), or a question (question mark). Let him do the punctuating, according to what he hears. Punctuation marks echo the way we read.

"Little Bull" (Figure 2.84) is a retelling of *Growing Up in Africa's Elephant Kingdom: The Story of Little Bull,* by Ellen Foley James. The conventions are Jessica's own, and they are impressive. This level of control represents a sufficiently high expectation for primary level, in my view, even though it is not flawless. Flawless is always a dangerous goal, even for adults. This is controlled, readable, and indicative of a wide range of conventional skills; we should not ask for more.

Figure 2.84

"Little Bull"

In a faraway land, shaped just like an elephant's ear, a baby elephant was born. His name was Little Bull. Wraped like a cabbage in his big elephant ears, Little Bull lay very still. Little Bull lifted one ear and heard a chater of birds. Little Bull's playground was the grassy plains. And in a distance, rising up like an elephant's back, was the Great White Mountain. Sometimes, Little Bull tried to get his mother's attention by standing on his head. His humpty dumpty body toppled over every time. That evening Little Bull saw a huge dark mountain move across the sky. That night, Little Bull saw a bowl of stars overhead. The dry season went on and on and on. One day, the rain boweld over the ground. That day, little Bull played with Keekay.

By Jessica (2)

Figure 2.85

If My Animals Could Drive and Wear Clothes By Kate (3)

If Lucy the cat could drive and wear clothes, Lucy would be a princess, in a golden carriage, and a coachman would drive her around. She would wear a pink fluffy party dress, high-heeled shoes, long white gloves, and a diamond tiara.

Cleo, on the other hand, would drive her catself in a mini car, wearing a tanktop, shorts, a visor, and sunglasses. The police would be stopping her at every corner for speeding and running red lights.

Buzzby, wellll . . . he's a different story. This cat would be kickin' back in a hot tub on a limousine, too cool for school.

Ah, Ricky the dog would drive a Durango. He'd wear anything my mom wears!

Well, Anna would drive a school bus (the only thing that will hold a bald python!), and non-matching clothes.

Lucky the bird = Motorcycle, leather jacket, and of course, leather pants.

Those are my pets.

Weird, huh?

Figure 2.86

Primary Checklist for Conventions

- ☐ You can read my paper without help.
- ☐ I have a title.
- ☐ I wrote my name on my paper.
- ☐ I wrote from left to right.
- ☐ I put spaces between my words.
- ☐ I have periods after sentences.
- ☐ I have question marks after questions.
- ☐ I used capital letters.
- ☐ I used my BEST spelling.

Kate (Figure 2.85) shows extraordinary facility with conventions for a young writer. Not only is Kate doing things correctly, she is experimenting, too. Notice the word *catself* in paragraph 2, the playfulness with *wellll* in paragraph 3, ellipsis, and the abbreviated word *kickin'*. *Ah*, opening paragraph 4, is a nice touch. I also like the equal sign in paragraph 6. This writer has discovered the truth about conventions: that they're not just about correctness. They shape meaning and reveal voice. Kate's clarity and personal voice will benefit from her insight.

See Figure 2.86 for a primary conventions checklist.

LAST THOUGHTS

One of the rewarding things about writing assessment is that through their voices, the writers are always present, always before us. As we learn to look within their writing, they become our teachers, lighting the way for us. As Carol Avery says, "When I focused on children rather than practices, teaching became not only more challenging but also more rewarding and, more important, more effective for the children. I was able to let the children shine through" (2002, p. 6).

CHAPTER 2 IN A NUTSHELL

- Look first for the positive—for what is *there*—not what is missing. Help young writers to grow by building on their strengths.
- Remember to look carefully at both text and picture forms of writing to capture every nuance of meaning and voice.
- Offer suggestions that are specific and manageable—for example, "Quotation marks are like shoes or gloves. They come in pairs and work together, like this. . . ."
- Create and use checklists that "speak" to children. They should address the concerns young writers have and incorporate language young writers can understand.

- Responding to children's writing (or to any writing) is an art. Teach yourself to see what is within the writing so that your students can know the beauty and force of what they create. You are a guide and must point out what will otherwise go unnoticed on the journey. Remember the words of Kathleen and James Strickland: "Assessment gets to the heart of teaching and lets us decide how and when to offer support to writers. Learning to assess students' writing can actually help us to become better teachers of writing" (2000, p. 66).

STUDY GROUP: INTERACTIVE QUESTIONS AND ACTIVITIES

1. **Activity.** Now that you have had a look inside the writing of numerous students, check out some of the writing your own students are doing. Trait by trait, make a list of the strengths you see. What are your students doing well in terms of clear message, detail, beginnings or endings, continuity, picture-text coordination, voice, exploration with new words, developing sentence fluency, or appropriate, primary-level conventions? For each strength you see, ask yourself, "*Very specifically*, what comment could I make to encourage the student?"

2. **Discussion.** In the chapter "Draw Me a Word—Write Me a Picture" (from *More than Stories—The Range of Children's Writing*), Thomas Newkirk suggests that several forces combine around the end of first grade (or the beginning of second grade) to move children away from picture writing and toward a more text-focused approach. Among these factors are the child's own increased fluency, the increased ease of letter formation, the child's in-

creasingly critical view of his or her own artwork, the use of lined paper, and a perception (perhaps fostered by society) that text is more "adult" than picture writing. What do you feel are the advantages or disadvantages of this shift? Based on the samples in this chapter and your experience with your own students' writing, do you see drawing as a legitimate form of written expression? For which children might this offer an advantage? How might these children be affected by a text-only approach to writing instruction? Discuss this with your group.

3. **Activity.** Choose two or more samples from this chapter and review them using the primary-level continuums in Chapter 8, pages 251–256. Make copies of the continuums so that you can write on them. *Using a highlighter,* mark all the strengths you see on each paper. Then, compare your responses with those of a partner. Do your responses match, for the most part? If the child's parent reviewed your continuums as part of a

parent conference, what would he or she learn about the child's writing performance? Now, do the same kind of analysis based on the work of one of your own students. If possible, review more than one piece of work. Paper clip the continuums to the student's samples (or copies of the samples), and include it in a portfolio.

4. **Activity.** With a partner, review (and if necessary, revise) one or more of the student checklists from this chapter. Use your own teaching experience and actual samples of student work from your class to make any modifications. Feel free to add items or to change wording. To the extent possible, involve your students in this revision process. Ask them, "Is there anything we need to add to this checklist?" Consider how you will use these checklists: handouts, posters, attachments to individual pieces of work, and so forth.

5. **Activity.** As an extension of Activity 4, work with a partner to simplify the checklists even further for use with younger students or those learning English.

6. **Discussion.** Kathleen and James Strickland suggest that assessment can help us become better teachers to the extent that it takes us inside students' thinking, enabling us to know them better so that students actually become our teachers. Reflect on and discuss this idea based on your own teaching experience. Create a journal entry based on your thoughts.

7. **Activity and discussion.** By this time, you have had some experience working with both the six-trait rubrics (appendix) designed for use with grade 3 students and older, and with the primary continuums developed for use with students from kindergarten through early grade 3. What nuances of performance do the continuums capture that are not reflected in the rubrics for older writers? Make a list, trait by trait. If a very young student, say a kindergartner, were assessed using the rubrics for grades 3 and up, what implications might that have for the student? Discuss this with your group.

 # SOURCES CITED

Avery, Carol. 2002. *And With a Light Touch*, 2d ed. Portsmouth, NH: Heinemann.

Calkins, Lucy McCormick. 1994. *The Art of Teaching Writing*, rev ed. Portsmouth, NH: Heinemann.

Cannon, Jannell. 1997. *Verdi*. New York: Harcourt Brace & Company.

Florian, Douglas. 1998. *Insectlopedia*. New York: Harcourt Brace & Company.

Florian, Douglas. 2000. *Mammalabilia*. New York: Harcourt Brace & Company.

Fox, Mem. 1993. *Radical Reflections: Passionate Opinions on Teaching, Learning, and Living*. New York: Harcourt Brace & Company.

Freeman, Marcia S. 1998. *Teaching the Youngest Writers*. Gainesville, FL: Maupin House.

James, Ellen Foley. 2001. *Growing Up in Africa's Elephant Kingdom: The Story of Little Bull*. New York: Sterling.

Johnson, Bea. 1999. *Never Too Early to Write*. Gainesville, FL: Maupin House.

Lane, Barry. 1993. *after THE END*. Portsmouth, NH: Heinemann.

Lane, Barry. 2001. *Reviser's Toolbox*. Shoreham, VT: Discover Writing Press.

Lewis, Cynthia Copeland. 1994. *Really Important Stuff My Kids Have Taught Me*. New York: Workman Publishing.

Murray, Donald M. 1985. *A Writer Teaches Writing*, 2d ed. Boston: Houghton Mifflin.

Newkirk, Thomas. 1989. *More than Stories: The Range of Children's Writing*. Portsmouth, NH: Heinemann.

Olshansky, Beth. 2006. *Picturing Writing: Fostering Literacy Through Art* and *Image-Making Within the Writing Process*. Durham: University of New Hampshire.

Ray, Katie Wood, with Lisa B. Cleaveland. 2004. *About the Authors: Writing Workshop with Our Youngest Writers*. Portsmouth, NH: Heinemann.

Strickland, Kathleen, and James Strickland. 2000. *Making Assessment Elementary*. Portsmouth, NH: Heinemann.

Figures 2.10, 2.11, 2.55, 2.66, and 2.71 from this chapter were inspired by the work of Beth Olshansky: www.picturingwriting.org

Teaching Traits Conceptually: Introductory Lessons

> Teaching masters like Janet Emig, Donald Graves and Jerome Bruner tell us students learn best when they mine their spontaneous knowledge for skills they already use. Simply put, we learn by doing; then we go on to do more through learning.
>
> **—Barry Lane and Gretchen Bernabei**
> *Why We Must Run with Scissors* (2001, p. 1)

> Writing allows us to hold our life in our hands and make something of it.
>
> **—Lucy McCormick Calkins**
> *The Art of Teaching Writing* (1994, p. 4)

> Poor horsemanship consists in suggesting that man and horse are separate. A horseman afoot is a wingless, broken thing, tyrannized by gravity . . . for that burst of poetry, horse and rider have one another to thank.
>
> **—Thomas McGuane**
> *Some Horses* (2000, pp. 18–19)

"NOTHING TO DO WITH MY CURRICULUM"

A primary teacher intrigued me one day when she said, "I can't work with these traits—they have nothing to do with my curriculum." When I asked her to describe her curriculum, she said, "Well, we talk about fun things we could write about. We make lists. Then we have time for writing, and sometimes I help my kids get started. Later, we share what we have written. Sometimes, we make displays." Fun things to write about? Those are ideas. Making lists? A way of capturing ideas on paper. Getting started? Organization. Sharing? Voice—and words, too, of course. Displays? Often, some attention to detail there that might connect to revising ideas or thinking about conventions. In other words, the six traits were embedded in everything this teacher was doing. She was seeing the traits as something separate, a new layer of instruction, an extra "workbook."

It is not like that at all. What the traits do, really, is get us organized. My mentor teacher, Ronda, turned the light on for me when I saw her sprawled in the middle of her classroom one August afternoon, her files in apparent disarray around her. When I asked what she was doing, she replied, "It's simple. I already teach all this stuff [the traits]. I'm just reorganizing my lessons so that when I want something on organization or voice or fluency, I can find it. See?" I did see. Ronda also inspired me to color code my files: red for ideas, green for organization, and so on. This is such a simple idea, but it is so helpful. Not new so much, you see, as *restructured*. Many of the best books on writing give us a thousand good ideas but never answer the one question we're burning to know: How do I get started? The traits make it simple. Start with ideas—a message, a topic, something you love to write about. Model it, read books that show how skillful authors express main ideas and details, and then add another trait (*writing*, of course, all the while).

Emphasize what students need. As Ronda told me, "Every class is different. Some are strong in conventions—some have wonderful voice or details. It's when I look at their writing that I know where to spend my teaching time." You'll know, too.

Two things are critical at the primary level:

1. Writing, reading, and just plain loving it.
2. Using writers' vocabulary so that such terms as *voice* or *fluency* are at least familiar—even if they are not integral parts of a child's own writing.

You can teach the first by being an enthusiastic writer/reader yourself, by providing time and a classroom environment in which students are immersed in wonderful literature and feel comfortable as writers. Teach writers' vocabulary by using the language yourself at every opportunity. And remember, if it is difficult for some students to grasp the notion of, say, fluency in the context of writing, you could start with the larger notion of fluency. What is it, really? This chapter is meant to give you an inside look at the *concept underlying each trait* as a way of making definitions clearer to young minds.

TEACHING IDEAS CONCEPTUALLY

Ideas can be taught conceptually in many ways, because they are many things. They are everything we think or imagine or picture in our heads. Ideas can begin with something huge: *Things that grow.* Then, by fine-tuning our mental binoculars, we focus in on our idea and bring it down to manageable proportions: *Plants . . . houseplants . . . my philodendron . . . the philodendron that is overtaking my file cabinet, keeping me out with its leafy arms.*

Let me suggest three key approaches, each of which can be taught separately—even to students who are not yet creating much (if any) text. They are

1. Ideas as *imagination* and *observation*
2. Ideas as *pictures in the mind*
3. Ideas as *messages*

Ideas as Imagination and Observation

Give students something interesting to observe—a rock, say, or a seashell or an orange peel. Ask them to look, sniff, touch, tap, and turn it around to see it from different sides. As they do so, they should ask themselves the questions "What do I notice?" and "What does it remind me of?" A simple object such as a rock may suggest to the imagination a mountain looming in the distance or the shape of an animal. It may take the observer, in his or her imagination, to a wooded glen or the flatlands of a desert. It may remind one writer of her aquarium and another of his grandmother's rock garden. The smell of an orange may take a writer to a kitchen, a picnic, or a grove in Florida.

Observations and associations, especially when recorded, teach children to be keen observers of the world—and mental recorders as well. A writer can have no greater gift. As writer James Dickey (in Calkins, 1994, p. 3) has observed, "A writer is someone who is enormously taken by things anyone else would walk by."

You can enhance this experience by recording your students' observations and rewarding them by appreciating the small details they notice—especially if you did not notice them yourself. Have you ever looked, *really* looked, at people's hands, for example? The shape, the look of the nails, and the lines and creases all tell us who the person is, even if we have no other details on which to rely. Author Rick Bragg wrote of his grandfather's hands, "They hung at the ends of his skinny arms like baseball mitts, so big that a normal man's hand disappeared in them. The calluses made an unbroken ridge across his palm, and they were rough, rough all over as shark's skin. The grease and dirt, permanent as tattoos, inked his skin, and the tar and dirt colored the quick under his fingernails, then and forever. He could have burned his overalls, changed his name and bought himself a suit and tie, but those hands would have told on him" (2001, p. 52). This is observational genius—coupled with supreme inferential skill. And it starts right in your classroom, looking at a simple object as you jot down what your children see and celebrating their skill in seeing.

Ideas as Pictures in the Mind

We see with our eyes, but we see within our minds as well. Ideas grow out of what students hear and what they visualize from what they hear. In *Twilight Comes Twice*, Ralph Fletcher (1997) creates image upon image, a mental collage that defines dawn and dusk in myriad ways. In what remains my favorite passage from the book, Fletcher tells us, "Slowly dusk pours the syrup of darkness into the forest. Crows gather in the trees for last-minute gossip before nightfall." Close your eyes and you can see the syrupy darkness falling slow and thick across the trees, covering them and blurring the shapes. You can see and hear the crows gathered on the branches, chatting with each other.

Now imagine your students creating pictures from what they see and feel and hear as you share a story, a poem, or a moment of your own experience. Students, who draw freely—without fear of "getting it wrong"—create as much meaning with pictures as with text. They incorporate details, and they let us know what meaning a passage has had for them. They may expand meaning, too. Part of Fletcher's art is that he never tells too much. So often our teacher comments include the suggestion, "Tell me more." What we really mean sometimes is, "Tell me the *right* thing—the *just right* thing." Encourage your students to speak through art. Sketching and painting are ways of discovering what that "just right" detail might be.

It is easy to sketch what Ralph Fletcher describes. His images seem to float right off the page and into our hearts and minds as if he were touching a spot within our brains that could take us to a time and place where we had once been ourselves. If a writer labors with every word, the mental pictures come less easily. Suppose that Ralph had written, "Everything got darker. Then some birds came." This would be tougher to sketch, don't you think? Just as writers can tell too much, they can also tell too little. Therefore, ask your students as they draw what they picture: "What do you see? Is it easy to draw? Do you see enough? You *do?* The little parts of what you see are detail." They hear, they see in their minds, they draw—and often, they expand. Expect their pictures to encompass more than Fletcher—or any author—provides a blueprint for. Their mental pictures will stretch and grow—as long as you let them form on their own and do not too quickly share the pictures from the books (however wonderful!). Oh, it's tempting. After all, we buy picture books partly (sometimes *mostly*) for the pictures. Now and then, however, it is refreshing for the mind to make its own movies.

Ideas as Messages

In the introduction to his wonderful book, *More than Stories*, teacher and author Thomas Newkirk (1989, p. 1) tells the delightful tale of his five-year-old daughter reading the long list of rules posted at the city's swimming pool. Why, Newkirk wondered, would this young child take such a long time in the cold winter air to study rules that she could only begin to read? The answer was that she wanted to go into the sauna—and could not. It was this print, these rules, that kept her out: "Here we were, about fifty swimmers in all, seemingly controlled by the words written on this poster, words that would, among other things, keep her out of the sauna bath until near the twenty-first century" (1989, p. 1).

The rules carried a message, and that message was, in essence, "You cannot do what you want because you're too young." Often, this is precisely what we mean by ideas—a message.

See how many ways your students can think of that we give messages to each other in our society. Here are a few (they will think of more):

✔ Conversation
✔ Television
✔ Radio
✔ E-mail
✔ Post-It notes
✔ Signs
✔ Letters
✔ Advertisements
✔ Newspapers
✔ Greeting cards
✔ Bumper stickers
✔ Labels
✔ Directions
✔ Product packaging

Figure 3.1 Imagination and clarity.
Rebecca (2)

It's spring. There is clean white glittery snow on the ground. It floats like a cloud. The blue electric sky is flashy. The trees are blowing swiftly among the wind. The stream's water waves everywhere as it flows down into a pond. I would like to go outside for the whole day. I think it's a great day. I hope tomorrow is like today.

Rebecca

What separates a good message from a poor one? Simple. You can understand it. It makes sense. This is just a simple way of saying that it has *clarity*. When you ask your students to line up, take out paper, give you their attention, prepare to go home for the day, remember something to bring for tomorrow, or take a notice to parents, you are giving a message. And when you ask, "Does everyone understand? Do you have questions?" you are checking for clarity.

Messages can be very simple, like "Stop!" Or they can be as complex as the Internal Revenue Service tax code. The greater the complexity, of course, the harder it is to maintain clarity. That's the test of a good informational writer, really; a truly gifted informational writer can make tax codes as understandable as traffic signs.

You might teach this message concept by having students write notes home—through pictures or print—about *one* significant thing that happened during the day. Ask them to write Post-It note reminders to each other; again using pictures, print, or a combination. Ask students to create posters for classroom rules, such as behaving courteously. Again, pictures or print—it does not matter. What matters is that the message goes from writer to reader in any way that makes sense. Clarity is the name of the game.

Ideas as "Something to Write About"

When students hear the word *ideas*, they often think of the age-old question, "What shall I write about?" Write what you know, we tell them, or write what interests you. What *is* that anyway? We ask these questions of our students, but the truth is, often we cannot answer them ourselves. Ever notice how a million things interest you until someone sticks an eight and a half by eleven inch sheet of paper in front of you? Then, amazingly, you cannot think of one interesting thing. So what do you do? As Anne Lamott tells us, there is no "magic formula my father passed on to me in a whisper just before he died." You just sit down and do it. "You begin to string words together like beads to tell a story" (1995, p. 7).

USING LISTS

We all have stories in our lives, things we notice, things that interest us, and opinions about this or that. Everyday events become the stuff of narrative, descriptive, expository, and persuasive writing—the basis for notes and letters, how-to pieces, essays, and stories. For example, ground squirrels routinely devour our flowers and plantings (right down to the root—and sometimes the roots, too). We are reluctant to kill them, however pesky though they may be, so we have engaged in a relocation plan, trapping them in a humane manner, and then taking them to a greener area rich with all manner of flora, near a river. It's a lot of work. We have to bait the traps, watch them carefully so the squirrels are not left without food or water for too long, and then drive a half hour each way to reach the river. Our neighbors think we are insane. They tell us we should drown the squirrels—or perhaps shoot them. Frankly, I would not have missed the experience of transporting them to new homes. I have learned to trap them successfully, to keep them calm during transportation, and to release them in places where they are most likely to survive and flourish. I've even learned to enjoy their antics, knowing I can successfully banish them from my flower beds. Best of all, I have wonderful fodder for writing. I could write a description of a ground squirrel's tunneling network, or a persuasive essay on the advantages of relocation. I could even write a story about the time my neighbor was bitten by an aggressive ground squirrel he tried to drown (OK, I made that one up, but I *could* write it). We need to model how everyday happenings become writing topics so our students see that writing ideas are all around us, all the time.

> *When we give the topic to our students, we assume a common experience that does not exist.*
>
> **—Donald Murray**
> *A Writer Teaches Writing* (2004, p. 96)

> *Every book, film, conversation, ride on the bus, glance out the window sparks a hundred possibilities for writing—if you have learned to think like a writer. If not, the whole world looks like a blank page.*
>
> **—Vicki Spandel**
> *The 9 Rights of Every Writer* (2005, p. 21)

What are three things you are thinking of writing about *right now?* Write them down. This is the beginning of a list you can share with your students. You can't share it just once, of course. You need to share your list frequently because it will change all the time. Here is my current list of things to write about (I am not going to write about all of these, you understand—or maybe any of them—it's just an idea list):

✔ How to entertain yourself when you miss a flight
✔ How to deer proof your yard
✔ What to do when a truly angry dog comes after you—and you are alone
✔ How to get up when you are cross-country skiing and fall into a deep snow bank
✔ The story of Jack (my grandson) and how toddlers and adults define the concept of "toy" differently
✔ The sheer joy of watching sea turtles at play—from underwater

This is my list. I would not assign *any* of these topics to my students because their experiences are different. The only person I can effectively choose topics for is myself—and that is how I want students to feel, too.

BORROWING

One good place to go for writing ideas is a writing group—or simply a friend who writes. Just as the fish are always better on the other side of the lake, so the other writer is always coming up with a better idea. Barry Lane (2002) is writing a series of stories based on fables, his first being *The Tortoise and the Hare Continued.* . . . I like this idea very much—the notion that stories aren't really over when they're over—there is always another episode. This is a good one to borrow. Author Anne Lamott advises her students, "Write down all the stuff you swore you'd never tell another soul. What can you recall about your birthday parties—the disasters, the days of grace, your relatives' faces lit up by birthday candles? Scratch around for details: what people ate, listened to, wore—those terrible petaled swim caps, the men's awful trunks, the cocktail dress your voluptuous aunt wore that was so slinky she practically needed the Jaws of Life to get out of it" (1995, p. 5). I love this advice because basically she is telling us, each of us, "Your life is fascinating, and because only *you* have lived it, only *you* know what to write."

Our students need to talk to one another *before* they write—and to help one another discover ideas for writing. In *Writing: Teachers and Children at Work*, Donald Graves suggests that we should know our students and their interests in order to help them find topics. Rather than assigning topics, he says, know the child well enough to explore his or her world. He even suggests making a chart (and if you have never tried this, it may surprise you to discover how hard it is) listing each student's name and special interests (1983, pp. 22–28). That way, the first conference can focus on topics—not topics we assign but questions that lead children to topics of their own: What is the most interesting thing that ever happened to you? What is your first really vivid memory? Do you have any pets? Do you have hobbies? What do you find fascinating? Annoying? As Graves tells us, "Writers who learn to choose topics well make the most significant growth in both information and skills. . . . with [the] best topic the child exercises strongest control, establishes ownership, and with ownership, pride in the piece" (1983, p. 21). Ownership and pride—that's a recipe for voice. Voice begins with having something to say. "Writers who do not learn to choose topics wisely lose out on the strong link between voice and subject" (Graves, 1983, p. 21).

TEACHING ORGANIZATION CONCEPTUALLY

When we connect organization to writing, we think immediately of leads, transitions, conclusions, orderly paragraphing, patterning, and so on. However, the concept of organization is much larger than writing. It can be taught in several ways.

✔ Organization as *patterning*
✔ Organization as *grouping*
✔ Organization as *making a plan*

Organization as Patterning

Many things in life are organized—and you might brainstorm a list with your students. The following is a list of things students have mentioned at various times—and no doubt your students will think of more:

✔ Grocery stores (and other stores, of course)
✔ Closets (not mine, but some)
✔ An ant colony
✔ Traffic

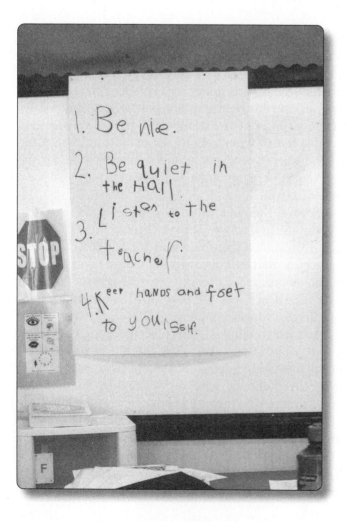

✔ City streets
✔ A buffet in a restaurant
✔ A hotel
✔ A sports team
✔ Colors in a crayon box
✔ Living room furniture
✔ Newspapers
✔ Telephone books
✔ Rows of crops
✔ The alphabet
✔ Dishes in a cupboard
✔ A calendar
✔ A blueprint for a house
✔ An eight-course dinner

Good. Think about how each thing is organized—what sort of pattern does it follow? Alphabetical? Geographic (like a map)? Little to big? Salad to dessert? And so on. Now, what about the things in the world that are disorganized (or random)? Here are some things students have mentioned:

✔ *Some* closets
✔ *Some* desks
✔ Clouds in the sky
✔ Weeds
✔ People running from a fire or accident
✔ A fight
✔ My hair in the morning
✔ Wrinkly clothes packed in a hurry
✔ My notebook!

✔ The laundry when it first comes out of the dryer
✔ My dad's calendar
✔ Our kitchen
✔ Our car

In one group, we see patterns; in the other, not. This is one underlying concept of organization: things in patterns. You can reinforce this basic idea throughout the day or the week by asking students to identify moments or events during which things or people fall into patterns—or not: People line up for the bus (that's organized); leaves blow off the tree in the wind (that's not). Soon your students will be seeing organizational patterns everywhere—and you can reinforce this with art. Ask them to draw a picture of something organized and a picture of something random. This reinforces their thinking about the basic notion of organization. Now it is time to extend it, if you wish.

Sometimes patterning is vital; at other times it really does not matter. For example, no one cares whether leaves fall from a tree in a precise pattern. We rather like the randomness. However, take one of the student examples—the grocery store. There, order matters a lot. Why, though? Ask your students this: What if you went to the grocery store and things were totally jumbled: paper towels mixed with oranges, soup mixed with toothbrushes. Would that work? Why? Suppose that you opened your calendar and the dates were out of order. Would a calendar like that be usable? How come? The question here is: How does organization make life easier? Your students will have creative answers, and their answers will provide the foundation for what you want to teach later—that organization in writing makes some writing easier to interpret and to follow. (A poem may be more random than, say, a how-to chapter on fixing your lawnmower.)

◾ Don't Forget Puzzles

Jigsaw puzzles make patterns—patterns that are not always immediately obvious. In many ways, assembling a puzzle is a way of solving an organizational challenge: What is the picture or pattern I am supposed to be seeing? Many people (young and older) solve puzzles by beginning with the outside framework. This is rather like coming up with a main idea that frames what follows. Puzzle pieces are linked together with colors or shapes; words, phrases, and sentences are linked together by common ideas.

◾ Pictures in a Series

Give your students three pictures, related or not, and ask them to put the pictures in order and tell a story based on the arrangement (There does not need to be any right answer to this—it's an exercise in imagination). The pattern they choose determines the story. When they have finished, see if they can shift the order to come up with a different story.

Organization as Grouping

Grouping is easy to teach. It is simply putting things together that go together. You can teach grouping with items of similar size, color, shape, texture, or any other common trait. This practice provides a foundation for creating paragraphs or chapters—for "chunking" information. You can do an interesting grouping activity with something like rocks or coins, where there are numerous possibilities for grouping. Coins, for example, can be grouped by color, size, value, or date—or in a number of other ways your students will surprise you by thinking of. The same is true for rocks and numerous other objects. Grouping can be done in teams, and when you are finished, ask students to share the various methods of grouping their teams have thought of.

Organization as Making a Plan

When you have an event coming up—a conference night, a school gathering, a field trip, or whatever—make a "plan" with students. You may decide to prepare invitations or posters, to celebrate, to write about the event, to take a class picture, or any number of things. Planning is an important component of organizing because it requires anticipation and prediction. When you plan as a group, you ask students to envision what will happen in the future.

This is the idea, really, behind prewriting: making a plan for writing (so what you are teaching is a precursor to the prewriting phase of writing process). Of course, in our lives, when the wedding plans do not work out, we amend them—or abandon them. Somehow, we forgot to give ourselves such freedom with writing, in which outlines can become tyrannical. Where we often go awry with prewriting is in forcing student writers to stick relentlessly to whatever plan they come up with (never mind if it's working!). This defeats the whole point. The planning sets thinking in motion; drafting continues the development of that thinking. An idea evolves throughout the prewriting, drafting, and revising stages—and must be given freedom to do so. Force students to adhere to a prewriting plan (whether a list, a web, or whatever), and you shut down their thinking. Lucy Calkins says, "I've come to think that it's very important that writing is not only a process of recording, it's also a process of developing a story or idea" (1994, p. 8).

TEACHING VOICE CONCEPTUALLY

Of all the traits, I love voice the most because voice is the person speaking to us from the page. Voice is the essence of the writing, the reason for the writing, and the reason for reading. Voice is the place where many students, regardless of technical skill in other areas of writing, are likely to shine.

Let me suggest several different ways of teaching this elusive but vital concept:

✔ Voice as a *metaphor*
✔ Voice as *individuality*
✔ Voice as *mood*

Voice as Metaphor

This first way to teaching voice is the simplest—and it is a good place to begin. One day, when I visited my friend Arlene Moore's K-1 classroom, she said, quite out of the blue, "Jennifer, that dress has so much voice!" Indeed it did. It was a bright rosy pink with yellow loose-petal flowers hand-stitched onto the front.

"I love bright colors," Arlene went on. "It makes me feel good just looking at them." She went on to ask her students what colors they felt had the most voice—and not surprisingly, the striking colors of purple, orange, yellow, and red were popular responses. We then talked about colors without voice—but this time, there was not so much agreement. Some children saw tan as voice-free, but one young writer said that tan was the color of beach sand, which he loved—so for him, tan did have voice. Many students felt that gray lacked voice, until one writer ran to the window and pointed out the number of different grays in the sky; a storm was brewing. "Gray can be a storm color, and storms have voice," he reminded us. Voice is personal.

Arlene likes to connect voice to favorite and least favorite foods, too—"strong voice" foods typically include the perennial favorite, pizza, as well as ice cream, chocolate, hamburgers, fruit, cotton candy, and so on. For students, "low voice" foods include tapioca pudding, leftovers of all kinds, liver, undercooked eggs, watery oatmeal, and "anything my sister makes in the blender."

Use your imagination in making metaphoric connections. Anything that taps into the senses will work, including music, art, dance, films, TV shows—even animals. "Zebras and chimpanzees have a lot of voice, and slugs don't," one first grader told me (or perhaps the "slug" voice is less appealing to us).

Voice as Individuality

> *Voice is the imprint of ourselves on our writing. It is that part of the self that pushes the writing ahead, the dynamo in the process. Take the voice away and the writing collapses of its own weight. There is no writing, just words following words. Voiceless writing is addressed "to whom it may concern."*
>
> **—Donald H. Graves**
> *Writing* (1983, p. 227)

Here's a question I like to ask students: "When you talk to a friend on the phone, how long does it take you to recognize that person?" Not long. Why? Because every voice is different. Try this. Have your students close their eyes, tap one student on the shoulder, and ask him or her to make a simple statement: "Guess who I am." Everyone will guess correctly. That's how individual voices are.

Voice shows itself in other forms, too, such as art. Show your students works by a few well-known artists, for example, Picasso, Charles Schulz, Bev Doolittle, William Steig, Jules Feiffer, and folk artist Charles Wysocki. What are the differences? What kinds of "voices" are these artists showing in their paintings? Don't worry about whether your students recognize the artists; that really makes no difference at all. You are simply looking for their responses to the voice within the art. Who *is* this person? You can also use art from the vibrant world of picture books, of course. Some *particularly* striking examples include

- ✔ Jean-Michel Basquiat [in Maya Angelou's *Life Doesn't Frighten Me* (1993)]
- ✔ Jannell Cannon [in her book *Verdi* (1997)]
- ✔ Lauren Child [in her book *I Am Too Absolutely Small for School* (2003)]
- ✔ Steve Jenkins [in his book *Actual Size* (2005)]
- ✔ Tom Lichtenheld [in his book *Everything I Know About Pirates* (2000)]
- ✔ Jackie Morris [in Carolyn Pitcher's *Lord of the Forest* (2004)]
- ✔ Margie Palatini [in her book *Bedhead* (2000)]
- ✔ Giselle Potter [in Toni Morrison's *The Big Box* (1999)]

✔ Lynn Rowe Reed [in Robin Pulver's *Punctuation Takes a Vacation* (2003)]
✔ Chris Raschka [in Norton Juster's *The Hello, Goodbye Window* (2005)]
✔ David Shannon [in his book *Alice the Fairy* (2004)]
✔ Lane Smith [in Jon Scieszka's *Math Curse* (1995)]
✔ William Steig [in *any* of his books, including but not limited to *Amos and Boris*, 1971; *The Toy Brother*, 1996; *Dr. De Soto*, 1999; *Solomon the Rusty Nail*, 1987; *The Amazing Bone*, 1993; *Brave Irene*, 1988; *Shrek*, 1993]
✔ Lauren Stringer [in Cynthia Rylant's *Scarecrow* (1998)]
✔ Stefano Vitale [in Alice Walker's *There Is a Flower at the Tip of My Nose Smelling Me* (2006)]
✔ Mo Willems [in his book *Knuffle Bunny* (2004)]

Pictures, like text, have mood and tone. Talk about this with your students. Ruth Wright Paulsen, for example, creates a hauntingly beautiful snowscape for Gary Paulsen's *Dogteam* that fits the adventurous, mysterious mood of the book perfectly. David Shannon's illustrations are playful, and sometimes outrageous. Giselle Potter creates unique details with eyes, mouth, and hair. She can sketch a character to make you laugh out loud or break your heart. Mo Willems combines photographs and cartoon-like characters for an artsy, modern look, while Stefano Vitale's work creates symbolic, almost surreal effects. Chris Raschka's childlike paintings of Nanna's kitchen window touch the heart, Lauren Stringer's paintings give a nostalgic sweetness to Cynthia Rylant's classic *Scarecrow*, while Jackie Morris's bold and dramatic tigers give breathtaking power to *Lord of the Forest*. Jannell Cannon is stylish, but leans toward a mix of reality and fantasy. Cannon relies heavily on texture and color to create the "voice" imprint of her work. In *all* his books, William Steig is humorous and unpredictable. Steig's artistic voice relies on facial expression and the interaction between characters, whose motives and intentions are immediately readable on their faces. Artistic voice is an important tool; it can lure us into the content. Lynn Rowe Reed's whimsical style makes punctuation seem an appealing, lighthearted topic. Tom Lichtenheld's jaunty, defiant pirates make us want to climb aboard for adventure. Steve Jenkins' stunningly colorful collage art bridges the gap between imagination and science, beautifully blending two interpretations of the world. The point is, voice can be as strong in art as it is in text, and no two artistic voices are alike. Once students begin to see voice in the artwork around them, they become more conscious of their own artistic voices—the individuality that makes their work unique. But you must *say* it, you must emphasize and applaud that individuality, or your students will not automatically value it. Help them notice and appreciate the differences among artists so that they will value those same differences among themselves.

Voice as Mood

Music offers an immediate way of helping students tune into mood. Think of a film you have seen recently—or at any time. How often did the music let you know what was about to happen? You know when the hero is in trouble, don't you? Or when something sad—such as the old, faithful dog dying—is about to happen? Think of the music *you* play when you are in a celebrational mood, at a party or wedding, versus what you might play as background music when you are reading or working. What do you play to cheer yourself up? To mellow out? What pieces of music speak to you?

Right now, while you are thinking of it, jot down three memorable pieces of music. (They do not have to be your three all-time favorites—just three that pop into your head.) Are they instrumental or vocal? Lively? Wistful? How do they make you feel?

With your students, explore the moods of music by playing a variety for them, marches, symphonies, folk music, Celtic music. Compare Willie Nelson; Bob Dylan; Rod Stewart; Sinatra; Peter, Paul, and Mary; Beethoven; Mozart; The Chieftains; Raffi; Greg and Steve; and Norah Jones. Compare Israel Kamakawiwo'ole's light, upbeat version of "Somewhere Over the Rainbow" (*In IZ World*, 1992) to Judy Garland's more heart-wrenching rendition (*Judy at Carnegie Hall*, 1967). Ask students to tell you how each piece of music makes them *feel*. Voice is ultimately about reader response—which begins with listener response. Music is vivid and embracing, but the response your students have to music as it engulfs them teaches them how to respond emotionally to poetry or to prose.

▓ Different Voices, Different Times

Most of us have a wide range of voices: one for pleading with a parent or child to please do *whatever*, another for cheering on the team on the football field, for conspiring with a close friend, for arguing with a petulant sibling, for greeting a stranger on the phone, or talking to an infant or a puppy. You may wish to actually have your students try this out. Set up a situation. Let's say that you want the door closed. First, have a student ask a parent to do this. Notice the words and the tone of voice. Then ask another student to imagine that his or her very annoying younger brother has left the door open for the "bazillionth" time—what do you say, and *how do you say it?* Then have a third student teach a toddler how to close the door—what do you say, and *how do you say it?*

If you tell first graders that mystery stories, business letters, and personal essays all have slightly different voices, you cannot really expect them to understand what you mean—yet. However, when you tell them that we all have many voices within us and that we use different voices at different times, they do understand. You are only planting a seed.

Figure 3.2 "Good Memories" is an expressive piece of personal writing by Skye (2).

When I was 2 or 3 I fed a BABy DEER. She was not I tell you not afad. My 3 birthday was a blast in Texas. At Bufflo Bills I ate wild wild wigs. Whats your favent food? Did I menchan about the time I ate hotapeaows I cyd 24 hourers. Man I cryed for a long time.

■ Wearing Many Hats

Clothing gives us clues about mood, tone, and purpose. I do not wear my jeans to a wedding or chiffon to the rodeo. If you're a hat collector, you can use a variety of hats to indicate various kinds of voice. A cowboy hat might suggest one thing, a gardener's hat another, and a wide fedora with a peacock feather something else. You can bet your students will recognize colorful versus drab, formal versus informal, playful versus serious. This same visual effect works for word choice, too—and later, for fluency. Sentences, like voices and word patterns, can come to the party dressed to the teeth or lounging in comfy clothes. Play "dress-up for voice" with your students. Ask each person to come to class with a hat of some kind, and talk about the kind of voice each one suggests.

TEACHING WORD CHOICE CONCEPTUALLY

Choice is the operative word here. You might begin with menus. Ask your students to view them and to make choices as if they were ordering food right now. Write their choices down, and explain that writers choose words much the way hungry diners choose foods from a menu or shoppers choose groceries or other things to purchase. We have hundreds of thousands of words in English; yet, for a particular moment, to create a particular picture in the reader's mind or a particular response, only the "just right" word will do—the way sometimes you *only* want hot fudge or a burger. Writers are picky or, we could say, *discriminating, selective, choosy, fussy, particular, demanding,* or *persnickety.* Some simple ways to teach word choice conceptually include these:

✔ Word choice as *weight*
✔ Word choice as *the target*

Word Choice as Weight

Some words carry a lot of weight. This is another way of saying that they have substance, meaning, impact. Vague words—*nice, big, happy, sad, great, fun*—are pebbles. They do not tip the scale because they do not tell us anything. You can illustrate this with a scale and a collection of rocks and pebbles. As your students encounter a new word, ask them, "Rock or pebble? What do you think?" Glue or tape the rock or pebble to a card with the word printed on it, and place it right on the scale. Be sure, though, to let your students make the choice.

To kick off this game, you need some examples. Start simply, with a word your students use often—such as *big*. We all use it, but it's a "pebble" word, really. It does not say much. What are some weightier alternatives? How about *enormous, vast, bulky, burly, robust,* or *weighty*? Of course, these words are not completely interchangeable. This is the tricky part, isn't it? We can say, "The *vast* landscape stretched before us," but "The *bulky* landscape stretched before us" doesn't work. So, you will need to provide sample sentences for clarification. By the way, lots of letters do not add up to more "weight"—it is more a question of how specific a word is. I am *glad* when a favorite movie is on television; I am *jubilant* when my daughter phones to say that she is coming for the weekend with my grandson Jack.

One of the best ways to show off heavy language is through literature. In *Verdi* (1997), Jannell Cannon writes about a young python being sent into the jungle to grow up "big and green" as all pythons must. Cannon could have written, "Verdi was a *nice* python. He wasn't *too big*. He was *slow*. He was *happy*. He had *neat* stripes *going down* his back." Instead, she used some heavy language: "Verdi dawdled. He was proudly eyeing his bright yellow skin. He especially liked the bold stripes that zigzagged down his back." We never hear a teacher say, "I'm just so tired of *zigzagged* and *dawdled*. There *must* be another way to say it!" We all like fresh language; we cannot get enough.

Word Choice as The Target

Precision is an important component of word choice. When one of your students uses a particularly precise word, you can paste that word right onto a "Word Choice Target"—right at the bull's-eye. In *Smoky Night* (1994), Eve Bunting describes a street riot. Following the turmoil, a street sign "lies crumpled in the gutter." Not bent. Not broken. *Crumpled.* Does that word hit the bull's-eye? You only have to ask your students, "What do you picture when you hear it? Does *crumpled* tell you more than *bent*?"

In *The Toy Brother* (1996), William Steig tells the tale of Yorick, a mischievous young sprout who hopes to become an alchemist, like his father—and who finds his brother Charles a real "pain in the pants." Charles cannot "fathom" why Yorick doesn't like him more and hopes they will someday become "palsy-walsy." When Yorick accidentally shrinks himself, Charles (who is on a ladybug hunt at the time) finds Yorick "thrashing" through the weeds: "It was indeed Yorick, down to the minuscule wart on his knuckle!" *Pain in the pants, fathom, palsy-walsy, thrashing, minuscule*—those are right-on-target words, bull's-eyes. Contrast this version: "Yorick wasn't much *fun*. He wasn't *nice*. Charles did not *get why*." We are on the outer rim of the target here.

What I like about the target is that it helps students to see that you can get the basic meaning across with vague words—like *nice*. Taking extra care to aim for the center, however, is worth it; bull's-eye words wake readers up.

TEACHING FLUENCY CONCEPTUALLY

Fluency is wonderfully rewarding to teach conceptually. It is all about rhythm, grace, and motion. Think for a moment how very many things this applies to in real life—everything from an Olympic ski jumper to your own way of climbing or descending stairs. It could be the ripple of waves or the flutter of a butterfly. Wind in the treetops or a dust devil darting across the fallow fields of the North Dakota farmlands. To teach this, start with your own graceful movement—again relying on music. This time, though, you are going for movement, not emotional response. Choose something lively, with a strong beat. Ask students to move to the music. They can march, twirl, wave arms, clap hands, snap fingers, stomp feet, sway—whatever has rhythm. You need to move with them. They need to feel the beat. You can teach . . .

✔ Fluency as *personal imagery*
✔ Fluency as *"come alive" poetry* (you can perform)

Fluency as Personal Imagery

Brainstorm. Ask students to brainstorm what in the whole wide world around you moves with rhythm. They will surprise you with their answers. As they speak, write what they say on an overhead transparency, creating a poem of possibles. Here is one third-grade version:

Fluency Is . . .

Geese in a giant V
Wild horses running
Whales sounding
Bats darting after insects
Clouds shifting, meandering
A rodeo clown
Dancers in a line
A parade
Wheat in the fields
Grasses bent by the wind
Trees swaying in the storm
Lightning flashing
A chef flipping burgers
Gravy dripping over mashed potatoes
Skaters gliding
Skiers flying
Water flowing down a mountain
Waves pounding on the shore
People walking down the street
A cat stretching
A spider spinning its web
A spider wrapping up its prey
Hair in the wind
Shadows flickering
Fire
Candlelight
A bride's dress
A pulse
A drum beat
A conductor's wand
A musician's fingers
A slowly widening smile
My mother's hands

This is fluency!

Fluency as "Come Alive" Poetry

Introduce poetry your students can act out. Good possibilities for "come alive" poetry that you dramatize on your feet come from Douglas Florian (*Insectlopedia, Mammalabilia, Beast Feast Zoo's Who*) or Shel Silverstein. Read a line and ask students to repeat it, moving, using arms, hands, eyes, and facial expressions to bring the poem to life. One poem I love is Douglas Florian's "Army Ants," from *Insectlopedia* (1998, p. 13). You will get the idea immediately if you stand up, right now, and march—left, right, left right—as you read aloud. This is a marching poem with a strong beat, and students love it. They can perform it in small groups or as a whole class. It is short, so they learn it quickly, but you can say a line first and then have your students repeat (the echo effect only enhances the rhythm):

> Left
>   Right
> Left
>   Right
> We're army ants.
> We swarm.
>   We fight.
> We have no home.
> We roam.
> We race.
> You're lucky if
> We miss your place.

A suggestion: To suggest an army of ants coming from far away, descending upon you, then fading into the distance, start the left-right, left-right in a whisper, slowly building to a crescendo. Then fade out again to a whisper at the end. Ask students to actually march around the room as they recite the poem. The marching feels good, and it reinforces the idea of fluency.

TEACHING CONVENTIONS CONCEPTUALLY

What are conventions, really? Rules, many student writers would say. (This is often what we think, too.) Actually, the word *conventions* signifies "traditions, customs, protocol"—the thing to do.

Conventions as Customs

Custom and tradition are woven through almost every part of our life. Ask your students to think about customs or traditions that go with eating a meal. These days, we usually eat with silverware, for example, not with our fingers—it was not always so! We eat from plates and bowls. Why? How do you suppose that became a mealtime convention? Each time your students identify a convention or custom, ask why? Why did that become the custom?

Look at other situations, too. Sports, for instance, are riddled with conventions. Conventions are the rules of the game in baseball, basketball, or whatever. But what of other conventions? Today it is customary to wear uniforms, have coaches, limit the numbers of players who can participate at once (whole towns once played football), limit the time of the game (once they played until everyone was wounded or exhausted), or have fans sit on the sidelines (years ago, "fans" and players were inseparable).

How about driving? What are the customs or conventions that govern our behavior on the road? What happens if we violate them? How about shopping

Figure 3.3

Expanding control over conventions. Jamie (2)

> But I don't want to move, Mom!
>
> Why do we have to move mom. What about Kyle? Kyle's a boy but he's also my friend! My only friend! My brother Ryan makes fun of me because he's a boy. But Mom says just to ignore him when he says that! the next morning, AHHHH, yelled my brother AHHH!!!! W-w what happend I asked. somebody stuck a frog down my pants AHH! Ha Ha I giggled. Grrr I'm gonna get you little pipsqeak!!! AHHH! I cried! AHHH. Well this was in the morning wile my mom was still sleeping. And both of us got in trouble! Grounded for the day! BORING!!! It turned out that we didn't have to move but my brother's still chasing me for puting that frog in his pants but he needed it so I'm not scared! Not one bit! AHHH. THE End!

at the grocery store? Visiting the library? Riding the bus? Walking a dog in the park? Dressing for school? Sitting in class? The possibilities are endless. The point is to help students see, first, what conventions *are* (customs or approved ways of doing things) and, second, how conventions *came to be* (to make life easier, to make people comfortable, and so on).

To consider conventions in writing, begin with writing that is as convention-free as you can make it. Write letters backward and upside down. Put no spaces between words. Spell words irregularly. Omit words, letters, or punctuation marks. Write from the bottom of the page up or right to left. Then ask your students the key question: Why? Why wouldn't it work if everyone wrote this way? Conventions evolve to make our lives, including our writing lives, easier.

A LESSON IN ANATOMY VERSUS JUST DOING IT

The lessons in this chapter, of course, are not a support, not a substitute for writing. Writers have to write. All the time.

Several years ago I watched a western horsemanship instructor giving a group of seven-year-olds their first lesson. They were excited when she led an ornery old paint horse, Willie, out in front of them, and it was obvious from their expressions that in *their* eyes Willie was not a broken down, sway-backed, best-days-behind-him nag. He was flat-out beautiful. They were virtually quivering with anticipation, wondering who would be the first to take Willie around the arena. They wanted to touch him and make friends, to climb aboard and storm the track and win ribbons—but they had been instructed to "stay on the benches."

Excitement dissolved into tedium as it became increasingly apparent that the teacher's intent—at least for lesson one—was to hold off on any actual riding until everyone had mastered the "anatomy of the horse." Her circle of pupils sat stone-faced and rigid as she pointed to various spots on old Willie's legs, head, shoulders, and back and asked the "riders" in turn to supply the correct terminology. "When do we get to ride?" one of her more intrepid pupils finally asked. The instructor looked vaguely perturbed, remarkably unaware that she had lost the attention and enthusiasm of her class.

Before they left (looking considerably less excited than when they had come in), the instructor handed each student a homework sheet with a sketch of a horse and arrows leading to "parts of the horse" labels many of them could not read. These were to go home to parents for more drill and practice. I was willing to bet the class would be smaller the following week—but then, perhaps that is what she was hoping for. After all, she had eight pupils and only four horses. Teaching is almost always like that.

I was lucky—I didn't have that instructor. Becky, who sat a horse as if she'd been born on one, taught me to ride. For a time, she didn't provide much direct instruction at all. She watched me ride, and she rode with me and asked me to watch her. She and the horse moved as one; I wanted to ride like that—to move like that. I wanted to stop bumping up and down, inelegantly smacking the saddle and feeling my feet fall sloppily out of the stirrups. As I think back now to her instruction, I feel the best word to describe it would be *subtle*. She didn't write evaluations or give me points for heel extension or drill me on terminology. She encouraged me to *ride*—in fact, I was on top of a horse within five minutes of meeting her. "Imagine," she would say, "that your legs are so long they could reach clear around the horse and meet underneath." I literally felt my legs grow. "Imagine," she told me, "that every move you make is felt by the horse and interpreted as a signal of where

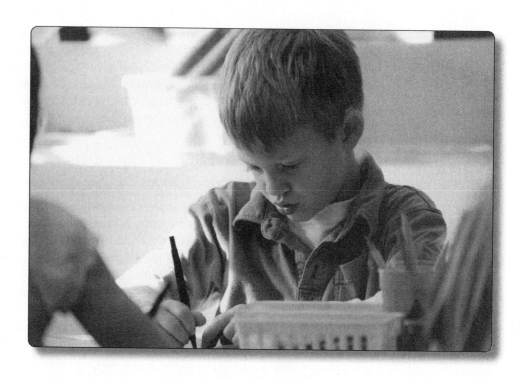

you want to go." And as soon as she said it, I felt it happening. Over time, she taught me about keeping my hands quiet, reading a horse's ears, thinking "down and back" when loping, keeping a center of balance so that I could ride with my eyes closed, extending my legs so that the weight would go into my heels, and feeling the horse's feet move beneath me. We never did get to the anatomy lesson, but I learned anatomy anyway. I do not remember that part of her instruction at all. What I do remember—what I will *never* forget— is Becky saying, "Trust yourself. Go with the flow." Great teachers encourage and suggest—then they trust.

CHAPTER 3 IN A NUTSHELL

- Trait-based instruction is centered around writers' language. For this reason, it is not a curriculum unto itself, nor a new way of teaching writing. It is a way of *thinking* about writing that supports process-based writing instruction.

- Because traits (characteristics of strong writing) are inherent in every piece of good writing, they are necessarily embedded in writing instruction, even when we do not realize we are teaching them.

- Understanding the core meaning of a trait, what it truly is that we are teaching, enables us to teach each trait conceptually—to teach the fundamental meaning behind the trait.

- Ideas are about imagination, pictures in the mind, clarity of meaning, or a central message.

- Organization is about patterning, grouping, planning—creating a sense of direction.

- Voice is individuality, personality, mood, expression, and connection to an audience—the right tone of voice for the message and the moment.

- Word choice is about precision, hitting the target, relying on verbs instead of modifiers, and using words that paint pictures in a reader's mind.

- Fluency is rhythm, grace, flow, music to the ears, going for the sound and not just the literal meaning.

- Conventions are traditions, customs, protocol, the sum of what's expected and accepted—whether in writing or in any context.

- Writers learn to write by doing it. The traits, therefore, are not an end in themselves but a means to making writing practice richer and more purposeful.

STUDY GROUP: INTERACTIVE QUESTIONS AND ACTIVITIES

1. **Activity and discussion.** Without looking back, ask yourself, "What is the main thing I am trying to teach, conceptually, for each trait?" Can you answer this in writing? If you can, you are ready to teach them. If you cannot, take time to review as necessary. Then try it again, working with a partner. If you can, expand my list of ways to teach each trait conceptually.

2. **Discussion.** Think back on the writing instruction you received as a student. What was it like? Which of the two "riding instructors" did you encounter most often? Describe one experience, positive or negative, for your group: What was it like and how did it affect you as a writer—and then as a teacher?

3. **Activity and discussion.** How would you analyze your own style of teaching? Begin with the following checklist and then expand your thoughts with a short paragraph, being as objective as you can. Be prepared to present your self-analysis to your study group.

Check each one that describes you, your teaching style, or your teaching philosophy:

___ I believe children learn to write by writing.

___ I believe children need some basic instruction in writing skills before doing any significant writing.

___ Primary students can and should write, in some form, from the very first day of school.

___ Students are ready to write when they can form whole sentences and spell a few high-frequency words correctly.

___ Young children benefit from seeing me model writing—and then doing it themselves.

___ Young children have much to teach each other about writing. They need to talk and share.

___ Very young students cannot distinguish between strong and ineffective writing. We need to tell them which writing is good.

___ Young students can comprehend the concepts of clear message, voice, and organization even before they know how to incorporate those things into their own writing.

___ In order to teach trait-based writing effectively, I need to understand the traits inside and out myself.

____ The way in which I talk about writing—including my students' own work—influences significantly the way they think about writing.

____ A writing classroom may sometimes look noisy and somewhat chaotic, but be highly productive.

____ The most productive writing classroom is one in which children are sitting quietly, attending to their writing.

____ In a successful writing classroom, each child's work will reflect an individual and unique voice.

____ Ideas and voice—expression and individuality—are the heart and soul of good writing.

____ Conventional correctness is the foundation of good writing, though other qualities are also important.

Add your own thoughts to the profile you have created with this checklist.

4. **Activity and discussion.** What would you say to a teacher who said, "The six traits have nothing to do with my writing curriculum"? Write a short (two to three brief paragraphs) response directly to this hypothetical teacher. Be prepared to share your response aloud with your study group.

5. **Discussion.** What, specifically, are the advantages in introducing primary students to the traits by teaching them conceptually, as opposed to simply handing out checklists or scoring students' work? Discuss this with your group.

SOURCES CITED

Angelou, Maya, 1993. *Life Doesn't Frighten Me.* New York: Stewart, Tabori, and Chang.

Bragg, Rick. 2001. *Ava's Man.* New York: Alfred A. Knopf.

Bunting, Eve. 1995. *Smoky Night.* San Diego, CA: Harcourt Brace & Company.

Calkins, Lucy McCormick. 1994. *The Art of Teaching Writing.* Portsmouth, NH: Heinemann.

Cannon, Jannell. 1997. *Verdi.* San Diego, CA: Harcourt Brace & Company.

Child, Lauren. 2003. *I Am Too Absolutely Small for School.* Cambridge, MA: Candlewick Press.

Collard, Sneed B. III. 1997. *Animal Dads.* Boston: Houghton Mifflin.

Fletcher, Ralph. 1997. *Twilight Comes Twice.* Boston: Houghton Mifflin.

Florian, Douglas. 1998. *Insectlopedia.* San Diego, CA: Harcourt Brace & Company.

Graves, Donald. 1983. *Writing: Teachers and Children at Work.* Portsmouth, NH: Heinemann.

Jenkins, Steve. 2005. *Actual Size.* Boston: Houghton Mifflin.

Juster, Norton. 2005. *The Hello, Goodbye Window.* New York: Hyperion Books for Children.

Lamott, Anne. 1995. *Bird by Bird.* New York: Doubleday.

Lane, Barry. 2002. *The Tortoise and the Hare Continued . . .* Shoreham, VT: Discover Writing Press.

Lane, Barry, and Gretchen Barnabei. 2001. *Why We Must Run with Scissors: Voice Lessons in Persuasive Writing.* Shoreham, VT: Discover Writing Press.

Lichtenheld, Tom. 2000. *Everything I Know About Pirates.* New York: Simon & Schuster.

McGuane, Thomas. 2000. *Some Horses.* New York: Random House.

Morrison, Toni (with Slade Morrison). 1999. *The Big Box.* New York: Hyperion Books for Children.

Murray, Donald M. 2004. *A Writer Teaches Writing.* Boston: Heinle.

Newkirk, Thomas. 1989. *More than Stories: The Range of Children's Writing.* Portsmouth, NH: Heinemann.

Olshansky, Beth. 2006. *Picturing Writing: Fostering Literacy Through Art and Image-Making Within the Writing Process.* Durham, NH: University of New Hampshire.

Palatini, Margie. 2000. *Bedhead.* New York: Aladdin Paperbacks.

Paulsen, Gary. 1993. *Dogteam.* New York: Delacorte Press.

Pitcher, Carolyn. 2004. *Lord of the Forest.* London, England: Frances Lincoln Children's Books.

Pulver, Robin. 2003. *Punctuation Takes a Vacation.* New York: Holiday House.

Romano, Tom. 1995. *Writing with Passion: Life Stories, Multiple Genres.* Portsmouth, NH: Boynton/Cook.

Rylant, Cynthia. 1998. *Scarecrow.* New York: Harcourt.

Scieszka, Jon. 1995. *Math Curse.* New York: Viking Press.

Shannon, David. 2004. *Alice the Fairy.* New York: Scholastic.

Spandel, Vicki. 2005. *The 9 Rights of Every Writer.* Portsmouth, NH: Heinemann.

Steig, William. 1996. *The Toy Brother.* New York: HarperCollins.

Walker, Alice. 2006. *There Is a Flower at the Tip of My Nose Smelling Me.* New York: HarperCollins.

Willems, Mo. 2004. *Knuffle Bunny.* Boston: Houghton Mifflin.

Figure 3.1 was inspired by the work of Beth Olshansky: www.picturingwriting.org

4 Trait by Trait—More Ideas for Teaching

Children want to write. They want to write the first day they attend school. This is no accident. Before they went to school they marked up walls, pavements, newspapers with crayons, chalk, pens or pencils . . . anything that makes a mark. The child's marks say, "I am."

—Donald Graves

Writing: Teachers and Children at Work (1983, p. 1)

Children have language, curiosity, and creative instincts. They have a voice that is often unique. But you have to believe in children's capabilities if you wish to entice the good ideas out of the crevices of their fertile minds.

—Ronald L. Cramer

Creative Power: The Nature and Nurture of Children's Writing (2001, p. 221)

TRAIT BASICS

There is no substitute for writing—for just doing it. So, we begin with an assumption that students, no matter how young, no matter how inexperienced, are writing in your classroom every day about a wide range of things. Having said that, within the context of all this writing, it is helpful for writers to have both strategies and language—language for thinking and speaking like writers.

Here is something I have learned about teaching: The closer you come to figuring things out, the smaller your lists get. So, here it is—my newly revised list of four (only four) general strategies for teaching traits at the primary level:

1. Ask *students* to be assessors, using the trait language you have taught them. Ask them to voice their opinions about which of two samples is stronger or more appealing.
2. Use literature to model what you want children to hear and see in good writing (and in weak writing, too).
3. Be a writer yourself. Model. Show students prewriting, drafting, revision, and editing in action (more on this in Chapter 6).
4. Use targeted lessons that help students strengthen specific skills (such as writing a lead or blending two sentences together).

In this chapter we will deal with the fourth method for teaching traits: *using targeted lessons.* As you go through this chapter, keep making the connections in your own mind, too: What am I *already doing* to teach this trait? If you are like most teachers, you will find numerous connections. Think of this chapter as helping you to recognize ways that you are *already* teaching traits.

In Chapter 5 we will look closely at publishing and the revision/editing process as it applies to primary writers. Chapter 6 deals exclusively with modeling—the importance of being a writer with your students. Chapter 7 is devoted to literature connections—books carefully chosen to help illustrate strong voice, good word choice, and so on. Chapter 7 includes additional lessons, too.

They Hear It Before They Do It

Here's another thing to keep in mind: For very young writers, traits are first learned aurally; that is to say, they *hear* ideas, voice, or fluency. These elements may or may not show up in their own writing, though, for some time to come. Never mind. "Listen to this lead" *is* a lesson in organization every bit as much as if you were asking your students to write leads themselves. You can learn a lot about writing without a pencil in your hand or a keyboard at your fingertips.

Teaching a Trait Is Not the Same as Assessing It

This is why it makes sense to teach each trait long, *long, long* before a student is ready to be assessed on that trait. If we wait for students to craft fifty-sentence essays (so that we can assess them) before teaching fluency, we are waiting too long. If we wait for students to stun us with quotable passages before teaching voice, we are waiting too long. We are gambling that they will "get it" while we wait. Why do that? Instead of hoping that students will stumble fortuitously upon whatever it is we are looking for, let's teach them to listen for it in the literature we share and to build a foundation on which skills relevant to that trait can grow.

TEACHING IDEAS
What You Are Teaching

✔ Main idea or message
✔ Clarity
✔ Detail (and interest)
✔ Noticing/observing

How to Get There

■ 1. Keep It Small

One of the greatest lessons to be learned about writing is keeping it small. This lesson has been taught to me by every truly good writing teacher I have ever encountered (meaning the ones who were writers and readers themselves) and by all my writer friends. Tommy Thomason, head of journalism at Texas Christian University, likes to keep his books for teachers under 100 pages. The hallmark of Tommy's books (other than wisdom and readability): They are all skinny. He always tells me, "If you have more to say, write another book. Teachers are busy people." I believe this. Barry Lane is also an advocate of "small writing"—by which he means focusing in. Barry says, "Don't write about how messy your brother is. Write about how you hate finding hair on the soap in the shower" (1999, pp. 52–54).

In coming up with good topics, you need to think about everyday events, the stuff of real life, what you are seeing and feeling right now—or something you noticed just ten minutes ago. Do not go epic. Do not do "world peace." Let someone else handle the big, brooding moral issues of our time. Cut a one-inch hole in a piece of paper, and peek through. On the other side you will find almost every topic you ever need to write about.

Here are some possible tiny topics (just to give students the idea—these are *not* assignments):

✔ Difficulty with a pet
✔ A pesky insect
✔ Falling down
✔ A troublesome brother, sister, or friend
✔ A time I wished I had stayed home
✔ Advice I would like to give a friend (or relative)
✔ A habit I wish I could break
✔ I thought it was lost for good
✔ I thought *I* was lost for good
✔ It's so boring, I can't stand it
✔ The worst weather ever
✔ A TV show not to waste your time on
✔ The advertisement that hooked me
✔ The toughest food to give up
✔ A chore I could do without

Model It.   Show students how to take a big idea down to size. Model this orally or on an overhead projector or chart paper. Start with a topic such as *animals*. Create a set of steps like those in Figure 4.1.

Write your topic on the bottom step: "Animals." Explain that you think this is a very *big* topic and that big topics lead to vague writing. Why? Because there is just too much to say. Whittle it down, making this overwhelming topic smaller and smaller as you go. On step 2, you might write "Wild Animals." Better, but still pretty big. On step 3, write "Wild Animals of Africa." Better, but still large. On step 4, write "Lions." Now we are getting somewhere. But isn't there something specific about lions you could write? How about hunting? Good. On step 5, write "How Lions Hunt."

Figure 4.1

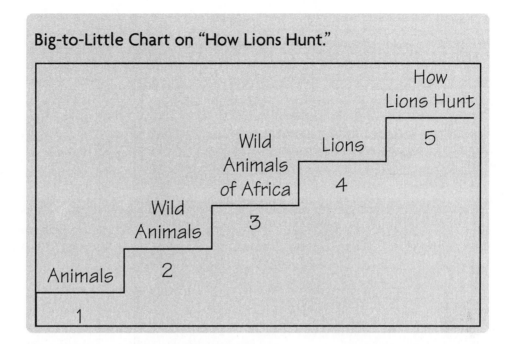

Big-to-Little Chart on "How Lions Hunt."

2. Hunt for Details

This activity builds on the concept of "ideas as observation" presented in Chapter 3. Begin by bringing in objects for students to examine closely, and asking them to work in pairs, just talking at first, then recording what they see. They can record with words or pictures—either way, they will need to look closely. Tell them that they are looking for *details*. Good things for examination include driftwood, shells, rocks, pinecones, moss or other vegetation, flowers, fruit, fabric, their own hands, insects and spiders, fish, or small animals.

If they have practiced observing before, it is time to push a little to make details more explicit. For example, if your students say a rock is "brown," ask what kind of brown—chocolate brown, hen's-egg brown, mud brown, baked-potato brown? Ask them to think in analogies and metaphors: *The cone was as prickly as a porcupine. The corn silk looked like hair. The rock was a small mountain.*

Once their recording is done, ask them to use their observations in a paragraph or poem (see Figures 4.2a and 4.2b).

Jewelers' Loupes. Have your students ever looked through a jeweler's loupe? If not, they are in for a treat! You can obtain loupes (and books of ideas, too) from many stores that carry educational or science-study materials. Details loom large through the loupes and invite students to make connections they could never make previously. In a book called *The Private Eye: Looking/Thinking by Analogy,* even very young students make telling visual discoveries examining their own hands: "craters of a meteor, a garden of cracks, rivers of lightning, elephant skin, threads woven together" (Ruef, 2000, pp. 86–87).

3. Study Pictures

Ask students to study a photograph, a painting, a drawing from a book, a sketch—anything. Postcards work particularly well. Start with a list of details, and turn it into a poem. Create a story. What's happening in the picture? Write

Figure 4.2a Using Detail. Erin (2)

The smooth snow is like a soft feathery pillow. The chirping birds are singing in the trees. The bumpy tree trunk is not so soft. The leaves are slowly swaying against the wind. The ocean colored sky is filled with shades of light and dark blue. The daisy yellow sun is shining brightly in the afternoon sky. The chirping birds are singing loudly. The spring snow makes me happy.

Figure 4.2b "What I See Through My Eyes."

The sun
glistening on a group of trees
A storm has just passed by
Millions of pinecones
laying on the ground
silent as can be.
Snow capped mountains
in the distance
Mount Rainier sitting alone
glittering in the sun
Birds chirping
As they look for their lunch.

By Michael (3)

about it, or put yourself into it—either way. If your students are not fluent writers yet, you can do the writing yourself, letting them supply the ideas. You will need to ask questions: "Who is the person in the picture? What just happened? What is he or she thinking? What's about to happen? Should this be a scary or funny story? How do you know? Are we telling the reader enough? Too much?"

■ 4. Teach Students the Art of Questioning

The first time you do this, you will need to supply the main idea and let students ask the questions. You can do this with a story—perhaps based on something that happened to you—or with an essay, description, or how-to piece. I have done this frequently with stories, most recently one based on a nasty little poodle named Pearl and her encounter with a coyote. I begin with a simple statement: "Pearl did not know she was in danger, but the coyote did." Then I invite students to ask me questions: "What do you want to know?" Here are the most frequently asked questions:

✔ Who is Pearl?
✔ Why is she in danger?
✔ Does the coyote attack Pearl?
✔ Were you in danger too?
✔ Did Pearl get hurt?
✔ Did she die?
✔ What happened to the coyote?
✔ Did you rescue Pearl?

✔ What was the coyote thinking?
✔ What were you thinking?
✔ Were you scared?

I do three things next:

1. I keep a list of the questions on an overhead transparency so that I can share them again with students later.
2. I explain to students that it is not my job as a writer to answer *every* question—I will pick the ones I find most interesting.
3. I write a draft based on the questions plus my own memory of the event and share it with students.

Students can also work with partners to come up with their own topics, generate questions, and use the best questions to begin a draft.

5. Use Oral Skills

For many writers, talking is an excellent form of prewriting. They need to talk over an idea *before* writing. Like sketching, talking helps writers think through connections, remember details, and put things into place.

Writers with big imaginations but limited keyboarding/pencil-paper experience can occasionally "write" an essay or story on tape. Playing it back helps young thinkers notice the details they have included or omitted, especially if you coach them to listen for this specifically. More advanced writers can write first, then read aloud to record, and play back to see if they have missed anything or have said all they want to say.

6. Say It—Then, Write It

Talk through a story first, and then write a sketchy version of the same story and read it aloud to your students. Once when I was stranded overnight because of a canceled flight, the airline bused us to a hotel where almost nothing worked. Only one light came on—and it was not in the bathroom. In the morning, tired as I was

> *When we sent the children off to share questions with a partner and later to write, ideas flowed. Some began by simply writing the questions. Others were able to take ideas inspired by the questions and write longer pieces. Others drew pictures related to their questions. No one had to be told what to write.*
>
> **—Ellin Keene and Susan Zimmerman**
> *Mosaic of Thought* (1997, p. 105)

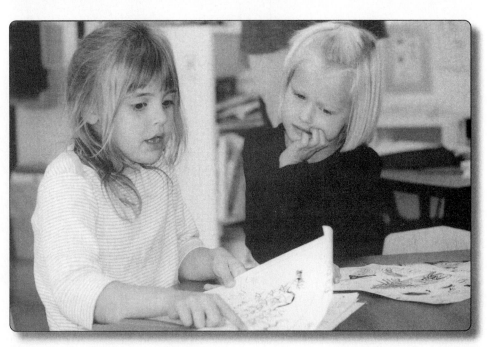

and trying to get myself together in a dark bathroom, I shampooed my hair with hand lotion, not shampoo (I couldn't read the tiny label in the dark). This treatment gave me a halo of greasy spikes that made me look as if I'd had a bad day on the "Star Trek" set. Students generally love hearing this story, but suppose I wrote it up this way: "One day I had a bad experience! It all started when we missed our flight. We had to stay in a hotel. The hotel we stayed at was not that good. A lot of things didn't work. Thank goodness, we left after only one night."

Notice any details missing? You can bet students will, too. It's the contrast that helps them understand the value of details. Students also enjoy illustrating a story like this for you—as you can see from Figure 4.3.

■ 7. Draw!

Your students can certainly draw on their own, of course, but now and then you can join in the fun, too. Figure 4.4 shows how simple it can be to use a series of geometric shapes to sketch an animal such as a fox. This idea comes from *Draw Write Now*, book seven, by Marie Hablitzel and Kim Stitzer (2000). The idea is to guide students through the sketching process as you discuss the subject of the drawing—in this case, the fox. Students can help you fill in background details by suggesting where foxes live, what they eat, and so on. They can also suggest details—for example, "Add some toenails"—that go beyond this simple geometric sketch. When you complete the sketch (remember, your students are drawing right along with you), you and they can do some research on foxes, making a list of details. Then use what you find to create stories or all-about papers (a simple kind of research paper). From this activity, students learn to use detail in both art and writing, learn to link text to illustrations, and also learn a bit about research.

Figure 4.3

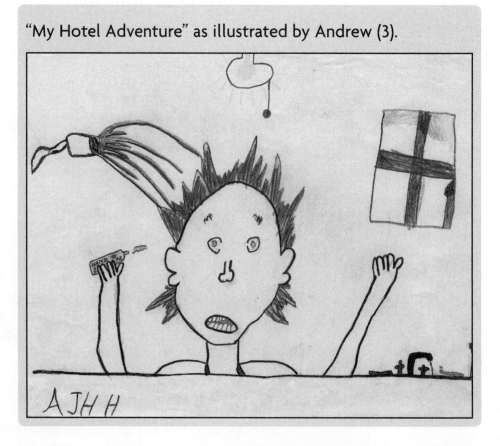

"My Hotel Adventure" as illustrated by Andrew (3).

Figure 4.4

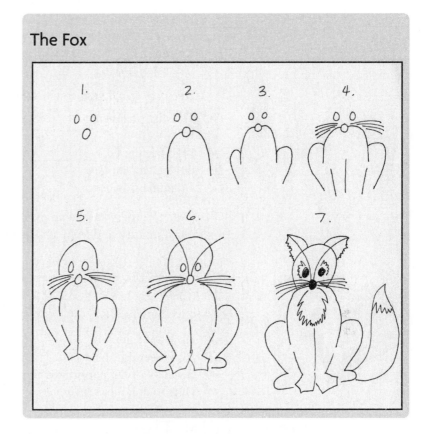

The Fox

■ 8. Use "Snapshots"

This idea comes from author/teacher Barry Lane, who explains it in great detail in his wonderful book *Reviser's Toolbox* (2000, Chap. 3, 74ff). It is a variation on an old theme: *Show, don't tell.* Unfortunately, students do not always understand what we mean by this. As teacher Laura Harper explains (Lane, 2000, p. 217), "I wish I had a nickel for every time I scrawled 'Describe' or 'Explain' or 'Give me more detail' next to an imprecise sentence. . . . Sentences such as 'I walked into my bedroom' actually became worse . . . turning into 'I walked into my big, blue, full, messy bedroom.' "

I like the snapshot idea because students can immediately picture what we mean: *I want to see it, like a photo in an album.* Instead of piling on adjectives, they create pictures. Delia, a second grader, created this snapshot of her family at dinner (Lane, 2000, p. 75):

> My supper is always the same.
> My sister won't eat.
> My other sister whines but I just listen to the crickets.

This is a simple snapshot, but it is extremely vivid. If this were actually in a photo album, it is the one you would point to and say, "That's so typical! That's *just* how Delia's family looks at dinner!" That's the purpose. Teach this with an example first; then have your students try it.

> *Vague sentence:* "I walked into my room."
> *Snapshot:* "I stomped into my room. I threw myself on the bed and punched my pillow hard. I had to blink my eyes to keep from crying." (*Do you see it?*)

Vague sentence: "It was hot."
Snapshot: "Our shirts stuck to us like plastic wrap. We tried cooling down with ice cream, but it turned to mush before we could get our tongues on it." *(Do you feel it?)*

Here are some vague sentences for your students to turn into snapshots:

✔ The dog was mean.
✔ He was tired.
✔ I felt frightened.
✔ She had a nice face.
✔ Grandma was brave.

Tip: Very young writers can do snapshots with pictures, dictation, or a combination of picture and text. It's the concept that counts.

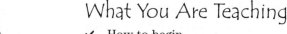

TEACHING ORGANIZATION
What You Are Teaching

✔ How to begin
✔ How to end
✔ Sense of order, patterning, sequencing
✔ How to link ideas together

How to Get There
◼ 1. Choose Strong Leads

> *What is the most boring way you could begin a research report . . . ? We all know. "In this report I will tell you about . . . ."*
>
> **—Barry Lane**
> *Reviser's Toolbox* (1999, p. 30)

In any kind of writing, leads are critical. They are equally important in visual media. Ask students how long it takes them before they know whether they like a TV program or a film. Most of us form an impression within moments, although some of us hang in there longer than others, hoping a dull show will improve. Like filmmakers, good writers know they have to hook readers quickly or lose them. However, young students may not even be aware of the time and effort writers have put into leads; it probably has never occurred to them to think about it. You can heighten their awareness first by comparing and contrasting different possible leads—then by simply asking, "Which one do you like better?" That's it; that *is* the lesson.

Of course, you need contrast to make this lesson work:

Lead 1: "This will be a story about picnics on our apartment roof. Ready? Here goes."
Lead 2: "I will always remember when the stars fell down around me and lifted me above the George Washington Bridge."

Which one do you like better? If you are like most readers, you picked the very magical lead 2, the actual opening to Faith Ringgold's classic *Tar Beach* (1991). Try another:

Lead 1: "The night Max wore his wolf suit and made mischief of one kind and another, his mother called him "WILD THING!" and Max said "I'LL EAT YOU UP!" so he was sent to bed without eating anything."
Lead 2: "In this story, I will tell you about Max, a boy who acts wild sometimes."

Another easy choice. Lead 1, of course, is from Maurice Sendak's 1963 book *Where the Wild Things Are*.

As you explore the leads from books you love to read to your students, you will find that most are strong. Here is one of my favorites from Fred Marcellino's *I, Crocodile* (1999): "Ah, what a contented crocodile I used to be. Wallowing around in slimy green water. . . . Snoozing on mudbanks in the hot sun. . . . Scaring the life out of anything that walked by." Imagine the difference if Marcellino had written, "Hi. I'm Fred, and I like crocodiles. Do you? In my book, I'll tell you everything I know about crocodiles. . . ."

■ 2. Use the Visual

As Lucy Dahl recounts in *James and the Giant Peach: The Book and Movie Scrapbook* (1996), "Every movie begins with a script. . . ." Writers guide the way a film begins, how the characters move and when and what they say, how scenes are set up, and so much more. You and your students may enjoy exploring Lucy's tale of how a favorite story became a film. In addition, though, encourage your students to look at visual media through the eyes of a writer and to ask questions such as these: Why does a film begin (or end) this way? If I were the scriptwriter, would I begin (or end) differently?

As a way of encouraging students to think visually, choose a favorite book, and ask your students to imagine that it is going to be made into a movie. Ask them to work in pairs to come up with an opening scene. How and where should the movie begin? They can sketch the opening scene, and even come up with music to set the mood.

■ 3. Make Predictions

Begin with a lead like this one from William Steig's book *Brave Irene* (1986):

> Mrs. Bobbin, the dressmaker, was tired and had a bad headache, but she still managed to sew the last stitches in the gown she was making.
>
> "It's the most beautiful dress in the whole world!" said her daughter, Irene. "The duchess will love it."
>
> "It is nice," her mother admitted. "But dumpling, it's for tonight's ball, and I don't have the strength to bring it. I feel sick."

Make a list of predictions, based on this brief opening. Encourage your students to guess what *might* happen next. It's like going on a journey, imagining what will be around the next bend.

■ 4. Put Things in Order

Take any piece of writing and divide it into five or more short sentences, writing each on a separate strip of paper. Stories work well for this activity, but you can also use directions, recipes (see Figure 4.5), expository writing, advertisements, letters, newspaper articles, or pretty much anything. Try to choose a piece in which sequence makes a difference. For example, order matters greatly in a recipe; it often matters in a poem— but not always.

Figure 4.5

Out-of-Order Recipe

1. Eat and enjoy!
2. Boil some water.
3. Cook till tender.
4. Drain the macaroni.
5. Pour in 1 cup of macaroni.
6. Add salt and pepper.

Give each strip to one student, and give the students time to meet in a group, sort themselves out (so that the sequence makes sense), and prepare to present the writing to the class. As they line up in order, you (or one of the other students) should read the whole piece aloud. When you have finished, ask the rest of the class (those who are not part of the sequence group) to comment on the order. Does it make sense? Is anything out of place?

■ 5. Use Idea Webs to Plan

Graphic organizers of all kinds are helpful to older or more experienced students in organizing information. You can model this by choosing any subject about which you have some knowledge and talking through a few elements that you might include in a report. Do not make your web too complex, or it may look intimidating.

Talk through the web (see Figure 4.6) as you sketch it: "My report will be about worms, so I'll put that right in the middle. Now I'm going to add some details I know about worms. For one thing, they were the first creatures on earth; they have been here for about half a billion years. They have no legs . . . and no bones either. Worms aren't very good fighters, so they need to hide. They live in the soil or under rocks. They hide there because worms are food for many creatures, including frogs, birds, and fish. People can eat some kinds of worms—they're usually not poisonous—but I don't think I'd want to! I also learned that earthworms can be huge! In Australia, they grow up to 12 feet long! Just think—as many as 90 thousand worms have been found in one apple!"

Put your web on chart paper, and post it where students can see it easily. Take this lesson to the next step and write a paragraph on worms (or whatever your topic may be) using the parts of your web to organize information. Read the paper aloud as your students study the web.

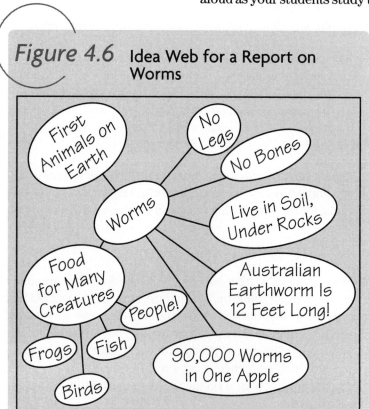

Figure 4.6 **Idea Web for a Report on Worms**

Note: Author/teacher Marcia Freeman reminds us that many students are not ready for something as advanced as webbing. "Primary writers are not ready for abstract graphic planners such as webs, clustering, mapping, timelines. Teach them to talk, draw, make lists, and make pictures while they gather thoughts before writing" (1998, p. 139). I agree with this core philosophy completely, and if you do find that webbing is beyond your students, by all means forget it. In my experience, though, some students *do* like it—and find it helpful. Perhaps it is just the right combination of picture making and writing for them.

Ellie, a first grader, for example, creates a fairly complex web to organize her thoughts for a paper on things she is thankful for (Figure 4.7a). In Ellie's case, the web becomes just an alternative to talking or listing—but this is not to say that it will work with all children. You must use your judgment. Figure 4.7b shows Ellie's finished paper, which follows the web very closely.

Figure 4.7a

"Things I'm Thankful For" Ellie (1)

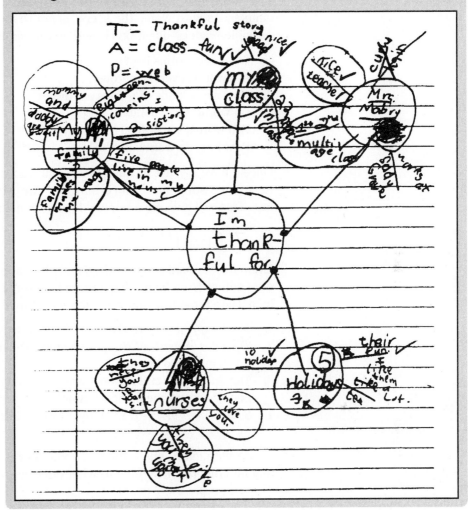

Figure 4.7b

I am thankful for my family. My family makes me laugh a lot. Five people live in my house. I have two sisters and 21 cousins. I love my mommy and Daddy.

I am thankful for nurses. They love you. They take care of you. And they give you check ups.

I am thankful for Mrs. M. She is nice. She teaches multi-age 1st and 2nd at Shady Grove.

I am thankful for my class. My class is nice and very fun too. There are older and younger people in my class.

I am thankful.

By Ellie (1)

■ 6. Use Lists

Like webs, lists help to organize information, and for many students, lists are simpler. As with webs, the secret is not to make them too big. Here's a list of possible readers' questions based on the same topic: worms.

1. Where do worms live?
2. Are worms ever dangerous?
3. How many kinds of worms are there?
4. Do worms have bones?
5. Can worms see or hear?
6. How long do worms live?

Once I have my list of questions, I can reorder them as I please and put the most interesting question (I think it's "Are worms dangerous?") either first or last. This will give me a punchy lead or conclusion.

■ 7. End It!

Even professional writers struggle with wrapping it all up, so expecting knock-out endings from beginning writers is asking a lot. Still, some suggestions may help. Here are a few that are fairly easy for younger writers to understand:

1. *What happened last?* Example: "Finally, we got home safely."
2. *The most important thing.* Example: "The most important thing when you ride a bike is to be safe."
3. *The thing I remember best.* Example: "The thing I will never forget is how far I could see out the plane window."
4. *Something I learned.* Example: "Fishing is harder and more fun than I thought."

As with leads, share the best examples from the literature you read aloud to your students. Listening to what other writers have done is very helpful.

TEACHING VOICE

What You Are Teaching

✔ Putting energy into writing
✔ Recognizing voice
✔ Selecting personally important topics
✔ Connecting to an audience

How to Get There

■ 1. Write Notes and Letters

Notes and letters work especially well for developing voice because voice is, in part, a writer-to-reader bridge, a way of connecting to an audience. With a letter, the audience is built in. In "How to Write a Letter," Garrison Keillor (1989, pp. 138–139) suggests this frame of mind: ". . . let your friend come to mind until you can almost see her or him in the room with you. Remember the last time you saw each other and how your friend looked and . . . when your friend becomes real to you, start to write." In short, picture your audience. Picture the person's face, the expression as he or she opens the letter. Ask your students to do this.

Students can write to each other, to you, to their parents ("Dear Mom—You are invited to an after-school conference . . ."), to sports figures, celebrities, favorite authors, or people in your community. If they can bring in a photograph to go with the letter (see Figure 4.8), so much the better.

Letters, even when written for a business purpose, are a way of putting ourselves on the page. Donald Murray (1990, p. 34) tells us, "Even in the corporate world, the writer is egocentric, obsessed with self. This is what each writer, no matter the mode or form of writing, has to offer: the individual view and the individual gift." Voice *is* a gift.

■ 2. Help Students Discover Personally Important Topics

It is important for students to find writing topics that they care about deeply, even passionately. If this does not happen, voice remains luke warm. If we want writing that excites us, we need excited writers to produce it. It is hard to come up with a topic that excites someone else; this is why assigning writing is such a thankless task. Restrictive, assigned topics sound something like this: "Think

Figure 4.8

"Dear Ann, I'd love to go riding with you this weekend. Remember how Smokey bucked you off two weeks ago? Ha, ha. What good times we had! Love, Vicki."

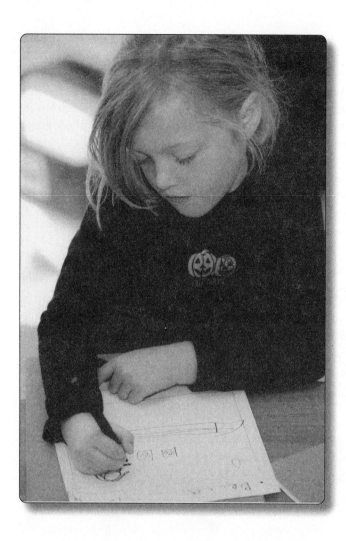

of a birthday gift you really liked. Write a story about receiving that gift. Be sure to tell what happened and how you felt."

There is nowhere to go with a topic like this. It's a form to be filled out. Suggestions, by contrast, often appear as pictures, single words, phrases, incomplete sentences, or quotations—anything that opens mental doors with just a hint or suggestion, but nothing more. Offer your students a "borrowing list" (and post it) *just* for those times when they find themselves staring at a blank sheet of paper and nothing—absolutely *nothing*—comes to mind.

✔ The hardest thing
✔ I can't forget it
✔ A good friend
✔ It made me angry
✔ Oops!
✔ I wish I never had to hear it again
✔ It almost worked
✔ I'm happy that . . .
✔ I'm supposed to like it, but I don't
✔ The trouble with _____
✔ Warning: Don't eat _____
✔ My advice
✔ Taking turns
✔ I'd love to do it again
✔ A book you should not miss
✔ Something worth saving
✔ You're old when . . .

Don't abuse your borrowing list—it's a resource for ideas when you're stuck, never a replacement for students' own topics.

What if you have a student who only wants to write about one thing? Don't despair. Some students have a few favorite topics on which they like to write repeatedly. There is nothing wrong with this. Adult writers do the same. Review several books by any favorite author, and you're likely to encounter recurring themes, settings, and even characters. As Regie Routman reminds us, "Students have to care about their writing to write well, and they care about things in which they are interested. One of the mistakes we make is to expect writers to come up with new topics all the time—every day, in some classrooms" (2000, p. 213).

> *The first consideration in writing or teaching writing is choice of topic. Real writers choose their own topic; therefore, children should be allowed to do the same. I chose the topic for this chapter. When I suggested it to the editor she didn't say, "No, you can't write about that. Write about this."*
>
> **—Mem Fox**
> *Radical Reflections* (1993, p. 36)

3. Show Students How to Put "Personal Self" into Their Writing

When you come up with a topic that is personally important to you, model the thinking you use to put yourself, body and soul, into the time and place where you need to be to write. Close your eyes, put yourself in the moment, take it in, get every sensory detail you can, and talk it through: "I am on a rocky cliff close to the beach. The surf is pounding

The worst paper we see in college writing is the paper in which "nobody's home." We do this to students. We do it to them in school by having them write about things they know nothing about. Worse, we have them write about things they don't care anything about. The writing is for only one person, the teacher. It's written "To Whom It May Concern."

—Donald Graves and Virginia Stuart
Write from the Start: Tapping Your Child's Natural Writing Ability (1985, p. 38)

the rocks so hard we have to scream, but we're laughing, too. I'm walking with my parents, and my mother has the wrong kind of shoes for climbing rocks, little white sandals with pink roses on the top. Why did she wear those? I think to myself. That was so stupid. Then, she slips, and before any of us can catch her, she has scraped her shin and is bleeding. She's crying, and I try to comfort her, hugging her, but she does not want to be hugged because she is afraid of falling again. All I want to do is put my arms around her, but I'm too short to hold her up. Suddenly, I am furious with the ocean for being so loud. My mother cannot hear my soothing voice. I want to help, but I can't, so I begin to cry. . . ."

Then I ask students, "What from this story do I absolutely *have* to put in my writing to make sure readers feel everything I feel?" And most often, they will say—

✔ The "stupid" shoes
✔ Your mother crying
✔ You try to hug your mother and she won't let you
✔ You feel mad at the ocean

I ached on that day at the beach—and I want the reader to feel that ache. In helping *me* identify the details and feelings and impressions that bring the moment back, students rehearse ways of putting *their own* heartfelt memories onto the page.

■ 4. Nurture Voice in an Atmosphere of Sharing

Some elements of voice can be taught directly; some can be *nurtured*. Sometimes teachers say, "If voice is about personality, how can you teach it?" Well, of course, it isn't quite that literal: "Today's lesson, kids—personality. When you finish this lesson, people will seek you out. Now let's begin with that smile. . . ." On the other hand, personality can most certainly be nurtured, rewarded, and fostered. The same is true of voice. You reinforce it by providing an atmosphere in which it feels safe to share and to experiment. You also reinforce voice when you value it and *show* that you value it by reading voice-filled pieces (whether by professionals or by your students) aloud.

Readers don't need commentary. They don't need detached description. They don't need big words. They don't need imitation Alice Walker. They need you, with your language, your rhythms, your story. They need your heart.

—Nancy Slonim Aronie
(1998, p. 32)

Writers need audience response. We should teach students to respond respectfully to one another, but we have to be careful. Honesty is also important. A kind of forced politeness comes through in comments such as "I really liked your paper" or "That was so good." When students are not sure what to say, here are some *kinds* of comments that can be helpful to a writer:

✔ Name a favorite word or phrase.
✔ Describe something you pictured in your mind as you were listening.
✔ Name something—a person, place, or experience—the paper reminded you of.
✔ Do you have an interesting question for the writer? What?
✔ Are you curious about what will happen next? Say so.
✔ Did anything surprise you? What?

✔ Did the voice in the paper sound like the writer's speaking voice? If so, let the writer know.

Sharing can be scary for some students (even though it is the high point of the day for others). You can create an atmosphere in which sharing feels safe by, first, sharing your own writing (often) and, second, coaching students on appropriate responses through modeling and examples. Sharing should never feel formulaic, but I think it is helpful to have some ground rules:

✔ Listen with your whole body—eyes, ears, posture.
✔ Think about what the writer is trying to tell you and show you.
✔ Focus on your feelings and thoughts as you listen.
✔ Be honest.
✔ Be kind.

It is helpful if your personal response comes last; it is often the one that will make the greatest impression. Some teachers encourage applause; some dislike it. I think applause is fine as long as it's not a measure of how well students liked the piece of writing—that creates tension and bad feelings. What we should applaud, really, is the writer's courage and willingness to share. This in itself is an achievement—and with this approach, everyone's applause meter is the same.

■ 5. Make Room for Alternatives

> *Students are perfectly capable of writing with voice if we show them how. The same is true for using conversation, meaningful detail, and verbs—even for young writers.*
>
> **—Regie Routman**
> *Conversations* (2000, p. 210)

Same old stories? Same old essays? How about a different form of writing? Instead of a book report, ask students to do a book review, giving the book one to five stars and stating why someone should or should not read it. What if a favorite character from a book escaped? Create a wanted poster. How about an advertisement—say, for chocolate from Willie Wonka's chocolate factory or for the services of Dr. DeSoto, the mouse dentist created by William Steig (1982). Résumés are a good way to get at character and to develop voice as well. Here is a start for a résumé for the witch in *Hansel and Gretel:*

Name: Corinne Johnson (nickname: Corie)

Address: The woods

Phone: No phone—people just stop by

Hobbies: Working with children, baking, singing, raising pet scorpions

Experience: Professional baker for 10 years, children's camp director for 20 years, home decorator for 15 years

Professional goal: To star in a movie about my life

Your students also can write poems, songs, journal entries, recipes, weather reports, or news articles:

Singer and songwriter Jonathan Wolf (who goes by the stage name of Big Bad) was arrested today for assaulting three local business people, owners of the Three Pigs Construction Company. Wolf admitted to being present when two buildings recently completed by Three Pigs Construction suddenly collapsed. However, he denied any responsibility. "I was just happening by," he said. "It was really quite lucky I was not hurt." The pigs, however, tell a different version of the story. "He deliberately flattened the buildings," said Herbert, oldest of the three pig brothers. Wolf admits that his years of singing have given him amazing lungs, but scoffs at the idea he could blow down a house. He called the pigs' charges "ridiculous." A hearing is set for next Tuesday following the grand opening of the Three Pigs Vegetarian Restaurant, built entirely of brick.

■ 6. Write in Character

Take idea 5 a step further and ask your students to write in character as someone else. Stepping into the shoes of another person—even for a short while—helps you appreciate that person's perspective, and perspective influences voice tremendously. My friend and colleague Lois Burdett teaches Shakespeare to her second and third graders in Hamlet School in Stratford, outside Ontario, Canada. Her students hear the stories of William Shakespeare and act them out as well. The sight of such young actors in beards, wigs, capes, caps, and boots is stunning and inspiring—but most striking of all is their ability to get inside the hearts and minds of the characters and even Shakespeare himself. "Imagine," Lois tells her students, "that you are on your way to becoming the most famous playwright the world has ever known—and your beloved Globe Theatre burns to the ground. How do you feel?" The children are touched by Shakespeare's plight and express their feelings in letters that might have been written by Shakespeare to his wife Anne. In the introduction to one letter (Burdett, 1995a, p. 56), seven-year-old Marijke writes, "I hve some dredful noos for you Anne. Our globe Theatre is histery! Gone capush!" Marijke's voice comes through loud and clear in her note. She *is* the playwright who has lost his theater. (For more examples, see Lois Burdett's books, listed under "Sources Cited" at the end of this chapter.)

■ 7. Act It Out

Get students on their feet whenever possible. The combination of speaking (or oral reading) and body language does wonders for developing voice! Choral reading and a readers' theater (in which students read parts aloud from a text) are excellent. The come-alive approach to poetry noted in Chapter 3 also works well. For truly boundless ideas on using drama in the classroom, I recommend Carol Glynn's imaginative book, *Learning on Their Feet* (2001). Carol describes games for dramatizing concepts (such as punctuation, immigration, or the seasons) and for using dialogue or monologue to express ideas of all kinds.

One of my favorites in her bag of many tricks is the use of statues that come to life. Selected students become statues of persons in the neighborhood, for example, a bakery clerk, postal clerk, police officer, teacher, firefighter, person waiting for a bus, person washing windows, person gardening, person walking a dog, and so on (Glynn, 2001, p. 190). Students can work with you in creating a setting; for example, "It was early Monday morning in the town of Summerville. The residents were just coming to life." Students who are not playing parts for this round work with you to create a story of the events of the day; for example, "Mr. Greely was walking his dog Grumbles. Grumbles was tugging on the leash, making it difficult for Mr. Greely to stay on the path!" Mr. Greely acts out his part for a short time; then it's on to the next character. Breathing life into the "statues" is an excellent warm-up for breathing life into writing. You will find your students using more verbs in their writing when they have actually acted scenes out, or when they create scenes for others to act out.

◼ 8. Keep It Snappy

Get a volunteer student to act out the concept/character of "bored" in front of the class. How does "bored" look? Tired eyes, perhaps poor posture (kind of a slump), listless expression, limp arms, and so on. Now ask your students to transform "bored" into "excited"—by telling the actor what to do. Movement is encouraged! Ask them to remember this difference when they write. Which person is likely to compose the piece that will keep you awake—"bored" or "excited"? Tell them, "I want to see an 'excited' face in my mind when I read your writing."

Show them that even factual writing can be exciting. Here are six facts about sharks, followed by two reports. Which was written by a "bored" writer? Which was written by an "excited" writer? Can your students tell?

Facts

1. Sharks have been on earth for millions of years.
2. Sharks get new teeth throughout their lives—up to 50,000 of them.
3. Some sharks have powerful tails and use them to kill prey.
4. A shark's skin is very rough.
5. Only a few sharks are truly dangerous.
6. Sharks sometimes mistake a swimmer for a seal.

Sample 1
"Bored" or "Excited"?

Sharks have been on earth a long time. They are very interesting. If they lose their teeth, they get new ones. Sharks have strong tails. They have rough skin. Some sharks are dangerous. Some aren't.

Sample 2
"Bored" or "Excited"?

Sharks are among the oldest creatures on earth. They were around even before the dinosaurs. Though people are generally afraid of sharks, only a few are dangerous. When sharks do kill a person, it's usually an accident. To a shark, a person swimming sometimes looks like a seal—and that means lunch! Unlike people, sharks get new teeth all through their lives, so if they lose one, it's no big deal. A shark can get up to 50,000 new teeth in its life. A shark's skin is as rough as sandpaper, and if you touch it, it could actually scratch you.

◼ 9. Encourage Students to Say What They Mean

Authentic writing on real topics is, in the end, the best (if not the only) path to voice. A teacher once said to me, "I love the papers about rainbows and blue skies. There is too much violence in the world. We need more students who write about happy things." I disagree. We need more happy students, this is true. But rainbows and blue skies, appealing as they are, are not reality for many students. If we cringe at their reality and force them into some phony fantasy world where all is well, we discourage voice instead of nurturing it. Donald Graves tells us that "People who write with their own voices are people who are not afraid to say what they mean" (Graves and Stuart, 1985, p. 38). Although I do not for a second advocate encouraging gratuitous violence in writing (e.g., alien planets warring with one another), it is simply a fact of life that

> *Voice is integrally connected to word choice. A strong voice and apt wording keep readers reading for little sparks of surprise and humor.*
>
> **—Donald Graves and Virginia Stuart**
> *Write from the Start* (1985, p. 38)

some students feel anger or depression and have a need to write about it. Delving into private lives is stepping over the line certainly, but at the same time, we should be open to honesty and authenticity, even when it does not come packaged in rainbows.

TEACHING WORD CHOICE

What You Are Teaching

✔ Being choosy about words
✔ Identifying favorite words
✔ Using strong verbs
✔ Knowing a verb from a noun—or adjective

How to Get There

◼ 1. Act Out Words (Pick One Out of the Basket)

Everyone is tired of the old vocabulary lists. There must be an easier, more interesting way. Here's one. Choose verbs and adjectives that your students are likely to really need and use (perhaps some come from books you are currently reading or discussions your class is having). Print each in big letters on a three-by five-inch card, and put the cards into a bag or basket. Pass the bag or basket around, and ask each student to draw one card. The student should come to class the next day ready to act out his or her word. Drama imprints meaning on the mind in a way that memorization alone cannot even touch.

◼ 2. Make Posters

A variation on idea 1 calls for students to make posters. Each poster should include the word itself, a definition, and a relevant drawing or painting. The word could also be used in a sentence. Display posters in your classroom or on hallway walls for everyone to see.

◼ 3. Play "Quick Five"

This game can work in numerous ways, depending on the ages of your students and their readiness. The basic game is always the same. Students form a circle and take turns tossing a ball, randomly, to anyone of their choice. The person tossing the ball gets to decide what the persons receiving must come up with. The game continues for five tosses; then, the fifth person (after contributing) can change the game by calling for something new. Possibilities include words beginning with *w* (or any letter), any action word (verb), any naming word (noun), any describing word (adjective), or the next word in a sentence (the person tossing the ball must say *all* the words so far). The game can be more focused, such as any word that rhymes with *ball*, any word that describes feelings, any word that names an animal, any word you could use instead of *nice*, or any word you are tired of! Use your imagination to vary the game each time you play.

◾ 4. Do a Sentence as a Play

Although we do not want *parts of speech* to become the whole focus for word choice, it is helpful if students know some basics, such as nouns, verbs, adjectives, and adverbs. If they do not know these basic parts of speech, it will be difficult to share important advice of this sort: "Use specific *nouns*. Use lively *verbs*." Here's a painless way to teach parts of speech—and it's one that students will remember. First, create a short sentence that has at least one noun, verb, adjective, and adverb. It can end with a period or question mark. Write each word or punctuation mark on a separate strip of paper or large card (see Figure 4.9). Be sure the print is big enough for the whole class to read. Here is a sample sentence:

Hungry dogs ran rapidly.

Students can hold the cards, but this game works better if they can hang them, by string, around their necks so that their hands and arms are free. Invite students to play the various roles—one student per word or punctuation mark. The actor playing *hungry* tells the *dogs* (you can have two students play this part because it's plural) how to look or act. Why? Because adjectives "boss nouns around," if you will. They tell them how to look, sound, smell, and so on. Similarly, *rapidly* bosses *ran* around (because adverbs control verbs). When it's his or her turn, *rapidly* should keep telling *ran* what to do: for example, "Faster—you need to move faster!" What does the "period" do? When everyone has successfully acted out his or her role, the "period" can decide it is time to "stop."

Figure 4.9

Five sentence cards—five parts to play.

◾ 5. Create Advertisements

People who write ads know it is often language that persuades us to buy things. Spend some time collecting ads you think have word power, and talk with your students about persuasive wording. Which products would they buy? Which words "speak" to them? Make a list and keep it in sight so that your students can use words they like. Then create ads of your own. You can use common items your children already have—for example, backpacks, pens, books, or clothing—or you can branch out, working in some art. As an alternative, write descriptions for items on a menu.

■ 6. Create Some Small Writing (Greeting Cards, Bumper Stickers, Tee Shirts)

Young students love writing books—of course! Yet some of the strongest writing is little: greeting cards, Post-It notes, bumper stickers, and so on. Why? Because the writer has only a few words with which to get the message across—not a word can be wasted. As with any writing, it helps to have a sense of purpose, so you might suggest ideas like these:

✔ A poster advertising our school play
✔ Post-It note reminders for people who keep forgetting things!
✔ A greeting card for someone who needs cheering up
✔ A bumper sticker for drivers who tailgate
✔ A bumper sticker for a driver who loves his or her car
✔ A thank-you card for someone who took care of your pet or your plants

■ 7. Revise "Weak Verb" Pieces

This lesson will emphasize the *choice* part of word choice and encourage students to be on the lookout for strong verbs at the same time. Start with a passage from a book you like—one with strong verbs. Here's a short passage from Chris Van Allsburg's *Two Bad Ants* (1988, pp. 4–5, underlining added):

> The news <u>traveled</u> swiftly through the tunnels of the ant world. A scout had <u>returned</u> with a remarkable discovery—a beautiful sparkling crystal. When the scout <u>presented</u> the crystal to the ant queen she took a small bite, then quickly ate the entire thing. She <u>deemed</u> it the most delicious food she had ever tasted.

Notice the strong verbs in this passage: *traveled, returned, presented, deemed.* You could rewrite this passage for your students (prior to showing them the original), replacing these strong verbs with weaker substitutes, for example, *went* (for *traveled*), *came back* (for *returned*), *gave* (for *presented*), and *called* (for *deemed*). Try reading the passage aloud now with these substitutions. Not nearly as satisfying, is it? Ask students to brainstorm some possible replacements for the weaker verbs you have come up with; for example, "What could we say instead of *went*?" See how many possibilities they come up with; then share Allsburg's original—just for comparison. The idea is not to match the author, but to consider how even tiny changes in word choice affect meaning. Compare these options: *The news went swiftly . . . The news traveled swiftly . . . The news journeyed swiftly . . . The news sped . . . The news shot . . . The news rippled . . . The news made its way . . . The news inched along. . . .* Word choice is not about the "right" answer; it's about the word that conveys the image or mood or impression the writer is seeking.

■ 8. Keep Personal Dictionaries

As students learn new words, from reading, from conversation, or from direct instruction, encourage them to keep personal dictionaries in their notebooks. These "dictionaries" do not need to be totally alphabetized, but it is helpful to keep all the *b* words together, all the *n* words together, and so on.

These dictionaries may be small at first, but they will grow! Encourage students to share words with each other, too, and to borrow. See Figure 4.10 for an example.

■ 9. Collect Favorites

In *Dr. DeSoto*, William Steig (1982) writes of a charming mouse dentist who refuses, at first, to take on a crafty fox as his patient. The fox, in terrible pain, finally persuades the soft-hearted DeSoto to remove his tooth—then stumbles home still under the influence of anesthetic:

> The fox, still woozy, said goodbye and left. On his way home, he wondered if it would be shabby of him to eat the DeSotos when the job was done.

I love the way an author like Steig with a million-dollar vocabulary chooses homey but underused words like *woozy* and *shabby*. Immediately, I want to add those to my personal dictionary.

■ 10. Create Alphabet Books

This is another thing to do with favorite words—or with words that go with a particular topic: vacations, math, school, siblings, pets, parents, sports, bad days. It is OK to have more than one word per letter! When you are finished, create an "Alphabet of Tired Words": *G* is for *great*, *B* is for *big*, *A* is for *a lot*.

Figure 4.10

Ali's Personal Dictionary

Aa aunt arch action	**Bb** brother beetle bother
Cc cruise careful correct clash chocolate	**Dd** dawdle draw
Ee excited elevator	**Ff** frighten forget favorite

You may not have a tired word for every letter; that's fine. Keep the book going, and by the end of the year, you may be surprised at how many of those letters you fill up!

11. Guess What It Means

Words do not always make sense the first time we hear them. However, we learn meanings from the way words are used—from context. Lists are an ineffective way to teach meaning because they rarely include examples of words in action. For in-depth understanding, we need to see and hear words—more than once. Students need encouragement to guess at word meanings, which in turn expands listening skills. Suppose that you gave your students this list of words:

✔ *despised*
✔ *avoided*
✔ *predator*
✔ *ravenous*

Would they know them all? Perhaps not. They might make some very good guesses, though, on hearing this passage from Janell Cannon's *Crickwing* (2000):

> Crickwing despised his nickname, and he avoided hearing it by staying far away from the other creatures. He would sneak out to find his food when the night was darkest, knowing that the forest was crawling with predators even worse than ravenous toads.

Notice how Cannon gently hints at word meanings. Notice too how completely unnecessary it is to know *every* word in order to get a strong sense of the text.

TEACHING SENTENCE FLUENCY
What You Are Teaching
✔ Sentence sense: What is a sentence?
✔ An ear for variety
✔ Different sentence patterns

How to Get There
1. Notice Sentences in Students' Writing

Students' early sentences typically do not *look* like sentences at all—until we decode.

Figure 4.11 shows a paper by Christopher about visiting the park. When confronted with a piece of writing like this one, it's tempting to see at once all the things that need attention: Capital and lowercase letters are mixed, spelling could use some work, punctuation is unconventional with periods and commas inserted randomly—and there is no period at the end. Spacing needs work, too. All true. Yet we need to ask ourselves, "What is the most important thing for Christopher to know about his writing right now? The answer is that he is writing in full sentences. This is the beginning of fluency. If we recognize this, we can say, "Christopher! You're writing whole sentences.

Figure 4.11

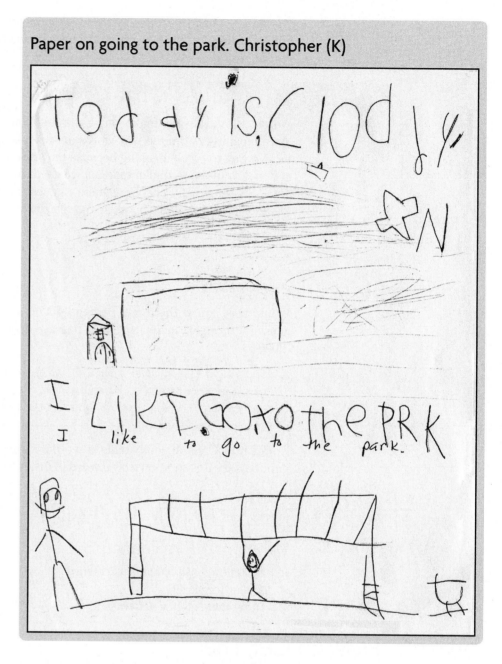

Paper on going to the park. Christopher (K)

Here you have two ideas combined in one sentence—*Today is cloudy and I like to go to the park. Terrific.*"

2. Keep an Open Discussion on "the Sentence" Going

Around the early part of first grade is a good time to begin asking students the big question, "What is a sentence?" Don't expect them to have the final answer, of course. Just put the question into their minds, and keep raising it. Keep in mind that this is not an easy concept to define, even for adult writers. Of course, we all have definitions swimming in our heads: A sentence is a complete thought. A sentence is a subject and predicate (*That* was a helpful one). The truth is, however, that we gain a sense of what a sentence is simply by listening to people speak—or read aloud. I like Bea Johnson's definition because it's simple and sensible: A sentence is "a group of words that tell about someone or something and what that someone or something is doing" (1999, p. 137).

To expand the students' understanding of this definition, write a sentence *slowly* on the overhead projector or chart paper and ask students to let you know when it becomes a sentence:

The . . . bear . . . found . . . the . . . berries.

Then ask: What is the sentence about? *A bear.* What did the bear do? *Found berries.*

> Note the sentences children write. They never use the simplistic sentence structure commonly used in the vast amount of the early-basal-reading series. Peruse the children's writings contained in [my] book. You will not find one "See Dick. See Dick run!" type communication. The children consistently use long flowing sentences to communicate their thoughts in a natural way
>
> **—Bea Johnson**
> (1999, p. 138)

3. Show How Punctuation Divides Sentences

Without end punctuation we would have a tougher time telling where sentences start and stop. You can show this to students with some easy steps. First, write just one sentence on the overhead projector (or chalkboard), and omit the final punctuation:

My dog had puppies

Ask your students if this is a sentence. (Yes.) Now ask if anyone knows what is missing. Someone likely will mention the missing period, but if not, you can answer for them and put one in. Explain how the period shows that the sentence is over. Now try a more extended piece of writing, with capital letters and periods (or question marks) missing:

My dog had puppies she had four puppies in all they were the cutest things I have ever seen in my life

Read this piece aloud with inflection and pauses, showing with your voice where the sentences end—where the punctuation should go. Ask your students to tell you as they read/listen where they hear each sentence end. Then show how capital letters and periods help make these endings clear:

My dog had puppies. She had four puppies in all. They were the cutest things I have ever seen in my life!

4. Read Fluent Passages Aloud

In Chapter 7 you will find numerous books that are excellent examples of fluency—and no doubt you have many of your own to add to the list. In order to emphasize fluency, you need to read with plenty of expression, and as students become ready, you need to ask them to listen for specific things:

1. Do you like the way this sounds when I read it?
2. How many different ways does this writer think of to begin sentences?

■ 5. Focus on Poetry—and Music

Poetry is *by nature* fluent, so, when you read poems aloud, you *are* teaching fluency. Share poems often. Give your students opportunities to compose poems, too. Rhyming is fun, but poems do not have to rhyme all the time. You can turn prose into poetry just by formatting it differently; for example,

> Rhyming is
> FUN.
> But poems
> do not
> have to rhyme
> all the time.

Students also have fun writing songs. They can borrow melodies from well-known pieces and write their own lyrics. It helps to sing one or two to get them warmed up. Then provide a list of well-known songs from which to borrow melodies and rhythms, and watch the lyrics flow. Do this as a group activity (with you as recorder and lead lyricist) if students are not ready to do it on their own. Here are a few melodies that are pretty well known (but your students may have favorites they prefer to use):

✔ "I've Been Workin' on the Railroad"
✔ "Row, Row, Row Your Boat"
✔ "Bingo (Bingo Was His Name-O)"
✔ "Yellow Rose of Texas"
✔ "Three Blind Mice"
✔ "Deep in the Heart of Texas"
✔ "You Are My Sunshine"
✔ "Twinkle, Twinkle, Little Star"
✔ "Down in the Valley"

■ 6. Break the Monotony!

Sentence patterning is quite typical with young writers, yet many manage to break free of this mold (usually at the end of grade 1 or the beginning of grade 2) when introduced to the possibility of varying sentence beginnings. A good way to begin is by modeling. Create a piece in which all sentences begin the same way; for example:

> We had fun over the weekend. We went to the beach. We met some friends. We went walking. We had a picnic.

The first time through, just read the piece to students and ask them what they notice about your sentences. Some may pick up the repetition right away. If not, read it once more, asking your students to listen to the beginnings. Let them know that you are not happy with every sentence beginning being the same. Invite them to help you to think of different ways to begin each sentence. Let them do as much as they can before jumping in with a solution. Here is one possible result:

Last weekend, we had a great time. Saturday morning we left for the beach. Some friends met us there, and we all walked together. Later, we had a picnic right on the sand.

See Chapter 7 for suggestions on books you can use to illustrate varied, interesting, and meaningful ways of beginning a sentence. For example

✔ *The turtle laid eggs* **becomes** <u>*Under the full moon*</u>, the turtle laid eggs.
✔ *The baby turtle headed to sea* **becomes** <u>*Moving quickly*</u>, the baby turtle headed to sea.
✔ *A ship appeared* **becomes** <u>*Far from shore*</u>, a ship appeared.
✔ *She never appeared* **becomes** <u>*For thirty years*</u>, she never appeared.
✔ *She floats on the sea* **becomes** <u>*Tiny as a cork*</u>, she floats on the sea.

We have only to look at the best literature to see models of the wondrous and inventive sentence patterns available to our student writers.

7. Use a Poem as a Model

Teacher Penny Clare has used the poem *And My Heart Soars* by Chief Dan George (1989, p. 41) to inspire her students to think about those things that touch their hearts. Students begin by listening to the poem, then creating a sketch of things that are important to them (Figure 4.12a). Penny models this first by doing her own sketch. Drawing triggers memories that are captured in a draft poem, which is then shared in a peer or group conference. Penny writes with her students, but stresses originality in both content and form. She does not want students to mimic her ideas. Further, students do not need to follow the pattern of Chief Dan George's original poem precisely; the emphasis is on writing from the heart, and making the final copy as fluent as possible (with help from a peer coach). Notice that the first four stanzas of Miriam's poem (Figure 4.12b) end with the refrain "Speaks To Me," while the final stanza closes with the line "And My Heart Soars." This is her choice. The poem has a gentle but forceful rhythm, while focusing on what matters most to the writer. Even a writer as young as Miriam has begun to gather memories that make her "heart soar."

> *When you read like a writer, you also notice and think about how a text is written, because you just notice things like that.*
>
> **—Katie Wood Ray**
> **—Lisa B. Cleaveland**
> *About the Authors* (2004, pp. 14–15)

8. Sentence or Fragment?

Students learn to hear the difference between a sentence and a fragment with practice—and many may be good at this right from the start. Make six sentence-fragment pairs by writing them on strips of paper and putting them into a paper bag. Each bag should contain a different set of twelve—six sentences and six fragments. Keep them short, simple, and obvious: for example, *The octopus*. Make the print *big*. Give one bag to each team of three or four students and ask them to sort the fragments from the sentences as quickly as they can. When they finish, ask teams to check one another's work. See if they have any disagreements. If they do, write the questionable "sentence" on the overhead projector or chart, and talk about it with the whole class. Keep asking that question: *What is a sentence?*

Figure 4.12a

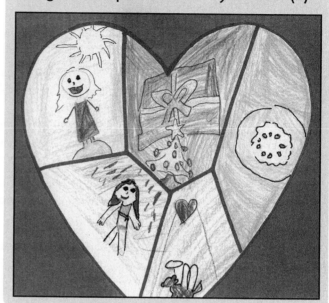

Things that "Speak to Me" by Miriam (2)

Figure 4.12b

And My Heart Soars by Miriam (2)

And My Heart Soars
By Miriam

Swimming in the rain
So refreshing water
Sounds of the raindrops
Speaks To Me

My cousin's smile
Giggling laughter
The sound of joy
Speaks To Me

Aunt Diane's blueberry pie
The warming scene
Cinnamon, crust, sweet blueberries
Speaks To Me

My dog up in heaven
His black silky fur
Him licking my face
Memories
Speaks To Me

Christmas morning
Pancakes
Delightful buttery taste
All the presents
They Speak to Me
And My Heart Soars

■ 9. Phone Yourself!

Out of three PVC joints from any home building and repair store, you can make a handy plastic "phone" into which students can read and speak—with amazing results! The pipe enhances the voice so that students hear themselves with exceptional clarity. "Phoning yourself" and reading your own writing aloud is a good way to check fluency. It builds voice as well. It is also an aid in conventions because many conventional errors are caught with the ear, not just with the eye. Shy students who do not feel comfortable sharing with a small group or even a single partner take comfort in being a "group of one" for that first reading. Not-so-shy students simply enjoy hearing their own voices. Figure 4.13 is a simple sketch of how the PVC "phone" looks when assembled; other configurations work just as well, so pick any pipe fittings you like.

■ 10. Use Imagination to Create Puppet Dialogue

Dialogue is a critical part of fluency, but one that is often overlooked. Before students are ready to create dialogue on paper, they can create it orally. Using puppets keeps them focused on "speech," with fewer side comments.

Figure 4.13

PVC joints create a simple "phone" on which students can speak to themselves.

You may wish to provide a hypothetical situation with which they can work; for example:

- ✔ Two friends meet who have not seen each other in a long time.
- ✔ Two people argue over who should get the first turn down the slide.
- ✔ One friend is upset and another is trying to comfort him or her.
- ✔ One friend does not like school and another does.
- ✔ One friend tries to talk another into sharing his or her lunch.

■ 11. Listen to Books on Tape

One of the best ways to teach fluency is to read aloud. It is wonderful, though, for students to hear other voices, too; each reader has his or her own special style. Besides, when you play a book on tape, you get to listen, too. (Don't forget to include music; it's an excellent way to teach fluency.)

TEACHING CONVENTIONS
What You Are Teaching

- ✔ A proofreader's "eye" and "ear"
- ✔ Awareness of conventions
- ✔ Sense of self as editor

How to Get There
■ 1. Let Students Edit Their Own Work

Very young students cannot (usually!) insert quotation marks in the right spots, use semicolons with skill, or spell ten-letter words correctly. Fortunately, this is not all there is to editing, though. Begin with what they *can* do, and gradually increase editorial responsibility to match their skills and knowledge. For example, even the youngest students can put their names on their papers. When they check to make sure that they have remembered to do this, this is editing. Later, you can add additional skills: putting a date on the paper, putting a period (or question mark) at the end of a sentence, putting spaces between words, starting a sentence with a capital letter, and so on. Figure 4.14 pre-sents a simple editing checklist that works well with young students.

■ 2. Model Instead of Correcting

We often make the mistake of thinking we are "teaching" conventions when we correct students' work. We are, of course—only we are teaching *ourselves!*

Figure 4.14

Simple Editing Checklist.

EDITOR'S CHECKLIST

_____ Name on paper

_____ Date

_____ Title

_____ Capitals to begin sentences

_____ Periods or question marks

_____ Spaces between words

_____ "Capital I"

Name:_____

Number of Checks: _____

Students may interpret substantially corrected pieces as a form of rejection rather than help. This inhibits writing. And writing—a lot—is the only way to get good at it. Consider the wisdom of Bea Johnson: "Celebrate kids' writing, rather than correcting it. . . . Remember, in kindergarten and first grade, the philosophy is to let children write. If you red-mark them, you will inhibit the vital freshness of their writing" (1999, p. 136).

This does not mean that you should not pay attention to the kinds of errors you see. Not at all. You can deal with a few in conferences (see idea 3). Deal with the rest by making yourself a list and then modeling each one for the class. Perhaps many of your students are running words together and putting no spaces between them. Model this problem and the way to fix it.

Thefatoldcatcouldnevercatchthatspeedybird.

Then say to students, "See how hard this is to read? Let me show you what happens when I write the very same sentence with spaces between the words. First, I'm going to mark this sentence with slash marks between the words. Then I'm going to rewrite it so that it is easy to read. Watch and read along with me.

The/fat/old/cat/could/never/catch/that/speedy/bird.

"Now let's rewrite it and read it aloud again."

The fat old cat could never catch that speedy bird.

Model just *one* problem at a time. I know—you want to fix it all—right now! Be patient. Focus on one thing; then let your students try it. Keep the editing challenge at their level, meaning not what they can understand but what they can *do*. Maybe our sample sentence is too difficult for your young editors to do by themselves. Simplify. Young editors are often stumped because the editing we ask them to do is too hard; this is why they often cannot edit their own work. Their writers' minds race ahead of their editors' skills. Let them work on simple text first—before they take on the complexity of their own work:

Isawabird.

Even young writers, in teams of two, will usually figure this one out. If not, you will be there to help—and they will get it soon enough. And remember, this is only one lesson.

■ 3. Share One Writer's Secret

Start with sincere praise for something the child has done well, including both picture and text, writing a whole sentence, writing more than one sentence, remembering to put his or her name on the paper, and so on. The achievement may be small, but your noticing it will make all the difference. Then you can share one "writer's secret" (a phrase I borrowed from Lois Burdett). This gentle form of making a suggestion says to students, "What I'm about to tell you is special—and will help your writing." A writer's secret can be anything at all— as long as it is focused. Here are a few possibilities, some very tiny and some a bit more significant: "Did you know that if you put a capital letter at the beginning of your sentence, it's easier for the reader to tell where your sentence begins? Could I show you?" *Or,* "If you . . .

✔ Put a period at the end of your sentence . . .
✔ End a question with a question mark . . .
✔ Put a title on your paper . . .
✔ Use a period sometimes instead of the word *and*, making two sentences . . .
✔ Spell the word *write* with a *w*, like this . . .
✔ Use quotation marks to show someone speaking . . .

If you like, you can use a large Post-It note to write a "writer's secret" reminder to the student. At the next conference, check to see what progress has been made. If the student is ready for another step, you're on your way! If not, you can always try it again. Either way, you are keeping editing manageable.

■ 4. Encourage Temporary Spelling

Temporary spelling scares some people who wonder if those early spell-ings will "stick." They will not. In fact, temporary spelling has some real benefits when explained to students as "using what you *know* and what you *hear* to spell each word as well as you can." First, it encourages students to try more expressive and interesting words by removing the obstacle of "I can't spell that one." And second, because students are continually trying to make letter-sound connections and to "get it right" without a crutch, temporary spelling actually *improves* later conventional spelling.

Bea Johnson (1999, p. 56) notes that educators' and parents' fears that temporary spelling will somehow "take hold" and prevent the development of more conventional spelling skills are unfounded. First, children rarely spell an invented word the same way consistently; they are *constantly* experimenting and teaching themselves *how* to spell, not latching onto erroneous spellings that will haunt their careers as writers. Moreover, our logical understanding of how learning occurs—and *must* occur—tells us that experimentation and mistakes are not only inevitable but also desirable. The child who is willing to stumble and take a few bumps learns to walk faster than the one who sits safely on a pillow perusing *Ten Steps to Correct Walking.*

> *Research says that temporary spelling helps the child learn the sounds more effectively than most phonics instruction, which comes at an inappropriate time. . . . Allowing the child to come up with temporary spelling and to produce written language by himself increases his understanding. Piaget wrote that in order for children to understand something, they must construct it themselves—they must reinvent it.*
>
> **—Bea Johnson**
> (1999, p. 56)

■ 5. Encourage Word Banks and Personal Dictionaries

Students need easy-to-use, convenient resources from which to draw. Primary students are hungry borrowers. The more you can fill their

> *We have known for a long time that to understand beginning writing, we need to honor the smart, theoretical thinking children have to do to approximate spelling and other language conventions.*
>
> **—Katie Wood Ray**
> **—Lisa B. Cleaveland**
> *About the Authors* (2004, p. 10)

worlds with print—print used correctly and easy to get at—the more borrowing you will see. An adult dictionary (or even one for older students) is an awkward tool for most primary writers. However, word walls and personal dictionaries (cards with names of colors or animals or days of the week) are user-friendly and encourage expansion of both vocabulary and spelling skills.

6. Brainstorm Word Possibilities Before Writing

When you have a topic in mind—a trip to Philadelphia, let's say—it is handy to know how to spell *some* of the words you are likely to be using: *Philadelphia, freedom, history, George Washington, bridge, monument, traffic, airplane, exciting, tourist, taxi, hotel, restaurant, shopping,* and so on. These words can be incorporated into personal dictionaries for handy reference later, too. You will not be able to write down every word for every child—there is never time—but you can allow ten minutes for creating a word wall from which everyone can borrow (this works well if students are writing on a common theme—animals, weather, food). If it works better for you, allow *each child* up to two or three words.

7. Celebrate the "Discovery" of Conventions

Students often "discover" periods, colons, semicolons, ellipses, dashes, and a host of other conventions before they know how to use them correctly. They simply like the look of them and feel that they have meaning. They want their own text to have meaning and significance, too. Text may be peppered with periods, for example, as a precursor to the writer's learning correct placement. This peppering is a *step toward correctness* and should be acknowledged.

8. Teach Editing Symbols Appropriate for Grade Level

Around the end of kindergarten or the beginning of first grade, you can begin working on some simple editors' symbols that will empower your students to feel like professionals when they edit their own or others' work. They will also open your students' minds to an understanding of what editors do. Editors' symbols are like a kind of shorthand—almost a secret code. If you teach them this way, you make editing fun and playful, not drudgery. And here's the thing: Very young writers do not have to rewrite. When they use editors' symbols, the corrections have been made. Job done. Figure 4.15 provides a simple list of editors' symbols appropriate for young writers. I have listed them in the order in which I would teach them—but you should feel free to change this order to suit your own instruction.

9. Provide Interesting Tools

Editing is much more fun with a favorite pen. Go for wild colors, bold shapes, or big, comfortable pens with an easy grip—even neon.

Figure 4.15

Easy Symbols for Young Editors

Symbol	It means	Use it like this
∧	Put something in.	Paul∧cats. *(likes)*
ℓ	Take this out.	Don is a ~~big~~ huge guy.
⫲	Put in a space.	Amy loves∧apples.
⊙	Add a period.	The horse saw us⊙
≡	Make this letter a capital.	We live in o̲r̲e̲g̲o̲n̲.
/	Make this letter lowercase.	Do you eat /Bacon?
_____	Underline this title.	Our teacher read the book C̲r̲i̲c̲k̲w̲i̲n̲g̲ to our class.

■ 10. Play the Treasure Hunt Game

Before students are even ready to work with conventions, they recognize them. Reinforce what they know, and teach them some new terminology at the same time by playing the treasure hunt game. Spend five or ten minutes simply hunting for a variety of conventions. You can use any text for this, but I like something with big print and a lot of variety. Because her text is generally rich with dialogue, Janell Cannon uses a wide range of conventions, including exclamation points, question marks, ellipses, quotation marks, and italics. Fred Marcellino's work (*I, Crocodile*, 1999) is also exceptional for illustrating how conventions help make meaning clear and put inflection into speech. Marcellino uses ellipses and dashes with flair. Show students a page of text from one of these authors or any author who uses conventions with skill (and voice—yes, conventions do enhance voice). Simply ask your students at first to find various conventions—and to put their fingers on an example when they find one. For instance, please find

✔ A comma
✔ A period
✔ A question mark
✔ Some ellipses
✔ An example of italics
✔ A name

✔ A capital letter
✔ The word *and*
✔ The word *crocodile*
✔ A word that ends in *e*
✔ Dashes

After playing the game this way a few times (and getting a little faster each time), ask students to tell you the meaning of the convention; for example, "You found quotation marks. Good! Why did the writer use them here?" Knowing the conventions by name and knowing why each one is used gives students a huge leg up on using them correctly in their own writing.

◼ 11. Keep Expectations Realistic

"As a society," Donald Graves (1983) tells us, "we allow children to learn to speak by trial and error. But when it comes to reading and writing, we expect them to be right the first time." Maybe it is because conventional errors are so noticeable. Maybe it is also because we know how to respond to conventions—they are either right or wrong. We are not nearly as sure-footed when it comes to responding to voice or ideas or (toughest of all) organization. When we correct everything on every piece of writing, though, we make our ultimate goal in conventions all too clear: perfect writing *all* the time, every time. How realistic is that? Do you achieve it? Do you know anyone who does? Although Chapter 8 deals with conventional expectations along a continuum, I would like to suggest some grade-level possibilities I think are realistic. They do not reflect perfection but rather focus on something more interesting and achievable—editorial growth (as always, please use your own observations and experience to modify these):

Kindergarten

✔ Playfulness with letters and numbers
✔ Some correct directionality with letters
✔ Ability to distinguish between capital and lowercase letters
✔ Ability to write one's own name
✔ Ability to write a growing body of sight words
✔ Incorporation of some punctuation (periods, exclamation points, commas) into writing, sometimes placed correctly
✔ Conscious attempt to put spaces between "words"
✔ Ability to write a complete sentence (even if in letter-string form)
✔ Ability to use at least one editorial symbol: the caret (∧).

First Grade

✔ Increasing experimentation with letters and numbers
✔ Correct directionality with most letters
✔ Ability to recognize and reproduce a reasonable facsimile of all letters of the alphabet
✔ Full ability to distinguish between capital and lowercase letters—and often to use one or the other appropriately
✔ Ability to write numerous sight words and to make good phonetic guesses at some more difficult words

✔ Readable spelling in most instances (i.e., reader can figure it out without the author's aid)
✔ Successful attempts to space properly in most sentences
✔ Ability to write a complete sentence—and often to compose in multiple sentences (usually with punctuation)
✔ Ability to recognize and use several editorial symbols: caret (∧), delete symbol (℘), caret with pound sign (⚛), symbol for inserting period (⊙)
✔ Ability to write (correctly or in recognizable form) many proper names: own name, names of family members, names of friends, names of pets, name of city and state, name of street, name of school, names of some other states or countries, names of some famous persons

Second Grade

✔ Experimentation with increasingly difficult words
✔ Correct directionality with letters in nearly all cases
✔ Ability to reproduce a readily recognizable facsimile of all letters of the alphabet
✔ Consistent, appropriate use of capital and lowercase letters
✔ Ability to write own name and names of friends, family members, pets, and most other familiar proper names
✔ Ability to write and spell an increasing number of sight words and more difficult words correctly and to make good phonetic guesses at others
✔ Readable spelling on virtually all written work (i.e., reader can figure it out without the author's aid)
✔ Consistent, correct spacing on all written work
✔ Ability to write and punctuate multiple sentences with relative ease
✔ Attempted use of paragraphing when needed
✔ Correct use of most terminal punctuation (periods, question marks, exclamation points)
✔ Incorporation of an increasing range of internal punctuation (commas, quotation marks, dashes, semicolons), sometimes used correctly, sometimes not
✔ Ability to create bulleted or numbered lists
✔ Ability to recognize and use the editorial symbols in Figure 4.15

Third Grade

✔ Continued experimentation with increasingly difficult words
✔ Consistent, correct directionality with capital and lowercase letters
✔ Ability to reproduce fully readable print and/or cursive writing *or*
✔ Sufficient keyboarding skills to compose multiparagraph pieces
✔ Consistent, appropriate use of capital and lowercase letters
✔ Ever-increasing personal vocabulary of correctly spelled words and use of fully recognizable phonetic spellings on new words
✔ Increasingly consistent distinction between common homophones: *to, two; know, no; their, there*
✔ Readable spelling on virtually all written work (i.e., reader can figure it out without the author's aid)
✔ Consistent, correct spacing on all written work
✔ Ability to write and punctuate multiple sentences with relative ease
✔ Ability to organize multisentence writing into paragraphs

✔ Increasingly correct use of terminal punctuation (periods, question marks, exclamation points) on virtually all written work
✔ Correct use of some internal punctuation (may include commas, quotation marks, dashes, semicolons)
✔ Ability to create bulleted or numbered lists
✔ Ability to recognize proper titles and to underline or italicize as needed
✔ Ability to recognize and use the editorial symbols in Figure 4.15 with ease
✔ Ability to write an increasing range of proper names correctly

Children vary tremendously in their skill with conventions and the rate at which they internalize conventions. Some writers are spelling numerous words correctly and using highly sophisticated grammatical constructions in grade 1. Others struggle with these same issues all their lives. Therefore, the lists I present here are general guidelines and cannot be more. I encourage you to modify them based on your own teaching experience and consultation with other teachers. What is helpful, I think, is not so much a list that is imposed as "must-achieve goals" but a set of guidelines that help us to watch for, recognize, and celebrate moments of growth in our children's writing.

> *If there is one rule that applies to every child, it is that progress is always uneven. Children never follow any series of stages exactly and sometimes appear to be regressing in one area as they advance in another.*
>
> **—Donald Graves and Virginia Stuart**
> *Write from the Start* (1985, p. 169)

12. Give Students Editing Practice— Often

Editors learn their craft by editing. Two things are critical: One is to do it often. Editing now and then will not get the job done. When students edit only what they publish, they do not get enough practice to become truly skilled. Second, young editors (all editors, in fact) need to practice on text that is *not their own*. This is so because they have no personal attachment to such text and do not mind making corrections; in addition, errors are much easier to spot in someone else's work. Ever notice a dusty table in someone else's house? So easy to spot, isn't it? Editing is just like that. Three, four, or five times a day, write a sample sentence or two about whatever you are currently doing or thinking— make one or two mistakes, and ask your students to find them. For example,

Im enjoying writing today

There are two mistakes here that will take your students anywhere from ten seconds to a full minute to find, depending on ability level. Make the corrections in front of them and go on. Do this often. Give them written text to edit on their own as well. Keep it short. Make it a game.

13. Invite Parents to Sit In on Editing Lessons

Parents worry over conventions endlessly. This happens for multiple reasons. Like it or not, society judges people on their conventions. When is the last time you became annoyed (I have friends who actually become enraged) when you heard a media representative make a grammatical error? Parents also worry because they remember their own writing instruction, and for many, it was a painful process of red ink–covered pages and cryptic, accusatory marginal comments. They lived through it, though, and feel it might be best if their children also traveled the rugged trail to conventional correctness.

Invite parents to sit in and watch as you teach your children to be editors. Watching young editors spotting errors, using editors' symbols, correcting text, and using editorial language gives parents much-needed confidence and a sense of relief that their children are not just being corrected but actually are learning the skills they need to edit on their own.

◼ 14. Include Samples of Students' Editing in Portfolios

> *Telling writers they've made a mistake is not teaching. If the child can already do what I've corrected, then correcting is only reminding. And reminding is not teaching. If the child doesn't understand the error, then correcting isn't enough.*
>
> **—Donald Graves and Virginia Stuart**
> *Write from the Start* (1985, p. 177)

Students need to recognize their improvement as editors, along with their improvement as writers. Therefore, make sure that portfolios include samples of editing practice—at least five (dated) from various points throughout the year.

◼ 15. Ask Students to Double-Space

This seems like such a simple thing, but we so often forget to ask students to leave room for editing. (It is like leaving room for cream in the coffee.) Text that is double-spaced and has wide margins is much easier to edit than text crammed together on a page. If your students use a word processor, have them double-space anyway and print out a copy for editing once they have made any other changes they wish to make. Most of us catch errors in printed text more readily than on a computer screen.

SOME FINAL QUESTIONS

Do I need to teach all six *traits to primary learners?* Yes—I think so. If you do not, it is like presenting writing as a fragmented rather than holistic concept. Writing is not *just* ideas or *just* conventions; it is a compilation of many things—and this is the whole point in working with the traits; to help students see what elements help shape writing and influence reader response. So, yes, teach them all, right from kindergarten. Do not have a *unit of instruction* on each trait, though. Relax! Just *talk about* voice and word choice. Read examples and ask students to listen for fluency or a good lead or detail. Weave the traits naturally, gracefully, into the instruction you are already doing.

Do I need to teach the traits in order, for example, ideas, organization, voice, and so on? Many teachers find this a comfortable approach because, again, it helps you organize how and when you will present various lessons or pieces of literature. Be careful, though. Do not get so locked in that you are afraid to comment on the wonderful voice in a student's piece just because you are working on organization right then. Balance is the key. It is mostly a matter of emphasis. Tell your students that they will be learning "some interesting things about how professional writers work." Perhaps you begin by emphasizing detail. Then leads (one important part of organization). Then personal voice. And so on. Stay flexible; flip back and forth as you need to.

What about conventions? Isn't that a special case? Absolutely. Do not wait to touch on conventions until you have *all* other traits in place. You will want to work on conventions *as you are working with other writing traits,* such as ideas or organization. Start simply, asking students to check for their names or names and dates on their papers. Gradually, add more conventions to match their editing skill.

How long should I spend on one trait? For older students, I suggest taking plenty of time, up to two weeks. For primary students, though, you may quickly lose the larger picture if you try this. Pick a feature or two of each trait to emphasize. With ideas, for example, your "key features" might be a main idea or message and details. For organization, they might be leads and endings. You may only need one or two lessons per trait to emphasize these key features as long as your students have lots of time to write. Keep in mind that the traits are only a key to unlock the mystery of what makes writing work; *writing itself is the thing!*

What if my students are struggling writers who find some of these activities difficult? How do I simplify writing activities for them? No matter what the level of your students, it is critical to view them as writers and to provide time for writing. This is the *only* way they will gain skill and comfort. In addition, though, use the tools they do have: speaking and listening, for example. As you model, they can respond and offer suggestions. They can talk to each other about their writing, your writing, or books you share. They can listen to literature and listen to you as you share writing samples—and talk about whether they have voice or detail. They can dictate pieces. Or they can talk as you (or someone) makes notes. They can use tape recorders and enhance their text with art. They can memorize poems and act them out or use drama to express feelings or characterizations or to practice dialogue. Writing *is* the focal point, to be sure, but it is not the only path to writing instruction.

 # CHAPTER 4 IN A NUTSHELL

- It is important to teach all traits at all grade levels in order to present writing as a coherent "whole."
- It is not, however, necessary to teach every element of every trait. Keep instruction simple.
- Focus on writing and process. Use trait language to help children "read" their own writing and understand process.

- At the primary level, put these goals ahead of others: gaining a writer's vocabulary (to build understanding) and experiencing joy in writing (to build passion).
- As you look at this book—or any book on teaching trait-based writing—you are likely to discover that *you are already teaching traits*, because they are nothing more than the foundation of good writing.

 # STUDY GROUP: INTERACTIVE QUESTIONS AND ACTIVITIES

1. **Activity.** List three of your favorite writing activities/ lessons. Connect each one to one or more of the six traits. (Do not be surprised if you are often teaching more than one trait.)

2. **Activity.** Create a detailed lesson plan for one writing activity. Identify the traits you touch upon in various parts of the lesson. Be prepared to share your lesson plan with colleagues in your study group.

3. **Activity.** Look again at the list you created for **Activity 1.** Which traits are you emphasizing most? Are there other traits you could emphasize more? For at least one trait you would like to focus on more, create a list of two or more lesson ideas you might try with your students. These need not be detailed, but include enough specificity so that you can share them orally with members of your study group.

4. **Discussion.** In this chapter, I recommend teaching conventions right from day one, rather than waiting to focus on this trait over a series of lessons. What advantages do you see in this approach? Does it match the way you currently teach conventions—or see yourself teaching this trait? Discuss this with members of your study group.

5. **Discussion.** Author Donald Murray said that writers learn to write primarily by building on their strengths. Do you agree? What influence might this have on the order in which you teach the traits? Discuss this with your study group.

6. **Discussion.** With older students, it may be desirable to present three, four—or even more—lessons on a single trait before moving on to the next. Some primary teachers, though, prefer to rotate lessons, giving primary students more of a "whole" sense of writing. With your study group, discuss the pros and cons of a trait-by-trait approach versus a rotating agenda of various traits.

7. **Discussion.** Some schools have tried a trait-per-year approach (for example, focusing on ideas in kindergarten, organization in grade 1, and so on). What impact might this approach have on students' understanding of writing and writing process?

8. **Activity.** One way to check whether your students understand the traits is to ask them to define each trait you have taught in their own words—not by reading or memorizing a checklist. If you are teaching the traits now, try this. How easy do your students find this task?

____ Very easy. They can describe each trait using their own language.

____ Somewhat easy. With a little coaching, they can articulate the basic idea behind each trait.

____ Fairly hard. It is difficult for them to describe the traits even with coaching.

9. **Activity.** Choose any lesson from this chapter and try it with your students. Discuss the results. What worked well? What would you modify, if anything?

10. **Activity.** Review at least ten samples of your students' work, and identify several problems common to three students or more. Design a simple modeling lesson you could use to address each of those problems, using just *one sentence* per problem. Begin in each case by writing a sentence that shows the problem clearly; then think what you will say, ask, or do to show how a writer solves the problem. Also consider how much coaching you can elicit from your students so that they take an active role in solving the problem with you.

SOURCES CITED

Aronie, Nancy Slonim. 1998. *Writing from the Heart.* New York: Hyperion.

Best, Cari. 2001. *Shrinking Violet.* New York: Farrar, Straus and Giroux.

Burdett, Lois. 1995a. *A Child's Portrait of Shakespeare.* Winsor, Ontario, Canada: Black Moss Press. Web site: *lburdett@shakespearecanbefun.com.*

Burdett, Lois. 1995b. *Shakespeare Can Be Fun Series.* Winsor, Ontario, Canada: Black Moss Press. Web site: *lburdett@shakespearecanbefun.com.*

Calkins, Lucy McCormick. 1994. *The Art of Teaching Writing,* rev ed. Portsmouth, NH: Heinemann.

Cannon, Janell. 2000. *Crickwing.* San Diego, CA: Harcourt.

Churchman, Deborah. 2000. "All About Worms." In *Ranger Rick,* Vol. 34, No. 7, pp. 32ff. Vienna, VA: The National Wildlife Federation.

Cramer, Ronald L. 2001. *Creative Power: The Nature and Nurture of Children's Writing.* New York: Addison Wesley Longman.

Dahl, Lucy. 1996. *James and the Giant Peach: The Book and Movie Scrapbook.* New York: Disney Press.

Fox, Mem. 1993. *Radical Reflections.* San Diego, CA: Harcourt, Brace & Company.

Freeman, Marcia S. 1998. *Teaching the Youngest Writers.* Gainesville, FL: Maupin House.

George, Chief Dan. 1989. "And My Heart Soars" from *My Heart Soars.* Saanichton, B.C., Canada: Hancock Publishing.

Glynn, Carol. 2001. *Learning on Their Feet: A Sourcebook for Kinesthetic Learning Across the Curriculum K-8.* Shoreham, VT: Discover Writing Press.

Graves, Donald H. 1983. *Writing: Teachers and Children at Work.* Portsmouth, NH: Heinemann.

Graves, Donald, and Virginia Stuart. 1985. *Write from the Start: Tapping Your Child's Natural Writing Ability*. New York: NAL Penguin.

Hablitzel, Marie, and Kim Stitzer. 2000. *Draw Right Now, Book Seven*. New York: Barker Creed Publishing. Web site: *www.dwnow.com*.

Johnson, Bea. 1999. *Never Too Early to Write*. Gainesville, FL: Maupin House.

Keillor, Garrison. 1989. "How to Write a Letter." In *We Are Still Married*. New York: Viking.

Keene, Ellin Oliver, and Susan Zimmerman. 1997. *Mosaic of Thought*. Portsmouth, NH: Heinemann.

Lane, Barry. 1999. *Reviser's Toolbox*. Shoreham, VT: Discover Writing Press.

Marcellino, Fred. 1999. *I, Crocodile*. New York: HarperCollins.

Murray, Donald M. 1990. *Shoptalk*. Portsmouth, NH: Heinemann.

Olshansky, Beth. 2006. *Picturing Writing: Fostering Literacy Through Art* and *Image-Making Within the Writing Process*. Durham, NH: University of New Hampshire.

Ranger Rick, Vol. 36, No. 7 (July 2000), p. 33. Vienna, VA: The National Wildlife Federation.

Ray, Katie Wood, with Lisa B. Cleaveland. 2004. *About the Authors: Writing Workshop with Our Youngest Writers*. Portsmouth, NH: Heinemann.

Ringgold, Faith. 1991. *Tar Beach*. New York: Crown Publishers.

Routman, Regie. 2000. *Conversations*. Portsmouth, NH: Heinemann.

Ruef, Kerry. 2000. *The Private Eye: Looking/Thinking by Analogy*. Seattle, WA: The Private Eye Project. Web site: *www.the-private-eye.com*.

Sendak, Maurice. 1991 (original 1963). *Where the Wild Things Are*. New York: HarperCollins (Harper Trophy Edition).

Steig, William. 1986. *Brave Irene*. New York: Farrar, Straus and Giroux.

Steig, William. 1982. *Dr. DeSoto*. New York: Farrar, Straus and Giroux

Van Allsburg, Chris. 1988. *Two Bad Ants*. Boston: Houghton Mifflin.

Figure 4.2a was inspired by the work of Beth Olshansky: www.picturewriting.org

Making Changes: Portfolios, Revising, Reflecting, Publishing

5

> My definition of a portfolio has evolved to this: a reflective selection of artifacts, work samples, and records that demonstrate who we are as literate beings.
>
> **—Regie Routman**
> *Conversations* (2001, p. 562)

> Acrobats start their children on the high wire as soon as they can walk, and a writer ought to begin before he has graduated to solid food.
>
> **—Robertson Davies, novelist**
> In Deborah Brodie, *Writing Changes Everything* (1997, p. 24)

> Making revisions to their pieces helps me see what students understand about good writing and gives me insights about how well they are internalizing instruction and managing writing independently.
>
> **—Laura Benson**
> "A Writer's Bill of Rights" (2002, p. 22)

> Be more interested in what is not on the paper.
>
> **—Barry Lane**
> *After THE END* (1993, p. 212)

> Revision is a ship. It is the vessel on which writers sail to discover what they have to say.
>
> **—Ronald C. Cramer**
> *Creative Power: The Nature and Nurture of Children's Writing* (2001, p. 98)

ARE PORTFOLIOS STILL WITH US?

Portfolios became hugely popular for a time in the late 1980s and early 1990s and then (for many) enjoyed a ride into the sunset for which some people, I think, actually stood and cheered. This is a shame—but it is understandable, really, to anyone who has visited classrooms where portfolios are or once were popular. Despite the valiant efforts of many portfolio champions—including Donald Graves himself—many teachers viewed portfolios as a mission, something quite separate from regular teaching, and they did _all the work._ I understand this. When my son left college, I vowed I would not spend five minutes cleaning his apartment for him. But you know? There was that cleaning fee at stake. . . .

As educators, we want our portfolios to look good—impressive. We want students to select their best, most shining moments to include—and how will they know which moments those are if we do not point them out? We also want them to reflect on their growth as writers, but how will they know what to say if we do not tell them? So, we select, we order, we stack and file, we reflect— and then we collapse. Well, who wouldn't? It's stressful to be wise and insightful about the writings of twenty-five or thirty students.

Of course, this do-it-yourself approach misses the whole point. The idea behind portfolios was never to create beautiful packages, although scrapbooking can be rewarding, if you like it. The point was to teach students to look thoughtfully at their own work, to make personal choices about what would be saved and why, and to write their own reflections, even if they were not perfect.

If we teach our student writers, including the youngest among them, to recognize detail, good organization, voice, strong word choice, or fluency when they see it, they begin to understand what, specifically, to look for—and out of _the writing they do each day as part of the classroom routine_, they can build a portfolio that will knock our socks off. Even more important, however, they will teach themselves (and us and parents) how they are growing as writers. As author/teacher Barry Lane points out from his experience with Vermont's large-scale portfolio-based assessment, "A portfolio is a window into a student's learning and can be as useful to the student as to the teacher" (_After THE END_, 1993, p. 203).

KEEP IT SIMPLE

The portfolio idea lost some of the popular vote, I think, because people saw it as huge. They imagined giant files in which students painstakingly collected and stored everything they wrote. By year's end, some would have had to tote their portfolios around in small wagons. This would be comparable to our saving every note, card, letter, e-mail, memo, grocery list, reminder, report, book review, poem, or story we created. What sane person would do this? If students are *selective* about what they save, a portfolio might be as small as five or six pieces. Then, if a student were to lay those five or six pieces out at the end of the year, he or she likely would see *big* steps in writing skill.

To see how powerful this overview can be, look at the following mini-portfolios, with just a *few* samples each. I am not suggesting that portfolios need to be *this* small either; I am including these examples to make a point. Although these are not giant collections, look how much they tell us. Add just one or two more items, and you would have a whole writer's biography.

Sample 1: Kiya's Journey

Kindergartner Kiya has four entries in her portfolio, running from November to April. In Figure 5.1 she is writing in a letter string and using her picture to carry much of the meaning. She is writing in full sentences

> *In one class that combined first grade and kindergarten, some of the first-graders were convinced on first glance that some of the kindergartners' work must have been put into their writing folders. They themselves could never have produced such a silly-looking jumble of letters.*
>
> **—Graves and Stuart,**
> (1985, p. 111)

Figure 5.1

November 20 entry in Kiya's (K) portfolio.

ILKSNDABEKS – M KPK
I like Sunday because we make pancakes.

and making numerous letter-sound connections. Notice her use of the blank for the word (*we*) she does not know. At this point, her writing includes all capital letters and no punctuation. The picture is full of detail; notice the high-flying pancakes and the happy faces of the pancake eaters.

By January, Kiya is constructing writing that we can decode without any difficulty (Figure 5.2). She is writing much more conventional text, with a mix of lowercase and capital letters and is using apostrophes and periods. She has learned to capitalize the pronoun *I*. Her picture and text are connected—just as they were in her November example. Both show early indications of organization.

In March, Kiya is writing more extended text (Figure 5.3). She continues to use punctuation, although, as this example shows, it is inconsistent. Writing is never a steady climb up the mountain; writers pause occasionally, hit plateaus, or even get sidetracked. Nevertheless, this expanded sentence shows a big leap in fluency and greater comfort with the generation of text. Kiya is also willing to experiment with new, less familiar words, for example, *slbt* (celebrate). She also has noticed that words are sometimes split at the end of a line, and so she is trying this technique out in her own writing, a reminder of what good borrowers young writers can be. Kiya still relies on pictures to carry a portion of her detail; we might infer that quite a large group will gather for Grammy's birthday and that they will be pretty happy about the whole thing.

Kiya's April example (Figure 5.4) takes an interesting turn. Here she puts much of her writing energy into her picture, which is far more detailed and expressive (this is voice) than any preceding. Compare this drawing with the figures in her November picture to appreciate the growth in her observational skills and sense of perspective. Here we even get bows on the shoes. On the other hand, Kiya is a bit less daring with the text, preferring to use blank lines for the sounds that she is unsure of in "new shoes." Never mind. She is very close to coordinating the text with the picture, and within a few weeks, we are likely to see the expanded text of Figure 5.3 combined with the detailed picture of Figure 5.4.

Figure 5.2

January 24 entry in Kiya's (K) portfolio.

I am going
to Angela's.

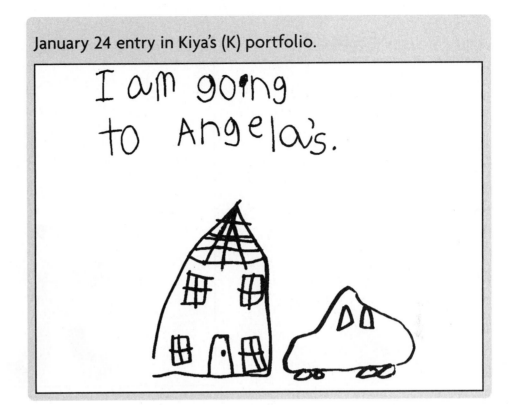

Figure 5.3

March 21 entry in Kiya's (K) portfolio.

Im go ing
To my Grammy
AnD Grampy House
To Slabt my Grammy's
Bir Thday

Figure 5.4

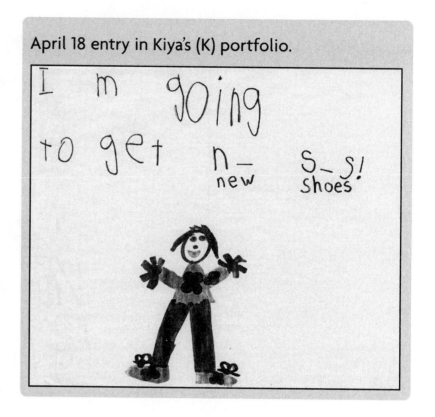

April 18 entry in Kiya's (K) portfolio.

Sample 2: Hannah's Journey

Figure 5.5 September 3 entry in Hannah's (K) portfolio.

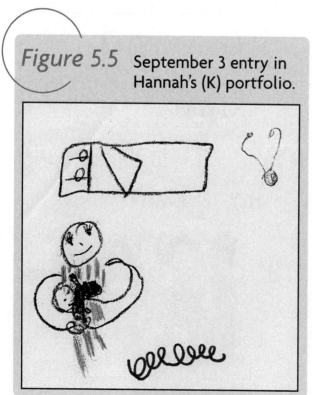

Hannah's very simple portfolio includes just three pieces of writing. Again, though, we can see signs of real growth and change. In Figure 5.5 Hannah creates a sketch of herself holding a baby. It is "labeled" with imitative writing that reads "My Baby Sister." The picture has detail. Both figures have smiling faces, and Hannah's arms embrace her baby sister. Notice the bed above, with covers turned down. Hannah has not yet begun to experiment with letter shapes.

In Figure 5.6 we see a change from October. Here Hannah is writing with letters and making many letter-sound connections in this complete sentence (a big step forward from the simple label in the preceding sample). Notice that although her text goes mostly left to right, she takes the liberty of running up the page when she runs out of room. Her drawings are more detailed than those from her first sample; we see lips, hair ribbons, and frills on the dress she plans to wear for this big event.

Big things have happened in Hannah's writing by April (Figure 5.7). She is writing more than one sentence and including detail—not just a tooth but a "wiggly" tooth. Her text goes left to right on the page, incorporates conventional spacing, displays both capital and

Figure 5.6

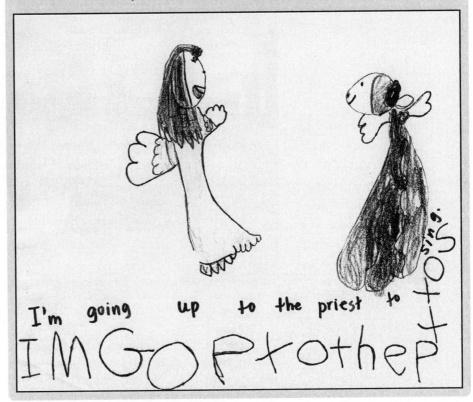

October 23 entry in Hannah's (K) portfolio.

I'm going up to the priest to sing.

IMGOPtothep

lowercase letters, and includes some punctuation. In addition, this text (compare Figure 5.6) includes many sight words plus more difficult words (*tooth*), all spelled correctly. Hannah can now convey her messages to a reader with ease. What a change from late October.

Figure 5.7

April 11 entry in Hannah's (K) portfolio.

I have a tooth in my wiggly mouth!

I like Molly M.

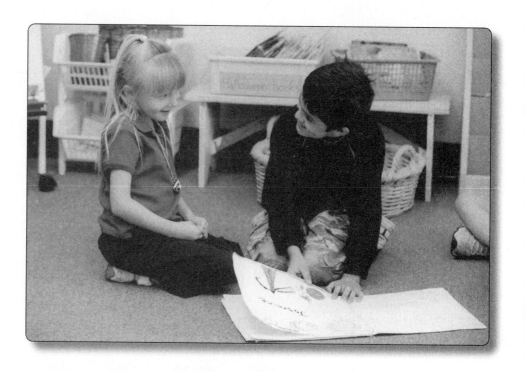

Small as these examples are, I think each clearly shows the value of preserving work samples at various periods in a writer's year and marking those periods with dates. No one example by itself tells us even a fraction of what we learn by putting those samples together and "reading" the story they tell. So, don't set out to do a "portfolio project" or launch yourself on a "portfolio mission," instead, do this:

1. Teach yourself the criteria within each of the six traits so that you know what to look for as you review your students' writing.
2. Teach students the traits so that *they* can see changes in their own writing.
3. Encourage your students to save and date a few pieces throughout the year, adding them to their portfolios/folders/writing collections.
4. Encourage students to comment on the changes they see, orally or in writing.

Suggestion: Just for practice, let your students review Kiya's and Hannah's portfolios and comment on the changes *they* see. Don't worry if they don't mention everything noted in this book. What's important is the practice of looking—a good warm-up for noticing changes in their own writing.

READY FOR REFLECTION?

When are students ready to do some serious reflecting on their writing? Sooner than you might think. Even very young students can notice and comment on things like these:

- ✔ I am using periods now.
- ✔ I am writing real words.
- ✔ You can read things I write.
- ✔ I can write a whole sentence.
- ✔ My picture has a face.
- ✔ I have two pictures, and they tell a story.

✔ In this paper I remembered to use a title.
✔ I have an ending.
✔ I describe things.
✔ My paper has details.

It is the *noticing* that matters, not the length of the reflection. You are simply teaching your students to compare individual pieces of writing and to comment on the changes they see. The more you talk about the six traits of writing, the easier this will be. It is easier to see or hear voice in your writing when you know the word and know what to listen for. It is easier to spot detail if you know what it looks and sounds like.

Michael, a third grader, likes to write mystery stories. He is in a class that has been working on the traits of ideas, organization, voice, and word choice. See if you can spot elements of each trait in his story "The Closet Monster" (Figure 5.8).

Michael's teacher asks her students to reflect on their writing, and to make this task easier, she provides some leading questions. They can, however, write about anything they notice. In Michael's reflection (Figure 5.9), you will hear some echoes of the traits, indicating his growing understanding of what makes writing—his or anyone's—work.

Figure 5.8

"The Closet Monster"

The Closet Monster

Hi, I'm Michael. I'm looking for what I call the closet monster.

I'm looking for the closet monster because last night around midnight I woke up from a rattling sound coming from my closet. I went over to check out what it was. I opened the closet door and nothing was there. I thought to myself it must of just been the wind. When I went back to get into my bed I saw a gigantic shadow move swiftly across my room. Then I was mabey thinking I had someone or something in my room that wasn't supposed to be here, and I had to get out of my room and quick because it was giving me the creeps. I stayed up looking around for whatever was in my room. Just then there was another rattling sound coming from the closet again. I creeped over to the closet and nothing was there. CRASH! My lamp came down on the other side of the room. Right after the lamp came crashing down I caught a glimpse of something scurry under my bed. My knees were trembling as I slowly crept over and nelt down in front. I pulled up the bed skirt and looked undernieth and there was something furry with big, black, round eyes. I jumped back in shock. My heart beat was going 10 times it's normal rate.

To be continued

What was under Michael's bed? Will Michael ever get it out of his room. Tune in next time for The Closet Monster.

Michael (3)

Figure 5.9

Michael's Reflections on His Writing

Something I did particularly well:

I think in this piece of writing I described things particularly well. Like "A gigantic shadow moved swiftly across the room."

If you were to work on this piece to make it better, what could you do?

I would try to yose different kinds of words to start off each sentence.

What did you learn from this writing that you can use in the future?

I learned if you write more description then more people understand your writing.

Notice that in answering the first question, Michael quotes from his paper to support his assertion about good description. This causes him to go back and take another look at his work, a vital step in teaching revision.

Celia (Figure 5.10) shares a brief reflection on a poem she wrote titled "The Blizzard." Notice how Celia's reflection focuses on her thought process and deliberate consideration of detail.

Figure 5.10   **Reflections on "The Blizzard." Celia (3)**

My Blizzard Poem.

Once I was thinking of writing a poem. (I usually made poems.) Whenever I made a poem I would think of a subject and write detals.

Today I thought about a blizzard being my subject I thought about the details

FINAL DRAFT

Name _____ Date _____ Grade _____
Title

and wrote them both scary and exciting. It took me two days and I used two papers. When I was done I was happy and I couldn't wait to share it.

REVISION: FROM ROUGH TO READY

Students tend to define revision in their minds in one of two ways:

1. Fixing the paper (especially the spelling)
2. Doing it over

Neither is particularly attractive, and how surprising is that? For a beginning writer, completing a piece of writing can feel huge, like completing a pyramid. Who wants to hear, "Would you mind *fixing* that pyramid? It's got a little tilt to the left." From the student writer's perspective, you (mean old reviser of pyramids) have two semireasonable choices:

1. Live with the writing as it is (clearly the more sane choice), or
2. I will write something *else* for you since you're so picky.

How do we deal with this? First, it is helpful to show students what revision really is. It is not fixing, correcting, or (necessarily) redoing—especially not at the primary level. Revision becomes more complex as writers get older and grow more skilled, but this is because both their writing and their thinking have grown more complex. Revision *is* thinking—and rethinking or reconsidering, if you will. If you have ever made a comment and wished you had said something else, left something unsaid, or used a different tone of voice, you have grasped the basic nature of revision.

To understand how revision works in writing, try this simple exercise. Think of someone (it can be a pet if you like—it does not have to be a person) that you see daily or at least very often. Right now, without thinking too hard about it, draw a one-minute sketch of this person (or pet). Go ahead—put the book down and *do* it. Then come back.

Got your sketch? Now, set your sketch aside for a moment and try to get a picture of the person (or pet) in your mind. Really try to bring his or her face and body into focus. Think of color, size, expression, attitude—little things like hair, hands, feet, way of standing or moving, eyes. Now look at your sketch again. Is there *anything*, any small detail, you missed? Anything you could add that would give more character or life to your sketch? Add it now. Do not take more than another minute.

Guess what. You have just revised your sketch. Revision is sometimes—often—as simple as adding or changing *one small detail*. Adding is an early (and significant) form of revision. Later, students also may choose to move things around. Later still, they may be ready to delete information or unneeded words. This is the most difficult stage of revision, and even adult writers fight it, so we should not be surprised if second graders are not wearing out pencils deleting extra words. Remember, a piece of writing is a hard thing to "build." You do not tear it apart without a lot of thought (and often some pain).

Revision Strategies

1. Make a Decision

Carol Avery teaches us that revision does not begin with marking up a paper, it begins with making choices. "Demonstrate returning to writing by reading what was written earlier, and ask children to reread their pieces from the previous day and decide whether to make changes, continue the piece, or start a new piece" (2002, p. 73). Read this one more time just to get the full impact: Make changes, continue, or start fresh. *This* is where it begins. Putting the writer in control over what will happen with the writing. Not every piece needs to go through the whole writing process. Some can be tossed aside. Some are unfinished, and the writer can pick up where he or she left off. Others call for change. Just knowing these three choices gives writers an enormous head start on revision.

■ 2. Learning Through Modeling

Model the sketching activity you just tried, and ask your students to do it with you. Share your sketches, and talk about the kinds of changes you made, big or small. Refer to your changes as *revision*.

Explain that revision is something you *get* to do as a writer—not something you *have* to do. It is a privilege, a right. Like deciding how you want your own room to look. Most of us do not like it when we are told that we have to keep our own personal space a certain way. We need to feel protective of our writing, too. This is not to say that writers should not be open to suggestions; however, there is a vast difference between suggestions and commands.

Ask students to help you with your revision of a simple piece. They can do this by offering suggestions or asking questions. Start with a very simple piece of writing, such as this one:

I was driving home. I saw a deer. It was very pretty.

Ask for questions: "What would you like to know?" Perhaps your students will have questions like these:

✔ Where was the deer?
✔ What was it doing?
✔ What did it look like (besides pretty)?
✔ What were you thinking when you saw it?

If they don't, though, you can encourage them: "Wouldn't you like to know...?" Then, answer the questions by writing a more complete version on the overhead projector, or chalkboard, as shown in Figure 5.11.

As you create a revision like this, talk through the changes you are making as you make them; for example, "I think I'll put these first two sentences into one longer sentence. I'm not sure I need to say the deer was pretty because most people know that. When I saw it, it was running along a fence, so I'll put that in. It had two very small fawns and was trying to cross the road with cars coming both ways. The poor

Figure 5.11

Revision of "The Deer."

A Close Call
~~The Deer~~

When I was driving home, I saw a deer. It was ~~very pretty.~~ running along a fence near the highway. It had two tiny fawns, and was trying to cross the road with cars coming both ways. The poor deer looked terrified! Luckily, it was fast, and darted across with both fawns. They were all safe.

deer looked terrified! Lucky for the deer, it was fast. It darted across with both fawns. They were all safe. Do I need to add anything else? [PAUSE] Maybe I should change the title. It was a very close call, so that might make a better title than 'The Deer.' Let's read it once from the beginning so that you can tell me what you think of my revision."

This revision is fairly long. You do not need to make yours this long—or even close. It's up to you. This revision adds a lot of detail. Another might focus on a specific feature, such as sentence beginnings.

When you model revision, several things are key:

1. Use as many suggestions from your students as possible.
2. Add your own ideas to theirs—being quite spontaneous as you do.
3. Do not try to do too much at once.
4. Talk as you go.
5. Read your revised paper aloud so that they can hear it as well as see it.
6. Let them know that you like having a *chance* to revise.
7. Do *not* expect their revisions to look like yours.

The preceding example may look complex, but it is actually quite simple even for very young students because you are doing all the writing. They are coaching you, watching, listening, and thinking. You can make your modeling even smaller, though, so that they see how manageable revision can be in some cases.

You might write—

I saw a bird.

Then you could say, "The word *bird* is a little vague. The bird was a hawk, so let me revise my sentence:

hawk
I saw a ^ ~~bird~~.

Let me revise just a little more by adding a detail about color:

golden hawk
I saw a ^ ~~bird~~.

Tiny examples put revision within reach, even for beginners.

■ 3. Delete and Insert (୯ and ^)

To make this strategy work well, you need to make one simple but very *important* suggestion to your young writers: *Double-space all work.* Do this as you model, too. It leaves room for revision. There is nothing like having room. *Big* margins are also a help. Trust me—if your students fill a page with text, side to side, top to bottom, they will not want to make changes and insertions. Would you?

Encourage use of the caret (^) to show the addition of a word, phrase, or whole sentence. Use the delete mark (୯) to show deletion of the same. Expect to see more insertions than deletions. It is difficult to get rid of language we have put to paper, much like tossing out favorite knickknacks. You encourage this if you model it and invite your students to egg you on a bit. As you begin your revision on the overhead, ask them, "What do you think? Shall I be timid or bold with my revision today?" What do you suppose they will say?

When children do not make progress as writers, we must look to ourselves. Giving our students layers and layers of modeling along with massive amounts of time to practice their writing are the hallmarks of successful writing programs.

—Laura Benson
(2002, p. 20)

4. The Beauty of the Arrow (→)

Some revisers are ready to move text around or to make larger insertions. There is nothing like the ever-helpful arrow for making this kind of change. Second grader Nina is quite an advanced reviser, using arrows together with crossouts to show changes in her draft (Figure 5.12). Notice how she replaces her comment about rolling in the leaves with the more relevant statement about feeling happy to get spring clothes. This deserves a response: "Nina, you made a great revision here, sticking with your topic and adding an important detail about your feelings. I like this revision."

5. Good Old Cut-and-Paste

My friend and colleague Tommy Thomason, author and professor of journalism at Texas Christian University, spends numerous days working with students in his wife Debby's kindergarten classroom. "It keeps me grounded," he likes to

Figure 5.12

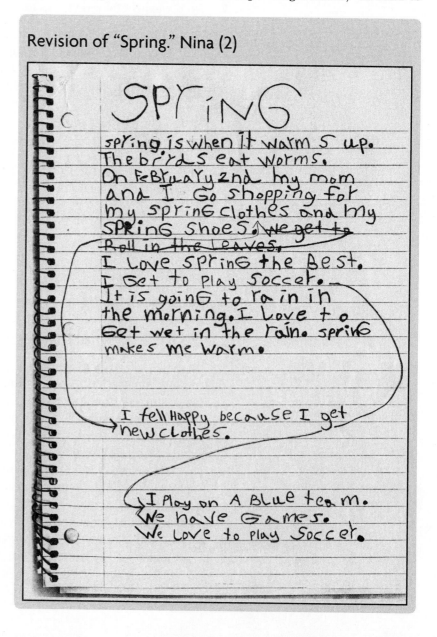

Revision of "Spring." Nina (2)

say. Like so many of us, Tommy has discovered that the problems writers face remain largely the same, from kindergarten right through college—and beyond. He is not surprised to see Debby's kindergarten students struggling with the same difficulties that plague professionals:

✔ How do I get started?
✔ What do I say first?
✔ How do I think up a title?

And so on. One advantage of experience is that we all learn little shortcuts that make writing easier. Among them is the much beloved cut-and-paste method of adding information. When Tommy stopped by for a two-minute conference with Sergio, the young writer announced, "I'm done. Wanna read it?" Tommy said, "I like to hear the voice of the writer—why don't you read it for me?" Sergio's first version (which we have edited) went something like this:

My Trip to the Zoo

Last Saturday I went to the zoo. My aunt took me. We went to mcDonald's first. I liked all the animals, especially the tiger. He was cool. I liked all the animals very, very much. I had a lot of fun. Later, we went home and I went to bed.

Tommy asked if the tiger was the white tiger at the zoo, knowing there wasn't one. "Naw," Sergio replied. "It was just a regular tiger." As he went on to describe it, Tommy pulled out his three- by five-inch notepad (the one he always carries with him when working with students) and made some notes. Sergio added four new sentences about the tiger (a lot for a writer so young).

When Tommy read them back to Sergio, he got a clear picture of the tiger in his head. "Know what they call that?" Tommy asked. "It's called good writing. When an author describes something so you can see it in your head, that's detail. Would you like to add these new sentences to your paper?"

Here's where Sergio hesitated.

So Tommy asked, "What if you could put those four sentences in your paper without rewriting? You know, a professional author wouldn't recopy this when you could put it together with a shortcut."

Sergio eagerly agreed. A few snips with the scissors, some tape and staples later, Sergio had a much expanded, highly detailed story to share with his friend Juan, who also loves tigers. He also had a new sense of revision.

6. Save It for Next Time

One of my all-time favorite suggestions comes from my friend Barry Lane, who says, "Understand that one method of revision is to write a new paper" (1993, p. 212). Sometimes this is the very best approach of all. Students can learn from the writing they are doing, the writing you are modeling, and the literature you share, and next time around, they can take another crack at it. Just the way you do when you say the wrong thing.

When Should Students Begin to Revise?

How old should students be when they begin to revise? This is an excellent question, one to which there is not, I think, any simple answer—but some common sense can guide us. It makes little sense, in my mind, for very young writers (or early beginners of any age) to extensively revise what is strenuously difficult to put on paper in the first place. At this age, revision, in the sense of "lessons learned," as noted in strategy 6, can be for next time. *Next time you write*, perhaps you will think to

✔ Add a detail.
✔ Create a picture to go with your paper.
✔ Think of a title.

You can (and should), of course, model revision for students of any age. Just because you model it does not mean you expect them to *do* everything you do. You are simply showing them conceptually what revision is all about. And it is often realistic even for young writers to add one detail to art *or* text or change one word.

Meanwhile, encourage young writers to develop some real fluency—comfort with the idea of writing. This (much more than revision) is the key goal for early beginners. Chances are that you do not remember learning to write. Very likely, however, you recall learning to drive (at least those portions you didn't mentally block out). Remember how important it was just to log miles, to get the feel of the car? If you are like most of us, you certainly did not do everything correctly at first. You forgot to signal a turn, or you signaled a quarter mile in advance. You cornered too sharply or too slowly. Or maybe, like me, you attempted to accelerate during your driving test without first turning on the engine (it is incredible how many points they knock off for *that*). Then one day it all feels comfortable—not *easy*, necessarily—but natural.

Writing needs to feel like this. When a writer stops thinking about how to hold the pencil and begins to think, "What do I really want to say next?" or "Does this make sense?" or "What is my main idea?", then the time has come for revision. How old is the student at this point? Probably mid-third grade, on average. As with anything, however, many students will be ready in grade 1 and others not until late grade 3 or even grade 4. The following behaviors can be a guide to revision readiness: The writer

✔ Is focusing more on the content of the piece than on the logistics of making letters or words.
✔ Has a main idea or message in mind.
✔ Is able to read his or her text aloud and ask, "Does this make sense? Is this what I want to say?"
✔ Has a conceptual understanding of revision as "rethinking," not as "fixing."
✔ Has seen the revision process modeled by the teacher and has in his or her mind some possibilities and strategies for revision.

Some Examples

I chose the examples shown here because I think they show clearly what early revision *can* look like. Although the changes in detail, voice, and fluency are significant, they do not affect the entire piece. Beginning writers do not (usually) discard whole pages of text, start over, rework the same topic, or set out to do extensive research because the detail is weak. Big changes like these are for later—when extensive practice has made writers not only faster and more fluent but also more confident about playing with their writing. Beginning drivers usually do not go from Maine to California. They go around the block. Yet, in these early revisions we see the promise of deeper thinking and larger changes to come.

Emma wrote a complex and moving story about her dog Lizzie (Figure 5.13). Notice the flow; this story surges along from event to event, heading toward its inevitable conclusion. I especially like the confrontation with Mom, who cannot help looking at her feet; this extraordinary role reversal between persistent but understanding Emma and her poor guilt-ridden mother creates restrained but powerful voice. Despite the strength of this piece, Emma was not totally happy. She felt the ending might be a little abrupt. It is a *good* ending, but yes, it is a little sudden. We learn the truth and *bam*, say good-bye. After

Figure 5.13

Original Draft of "Lizzie"

Good-bye, Lizzie

By Emma (3)

Lizzie was a wonderful dog. She would skip around everywhere. She was always so energetic.

Once I got so tired from playing with her I plopped down on the couch; she leaped up onto me and started licking my face until I woke up. She was always funny.

One day a few days after we got her, my granddad reached down to pet her and she bit him! And one day Lizzie bit me, that's why we had to get so many chew toys.

Another day when I came back from school I started looking for Lizzie.

I asked my mom, "Where is Lizzie?"

"Let's just say she isn't in the house with us any longer," she answered mysteriously.

My throat burned with sadness as I asked, "Did she die?"

My mom looked at her feet and said, "No."

"Then where is she? Did she run away? She could have been killed if she did."

My mom stared at her feet with wide eyes and said, "No, of course not."

"Then what happened?" I wailed.

"I put Lizzie in a shelter," she said.

"Oh."

I knew why she had. We had a baby cousin staying at our house and we did not want her to get bitten. I know it was definitely the absolute best thing to do, but I still miss Lizzie SO much.

I love Lizzie.

Good-bye, Lizzie.

Figure 5.14 Revised Conclusion to "Lizzie"

Good-bye, Lizzie
By Emma (3)
Lizzie was a wonderful dog. . . .

. . . . I knew why she had. We had a baby cousin staying at our house and we did not want her to get bitten. I know it was definitely the absolute best thing to do, but I still miss Lizzie SO much.

I looked at Lizzie's picture. Over the top of the picture I saw Lizzie's bed. I put the picture down. Suddenly I saw a movement in the corner of my eye. I smiled because what I was seeing was priceless, one last time I was seeing the friendship of a girl and a dog that no one could EVER separate even if we were apart.

some reflection, Emma chose to end her piece a little differently (Figure 5.14), celebrating a last memory captured in a photograph. She changed nothing in the original up to the line "I still miss Lizzie SO much," but note her stunning revision, printed in italics. All Emma's revision energy focused on her ending, the part that most needed her attention.

Olivia, a second grader, has created a descriptive piece about a snowy day. Her rough draft (Figure 5.15) focuses primarily on capturing the details from her brain-storming chart. By the time she creates her revision (Figure 5.16), she has used both her picture and reading aloud to help her rework sentence patterns, making the result smooth and lyrical. Read both versions aloud to hear the subtle but important differences.

Figure 5.15

Rough draft. Olivia (2)

Name Olivia   Spring snow   Picturing Writing   page # 3/21/02

Snow	Sky	Trees	Sounds
smooth	Celeste blue	Swaying	Chirping birds
feathery	blue		
pillow	glittery blue		
softly	ocean blue		

As the feathery snow fals from the sky and chirping birds sing a song. As the orange sky trns to celeste blue. as the trees swaying and my Dags run all arould. as there feet push the soft pillow like snow In to the gronud. I say My Day was the best.

Figure 5.16

Revised draft. Olivia (2)

As the feathery snow falls and chirping birds sing a song, the orange sky turns to celeste blue. The trees sway and my dogs are running all around in my snowy yard. Their feet push the soft pillow-like snow into the ground. I say this day was the best.

Cameron's piece (Figure 5.17), interestingly titled "Ago" (versus "*Long Ago*"), began as a four-line poem, the fourth line reading "My land," rather than "The new world." Cameron changed this line and added three more, for reasons he explains himself. Asking students to "think through" their revisions, whether orally or in writing, is a simple but powerful way of teaching the concept.

■ Inside Revision

If we remember what revision really is, it helps us be more patient about seeing it appear in children's writing. If we think of it as correcting or improving, then all our attention goes to the draft, not to the writer. When we remind ourselves that revision is "reseeing," or revisiting in our minds, then our attention goes to the writer's thinking. It is important to teach revision not so much because we want dazzling writing (although this is often the bonus) but because we want young writers who can *think*. Writers who revise learn the invaluable habit of thinking

Figure 5.17   **Cameron's Poem with Revision Comment.**

> I Revised the ending because I thought my land would be to Small and adding more detail would make it Sound more like a Poem.

Ago
By Cameron (3)

Ago we crossed the land,
Seeking our goal
The treasure of a lifetime
The new world
This journey is the journey of us all
This is Ago.

like readers. They learn to ask whether a message is likely to make sense to a reader, whether an image is clear, whether the voice is appealing or appropriate, or whether a phrase is sparkly and fresh or worn from overuse. Even very young writers can get in the habit of taking one more look, reading their writing aloud and "just thinking about it for a minute," *even if no actual changes result*. This thinking lays a valuable foundation for the time when they are ready to put the new vision on paper.

We in turn can be realistic in our expectations, remembering that revision grows through stages. Here is a quick overview to help guide *general* expectations (add to this list based on your own observations):

✔ *Beginners* (about kindergarten to early grade 1): Adding pieces and parts—such as missing words, a name, a title, a cover page, a small detail.

✔ *Experienced revisers* (at or about grades 1 and 2): Making substantive changes—such as selecting a new title from several possibilities, changing a sentence beginning, adding sensory detail, or making a sentence show more than tell.

✔ *Advanced revisers* (at or about grades 2 and 3): Basing revision on the whole piece, not only individual parts—reworking the lead (or ending) once the piece is written, making sure the piece focuses on one story or theme, not two, changing a word or phrase, making sure details connect to a main idea, strengthening voice, combining sentences to heighten fluency.

Suggest, model, encourage, and applaud revision. Do not demand it from beginning writers. Opportunity for revision results in creative, spontaneous new thinking. Required revision often produces mechanical, forced change that has little to do with what the writer thinks or feels. Which do you want from your students?

PUBLISHING

I once had a student ask me why "Being done" did not appear in my circular model of *The Writing Process*. "It's the best part," he said, and I thought of how often in my life I would have agreed with him (and not just about writing either). For a sense of closure, being done is tough to beat. Many students love publishing, in part, I think, because they equate it with "being done." They enjoy seeing their work in print and are pleased to have their efforts celebrated, whether publishing involves book making or simply posting work on a wall.

Publishing can take several different forms with children, and so it is important to clarify expectations in your mind before you set out to "publish." Some teachers publish only clean copy, and so everything must go through a final editing stage prior to publishing. This final editing usually involves the writer but is done with the help of the teacher or assistant or sometimes a parent or older student. Some teachers publish the draft just as the writer created it but may include a "book language" translation so that it will be readable to others as well as (in the future) to the author.

Published "books" may be done on regular eight-and-a-half by eleven-inch sheets of paper or on other paper selected by the child. They may or may not be formally bound, may or may not be illustrated. Many teachers like to include features that model the way published books are put together by publishing houses:

✔ A title page
✔ Credits for author, illustrator, and editor(s)
✔ A dedication page
✔ An "About the Author" section
✔ Illustrations or other graphics
✔ A cover

Including these features encourages student writers to notice the same things in the books they read and also parallels the way real-world publishing usually occurs.

As for editing, publishing houses are sticklers about it, and so I think it is realistic to ask for a higher standard of "correctness," plus attention to layout, when books are being prepared for this more formal sharing. Think of it this way: There is *functional editing*, which makes copy readable and reasonably correct for purposes of sharing it with a general audience. Then there is *editing for publication*, which makes copy as clean and correct as we can get it and also includes significant attention to layout—making pictures (or other graphics) and text look appealing on the page. The *way* in which you choose to publish depends on two things:

1. The ages and readiness of your students
2. The frequency with which you publish students' writing

Clearly, younger students are less ready to take on many publishing and final editing tasks for themselves, and so if you want correct copy for their published work, you just volunteered for extensive editorial duty (unless you are lucky enough to work with assistants or parents who are exceptionally good sports). Older students can do much of their own editing before the final run-through, and if they have access to word processors, they can even experiment with layout and use of different fonts (which most love). Spell-check programs and other computer aids make both revision and editing much easier and faster, but student writers of all ages and abilities still need some help, and almost all need a second pair of experienced eyes for final editing (just as we ourselves do).

Keeping It Manageable

The following are my suggestions for keeping the publishing process manageable:

1. *Do not publish everything.* In our zeal to include every stage of the writing process, we sometimes have felt compelled to publish everything our students write. This puts pressure on them as well as on us or else diminishes the significance of publishing by rendering it little more than a stapling together process. Neither extreme is desirable. Encourage the author to select a few pieces for formal publication, and give those the extra needed attention publication warrants.

2. *Review selections together to see what needs to be done.* Keep in mind the capabilities of the author. For a very young child, creating a cover and adding a name as author of the piece may be quite sufficient. For older writers, a more thorough revision/editing step may be quite appropriate, with help from an assigned, experienced editor (who may be you). Pictures also can be added, and if the document is word-processed, of course, the author may wish to choose an appropriate font—or fonts.

3. *Edit to suit the writer's skill level.* With older, more experienced writers, it may be quite sufficient to produce a final, edited draft. If the corrections are small and few, there is little to gain by saving the rough draft unless, of course, the author chooses to do so. On the other hand, for very young or less experienced writers, it may be helpful to do a "book language" translation that accompanies the original text. In this case, you may choose to save both copies so that the writer can read the text (from the book print version) but also track his or her own growth by looking at the original. This honors the child's own writing while still preserving it in a form that allows everyone to read it later.

4. *Ask for students' permission to include editorial changes.* In real-world publishing, an editor sends the author edited copies and then galleys (corrected versions of the original) to review. This gives the author a chance to look over the changes—and to learn from them. Why not give students this same opportunity? Most young writers are eager to know the "right way" of doing things—yet it can be discouraging to be handed a paper full of corrections that you must then deal with yourself. On the other hand, when you act as the student's editor and then ask for his or her approval of your changes, you put the power right back in the writer's hands while still showing him or her what needs to be done differently. A simple initial on a Post-It gives the author's OK to proceed with corrections as marked.

5. *Give credit where credit is due.* Indicate the author, illustrator (who may be the same person), and editor(s), including yourself if you participate in this way. It is fair, and it parallels the world of publishing. For example, you might have a front page for a book that reads:

   Written by Judy Becker
   Illustrated by Stefano Marco
   Edited by Judy Becker and Mrs. Kent

6. *Think beyond stories.* So many of the books we publish are stories. Some children prefer to write expository pieces, how-to pieces, recipes, travel brochures, alphabet books, or any number of other things. Encourage this. A classroom with variety inspires everyone.

7. *Include basic features, such as a title page, cover, dedication, and so on.* Such features enrich the publishing process and make the book more fun to put together.

8. *Give reluctant or challenged writers a way of participating.* Some writers are intimidated by the thought of a whole sentence, much less a whole book. What about them? They can do several things:

   ✔ Serve as an illustrator for another author
   ✔ Write a wordless picture book
   ✔ Dictate a book
   ✔ Dictate a review of another author's book (which can then serve as a back cover)

   Note: You may wish to encourage second-language students to work with native English speakers on a bilingual book and then share it aloud. Everyone benefits!

9. *Give highly skilled writers a challenge.* More skilled writers also can help in the publication process. They may write slightly longer books, even chapter books. They also may serve as editorial assistants (with credit) to other authors in the class. They may wish to be

   ✔ Copy editors, helping with corrections or layout
   ✔ Content editors, offering suggestions on detail, organization, or voice

Some Examples

The following samples show just a few of the many formats published works can take. "The Trip to Africa" (Figure 5.18), written by second grader Amity May, is exceptionally complete, with a wonderful sense of story. It is the tale of a clever kangaroo, Tom (formerly known as Sally, presumably in another story), who escapes a gruesome fate by tricking a crafty leopard. The text is thoroughly illustrated with expressive characters. This extended text surely lends itself to book binding and also could include credits for writing, illustrating, and editing—all of which go to Amity May herself (with the exception of a little help in editing).

"The Chocolate Mouse" (Figure 5.19) is written and illustrated (the cover) by Nikki. She had some help with the editing, and as we can see, she dictated her "About the Author" page to the teacher, who wrote it in the third person. This delightful story of a chocolate-loving mouse who turns into a chocolate "artifact" has rich detail and word choice. It also has strong moments of fluency

Figure 5.18

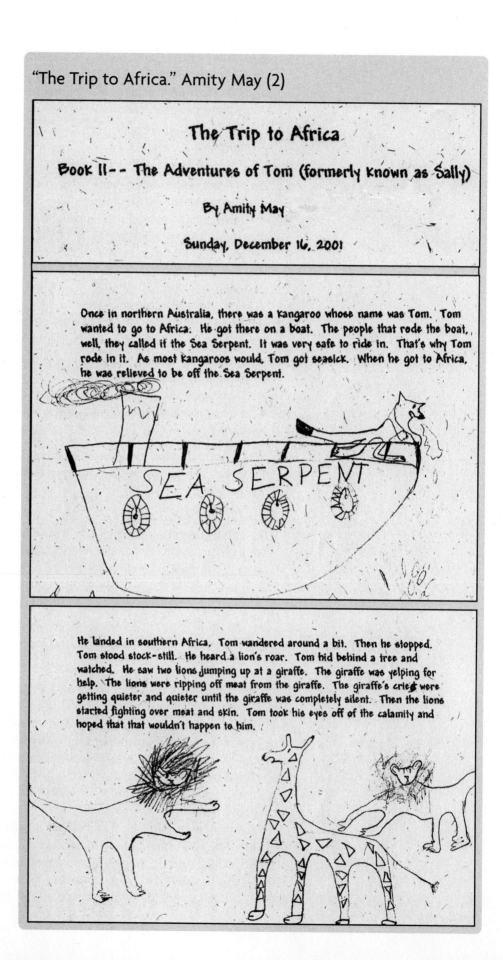

"The Trip to Africa." Amity May (2)

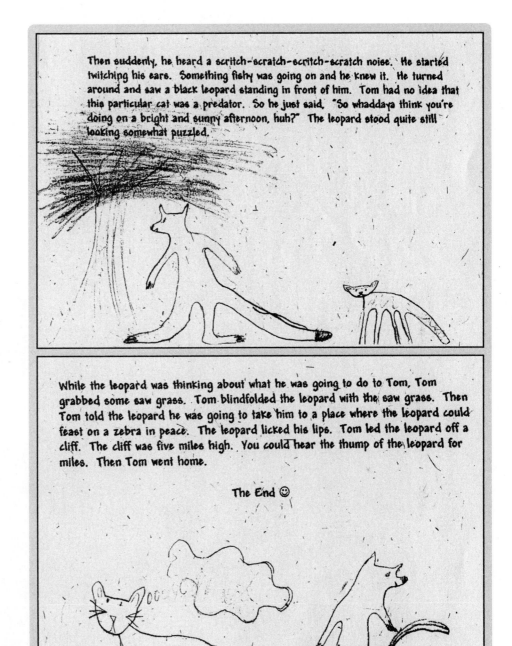

Then suddenly, he heard a scritch-scratch-scritch-scratch noise. He started twitching his ears. Something fishy was going on and he knew it. He turned around and saw a black leopard standing in front of him. Tom had no idea that this particular cat was a predator. So he just said, "So whaddaya think you're doing on a bright and sunny afternoon, huh?" The leopard stood quite still looking somewhat puzzled.

While the leopard was thinking about what he was going to do to Tom, Tom grabbed some saw grass. Tom blindfolded the leopard with the saw grass. Then Tom told the leopard he was going to take him to a place where the leopard could feast on a zebra in peace. The leopard licked his lips. Tom led the leopard off a cliff. The cliff was five miles high. You could hear the thump of the leopard for miles. Then Tom went home.

The End ☺

combined with numerous sentences that begin with "The doctor. . . ." Changing this one feature would bring out even more voice.

Kindergartner Jacque has created a very extended text for her age, "The Horse and the Duck" (Figure 5.20), the tale of an unusual friendship. Each page is illustrated, adding to the detail. Notice the very satisfying ending. Jacque also has included a cover page (word-processed) and a good bit of detail on her dictated author's page, which helps us to know her better. Her teacher includes a book version to help Jacque read her text in years to come.

Figure 5.19 "The Chocolate Mouse." Nikki (3)

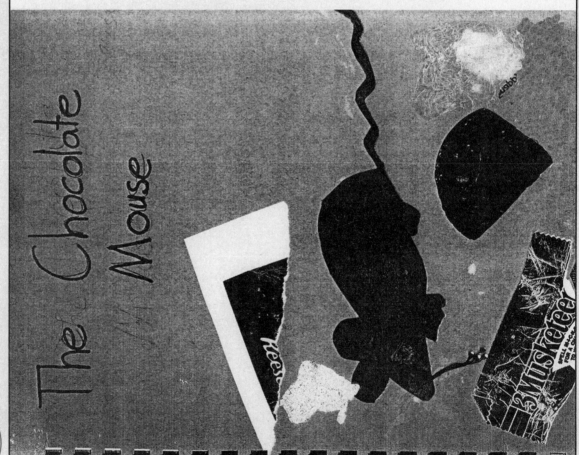

The Chocolate Mouse

Dedication

This book is dedicated to my Grandpa because he loves chocolate and I love him!

Once upon a time there was a greedy mouse named Scamper. Now, Scamper's favorite thing in the whole galaxy was CHOCOLATE! If he was with one of his friends and found a Cheerio, jelly bean, cheeseball, or especially CHOCOLATE, he would never share it.

One day Scamper woke up to find that he had brown spots and gold rings all over his back! He just thought it was mud until . . . . he tried to wash it off! It wouldn't come off! All of his friends asked why he was so dirty, but he didn't reply because he didn't know himself.

The next morning Scamper found more spots all over his back. He was very puzzled! He called the doctor and asked what was wrong with him, but the doctor wasn't much help. All he did was think, put his hand on his chin, scratch his head, and think some more. Very puzzled, he said he didn't know either. He said he would come back tomorrow and bring his doctor bag.

The doctor came over the next morning to find the mouse still in bed. The doctor took out his stethescope to listen to the mouse's heart beat, but there was none! The doctor was shocked and almost fainted.

The doctor put Scamper in the Museum so everyone could see him. He had to put Scamper in a very cool room so he wouldn't melt.

Inside the room was a sign that said, PLEASE DO NOT TOUCH!" And then, in smaller print it said, "Please do not eat either!" Mice and rats from around the world came to see this food artifact.

The doctor got a lot of cheese for bringing Scamper in the museum. The doctor thought about the mouse, whispered and said, "I didn't even know his name."

By Nikki
Grade 3

About the Author

Nikki lives at home with her mother, father, and little brother. She gives credit for her writing success to her mother, who also loves to write. Someday, Nikki thinks she may want to be a teacher! Nikki plans on writing more stories this year. Her friends (and her teacher) can't wait to read them.

Figure 5.20 "The Horse and the Duck" *(6 pages)*. Jacque (K)

Lah is a hrss.
Lah has a frunb
nuambshrah.

Shrh is a duk. Lah
anb shrh phih e toqhtl
tha phih e th ag.

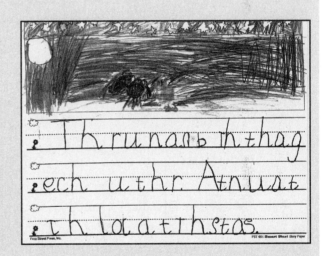

Th runaob h thag
ech uthr. At nuat
ih loa eth stas.

The Horse and The Duck

By Jacque

Lucy is a horse. Lucy has a friend named Sarah. Sarah is a duck. Lucy and Sarah play together. They play tag. They run and they tag each other. At night they look at the stars.

About This Author

My name is Jacque and I am 6 years old. My parents are Joe and Diane. I have 2 sisters. They are Sharon and Katie.

My home is in Texas. I was born on November 24, 1994, in Odessa, Texas. I lived in Greenwood for the first 3 years of my life.

My kindergarten teacher is Mrs. Stobaugh. My favorite thing about school is center time. When I grow up, I want to be a teacher.

My favorite food is pepperoni pizza. My favorite book is <u>Barbie Went Camping</u>. I like to swing and to play soccer.

I made up my book on my own.

Brady, a first grader, has written an all-about book on insects (Figure 5.21). This organizational pattern is a favorite with young writers and gives them an opportunity to show off what they know or what they have observed. As you will notice, Brady's word choice is running well ahead of his conventional spelling, which is as it should be. In case you need a "book copy," here it is: *Insects, by Brady. Ladybugs pretend to die. Ants get food for their colony. Bees get nectar for their hive. Butterflies can be beautiful. Dragonflies can be big. Some can be small. Praying mantises can be camouflaged on the leaves.*

One Last Thought

While publication is very gratifying, it is not the only reward for writing or writing well. Sometimes, as that student writer pointed out, just finishing is enough. Take your cue from students, however. If they feel the urge to publish fairly often, and if they are willing to give a little extra attention to a published piece (which is appropriate, I think), then go for it. If you (or they) are feeling some

Figure 5.21 "Insects." Brady (1)

publishing burnout, do not feel guilty if you cut back. It is the writing itself that is most important, not the publishing. Other ways to celebrate writing include the following:

✔ Taking it home to be shared with parents (or others)
✔ Sharing in a response group
✔ Sharing writing from an author's chair
✔ Simply posting a writing sample for display, even if it isn't formally published
✔ Adding a piece to a personal portfolio
✔ Hosting a writer's workshop evening, which parents or other community members can attend to hear children read their work and to celebrate your writing community

FINAL REFLECTIONS

We so often think of reflections as being linked to specific pieces of writing. It is interesting, though, to ask student writers themselves what writers need. Figure 5.22 shows Andrew's answer. Notice how many different things he identifies: reflecting time, an idea, pictures to prompt your thinking—and of course, good books. As it turns out, this is an insightful reflection, as the work of other student writers shows. In Figure 5.23, kindergartner Katie shows off the thinking she has done about her older sister Sharon, who seems to have a talent for music as well as a love of butterflies and flowers. How much detail and voice she manages to work into her art. In Figure 5.24, Justin begins by painting a hammerhead shark,

Figure 5.22

"What Does a Writer Need?"

You need thinking time and an idea before you start writing. It helps to know what you want to write about before you start. Jonathan shows me some of his pictures he's drawn and that gives me a good idea. It helps if you've read some good books, too.

By Andrew (2)

Figure 5.23

Portrait of Her Sister. Katie (K)

Figure 5.24

"Hammerhead Shark." Justin (2)

The gray hammerhead shark is cruising in the cold Pacific Ocean. The seaweed is swishing against hammerhead and he is very hungry. He is swimming between rocks and seaweed to look for crabs.

Figure 5.25

A Teacher's Favorite Among Mia's Poems.

Daffodils
By Mia (3)
Yellow
laughing
saying
spring is coming.
Be happy.
They dance in the wind.
Providing shelter for bugs
and
newborn kids.
They give
color
scent
and
light.

Figure 5.26

Mia's Choice for Poetry Night.

Spring
By Mia (3)
As the sun shines
I fetch the blue sky
My sister fetches the river
We put it in a bowl
And mix it up.
We come up with
the Earth,
the trees,
the rocks,
everything . . .
except
for you.

and the picture itself causes him to explode with ideas: the swishing of the seaweed, the hunger of the shark, and the hunt for crabs (notice the small one hiding on the ocean floor).

Reflection had a profound effect on Mia's selection of a piece to share for Poetry Night. This was to be a special form of publishing, in which Mia and other students would share their writing with parents at a celebration sponsored by Barnes & Noble Booksellers. At the last minute, Mia announced to her teacher that after thinking it over, she had changed her mind about the piece she would present. "Oh, but what about 'Daffodils' [See Figure 5.25]?" the teacher asked, unable to mask her disappointment. "That's a beautiful poem—I thought you were going to read it for Poetry Night."

"No, I want this one," Mia insisted (referring to Figure 5.26). Upon reading the poem, the teacher agreed Mia had made the right choice. I agree. What is even more impressive than the beauty of Mia's writing—which is mature, elegant, visually simple and stunning—is her unwavering belief in her own judgment. Writers who trust themselves have achieved an important level of success. Congratulations, Mia.

CHAPTER 5 IN A NUTSHELL

- Growth is about change. Revising and publishing are ways of making significant changes in writing. Reflecting and keeping portfolios are ways of noticing, recording, and documenting change.

- Portfolios do not need to be huge and complex. They serve us—and our students—better if they are simple and manageable.

- The primary purpose of a portfolio is to encourage the student writer to look carefully within his or her writing and to notice signs of change, growth, and risk taking. In this way, the student traces the journey of himself or herself as a writer.

- Reflection (which often plays a significant role in completing a portfolio) is mostly about noticing change. Students who know the six traits of writing have specific elements to look for as they reflect on who they are, where they began as writers, and what they can do now.

- Revision is not about fixing but about *rethinking* a piece of writing.

- Students are ready for revision when they begin to think of their writing conceptually (Does this make sense?)

rather than thinking at a more elementary level of how to form letters or spell simple words.

- Revision begins with a simple choice: Continue the writing, change the writing, or move on to a new piece?

- Revision skills progress in stages from simply adding an element (a word, name or title) to making substantive changes to rethinking the whole piece (leads, endings, details, voice).

- Publishing occurs in many forms, from simply sharing a piece publicly to making a book.

- Formally published books require a slightly higher level of attention to detail and editing and may include such elements as a title page, credit page (for author, editor, and illustrator), dedication page, cover, illustrations, and so on.

- Publishing every piece of writing is not essential—and can even lead to burnout for both teacher and students. Many teachers find it makes sense to publish carefully selected pieces so that publishing remains special and celebrational.

- One of the most important lessons to be learned through revision or publishing is the art of reflection.

STUDY GROUP: INTERACTIVE QUESTIONS AND ACTIVITIES

1. **Activity.** Do you keep a portfolio of your own? If so, you might reflect on how you choose pieces to keep, and share that with your group. If you do not, this is a good time to begin! Choose one piece of writing right now and let that be a beginning. Continue to add to your portfolio for the next six to eight months. Then write a reflection on who you have become as a writer and teacher. Ideas for things to include: personal writing of any kind, reviews or covers from favorite books, letters (to you or from you), any commendations or reviews of your work, journal articles you have contributed—or that have influenced your work or thinking, samples of art, lists of favorite artists or writers, favorite films or books, snapshots of you with your students, samples of student work you feel reflects your influence—anything that is *you.*

2. **Activity and discussion.** This chapter recommends keeping portfolios or at least folders of student work so that assessment can be based on a body of work rather than on individual samples. With your study group,

make two lists: (1) the advantages of this practice and (2) roadblocks to this practice. Discuss the two lists and see how close that discussion takes you to a decision about whether portfolios are right for you.

3. **Activity and discussion.** Write a definition of "revision" that is realistic for the grade level you teach. Share your definitions and discuss them along with these questions:
    - ✔ Are primary writers capable of revision?
    - ✔ Can too much emphasis on revision too soon discourage students' enthusiasm for writing?
    - ✔ Is it useful for us as teachers to model revision—even if we do not ask it of our students?

4. **Activity and discussion.** Look again at Figures 5.12 through 5.17. If you are currently teaching, would you say that your students

    ___ revise more than this.

    ___ revise at about this level.

    ___ revise less than this.

    Discuss this with your study group.

5. **Activity and discussion.** With your study group, brainstorm a list of all the things you do, as a writer, when you revise. Which strategies are most helpful to you? Which could you model for your students? Which could you ask them to try? How would you characterize yourself as a reviser of your own writing?

___ I am a timid reviser. I hardly change a thing.

___ I'm a procrastinator. I put it off for as long as possible!

___ I plunge right in, hacking, moving, tacking on inserts—the works!

___ I *love* revision; it's the best part of the whole process of writing!

___ I hate revision. I can barely stand to re-read my own work!

With your group, discuss how your feelings about revision might influence your teaching.

6. **Activity and discussion.** What if you had a colleague who said, "No student writing should be published—or even hung on a wall—unless it is editorially flawless." How would you respond? Write a short note to this person expressing your feelings. Be prepared to share your response in your study group.

7. **Discussion.** In your view, is publication a vital step in the writing process? Is it necessary for every child to publish in some form, in some way? Discuss this with your group.

8. **Activity.** Assume that publishing, in some form, will be part of your classroom instruction in writing. List three (or more) things you could do to ensure that every student could participate, in some way, in this process:

1.

2.

3.

4.

5.

9. **Activity and discussion.** Have you ever had a book or article or poem published? If so, consider sharing that experience with your students. Even if you have not, make a list—with your group—of ways that classroom publishing can (or should) parallel the real world of publishing.

SOURCES CITED

Avery, Carol. 2002. *And with a Light Touch.* 2d ed. Portsmouth, NH: Heinemann.

Benson, Laura. "A Writer's Bill of Rights." In *Colorado Reading Council Journal*, Vol. 13 (Spring 2002), pp. 22–23.

Brodie, Deborah. 1997. *Writing Changes Everything.* New York: St. Martin's Press.

Cramer, Ronald C. 2001. *Creative Power: The Nature and Nurture of Children's Writing.* New York: Addison Wesley Longman.

Graves, Donald, and Virginia Stuart. 1985. *Write from the Start.* New York: Signet Books.

Lane, Barry. 1993. *After THE END.* Portsmouth, NH: Heinemann.

Olshansky, Beth. 2006. *Picturing Writing: Fostering Literacy Through Art and Image-Making Within the Writing Process.* Durham, NH: University of New Hampshire. Web site: *ww.picturingwriting.org*

Routman, Regie. 2001. *Conversations.* Portsmouth, NH: Heinemann.

Figures 5.15, 5.16, and 5.24 from this chapter were inspired by the work of Beth Olshansky.

Modeling

Write in front of your students. Think aloud as you write. If you have never done this before, close your classroom door and risk it. It will get easier, I promise. When you write, you see firsthand the struggles, doubts, thoughts, and processes that writers (including your students) go through. When you write, you share not only your composing process but part of who you are and what matters to you. Your own insights as a writer will make you a more effective teacher of writing.

—Regie Routman
Conversations (2000, p. 232)

Your philosophy of writing is determined by your personal experience as a writer. That means your own life as a writer is ultimately reflected in your classroom. And it means if you want to change your classroom, you begin by changing you.

—Tommy Thomason
More than a Writing Teacher (1993, p. 2)

If you had asked me, when I was a child, to give a generic description of a teacher, I would have said someone who wears nice clothes, stands in front of the room next to the chalkboard, and knows everything.

—Nancie Slonim Aronie
Writing from the Heart (1998, p. 171)

Nothing, absolutely *nothing* you will ever do as a teacher will be more powerful than modeling writing in front of your students. It is vital to the successful teaching of writing, yet it does not happen nearly as often as it should. Do you recall ever seeing one of your own teachers write? Not lesson plans or comments on students' writing—but actual original writing? A story perhaps or a poem? If you do, you are among the lucky few, and odds are good it made a strong impression on you. I never saw a single teacher write, kindergarten through college. My teachers, for the most part, fit Nancie Slonim Aronie's (1998) vision: powerful figures dispensing knowledge from the front of the room.

Talking *about* writing only takes you so far as a writer, though. How much I would have loved to see exactly how to

✔ Choose a topic
✔ Take notes
✔ Write a good lead (or ending)
✔ Get rid of unneeded detail
✔ Come up with a good title
✔ Plan my organization
✔ Put more voice into writing

My colleague, Jeff Hicks, who is one of my writing and teaching heroes, always writes with and in front of his students. "I really would not ask my students to write anything I don't attempt myself," he says. "And besides, it's hard enough to get across to kids what it is you really want from them—when they see it, it's like some kind of magical door opens in their heads, and they say, 'Oh, *I* get it.'"

Briefly, these are the advantages to modeling:

1. To learn more about writing process *as writers*
2. To show students the writing process *as it is happening*
3. To show students how to deal with writing challenges and problems
4. To give students an opportunity to be coaches for us

In this chapter we'll consider each of these individually.

BENEFIT 1: LEARNING ABOUT WRITING PROCESS AS A WRITER

Most of us have read books about the writing process. Most of us have been to seminars and workshops. We have *taught* writing as a process, allowing time for prewriting and drafting and encouraging students to revise and edit their work. None of these activities, however, provides the in-depth understanding of the writing process that comes with being writers ourselves. Doing it. Prewriting, drafting, sharing, revising, editing—all of it.

It does not really help me as a teacher, for instance, to know the importance of choosing personally significant topics if I do not select some topics that are personally significant to me—and then write about them. It does not help me to know about the power of revision if I do not revise my own work, hoping an audience will like it, hoping it will be published. Here are just a few of the many things I have learned by modeling writing:

Think back. When was the last time you observed another person write? You would be unusual if you could recall more than two incidents in a lifetime.

—Donald H. Graves
Writers (1984, p. 43)

✔ On some days the writing does not come easily. Fortunately, you don't die of it.
✔ A lot of what I write is not as creative as things students come up with.
✔ The lead and the conclusion are usually the most difficult parts of any piece of writing.
✔ Titles are tough, too.
✔ Not all prewriting techniques work for everyone. I like the look of webbing, for instance, and I even like doing it—but I do not use webs when I write. Lists (mostly lists of questions) are more helpful to me.
✔ Conversation and drafting (just starting in) are my most effective prewriting tools.

✔ Reading certain writers influences my personal voice.

✔ The problems I experience most often as a writer are making the introduction too long, repeating words or phrases I've "fallen in love with" while writing, and going down a side road because I think of an anecdote I want to share even though it does not fit.

✔ You really should listen to the audience, even when you do not like what they say.

✔ Student writers usually do not want to criticize; they want to *help*—and they are good at it.

✔ You can tell more about an audience's reaction from how they sit and how they look at you than from what they say.

✔ Organization is, overall, my weakest trait.

✔ I like sentence fragments and will always use them in my writing, even though some people do not like them.

✔ I like to start sentences with *And*—even though *lots* of people do not like this either.

✔ *-able* and *-ible* words are very hard for me to spell.

✔ A lot of my writing takes a humorous turn, even when it does not start out that way.

✔ Almost nothing I write follows my original plan (including this book).

✔ Almost *all* my writing takes longer than I thought it would (including this book).

✔ Leaving writing alone for a *long* time (two or three weeks or more) improves revision 1000 percent.

If you write with/for your students, you probably have made discoveries very much like these. It occurs to me that without the benefit of writing my way through the writing process, I might very well feel comfortable teaching writing by

✔ Assigning topics that are uninteresting or that make little or no sense to students

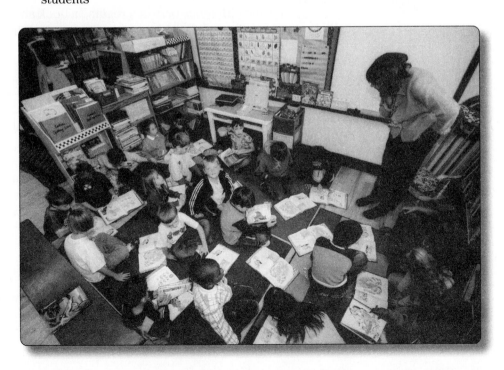

✔ Expecting students' writing to match some preconceived picture in my mind—without showing them what that might look like

✔ Having very unrealistic expectations regarding the amount of time it takes to write

✔ Having unrealistic expectations about the quality of student performance

✔ Imagining that students will do more than neaten up or fix spelling when they revise

✔ Imagining that titles and leads will offer genuine hints of what follows

✔ Assuming that students know such skills as cutting extra wording, making word choice more interesting, or listening for voice in their writing—when, in truth, it never occurs to them to do these things

The assumptions we make as teachers of writing often come from our sheer lack of experience as writers. Would you want to take a driver's test or be taught to drive by someone who had never been behind the wheel but had only observed other drivers?

BENEFIT 2: SHOWING STUDENTS THE PROCESS IN ACTION

We can show students all the writing process wheels we want, and we can even walk them through the steps of the writing process one by one, but nothing is as powerful as an actual demonstration of how it looks *while it is happening*. Remember, we have two kinds of models to show students:

✔ The *products* (samples of writing from other students, professional writers, or ourselves)

✔ The *process* (writing unfolding before their eyes)

It is the difference between reading a book about birthing and watching a birth. Of course, they are related experiences, but they are *not* the same.

BENEFIT 3: SHOWING STUDENTS HOW TO DEAL WITH SPECIFIC WRITING CHALLENGES AND PROBLEMS

There are two kinds of challenges you can deal with: (1) the struggles and decisions all writers face and (2) the challenges your own writers are facing. Sometimes these are the same—but not always.

Challenges All Writers Face

All writers, regardless of experience or ability, must do certain things—choose a topic, for instance, or write a lead, or decide when a piece is finished. You will

> *As teachers of writing, we can't just write. We have to write so that we come to understand what it is that we are teaching. We have to push ourselves to notice and to understand what's happening when we write, so that our writing becomes a powerful curriculum tool for our teaching.*
>
> **—Katie Wood Ray**
>
> *What You Know by Heart* (2002, p. 6)

not have time or opportunity to model every single writer's decision, but the more of them you deal with, the more opportunities your writers have to grow.

Take finding good topics, for instance. In *Conversations*, Regie Routman tells of a second-year teacher, Neal Robinson, who said two things helped his students write well: seeing models of other students' work and "finding a topic that mattered to them" (2000, p. 221). Our students' lives are filled with possible writing topics—but often they do not know it.

Remember our discussion of small topics in Chapter 4? One third grader wrote a charming piece about how to keep goldfish healthy. She had just purchased a goldfish and so had some expertise. A second grader who had been to a tea party wrote a how-to piece on proper behavior and etiquette at a formal gathering. Other small topics that have worked well for students include

✔ A letter to the tooth fairy about a lost
✔ A story of a stray cat who stayed—and became a fine mom to four kittens
✔ Spending winter break having an appendectomy
✔ Having a grandfather as a best friend
✔ Moving—when your friends can't come with you
✔ Being afraid to get on an airplane

Writing is about passion. When our students moan, "I have nothing to write about," it's time to ask them, "Ever feel afraid? Anxious? Annoyed? Downright furious? So bored you thought you'd fall asleep? So worried that you *couldn't* sleep? So happy you wanted to scream out loud? Well, what made you feel that way? Those are the moments to write about." Teaching writing well requires knowing our students and knowing what touches their lives. We can also show them that their favorite topics and ours are sometimes the same.

Most students love papers about teachers. Like many of them, I have had several teachers who were worthy of whole books. My kindergarten teacher was a character. She loved to dress up and refused to sit on the floor although we had to take naps on that same floor—which was disturbing to me, so I never let my head touch the ground. I recall her saying that she was "sick and tired of putting our boots on for us and blowing our snotty little noses." I also recall that she wore very high heels and very red lipstick and smelled better than most of us. She liked schedules and hustled us off to the restroom right on time, whether we had to go or not. Since I virtually never had to go, this was a recurring problem for me in school (my nickname was "the camel"), especially since we had to "perform" before we could leave the restroom. I spent hours there.

My first and second grade teachers were saints and so are less interesting to write about. My third grade teacher was a wanna-be model who fell back on teaching because she had such trouble getting her weight under 100 pounds (we all found this fascinating and loved to see what she would bring for lunch—nothing, usually). She was so busy job hunting that she had a hard time focusing on us.

Then, in fourth grade, all hell broke loose. Of course, at the time, I wasn't thinking, "It's good I'm living this nightmare because later I'll have this to write about." It took years of writing for me to begin thinking that way. When I tell students even a tiny detail about this blood-thirsty woman, who left sobbing and screaming children in her wake, they are eager for me to write something about her—and so I do. This is an ideal time for me to model two important things: how to write a good lead and how to choose a good title. I start with the lead and write several on the overhead, reading them aloud as I go. "I want you to help me choose the one you think is best," I tell them. Usually I will write at least one lead that I think is pretty weak, one that nearly everyone will recognize as weak. Often it is a lead that students are likely to use in their own writing—only it sounds worse when I write it. Here are some possibilities:

✔ "If I had known how bad fourth grade would be, I might have failed on purpose and stayed in third."
✔ "Have you ever known someone who was so mean that you could hardly stand to be around her? I have. In this paper I will tell you about her."
✔ "My fourth grade teacher was not the nicest person in the whole world. In this paper, I will explain why."
✔ "We could feel her coming before we heard her."

I make the print big, and I read each lead aloud. Then we talk about which one(s) they like best and why—and which ones do not work as well and why. Sometimes they have other suggestions. I record those, too. One lesson we learn together is that the first lead you think of may not be the best one. *As you write*, you often think of a better way of saying something.

Wait a second, though. What about those kids who are only writing single sentences. Is this lesson lost on them? Absolutely not! Think of what they are internalizing about leads. They are listening, advising, and making choices, even if they are not writing leads themselves—yet.

Next, we work on titles. I begin to brainstorm, and invite them to join in. I start with the teacher's name, because that is perhaps the most obvious title:

Miss Sader

Or, I tell students, I could describe her:

The Meanest Teacher on Earth

Or I could describe the experience:

Grade Four—A Tough Year

"What about her shoes?" someone will say. "I like the part where you feel her coming. Use that!"

Good suggestion. From their coaching comes my working title:

Battle Shoes

I mark it W T for *working title* and put a circle around it. This means, I explain, that after I finish my story, I will come back to the title to see if it still works. It is almost always easier—and better—to write the title last.

As I work on the draft about Miss Sader, and then later when I revise it, I can model many other things, including

✔ Putting voice into writing
✔ Choosing lively words

✔ Making sentences more fluent
✔ And so on

As I model these things, I will not write badly on purpose, but I will not create the all-time flat-out best writing I can either. I want to make room for students to offer suggestions. For example, in describing Miss Sader, I might start out something like this (notice that this copy is double-spaced):

> We could feel her coming before we heard her. Were her shoes hitting the floor that hard, or did we have the shakes? She had a HUGE voice and used it like a weapon, especially when she caught us doing something wrong.

I will ask students what questions they have, and I will use their questions to add details—and usually, voice.

Note: It is not necessary to write voluminous drafts to model writing. Little snippets work fine. Do a bit now and more later. In this way, you do not feel overwhelmed, and neither do your students.

Challenges Your Writers Face

✔ *"I have a student who will only write one sentence."*
✔ *"So many of my students start all their sentences the same way."*
✔ *"My students put no details in their writing!"*

Any of these sound familiar? You can probably make a list of your own. Do that. List everything you can think of that is a problem for your students—it may be a problem for *most* writers. The answer, in almost every case, is model the problem and its solution. Model it more than once if you need to. Attack it in slightly different ways, with different pieces of writing. Be creative. Here is just one example. You can easily invent more. The more you model, the more natural it feels, and the more relaxed you will be about tackling virtually any problem right on the spot.

Modeling Example 1: The Single-Sentence Syndrome

For some students, a single full sentence is a lot. So instead of despairing because there isn't more, we should be celebrating. It is also true, however, that some students will persist in writing just one sentence for a long, long time, as if they feel no special need to stretch. You need to model this problem, then its solution. Start by writing a single sentence on an overhead or chart paper:

I visited Alaska.

Now say something like this: "Sometimes, when you write one sentence, it's enough. But this time, for this topic, I think I need more details. Help me out. What would you like to know?" Use students' questions to create a detail or two that will expand your writing:

Last summer, I visited Alaska. There were so many mountains you could never count them. I ate Alaska king crab for the first time. It was cooked on an open campfire, and we dipped it in melted butter.

Now ask students, "What is different about this piece? How many sentences did I write? Let's count—OK, four. Did I give you a lot more information? What do you picture? Which piece of writing do you like better? *This* one? Me, too. You know what? When I read your writing, I like details, too. I need details to understand what you are trying to tell me. Let's try this: After you write, ask yourself if you could add just *one or two* more details. That might take three or four sentences."

Do not be afraid to give students your honest reader response to writing. You aren't throwing personal darts at anyone. You are just stating your preferences. Be opinionated. If you dislike violence in writing, say so. If you are bored hearing the same words over and over, tell them. And when you encounter a poor piece of writing (not one of your student's pieces, but a published work of any kind), bring it in and read it to them. Don't hem and haw. Say exactly what you think. You can be gentle and be honest at the same time, especially when you are showing them, time and again, that you find reasons to revise your *own* writing, too.

■ A Question

If you model ways to solve writing problems, won't your students quickly catch on to the fact you are writing badly (or not as well as you could, anyhow) on purpose? Yes—of course, but as long as you do not overdo it, it's fine. What you are modeling in this instance is how to *solve* a problem, not how to create one. You need to demonstrate the problem to do this. Writer/teacher Carol Avery talks about modeling haphazard placement of periods (just slamming them into the text in any old place), and her students laughingly telling her the text makes no sense that way. They know what she is up to. "I play the inexperienced writer, allowing them to be the experts who teach me," she explains (2002, p. 115).

In other instances, you *will* be doing your best. In that case, you are modeling for another purpose: to show your thinking in action. Do not be surprised, though, if you encounter an unanticipated problem or two on the way!

Modeling Example 2: All Sentences Begin the Same Way

This is a problem even for experienced writers simply because so many of us think in patterns. Luckily, it is one of the easier problems to solve, often requiring little more than awareness of the patterning. Always, problems are easier to see *in someone else's work*, so again, begin by modeling the problem, just as if it were *your problem*, using text something like this:

> My cat is pretty. My cat sleeps a lot. My cat is cuddly and loveable. My cat's name is Suki.

Already I have modeled two important things about revision: big print and ample space for new ideas and details. Call it "thinking space."

Now, since I am not literally standing in front of you (my reader) right now but sitting here at my desk, writing this book, I cannot show you how the revision unfolds as I would like to—as I would show it to students—inch by inch. But I will show you what the finished revision looks like (see Figure 6.1) and replicate as best I can what I might say as I was actually doing the revising:

How it looks:

Figure 6.1

My Cat Suki

What I say as I create this revision:
Let me read my piece aloud to you first—so I can hear it, too: *My cat is pretty. My cat sleeps a lot. My cat is cuddly and loveable. My cat's name is Suki.* Do you notice anything about my sentences? [Sometimes students will notice that all the sentences begin the same way, and sometimes they will not hear this unless I point it out—which I may do by reading it again.] I really don't want every sentence to begin with the words "My cat." Since her name is Suki, what could I say instead of *My cat is pretty?* Yes—*My cat Suki is pretty.* I can insert her name with a little arrow editors call a caret. Now here I am with another *My cat* sentence: *My cat sleeps a lot.* I wonder if there's another way to say that. [I will give students a chance to make suggestions.] Whenever I overslept, my mom used to call me a "sleepyhead," and I think that could be a good nickname for Suki. Let me show you a way to combine those two sentences: *My cat Suki is pretty*—comma—*but she's a real sleepyhead*—and since I am saying this with emphasis, let me end with an exclamation mark. Good. Here comes another *My cat* sentence: *My cat is cuddly and loveable.* I'm going to cross out the words *My cat* and think of what else I could say. [Again, I invite suggestions.] Yes, I could use her name, *Suki*—or I could say *She* since Suki is a girl. So—*She is cuddly and loveable.* Good. Now, let's look at my last sentence: *My cat's name is Suki.* Do I still need this sentence? No, because I already told my reader the cat's name—right in the first sentence. So, let's delete it. This writing looks messy now, and you know what? That's what I like. The messier it looks, the more *thinking* I am doing. Revising is thinking.

Modeling Example 3: Missing Details

This is a little different from the single sentence problem. With this kind of writing, a writer often presents us with multiple sentences, but they are a little bare bones. Since I present the writing as mine, it is really up to me to provide details, but I will ask students for suggestions, and then we own the writing together. I might begin with an example like this one:

> We went to the lake.
>
> We had fun.
>
> We rode on a boat.

I have left even more space for this activity because it is likely I will have more to write, based on my own ideas and students' suggestions. Notice also that this piece also has the "all sentences sound alike" problem, but much of this will likely be resolved as we add detail. If it is not, we can always work on that when we finish. When you model, keep the focus on one kind of problem at a time or you may create some confusion with beginning writers. What I like about this modeling activity is that it challenges students to do the thinking part of the writing, but I am doing the actual recording, so they do not need to really *write* anything. Because they think, watch, speak, listen, and suggest, though, this modeling is highly interactive, and still entirely do-able for writers of any age. Again, I will show you what the finished revision (see Figure 6.2) looks like and then talk you through my thinking process:

How it looks:

Figure 6.2 Lake Chinook

My family
^ ~~We~~ went to ~~the~~ lake Chinook.
  camped, hiked around the lake, and
We ^ ~~had fun~~ roasted marshmallows.
On our last day,   speed
^ We rode on a ^ boat,
  and I got quite ^ a sunburn!
                              ↳Those were delicious!

What I say as I create this revision:

Let me read my piece aloud to you first—so I can hear it, too: *We went to the lake. We had fun. We rode on a boat.* Can you picture me at the lake? [Some students will say they can. If they do, I ask if they have any questions about my trip to the lake. This usually triggers a good discussion.] I really want my reader to see this clearly. I need to add enough detail so my reader feels as if *he or she* took a trip to the lake, too. Let's start with the first sentence: *We went to the lake.* Who is "We" do you suppose? Right, my family. I think I should say that, don't you? And maybe I should tell the reader the name of the lake. So I'm going to write *My family went to Lake Chinook.* Better. The next sentence says *We had fun.* That doesn't tell the reader very much! What kinds of things do people do to have fun at the lake? [Students will have many ideas here, of which I will take those that best apply and show them what a difference specifics make.] All right—we have many good ideas to use. I am going to redraft my sentence to incorporate some of those ideas: *We camped, hiked around the lake, and roasted marshmallows.* Wow, what a difference! Can you picture us doing those things? Your ideas created wonderful images. You are thinking like writers. You are telling the reader so much more than I did in the sentence *We had fun.* Now let's tackle the last sentence: *We rode on a boat.* Do you think I should tell the reader when we did that? I'm going to add that detail, using a caret: *On our last day, we rode a boat.* What else do you want to know? [Students will have questions here, and I will use their questions to guide my final revision.] It was a speed boat, and what happened was that I got sunburned. So, here's my final sentence: *On our last day, we rode a speedboat, and I got quite a sunburn!* Now, let's read the *whole* revision we did together and ask ourselves how much stronger it is.

OTHER THINGS TO MODEL

Here are some other things you could model for students:

✔ Planning and developing a novel
✔ Researching the definitive autobiography
✔ Writing a screenplay for a video documentary

I'm *kidding.* See—that's the thing. Often, the reason we do not model is that we are thinking too big. Let's get real. Here are some down-to-earth, manageable things that you can readily model:

✔ Writing on just one side of the paper
✔ Putting spaces between words
✔ Writing on every other line to allow room for revision or editing
✔ Leaving margins
✔ Adding a title
✔ Changing the title when you finish—if it no longer fits
✔ Using an apostrophe
✔ Reading the lead aloud to see if it's a grabber
✔ Reading the ending aloud to see if the piece feels and sounds finished
✔ Combining two short, choppy sentences to make one smooth one
✔ Getting rid of too many *ands*
✔ Changing a sentence beginning or two to avoid monotony
✔ Including some sensory details—sounds, smells—to enrich the text
✔ Putting in dialogue to add spice
✔ Keeping tense (past, present) consistent
✔ Saying something directly and honestly to boost voice
✔ Making sure questions end in question marks
✔ Using quotation marks to show speech
✔ Deciding where a new paragraph should begin
✔ Taking out a bit of information that is not needed
✔ Working effectively with a writing partner (writing buddy)
✔ Reading a whole piece aloud to see if it is clear and fluent

Small is good. Small is do-able.

SECRETS TO GOOD MODELING

1. Base *some* modeling activities on specific problems you see in your students' writing. This makes your examples relevant.
2. Base other modeling activities on personal pieces *you* are actually working on at the time. Let students see you struggle with work that is important to you.
3. Model *everything*—from choosing a title to editing spelling or wrapping text from line to line. No writer's question is too small for modeling.
4. Talk as you go, but do not make the mistake of thinking that explaining alone *is* modeling. It isn't. Explaining helps make modeling clear, but you must *write*, revise, insert, and delete. Cross out, draw arrows, cut and paste.

5. Illustrate problems and struggles, but let students know that you are purposely modeling a problem many writers have. If you pretend that you do not know where a sentence ends, they will not believe you.
6. Get over being self-conscious. Modeling is good teaching. You are showing process, not award-winning text. Relax. Have fun.
7. Read the text aloud as you go. Remember that some of your students may not be able to read what you write with ease, so read it for them (sometimes more than once), talking about changes as you make them.
8. Keep examples short and focused.
9. Give students choices: Which is the best lead? Which is the best title? How should I end this?
10. Keep it interactive. Constantly ask for students' opinions.
11. Use shortcuts: carets, arrows, deletion marks, tape-on additions, or anything else that saves you time and effort.
12. Do not forget to read the final version aloud.

CHAPTER 6 IN A NUTSHELL

- Modeling is among the most powerful strategies we have for promoting strong writing among our students.
- Through modeling, students learn how to solve writers' problems and see thinking (writing and revising) in action.
- No part of the writing process is too small to model, from coming up with an idea to knowing where periods or commas go.
- Base some modeling on personally important work so that your students can see you making decisions that affect your own writing.
- Base some modeling on problems your students are having so that they can learn strategies of immediate help to them.

STUDY GROUP: INTERACTIVE QUESTIONS AND ACTIVITIES

1. **Activity and discussion.** What specific problems have you noticed in your own students' writing? Make a list of up to five. Choose two and create a modeling activity by following these steps:
   - ✔ Write a very brief passage that shows the problem plainly (e.g., repeated words).
   - ✔ Print the passage in very large letters with double-plus spacing on chart paper (or print to an overhead transparency if you use an overhead).
   - ✔ Practice reading the passage aloud and rehearse the questions you will ask students to encourage them to coach you.
   - ✔ Present your passage to students, and solicit their help.
   - ✔ Revise the passage with students acting as coaches.
   - ✔ Read your revised version, asking students to compare it to the original.

   Discuss your results with members in your study group. What went really well? What did students learn from your modeling activity? What things might you do differently next time?

2. **Activity.** Present one modeling activity to your group, as a way of rehearsing what you will do with students. Use their coaching and suggestions to improve your modeling strategies.

3. **Activity.** With your group, brainstorm a list of common problems that might make good subjects for modeling. Remember to keep in mind that lessons should be short

and focused! *How to come up with a good title* is a wonderful example of something you can model manageably. *How to write a story* is too big for one modeling lesson; you can divide it into multiple lessons, though, and model one of them or all of them: *How to come up with an idea, How to create dialogue for a character, How to describe a character, How to create a good setting, How to write a good ending,* and so on.

4. **Activity.** Are you working on a personal piece of writing right now? If so, you have a perfect opportunity to model something that is authentic. Consider a real problem you are encountering with your writing and ask for your students' help. Even if you think the problem is over their heads, you may be surprised by how much their response helps you in making decisions.

5. **Discussion.** Review the list of suggestions for successful modeling. Then, with your colleagues, brainstorm a list of things that get in the way of good modeling. Be honest!

SOURCES CITED

Aronie, Nancy Slonim. 1998. *Writing from the Heart: Tapping the Power of Your Inner Voice.* New York: Hyperion.

Avery, Carol. 2002. *And with a Light Touch,* 2d ed. Portsmouth, NH: Heinemann.

Graves, Donald H. 1984. *Writers: Teachers and Children at Work.* Portsmouth, NH: Heinemann.

Ray, Katie Wood. 2002. *What You Know by Heart.* Portsmouth, NH: Heinemann.

Routman, Regie. 2000. *Conversations.* Portsmouth, NH: Heinemann.

Thomason, Tommy. 1993. *More than a Writing Teacher.* Commerce, TX: Bridge Press.

Thomason, Tommy, and Carol York. 2000. *Write on Target: Preparing Young Writers to Succeed on State Writing Achievement Tests.* Norwood, MA: Christopher-Gordon Publishers.

Loving Books

We also have to be readers to write well. To write using rich, compelling language, we need to hear and read rich, compelling literature. Only a love of reading will promote an understanding and awareness of imagery, tone, voice, and other nuances of good writing. There is no shortcut.

—Regie Routman
Conversations (2000, p. 221)

When we first start trying to teach ourselves to read like teachers of writing, we often struggle because we've never really looked at texts this way. . . . We have to move forward and trust that once we train our eyes to look at how texts are written (in addition to what they're about), it will get easier and easier, and before long it will start to snowball. We'll know more about how to write well than we'll ever need.

—Katie Wood Ray
What You Know By Heart (2002, p. 109)

We need to be seen laughing over books, being unable to put books down, gasping over horror stories, and sighing over love stories—anything, in fact, that helps our students to realize that there is some reward, that there are many rewards, to be had from the act of reading.

—Mem Fox
Radical Reflections (1993, p. 63)

INTRODUCTION

If you love reading to your students—and what teacher does not?, you already have in your hands one of the most powerful ways to teach writing, and to show the traits of good writing in action. Everything we have talked about—good details, enticing leads, voice, word choice, fluency—is right there, waiting, within the world of books. In this chapter, I'll review some of my favorites and suggest some ways to connect them to writing. You do NOT need to use these very books. The ones you already know and love will do nicely. I simply include this *very* short list to give you a sense of how I use literature to

> *All children need literature. Children who are authors need it even more.*
>
> **—Donald H. Graves**
> *Writing* (1984, p. 67)

> *We believe that all there is to know about how to write well is found in well-written texts.*
>
> **—Katie Wood Ray with**
> **—Lisa B. Cleaveland**
> *About the Authors* (2004, p. 16)

make connections to writing traits. To do this, you must look at authors *as writers*, modelers of good writing. So much of reading aloud is done just for the sake of plot—not that that is an unworthy reason. We all want to know what happens next. Sometimes, though, we forget to appreciate writers' skill in touching our imaginations and shaping our thinking. Some books, you know, sing with voice. Some are rich with detail—or the fluency is so smooth you want to hear the phrasing again and again. Some books present us with new words, or words used in ways we'd never thought of. So when you say to a child, "Listen to this passage—don't you love the sound of it?" you are teaching writing *through reading* by sharing the writer's craft. And this enriches your reading time together. (For additional ideas, see my book *Books, Lessons, Ideas for Teaching the Six Traits*, 2001, Wilmington, MA: Great Source Education Group, Inc).

The following are some of my favorite books for sharing and for modeling good writing. They are listed alphabetically by author under the trait where I feel the connection is strongest, but clearly, *any* book can be used to illustrate any trait.

Books for Teaching IDEAS

Baylor, Byrd. 1974. *Everybody Needs a Rock*. New York: Simon & Schuster.

Summary

In this lyrical, visually beautiful book, Byrd Baylor celebrates the joy of simple things—such as finding a rock that is special. What makes it special? That is something each person must decide, but she gives us wonderful guidelines for finding just the right rock, and knowing how special it is.

Writing Connections

> *We must immerse our students in outstanding literature every day, help them notice how the author has dealt with the topic, genre, organization, setting, mood, word choice, sentence construction, more.*
>
> **—Regie Routman**
> *Conversations* (2000, p. 221)

✔ After reading the book, ask students to hunt for their own special rocks. Write descriptions that help students tune in to the details. Be sure they look, touch, smell—and reflect before writing.

✔ Make a rock display, featuring poems, descriptions, or stories based on the rocks your students find.

✔ Ask students to imagine what it would be like if a rock could speak. What things has it seen in its "life" on earth? Where has it been? What would the rock write if it could tell its own history of sights, experiences, and travels?

Collard, Sneed B. III. 2002. *Beaks!* Watertown, MA: Charlesbridge.

Summary

Sneed Collard is one of our finest nonfiction writers for young people. His books are filled with voice and precise word choice. In this inviting, highly readable text, he shows how birds eat, survive, and hunt using their beaks.

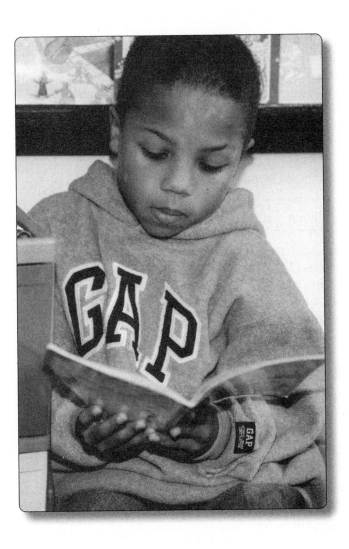

Writing Connections

✔ Point out the differences between the large-print main ideas and small-print details. Then, copy Collard's format in some writing you and your class do. Create a main idea (on any topic) in large print. Then, in smaller print, add details.

✔ Notice the striking illustrations by Robin Brickman. They're not only beautifully done, but informative as well, adding meaning to the written text.

✔ Point out Collard's very focused approach: He does not try to tell "all about birds," but focuses on one detail: *beaks!* This kind of focus, you can tell students, makes big writing small and manageable.

 Emberley, Ed. 1992. *Go Away, Big Green Monster!* New York: Little, Brown and Company.

Summary

If you pictured a big green monster in your mind, what might he look like? Ed Emberley shows us, step by step, how to construct him, from his "two big yellow eyes" right up to his "sharp white teeth." Luckily, as soon as the monster is fully assembled, he retreats—one feature at a time. And he doesn't get to come back until we say so! Young students will love this simple text with see-through pages that allow readers to make the monster come and go at will.

Writing Connections

✔ Read the book slowly without showing the illustrations to students. Let them sketch and color (or paint) their own monsters, listening to Emberley's descriptions. Then, compare Ed Emberley's monster with theirs. Which one is funniest? Spookiest? Craziest?

✔ Invite students to make up their own stories about the monster who appeared—then disappeared!

✔ Have students create their own step-by-step come-and-go books for other subjects: a growing plant, for example; a storm approaching from the distance; the sun rising and setting—or your own idea. Students can illustrate their own books or trade text and have partners try the illustrations.

 Heide, Florence Parry. 2000. *Some Things Are Scary*. Cambridge, MA: Candlewick Press.

Summary

Pulitzer Prize–winning cartoonist Jules Feiffer lends his considerable talent to this honest and often funny exploration of the little things in life that frighten us all. This is not a book of horrors. Instead, it is a whirlwind review of the many small encounters with fear and trauma we all face daily—things like forgetting where you parked the car, watching as you get a bad haircut, holding onto the wrong person's hand, and so on. Florence Parry Heide says of herself, "What scared me as a child was that I'd never learn how to be a real live grown-up—and the fact is, I never did find out how it goes."

Writing Connections

✔ Make a list—with your students—of little things in life you all find scary. Be sure to add your own fears to this list. *Keep it light, though.*

✔ Create a class book of "things that are scary." Each person can add a page, using text, illustrations, or both.

✔ Talk about the pictures in this text. What kind of "voice" do they suggest? What kind of person draws pictures like these?

✔ Any one of the possibilities Florence Parry Heide suggests could be the focus of an essay or story. Ask students, if they are ready for this kind of extension, to take one example from the book and write a longer piece, using personal experience to fill in details.

Jenkins, Steve. 2005. *Actual Size.* Boston: Houghton Mifflin.

Summary

Has factual information ever been presented in a more interesting format? You can compare your hand to that of a gorilla, look a giant squid in the eye, or squint at the world's smallest fish—all in real-life size. This is one book in which illustrations outstrip text when it comes to presenting information. The student artists in your class will love it.

Writing Connections

✔ Have fun making predictions as you read: Just how large *is* a tiger's head? How large *is* the largest spider on earth, anyway?

✔ Create an "actual size" class book of your own, based on students' own observations. If you can coordinate this with a zoo or museum visit, terrific, but if not, humbler subjects like caterpillars, birds, frogs, lizards, snakes, and insects will do. The point is to sharpen observation skills, then present the results artfully.

✔ Extend your "actual size" research to the human body. You could look up information on the tallest human, the biggest human foot (or the smallest)—or the average size of a brain, human heart, or human hand, the length of a nerve cell or artery—the longest hair or fingernail ever measured—or whatever piques your students' curiosity.

Alternate Text

Jenkins, Steve. 2005. *Prehistoric Actual Size*. Boston: Houghton Mifflin.

Jenkins, Steve. 1998. *Hottest, Coldest, Highest, Deepest.* Boston: Houghton Mifflin.

Summary

Where is the deepest part of the ocean? The windiest spot on earth? What's the wettest place on earth—and just how much does it rain there? If you find such questions intriguing, this is your book. Steve Jenkins' compelling nonfiction shows students how to use questions to structure informational writing, and how to make the factual fascinating.

Writing Connections

✔ Pose several (or more) of the book's questions to your students prior to reading. Ask them to make their best guesses in writing. Then read the book so they can compare their predictions with reality. They can write about that, too, using an *I thought–I learned* format. (You participate, too!)

✔ Create some additional questions to which your students would like answers. If you have access to a computer, show them how to find the answers to their questions, or—you can do it the old-fashioned way, using your library!

✔ Use the information from your research to create your own class book of informational tidbits. Don't forget to create illustrations!

Alternate Text

Jenkins, Steve. 1995. *Biggest, Strongest, Fastest*. Boston: Houghton Mifflin.

Juster, Norton. 2005. *The Hello, Goodbye Window.* New York: Hyperion Books for Children.

Summary

In this beautifully illustrated (by Chris Raschka) book, a little grandchild learns how much of the world she can discover—or imagine—by looking out of Nanna and Poppy's wondrous kitchen window. Juster's simple story celebrates both childhood imagination and the special relationship children often have with their grandparents.

Writing Connections

✔ After reading the book, ask students to draw or paint windows of their own, and to imagine what they might see of the world on the other side. Use ideas to write stories or poems.

✔ Choose an actual window in your classroom or somewhere in your school. Keep a record of people, things, and scenes observed through this window.

✔ Have students replicate the preceding activity with windows of their own—at home or elsewhere. Use the records to create stories or poems.

Perry, Sarah. 1995. *If. . . .* Los Angeles: The J. Paul Getty Museum.

Summary

What if . . . ants could count? Cats could fly? Or music could be held in your hands? Through extraordinary visuals and much imagination, sculptor Sarah

Perry explores a wide range of intriguing, sometimes outrageous possibilities guaranteed to startle and amuse readers of all ages.

Writing Connections

✔ The book provides numerous possibilities for imagining what might happen if certain incredible things came true. Consider writing on any one of these, or. . . .

✔ Invent your own "what if" possibilities, complete with illustrations. Here's a task guaranteed to stretch any imagination to its cosmic limits.

Rosenthal, Amy Krouse. 2006. *Cookies: Bite-Size Life Lessons*. Cambridge, MA: Candlewick Press.

Summary

What does it mean, really, to be patient, proud, modest, wise, courageous, compassionate, respectful—or envious? As students define such terms in their writing, we often tell them, "Show me, don't tell me." Here's a book that models just how to do that, using a subject almost everyone can relate to: the baking, sharing, and enjoying of cookies.

Writing Connections

✔ Read the book more than once. Talk about the meanings of the words. Some are easier than others, so build understanding through discussion.

✔ Ask students to think of one word that describes them or someone they know. Ask them to think about how they—or a friend—acted out what it means to be compassionate or patient, or whatever. Create illustrations and sentences or stories to show the meaning of each selected word.

✔ Ask students to watch for words in action. Maybe they'll see kindness, helpfulness or courtesy—or perhaps an example of impatience, rudeness, or unfairness—in everyday life. Invite students to write about what they observe and to create illustrations to expand their text.

Sayre, April Pulley. 2005. *Stars Beneath Your Bed*. New York: Greenwillow Books.

Summary

Students sometimes think they cannot write on a particular topic because it's just too—well, dull! Dust might seem to fit into that category. Could anything be more mundane? As it turns out, dust is quite fascinating. How many people know that the very dust that made King Tut sneeze is still around? Or that everything from sea salt to volcanic ash contributes to dust? Perhaps there are no dull topics after all!

Writing Connections

✔ Invite students to create some before and after pages on the topic of dust. Ask them to write their "before" pages prior to sharing the book—just writing everything they know about dust. Share their perceptions aloud. Your students might know more about this topic than you—or they—think!

✔ Now share the book and talk about what you learn together. This is what good informational writing is; it teaches us something. Then, write your "after" pages—what your students know about dust now. Read these aloud, too.

✔ Choose another topic to research. If you work with second or third graders, they can do some of the research themselves. If you work with younger students, you may wish to do some or all—but let students choose the topic: anything from stars to mud. Create enough facts so you have (at least) one fact per student. Then, distribute them, and ask students to create writing and an illustration to accompany this bit of information. Assemble your pages into a class book. Read it for an audience (other students, parents) and celebrate your ability to make any topic fascinating!

Shannon, David. 2002. *David Gets in Trouble.* New York: The Blue Sky Press.

Summary

The latest of the "David" series has the same whimsical style and laugh-out-loud humor. In this book, David is forever in trouble—but has a million excuses: *I didn't mean it; It was an accident; But she likes it.* . . . It's what we *all* do—and that's why we laugh.

Writing Connections

✔ We all do things we shouldn't—sometimes on purpose, sometimes by accident. What are some excuses we make? Brainstorm a list.

✔ Invite students to use one of the excuses and write a short paragraph (with or without an illustration) showing how or when this excuse might be used.

✔ Compile a class book of the results.

✔ Interview others (older students, teachers) in your building about a time they have used an excuse for something said or done. Write the stories of what happened, using text and pictures. Create a school book called *Our Excuses* or *We Didn't Mean It!* (Be sure interviewees know their stories are going to press!)

Waber, Bernard. 2002. *Courage.* New York: Houghton Mifflin Books.

Summary

What is courage anyway? We all hear of heroic efforts in films or on television, of course, but the truth is, many people demonstrate courage in small ways in their everyday lives—and this is just as important, as this insightful book shows. We all have opportunities to be heroes.

Writing Connections

✔ Ask students to think about the heroes in their lives—humans and animals, too. Who's done something brave? Talk about this in small groups or as a class.

✔ Draw pictures or write about some everyday heroes who have done small, brave things that do not make the news, but are still important.

✔ Create a class book celebrating "heroes." (It is OK to write about yourself if you have done something brave!)
✔ Create a class poem about what it means to be a hero. Each student only needs to contribute one line. You record the results, then read the whole piece aloud.

Books for Teaching ORGANIZATION

Banyai, Istvan. 1995. *Zoom.* New York: Puffin Books.

Summary

This wordless book (like Banyai's sequel *Re-Zoom*) is truly unusual and extraordinary. If you have ever looked through the zoom lens of a camera, you know the basic premise: The whole world changes as we move up close or far away. Earth is different from outer space. Philosophically viewed, what we see as overwhelming and critical may be tiny or remote or unnoticeable from a different perspective. (Compare *The Red Book*, in this section.)

Writing Connections

✔ Like many wordless picture books, this one is best shared with a smaller group of, say, 6 to 10 students. Depending on their ages, you may need to go fairly slowly at first, asking them always, "Are we zooming in or out? What are we seeing from the previous picture? What do you think we'll see next?"
✔ To really have some fun with this book, you need to literally take it apart. Once you do that, you can—to make them hold up—*laminate* the pages. Then, you can shuffle them like cards to see if your students can put them in order. As imposing as this task sounds, you will

> *When you read informational books, not only are you helping children develop an ear for expository genre, but they are also learning facts about nature, science, history, social studies, cooking, art, music, books, sports, etc. Your reading aloud does double duty.*
>
> **—Marcia S. Freeman**
> *Teaching the Youngest Writers* (p. 95)

find that young students do it quite adeptly, and gain a true sense of order from doing the activity.

✔ If you try the ordering activity just described, talk about the clues your students used to determine the order of the pictures. They will likely mention details, figures, colors, backgrounds, and so forth. These visual clues correlate to textual clues writers use: details, staying on the topic, using words like *next* to make a link, and so on. If the artist had begun with a picture of a rooster and then drawn an elephant, it would have been harder to put the pictures in order!

✔ Consider using jewelers' loupes to practice the art of zooming in. Ask students to take any object—a shell, a flower, an orange, or their own hand—and describe it by drawing it and by writing. Then ask then to view the same object through a jeweler's loupe and to describe it again. What does zooming in do for detail?

Brown, Margaret Wise. 1949. (Renewed 1977) *The Important Book*. New York: Harper Trophy.

Summary

This little classic has stood the test of time; many teachers who use it (with delightful results and responses from their students) were not yet born when it was written. The book has a strong central theme: each person, each thing on earth, has some important, special quality. We have only to look to see what it is. Because it pays homage to individuality, the book is also excellent for teaching this aspect of voice: the uniqueness of self. I have chosen it for organization because it is a pattern book with a readily recognizable format that is fun and easy to imitate. Almost as soon as you begin reading, your students will begin to anticipate what is coming.

Writing Connections

✔ As students begin to recognize the pattern in the book, ask them to fill in the blank as you go along: *The most important thing about _____ is that it's _____.* (Most will find this both easy and fun.)

✔ As a class, create a "most important" chapter about anything in your lives: a house, a teacher, a pet. Write the section together.

✔ Next, ask students to do a "most important" piece about a friend. They will need to tell several things about the friend, and then to choose the most important. Go over this format before they begin so they can remember it and feel comfortable with the writing.

✔ Ask students to do a "most important" piece about themselves. In doing so, they should really think and reflect. A most important characteristic might be a special talent, or something they value (or someone else values), or something not everyone knows about them—for instance, *The most important thing about me is that I love turtles.* Students do not have to be Olympic champions or award winners to have a "most important" quality!

✔ Write your own "most important" piece about yourself—and share it with your students. They will love it.

Carle, Eric. 1997. *From Head to Toe*. New York: HarperCollins.

Summary

Writer and artist Eric Carle introduces us to a wide range of movements and dance steps in this lively and colorful pattern book. Big print and easy-to-read text make this a book even young readers can tackle on their own. Do not miss the dedication; it expresses Carle's love of art.

Writing Connections

✔ Brainstorm a list of other animals Carle might have written about, and talk about the special movements each one makes: for instance, *I am a turtle and I can pull inside my shell. Can you do that?*

✔ The pattern within the book is simple and easy to imitate. Let students try it with some writing and sketching of their own. Be sure to focus on animals Carle has not included.

✔ Act out the various portions of the book, with one child playing each animal part—or (a variation) everyone doing everything as you read the parts. This is a real on-your-feet kind of book.

✔ Provide some samples of cloth or colored paper from which students can cut pieces to make some art like that shown in the book. They can make animals or anything at all. Write sentences, labels, or poems to go with the pictures.

✔ Use the art form shown in Carle's book to create illustrations for greeting cards. Send the cards to friends or parents.

Curtis, Jamie Lee. 1993. *When I Was Little: A Four-Year-Old's Memoir of Her Youth*. New York: HarperCollins Publishers.

Summary

This book offers a charming illustration of the comparison-contrast format. Here's how life was back when I was only four versus how things are now. The paintings (by Laura Cornell) are whimsical and filled with voice, as is the text. Young students will recognize their own thoughts and feelings and identify at once with this simple, easy-to-imitate format for organizing comparative information.

Writing Connections

✔ After sharing the book, discuss some of the contrasts the author makes. What did she do or think when she was younger? How are things different now? Brainstorm some differences your students recognize in themselves. You do not need to go back to age four; adjust the age to suit your students.

✔ Create a comparison book of your own (perhaps using some photos to illustrate) and share it with students. They will enjoy the contrast you create and the memories you share!

✔ Extend your students' understanding of comparison by asking them to interview someone who was little a long time ago: a parent, grandparent, aunt or uncle, or neighbor. Create a list of questions students may enjoy asking: for example, *How did you get to school? What did you do for fun? What was your favorite toy? What was your least favorite chore? What did you like (or not like) to eat?* Then, create writing based on the contrast: *When my uncle was in second grade, he . . . Now, we . . .*

Jenkins, Steve. 1997. *What Do You Do When Something Wants to Eat You?* Boston: Houghton Mifflin.

Summary

Jenkins uses a wonderfully simple organizational structure to present a wide spectrum of information: one central question with many possible answers. This is an organizational structure young student writers can appreciate and use themselves—in many contexts.

Writing Connections

✔ As you are showing students the cover, ask them, "What is the main question this book will answer?" This is an easy one—it's right there in the title! But in asking the question outright, you are tuning students in to the organizational strategy the author uses. Now ask how many answers there might be to this question: Just one? One or two? Three or four? Or many? Emphasize the value of question and answer as a good organizational structure.

✔ As you share the book, you will see it is formatted in a way that encourages readers to make predictions. For example, what does the glass snake do when it is grabbed by the tail? You must turn the page to find out! Your students can use this format in their writing, too.

✔ Use Jenkins' question-and-answers organizational structure to create an informational piece on any topic that has more than one answer. For instance, students might write answers to this question: *What do you do when you're late for school? What do you do when you're hungry? What do you do when you can't fall asleep? What do you do when you're caught in the rain?* . . . and so on. Create individual or class books of answers.

Jenkins, Steve. 1996. *Big and Little*. Boston: Houghton Mifflin.

Summary

In this excellent and beautifully illustrated text, Jenkins uses comparison-contrast as the design structure for presenting his information. The animals he compares have much in common, and are sometimes even related, yet differ dramatically in size, as well as in other ways—behavior, habitat, disposition, and so on. This book subtly and effectively illustrates that comparisons are not random; in order to work, they must be based on common ground. Thus, it is possible to compare a Cat Shark to a Great White—but not to a zebra!

Writing Connections

✔ Share the book and ask which comparisons your students enjoy the most. which were the most surprising? What did they learn that they recall most vividly?

✔ Brainstorm some comparisons that could work in your own writing. For example, you could compare a goldfish to . . . ? But not to . . . ? You could compare a bicycle to . . . ? But not to . . . ?

✔ Use your brainstormed list as the basis for writing comparison papers based on things that have something important in common—a basis for the comparison!

Lane, Barry. 2002. *The Tortoise and the Hare Continued.... Shoreham, VT: Discover Writing Press.

Summary

We've all heard Aesop's well-known fable of the *Tortoise and the Hare*, but do you know what happened the next day? Or a week later? Or 30 years later? Let Barry Lane spin the tale for you with his own inimitable brand of humor. His . . . *Continued* version is a delightfully readable set of tales—for each story suggests yet another to come. Use this book to help students see that embedded in any good ending is the suggestion of another essay, poem, or story down the road.

Writing Connections

✔ Make predictions. As you finish each of the six back-to-back fables, ask students to predict what might come next. This encourages them to use endings to launch new thoughts and ideas.

✔ Guess what the moral of each story might be, too. Morals are one way of summing up the main idea.

✔ Pay attention to leads as you read. This book—with its unusual format— is full of leads. As you read each one, ask students, "What do you like about this lead?"

✔ Try Barry's format with another fable. You may wish to read several fables so students can choose. Then ask them to write a "What happened the next day" paper, extending the story. Each should have a moral, too.

Lehman, Barbara. 2004. *The Red Book.* Boston: Houghton Mifflin.

Summary

Did you ever become so engaged in a book that you felt you actually became part of it? That's what happens in this wordless picture book that truly challenges students to consider what is happening from one illustration to the next. Organization is indeed the connection of text to illustration, but in this book, students must create their *own* text, and the answers are anything but obvious. They will need to be inventive and observant.

Writing Connections

✔ Because this book demands such close attention to the illustrations, you may wish to share it with a relatively small group who can come in close to see everything—perhaps 10 students at the most. Turn the pages fairly quickly the first time through to give students a sense of the total story. Most will be wondering, "What happened?" Then, go back through, more slowly this time, allowing for discussion of the plot. Give students time to piece the story together. You may wish to record their ideas and read them at the end to see if they have created a coherent story. Feel free to add your own ideas, too.

✔ Create your own wordless picture books. Suggest this strategy to students: Draw three pictures on three separate sheets of paper. The pictures should show a sequence of events. Then write text to go with the pictures—but keep your text on a separate page so it cannot be seen by someone looking at the pictures. Trade pictures with another student and see if he or she can invent text to go with the pictures. Compare partners' texts with the originals.

Palatini, Margie. 2006. *Oink?* New York: Simon & Schuster Books for Young Readers.

Summary

Like many of Palatini's books, this quirky and hilarious tale follows a problem-solution format. This is another organizational structure quite easy for young readers to grasp. In this case, the pigs, Joseph and Thomas, are the curse of the barnyard. They won't pick up, spruce up, or clean up. The hens, the duck, and the rabbit are pretty *fed* up—but can't seem to get the pigs to cooperate. What's to be done? And who winds up solving which problem? This gem of a book is wonderful for word choice as well. Notice the verbs.

Writing Connections

✔ As you share the book, ask students to imagine things from two perspectives: First, how do Joseph and Thomas (the pigs) feel? What is *their* problem? Second, how do the chickens, duck, and rabbit feel? What is *their* problem? Ask them to guess which side might find a solution—or will both sides solve their problem?

✔ As you continue reading, focus on the solution—for both sides. How do things turn out?

✔ Brainstorm a list of problems students might write about. These do not need to be personal problems! For example, a school problem might be choosing pets that are interesting but appropriate for a classroom, or making sure school lunches are nutritious and still appealing. A personal problem might be coaching yourself into reading aloud when you feel pretty shy, or finding time to clean your room when there are so many other interesting things to do! Come up with a list of problems small enough to be solvable, and then try the problem-solution format for organizing writing.

Alternate Text

Scotton, Rob. 2005. *Russell the Sheep*. New York: HarperCollins.

Schneider, Judy Mullen, and Mary Konrad Weeks. 2004. *But Not Quite*. Seattle, WA: Peanut Butter Publishing.

Summary

This book is a cleverly illustrated visual guide to the similarities and differences found in everyday objects: for example, "A mitten is almost like a glove. But not quite." The text offers no clues; readers must use their powers of observation to note the commonalities and differences.

Writing Connections

✔ Discuss some of the similarities and differences to strengthen students' observational skills.

✔ Over a period of time (a week or so) create, with your students, a running list of things that are very much alike, but have one or more critical differences. You may wish to target specific groups of things: for instance, numbers, letters, plants, animals, coins, punctuation marks, articles of clothing, kinds of food—or anything your imaginations can dream up.

✔ With young students, create a class book of your own *But Not Quite!* examples, perhaps imitating the fold-over illustrations that make the book's visual comparisons so intriguing.

✔ Older students may enjoy creating a book for younger readers.

✔ For more ideas, explore the Web site: www.toucancreations.com

Steig, William. 1982. *Dr. DeSoto*. New York: Farrar, Straus and Giroux.

Summary

A much-loved story that captivates readers of all ages—wonderful for word choice and voice as well. This book has a strikingly good lead and conclusion; you may wish to capitalize on that as you share it. Notice how Steig manages to tell a complex story in a very few words.

Writing Connections

✔ Try modeling some other possible leads for this same story and ask students to make comparisons: for example, *This will be a book about a mouse, who is a dentist, and a fox, who is his patient.*

✔ Ask your students, "How important are the pictures in this book? Do they tell or show things we do not learn from the words alone?"

Stojic, Manya. 2000. *Rain*. New York: Crown Publishers.

Summary

This book displays excellent word choice, and is a gem for teaching sensory detail. It's also a good choice, however, to illustrate the power of organizing information in a recurring cycle. Rain comes to the parched African savannah, transforming the landscape and awakening the animals' senses. Soon, however, warm sun dries the land, rain is but a memory, and a tiny crack appears. The cycle begins anew.

Writing Connections

✔ After sharing the whole story, ask students to listen for the moment when the cycle begins again. What is the beginning point?

✔ Brainstorm a brief list of things in your students' lives that occur in cycles: a school day, for example, or a year. What event begins the new cycle? Note that this could be different for different people.

✔ Choose one of those cycles to write about, remembering to bring the writing full circle—back to the beginning point. Notice that Stojic spans a full year, but gives us only *a few events* to measure the passing of time. Your students can do that, too, keeping the cycle great in scope, but simple in detail.

Books for Teaching VOICE

Bloom, Becky. 1999. *Wolf!* New York: Orchard Books.

Summary

Use this book to illustrate the importance of reading aloud with *voice*. In Bloom's delightful story, Wolf is anything but typecast. He tries to live up to his legend, but the other animals are having none of it. They're educated—avid readers, actually—and Wolf doesn't fit in. He's loud, brash, a nuisance, and above all, not much of a reader. As Wolf learns to read, first basal style, then with mechanical monotony, and finally with true inflection and engagement, we see his voice unfold, and gradually captivate his listeners, who find his new voice irresistible.

Writing Connections

✔ Voice often comes from an unexpected twist in a story, or the unpredictable behavior of a character. Ask your students how they would expect the wolf in any story to behave. Make some predictions. Then share the story. Does this wolf have some surprises for us? What does he do we might not expect?

✔ Through the story, Wolf models three different ways to read. First, he reads simple sentences from a basal reader: for example, "Run, Wolf, run." Then, he reads more advanced text, but with no voice. Finally, he gets it. His voice comes to life and the other animals actually listen. Talk about these different ways of reading and which shows the most voice. Model the different voices for students. Then, ask them to try it for themselves. Can they create a real contrast between flat reading and expressive reading—even when reading the same text? Emphasize that reading with expression helps us to write with expression—which is to say, with voice.

Browne, Anthony. 2001. *Voices in the Park.* United Kingdom: DK Publishing Inc.

Summary

Here's a simple story of a walk to the park told in four different voices, from four different perspectives. And while it's recognizable as the same tale each time, it definitely unfolds differently through the eyes of each teller. This is an excellent book for showing how voice depends very much on who is telling the story and how he, or she, sees the world. (See *Loki & Alex*, this section.)

Writing Connections

✔ Read the story, perhaps more than once. Ask students to talk about how the four versions differ.

✔ Talk about why each person has a slightly different take on what happened at the park. Which version do your students think is closest to the truth? Why do they think so? (There is no right answer to this, of course!)

✔ What's likely to happen next? Will these characters meet again? Invite students to tell the tale of another encounter in different voices.

✔ Ask students to write *any* simple story in someone else's voice. For example, how would a visit to the dentist sound in the voice of a tropical fish in the waiting room? How would a visit to the zoo sound in the voice of a lion or zebra?

Child, Lauren. 2006. *The Princess and the Pea.* New York: Hyperion Books for Children.

Summary

It isn't easy for a prince—even a handsome one—to find a princess. Good ones don't grow on trees, and when you're looking for someone "mesmerizing and fascinating," it's a challenge. This delightful retelling of the old fairy tale (with new twists on familiar characters) rings with voice and is as appealing to adults as to young listeners. Note the extraordinary artwork (from award-winning Polly Borland) that graces this book: paneled rooms cut from cardboard boxes and painted (like dollhouse rooms) to look realistic, furnished with dollhouse furniture and peopled with cutouts dressed in layered clothing. It's a feat that yields captivatingly unique results.

Writing Connections

✔ Find a copy of the original fairy tale version first and share it with students. Then read Lauren Child's humorous updated version. Do your students notice the difference? Talk about the charm of retellings. Why do people retell stories? Does the retold story take on the teller's special voice?

✔ Share another fairy tale or fable of your choice—any one at all. Or share several. Ask students to pick one and retell it in their own words, letting their own voices in. Invite them to do their own illustrations, too. They may not wish to go to quite as much trouble as Polly Borland, but they'll love hearing about her technique!

✔ If you and your students feel inspired, create (together) one illustration á la Borland. You will need to create a kind of stage set, paint it, and complete it with furnishings of all kinds—miniatures or pieces you make yourself. Then you can cut your characters from cardboard (as Borland did) and dress them in paper or cloth. Take a photo of your finished masterpiece, and your students will have true appreciation for how Borland makes her magic.

Child, Lauren. 2005. *I Am Too Absolutely Small for School*. Cambridge, MA: Candlewick Press.

Summary

As she explains to Charlie, her older brother, Lola is "too absolutely small" for school, not to mention the fact that she is very busy. Besides, why would she need to learn letters? She talks on the phone. Numbers? She has fingers and toes for that. Wait a minute, though: If Lola doesn't go, her (invisible) friend Soren Lorensen will have to go alone, and he will be quite nervous. This is a delightful book for exploring the power of voice in persuasive writing. It can also open the door to discussions of new or uncomfortable situations.

Writing Connections

✔ Enjoy the story together. Ask students if they have ever felt like Lola. Have they ever worried about a new adventure? How many have felt like Charlie, and helped someone *else* who was worried?

✔ Think about the next "adventure" that awaits your students. It might be first grade, second, third, or fourth. What are some things Lola might worry about in making this big move? What would Lola say? Invite students to write as Lola, thinking of one or two things they (or Soren Lorensen) might worry about when moving to the next level.

✔ Then, invite them to write back as Charlie, explaining why it will be OK.

✔ If Lola kept a diary, what do you think she would write after her first day of kindergarten? Create an entry, using text and/or drawings.

Curtis, Jamie Lee. 2002. *I'm Gonna Like Me*. New York: HarperCollins.

Summary

Sometimes it can be hard to like yourself. Those are the very moments when self-esteem is so important to carry you through. This gentle but powerful little book is all about learning to like yourself so that you can share the wealth and like others too.

Writing Connections

✔ Are there ever moments when it's hard to like yourself? Brainstorm a few. Then write or draw pictures to show what these times are like. (The point: Everyone has moments like these!)

✔ What do your students like about themselves *especially*? Brainstorm some of your best qualities—it's OK to love little things: not losing your cool when your shoelace breaks, being kind to animals, a sense of humor, ability to make your mom (or someone) laugh, willingness to spend time with a small brother or sister, ability to appreciate a rainy day. If you share a few small things you like about yourself, it will be easier for your students to think of some, too. Write or draw about your thoughts.

Drachman, Eric. 2005. *A Frog Thing*. Los Angeles: Kidwick Books LLC.

Summary

Frank wants to fly. Unfortunately, he's a frog—and flying just isn't . . . well, a *frog* thing, like, say, hopping or swimming. Should Frank give up? Or hold tight to his dream? Are there ways to make the seemingly impossible happen?

Writing Connections

✔ How does Frank feel through this story? What do the illustrations tell us about his feelings? Imagine that Frank kept a journal, and write what he might have to say at various points.

✔ Is Frank successful in the end in realizing his dream of flying? What do your students think? Write about this.

✔ Don't miss the CD presentation of *A Frog Thing* (sold with the book). Notice the multiple voices, and talk about how this production brings the story to life. Consider making a multiple-voice CD of your own, based on this or any text. Add music, background noises and sound effects, laughter—or whatever turns your production into audio theater.

✔ Consider asking older students to create an audio book (based on a fairly simple text) that could help younger children read.

Egan, Tim. 2003. *Serious Farm*. Boston: Houghton Mifflin.

Summary

Despite the serious faces on the characters, you will be laughing before you are two pages into this book—even if there is "nothing funny about corn." The trouble is, Farmer Fred has gotten too serious for his own good or anyone else's, and the animals, under the direction of Edna the cow, are determined to help him snap out of it. It isn't easy. No one on Serious Farm has laughed for quite some time. Perhaps they've forgotten how. You and your students will enjoy the expressions on Egan's very funny drawings (the eyebrows alone are worth a chuckle or two) as well as the antics of the well-intentioned animals.

Writing Connections

✔ Talk about the expressions on the faces of the characters as you share this entertaining story. What do they show?

✔ Have your students used facial expressions in their drawings or paintings to show emotion? Ask them to try this, thinking about how eyes and eyebrows, mouth, and nose look when one is serious—or not so serious.

✔ Farmer Fred really is a serious fellow—but does he care about his animal friends? How do we know this? Not all voices in the world are humorous. Farmer Fred has his own individual voice. What sort of voice is it?

✔ What would your students do to make Farmer Fred laugh? Make a book of things they might try. For each idea, add a page showing what Farmer Fred might say.

Falconer, Ian. 2000. *Olivia Saves the Circus.* New York: Atheneum Books.

Summary

If you loved Falconer's earlier book, *Olivia*, you'll love this one, too. Olivia is an independent spirit, and her voice shines through in everything she says and does. In this adventure, she arrives at the circus only to discover that everyone is suffering from ear infections—and cannot perform. Olivia to the rescue! She is more than willing to play all the parts, from lion tamer to acrobat, and even more willing to share her story with her classmates later. A story, she assures her teacher, that is "mostly true."

Writing Connections

✔ Have you ever "saved the day" in a large or small way? Write about it and share the story with your students.

✔ Invite students to share stories (or pictures or both) of how they saved the day for someone—even in a tiny way.

✔ Put Olivia in another adventure. What if Olivia—got lost shopping? Got left at the zoo by mistake? Went home with the wrong family? Or, let your students invent a "what-if" situation of their own. Draw sketches or write a story to get Olivia out of her predicament.

Haseley, Dennis. 2002. *A Story for Bear.* San Diego, CA: Harcourt, Inc.

Summary

A heart-warming tale of a bear who is enchanted with books and loves being read to. As he listens to the voice of the woman who gently shares stories with him, he falls in love with the very sound of her voice, with the whole peaceful feeling that engulfs him as he listens. Though not a word is intelligible to him, he nevertheless derives meaning from the very tone of voice with which she speaks the words. Use this book to teach the concept of voice through intonation and emotional response.

Writing Connections

✔ Ask students about their personal responses to the experience of having someone read to them. Write about this.

✔ Talk about specific things the woman says or does that enchant the bear. Why does he love his time with her so much?

✔ How does the bear feel at different points in the story? What are the clues in the text or in the pictures that let you know?

✔ If the bear could speak to the woman in words, what would he say? Ask students to write *in the voice of the bear* about this.

Hoffman, Mary. 2002. *The Color of Home*. New York: Phyllis Fogelman Books.

Summary

Hassan, who has just come to the United States from his war-torn Somalia, speaks little English. He uses art to convey his emotions, and the colors he chooses reflect his mood—which is dark, at first. He is plagued by difficult memories, one being the loss of his little cat, Musa. As he adjusts to life in new surroundings, his face, his heart, and his paintings reflect new colors and new hope. The text is gentle, but honest and unflinching. This is a fine book for introducing discussions of moving, coping with stories of war, and learning a second language.

Writing Connections

✔ Hassan paints his home as he remembers it. Talk about the contrast between his two paintings in terms of detail and color. Why are they so different? What do the differences show?

✔ What does the word "home" mean? Why does this word touch our hearts so much? Talk about some of the associations your students have with the word "home."

✔ Paintings can reflect voice as much as words. Before Hassan can use many words, he conveys his feelings through his art. Give your students a chance to do this, too. Ask them to create something about which they have strong feelings and to let the feelings show in their details and colors. They could do paintings of home and family—or something else: a friend, a relative who is important, a pet, a place they love even if it is not home.

✔ Share your paintings and talk about what the colors "say." How many ways can art reflect feeling?

Palatini, Margie. 2003. *Bedhead*. New York: Aladdin Paperbacks.

Summary

Is there anyone out there who *hasn't* had a bad hair day? Oliver is experiencing one of the worst ever, and to his chagrin, his whole family is on the case, trying to help. Ouch! The treatments may be worse than living with bad hair! Worst of all, it's picture day at school. Maybe a hat is the way to go—or is it?

Writing Connections

✔ Enjoy the story and have some fun creating your own drawings of Oliver and his wild hair. Illustrations by Jack E. Davis are quite zany, but your students may go to even further extremes.

✔ Think of all the ways you can to cure "bedhead." What have your students tried? What have *you* tried? Make a list, then use it to write a "how-to" piece on getting through a bad hair day.

✔ What if there were a hair dressers' salon that specialized in coping with bedhead. What might they call themselves? Give them a name and create some posters (with illustrations, of course) they might use to advertise.

Rylant, Cynthia. 1998. *Scarecrow.* New York: Harcourt, Inc.

Summary

This is a book to treasure, and to read over and over. It is the story of a scarecrow who understands that he is fashioned from bits and pieces of others' lives, but doesn't mind. He makes the most of every life experience, enjoying everything from the mice in his hat and the birds on his arms to the morning glories winding up his patchwork quilt legs. It is a gentle but passionate tale, the story of ourselves and a celebration of life's tiniest moments.

Writing Connections

✔ Share the book, enjoying the tale of the scarecrow and talking about all the things he finds most special in life.

✔ Ask students to draw or paint their own scarecrows or to fashion three-dimensional scarecrows from cloth, buttons, and stuffing. You can use white sacking for faces, colored markers for features, clothes pins for noses, buttons for eyes, yarn or raffia for hair, and so forth.

✔ Write in the voice of the scarecrow. What if he kept a journal? What does he think about, dream about? How does he see the different seasons? Does he ever wish he could just hop down and take off—like that other famous Scarecrow?

✔ There's something interesting about Cynthia Rylant's scarecrow: He's not very *scary!* In fact, birds love him. If different creatures wrote notes to Scarecrow, what might they say? Create some notes in different voices.

Smith, Charles R. 2001. *Loki & Alex: The Adventures of a Dog and His Best Friend.* New York: Dutton Children's Books.

Summary

Like all best friends, Loki and Alex love each other, but see the world a bit differently. In Smith's charming tale, these two appealing characters tell their story in their own very different voices, alternating to give us one take on a given situation, then the other. They do not always understand each other perfectly, but in the end, friendship prevails.

Writing Connections

✔ With younger students, you may wish to focus on the pictures first, imagining what each of the characters might be thinking, prior to sharing the text.

✔ Sometimes, one character humorously misinterprets the other's intentions or body language: for instance, Loki thinks Alex is happy when Loki helps himself to treats—but Alex's face tells a different story! With your students, talk about each character's "reading" of the other, and the reality revealed by the illustrations.

✔ What other sets of characters might see the world differently—just as Alex and Loki do? Consider student and teacher, child and parent, two siblings, two friends, cat and dog, cat and fish—the list is endless! Brainstorm a list. Then . . .

✔ Create some two-character stories of your own, with each character giving voice to his or her view of the world. Students may choose to have one animal and one human character, as in this book, or any combination they like.

Willems, Mo. 2005. *Leonardo the Terrible Monster.* New York: Hyperion Books for Children.

Summary

Leonardo is indeed a terrible monster. Not in the usual sense. He's a monster who's flat out *terrible* at being monstrous. Then he finds the perfect victim (or so he thinks): Sam. Will Leonardo's best efforts "scare the tuna salad" out of Sam? Let yourself be charmed by this (sorry, Leonardo!) very *unscary*, downright friendly tale of monsterhood.

Writing Connections

✔ Talk about how author Mo Willems is using the word "terrible." What does "terrible monster" usually mean? What does it mean in this story?

✔ Craft some "scary" would-be monsters of your own, by drawing, painting, or assembling them from paper, yarn, and cloth. They might look scary, but underneath, are they marshmallows like Leonardo? Have students write in their monsters' voices to show who they are inside—perhaps not that scary after all.

✔ Leonardo makes a decision in this story. Because he's not that good at being a monster, he decides to try being a *very* good friend. Is this a good choice? Why? Invite students to share their thoughts about this in writing.

Willems, Mo. 2003. *Don't Let the Pigeon Drive the Bus!* New York: Hyperion Books for Children.

Summary

Get ready. The pigeon is here, he wants to drive, and he has some pretty convincing arguments. Are your students strong enough to say "No!" in the face of all this feathery blustering?

Writing Connections

✔ As you read, notice the expressions on the pigeon's face. Pay attention to his body language. What do these clues tell us about his feelings?

✔ Make the story interactive by letting students talk back to the pigeon. They can do this as a group: "No!," or you can ask individual students to answer each one of pigeon's pleas—which grow more desperate through the book!

✔ Have you, or your students, ever wanted to do something and just been told "no!" Did you put up a fuss? Make an argument? Create some written arguments now for something you would really like to do—but probably won't get a chance to try, such as—*driving the bus!* Or, . . . *driving the family car . . . sleeping overnight in a tree . . . riding a space shuttle . . . having a pet rhinoceros . . . joining the circus . . .* the more outlandish you make your wish, the more fun the writing (and arguing) can be. *Shhhh. Don't look now, but this is persuasive writing.*

> *In picture books, particularly, the choice of words is as crucial as the choice of notes in a fugue. I constantly read aloud what I've written in order to feel and hear the rightness of phrases or sentences. I know from experience that a rhythm that seems fine on the silent page often turns out to be clumsy or unwieldy when it's spoken.*
>
> **—Mem Fox**
>
> *Radical Reflections* (1992, p. 165)

Alternate Texts

Willems, Mo. 2004. *The Pigeon Finds a Hot Dog*. New York: Hyperion Books for Children.

Willems, Mo. 2006. *Don't Let the Pigeon Stay Up Late*. New York: Hyperion Books for Children.

Books for Teaching WORD CHOICE

Cronin, Doreen. 2000. *Click, Clack, Moo/Cows that Type*. New York: Simon and Schuster.

Summary

You and your students will laugh at this delightful story of a stubborn farmer and the persistent cows and hens who threaten to go on strike if they are not given electric blankets. At length, they resort to writing to get their way, using an old typewriter. This simple book contains some surprisingly sophisticated language you can easily overlook if you aren't on the lookout for it: *typewriter, sincerely, go on strike, background, impatient, demand, furious, ultimatum, snoop, neutral*. What if your students knew all these words well enough to use them in their own writing? They can, you know!

Writing Connections

✔ Pass out words ahead of time and ask students to guess at their meanings.

✔ Share the story and invite students to listen for the words you passed out. Do they recognize them? Can they tell the meanings from the way words are used in the story?

✔ See if you can find a typewriter and bring it into your classroom—especially for students who have not seen one. Talk about the differences between a typewriter and a computer in word processing.

✔ Ask students to think about the story and Farmer Brown's side of things. Is it fair for the cows and chickens to go on strike if they need blankets? What about Farmer Brown needing eggs and milk? Ask them to take a side and write a short reflection on how they feel. It can be as short as a sentence or as long as several paragraphs.

Facklam, Margery. 2001. *Spiders and Their Websites*. Boston: Little, Brown and Company.

This is the fourth in Margery Facklam's impressive and acclaimed natural history picture book series. It is a model of what good informational writing should be: clear, educational, and filled with voice. Her words are simple but precise. She creates images and takes us right into the world of the spider:

> All the 4,000 different jumping spiders stalk their prey like cats. When they leap, they push off with strong hind legs, like a swimmer taking off from a starting block.

Her animated text has the reader appeal of any story.

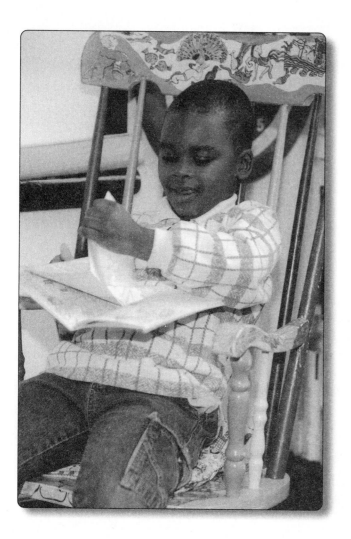

Writing Connections

✔ Draw any of the spiders Facklam describes in her book. This is great practice in noticing detail.

✔ After reading/hearing one chapter—say, on the black widow spider—ask students to recall information first, then try writing it in another form: a story, news article, or poem on the same topic.

✔ Keep a pet spider in your classroom for a time. Watch its habits. Compare your pet spider to the description in Facklam's book. Ask students to write a comparison paper, drawing one or more comparisons between the book and the real thing.

✔ Create a glossary of spider terms. Ask for students' help as you finish a chapter in identifying important terms to remember. Create a spider word wall. Use the terms later in writing about spiders.

✔ Invite students to label spider drawings. Ask them to watch for labeled drawings in other informational writing. (Not all writing is done in sentences.)

✔ Some of the longer words in Facklam's book are accompanied by pronunciation guides. Work through one or two of these with your students. Invite them to incorporate pronunciation guides into their own writing. Yes, this will be a challenge at first—but it's wonderful practice for thinking about how to pronounce a word correctly.

 Frasier, Debra. 2000. *Miss Alaineus*. San Diego, CA: Harcourt, Inc.

Summary

A charming, highly original book, the hero, Sage, catches a cold and has to miss Vocabulary Day. When her friend gives her the list over the phone, she mistakes *miscellaneous* for *Miss Alaineus*—with very funny (but also mortifying, for Sage) results.

Writing Connections

✔ So many new words are introduced in this book, you may wish to read it more than once so your students can "take in" a few more each time. As you go through, identify favorites and add them to the word wall.

✔ Create an alphabet book of the kind modeled in *Miss Alaineus*. Ask each student to write one sentence about him- or herself using three words that all begin with the same letter.

✔ To bring in some drama, ask students to dress up as favorite words—the book provides some pictures to inspire them.

Lionni, Leo. 1967. *Frederick.* New York: Alfred A. Knopf, Inc.

Summary

Your students will delight in the story of Frederick, the little poet mouse, who—while his friends are gathering grain and other staples for winter—gathers ideas, memories, and *words*. As winter howls outside their den, and the food diminishes and the chill sets in, Frederick warms his friends with stories, recollections, images—and words they love. A delightful book for showing the power of language to sustain us in less-cheery times.

Writing Connections

✔ Frederick gathers favorite colors and images to take with him into their winter den—things he does not want to forget. What if your students hibernated for winter. What would they take to cheer themselves up and share? Draw or write your answers.

✔ The "Fun Facts" in the beginning of the book tell us that "mouse" comes from a Sanskrit word meaning "thief." Why would this be? Invite students to write or talk about this.

✔ We also learn from the "Fun Facts" that a mouse's teeth grow all its life. That could be a problem, couldn't it? Ask your students to write about how they might solve this problem if their own teeth kept growing forever.

> *Remember that you do not need to read an entire book to make a point about detail or voice or whatever. Bits and pieces can be magical—and sufficient.*
>
> **—Vicki Spandel**
>
> *Books, Lessons, Ideas for Teaching the Six Traits* (2001, p. viii)

Pinkney, Sandra. 2002. *Shades of Black: A Celebration of Our Children.* New York: Scholastic.

Summary

A visual feast. Rich in text and in presentational style, this collage of photographs and poetic text celebrates the uniqueness of each child. The children pictured are not just "black," but "the creamy white frost in vanilla ice cream" or "the velvety orange in a peach." If ever there was a book to teach precision in word choice (and in thinking), this is it.

Writing Connections

✔ Use this book for description. Leaves are green, the sky is blue—but what *shade* of green, what *shade* of blue? Explore shades of meaning by expanding ideas about and definitions of color.

✔ What makes each person unique? This book explores unique colors—but of course, that's only part of the story. Use drawings or photographs to capture the uniqueness of each child. Then using poetry or prose, write about the unique qualities that make each person special. Students can write about themselves or about each other—or both.

> *Writing enhances all the concepts a child needs to become a skilled reader. . . . The child who writes first will actually read earlier because writing furnishes practice using word forms and sentence patterns.*
>
> **—Bea Johnson**
>
> *Never Too Early to Write* (1999, p. 10)

Pritcher, Caroline. 2004. *Lord of the Forest*. Great Britain: Frances Lincoln Children's Books.

Summary

Dramatic artwork (by Jackie Morris) graces this masterful coming of age tale focused on young Tiger, whose life is a quest—a search for the elusive Lord of the Forest. It's a short but mighty tale, visually satisfying, and rich with imagery, original phrasing, and alliteration.

Writing Connections

✔ Listen for favorite words and create sketches or paintings to accompany them.

✔ Use the book to teach the concept of alliteration: "slither of zig-zagged snakes," "creep of crabs," and "flip of fish." Brainstorm your own list of alliterative phrases and accompany them with drawings or paintings.

Recorvits, Helen. 2003. *My Name Is Yoon*. New York: Farrar, Straus and Giroux.

Summary

Lush illustrations and simple but poignant text go right to the core of human feelings—for not much is more personal than our names. *Yoon* means *Shining Wisdom* in Korean, but she does not feel shining or wise when she first comes to the United States, and she wonders whether another name might not suit her better and gain her the love of her friends and her teacher.

Writing Connections

✔ After sharing the story, ask students to write about their own names. Write about yours, too. (Not all students may wish to share this, and it is a personal topic, so that's fine.) Invite those who wish to share to do so. Their writing may discuss what they like (or dislike) about their names, names they might give themselves if they had a choice, nicknames they prefer, or the special history or ethnic origin of a name.

✔ If you are fortunate enough to have access to someone who can write names in a second language, invite your guest in to do that for your students. It can be fun and enlightening to see your name in another language.

Schotter, Roni. 2006. *The Boy Who Loved Words*. New York: Schwartz & Wade Books.

Summary

Someone, somewhere in the world, is forever in need of a new word. How lucky that Selig, hero of this charming book, collects them, and loves to share. His passion for words, the very sound, taste, and feeling of them, just may be contagious and prompt your students to start their own collections. This delightful book includes a very helpful glossary.

Writing Connections

✔ Read the book once just for fun, then again to explore word meanings.

✔ Ask students to identify favorites from the book, and add those to your own word walls. Practice saying them aloud together, and encourage students to use them in their writing. Talk about why we are drawn to some words. Is it the meaning—or just the sound? Or is it both?

✔ Start your own collection, perhaps writing your words on colored slips of paper, as Selig does. Post them in your room or better yet, give them as gifts to other students or teachers at your school.

Seeger, Laura Vaccaro. 2005. *Walter Was Worried.* New Milford, CT: Roaring Brook Press.

Summary

Walter might be *worried*, but Elliot finds himself—*ecstatic*. You can see the al-literative connection, and soon your students will, too. What's more subtle, and even more delightful, are the slightly camouflaged alphabetic symbols on the faces of these emotional characters. Your students will have great fun de-coding—then using—Seeger's creative idea to fashion some emotional faces of their own.

Writing Connections

✔ As you read the book, use the expressions on the characters' faces to explore the meaning of each word.

✔ Look for letters of the alphabet that help create each expressive face and spell out the word being depicted.

✔ Help students explore some emotionally descriptive words to go with their own names, choosing several possibilities for each name. Carlos could be *calm*, *creative*, or *capable*. Sara could be *silly*, *sagacious*, or *sensible*—and so forth. Then give students a chance to create self-portraits based on a word of their choice (make sure each child really likes his or her word!). Those who feel creative might try using one or more letters from the chosen word to help shape the features of their face.

Stevens, Janet, and Susan Stevens Crummel. 2006. *The Great Fuzz Frenzy.* New York: Harcourt, Inc.

Summary

The fantastic fuzz frenzy and fiasco all begins when Violet (a dog) loses her ten-nis ball down the prairie dog hole. Look out below! What *is* that wonderful fluffy stuff anyway? Look—you can nab it, poke it, jab it, put it in your hair, fashion coats of it—and hoard it: "That's *my* fuzz!" Will the madness ever end? Find out in this tale that makes good use of verbs to show how many creative ways prairie dogs can find to manipulate tennis ball fuzz.

Writing Connections

✔ Read the book just for fun, then go back to notice a few of the verbs. You don't have to painstakingly point out every one, but do listen for a few favorites.

✔ Draw your own prairie dog illustrations to showcase favorite verbs.
✔ Imagine something else that might be lost down the prairie dog hole—chewing gum, a small shoe, a deflated balloon, or something of your own invention. Write poems or stories to show what might happen.
✔ Where did Janet Stevens come up with this idea, do you suppose? Talk about this with your students; then read the account on the back flap of the book.

Books for Teaching SENTENCE FLUENCY

Cannon, Janell. 2000. *Crickwing*. New York: Harcourt, Inc.

Summary

Like Cannon's other beloved books *(Verdi, Stellaluna), Crickwing* is a model of outstanding word choice:

> The next morning the ants found Crickwing fussing with his latest ant trap. He had no chance for escape as thousands of leafcutters swarmed over him, dragged him back to the anthill, and marched him down its dark, winding corridors.

It's the tale of a cockroach with a damaged wing (hence the nickname) that is plagued by a barrage of predators, and ultimately captured by an army of ants, that he eventually saves from a fearsome anteater. You can use this book to teach any trait. The ideas are imaginative, the organization easy to follow, and the voice irresistible. It's also a fine example of fluency, with carefully crafted, flowing sentences.

Writing Connections

✔ Cannon begins sentences in many different ways. After reading the book once just for fun, read it again, this time focusing on sentence beginnings. How many different ones do you hear? Write some down.

✔ Many portions of the book contain speech. Read one or more samples aloud and ask your students "Does this dialogue sound real? Is it the way real characters would speak?" (Yes! Hence the voice.)

✔ Bring an actual cockroach into class for your students to study. How does the real thing resemble Cannon's drawings? How is it different?

✔ Make some cockroach sketches of your own. Encourage students to incorporate as many details as they can.

✔ Most people do not like cockroaches *at all!* Choose some other not-so-well-liked creatures and try writing in their voices. It's a good lesson on perspective!

Curtis, Jamie Lee. 2004. *It's Hard to Be Five: Learning How to Work My Control Panel.* New York: HarperCollins Publishers.

Summary

It *is* hard to be five—just ask anyone who's tried it. You have to control your mouth and your emotions, put up with baths, and worst of all, sit still—for hours! Of course, there's the good side: You can make some decisions on your own, reach more shelves, and walk yourself to the bus stop. Plus, you're still growing, so who knows what lies ahead?

Writing Connections

✔ Enjoy Curtis's rhyming text together. It's rhythmic and bouncy—and lively illustrations by Laura Cornell make this book even more appealing.

✔ Brainstorm some of the best—and hardest—things about being five—or whatever age your students are. Then write about it, making a class book: *It's Hard to Be* _____ (fill in the right age). Don't worry about rhyming!

✔ Illustrate some moments from your class book. Use Laura Cornell's paintings for inspiration. How many different kinds of faces does Cornell portray in her paintings? What details do your students like best? You'll need to look more than once to take it all in!

Davies, Nicola. 2004. *One Tiny Turtle.* Cambridge, MA: Candlewick Press.

Summary

The Loggerhead goes to such pains to find her home beach, dig her nest, and lay her eggs that surely, *surely*, she will be rewarded with a large and prosperous family. The truth is, on average only "one tiny turtle" survives, racing past predators, across a treacherous beach, and "into the arms of the sea." In this extraordinary nonfiction account, Davies shows off her remarkable verbal agility, finding ever-changing ways to fashion sentences that flow with the rhythm and grace of the Loggerhead herself.

Writing Connections

✔ Enjoy the book, asking students to listen for different sentence beginnings. They don't have to remember how she does it—it's enough to notice that Davies finds many ways to begin.

✔ Point out some of Davies' strategies for making a sentence interesting—and see how many you and your students can imitate. Here are just a few of her opening phrases:

Far, far out to sea . . .
Just beneath the surface . . .
Passing in a boat, . . .
Then she's gone, . . .
Steadily . . .
Bigger than a dinner plate . . .
Scooping carefully, . . .

✔ Ask older students to notice the differences between the lyrical text of the main story, and the more direct sentence structure found in the "fine print," the factual information that underscores some sections. This leveled text gives Davies a chance to try two quite different styles. Do your students hear the difference? Try reading one aloud, then the other. Discuss what you hear. Why might short, direct sentences be good for factual information?

Alternate Texts

Davies, Nicola. 2004. *Bat Loves the Night.* Cambridge, MA: Candlewick Press.
Davies, Nicola. 2001. *Big Blue Whale.* Cambridge, MA: Candlewick Press.
Wallace, Karen. 2002. *Gentle Giant Octopus.* Cambridge, MA: Candlewick Press.

Dr. Seuss. 1990. *Oh, the Places You'll Go!* New York: Random House, Inc.

Summary

This wise and humorous graduation speech from the grand sage himself is a celebration of life—and a wonderful send-off for explorers of all ages, from preschoolers through college graduates, and beyond. Explorers of five may have more in common than they know with explorers of twenty-one—or ninety-one! We all face the unknown and the unexpected. We all wonder how we'll do, what we'll discover, and whether we'll survive it all and find success.

Writing Connections

✔ Read the book more than once to appreciate the rhyme and rhythm of which Dr. Seuss is a master.

✔ Dr. Seuss's book is about a journey, and is illustrated as if it's a hike along a trail. Invite students to create some "hiking trail" illustrations of their lives. You need a good-sized piece of paper (8½ by 11 or bigger) with a trail right up the middle: Picture a giant letter "S" on its side. Along the trail, create three or four (or more) simple illustrations to signal life events. Examples might include these: the student's birth, birth of a sibling, a move, getting a pet, doing something memorable—playing ball, climbing a tree, making a friend, getting a first haircut, finding or losing something important, starting school. Invite students to talk through their hiking trail adventures.

✔ Think of the "places you'll go" more literally. What places on the map would your students like to visit? Explore a U.S. map or world map together. Talk about a few places—near home or far from home—*you* have been. Tell students about any you have experienced. Invite them to discuss any they know about. Ask each student to identify one place he or she might like to go—one day. Write about your "someday" places, and mark them on a map. If possible, gather some information on each special place.

Florian, Douglas. 2001. *In the Swim*. San Diego, CA: Harcourt, Inc.

Summary

Like his previous and subsequent books *(Mammalabilia, Insectlopedia, Beast Feast, Bow Wow Meow Meow, Zoo's Who)*, this book is a masterpiece of word choice presented in fluent, playful poetry. It features highly original use of fresh language—and should certainly be used in teaching that trait as well. I've put it in the fluency section simply because the poems are so rhythmic and delightful to read aloud, it would be a true shame not to use it in that way. It's ideal for choral reading.

Writing Connections

✔ Read the poems aloud first—then teach one or two to your students. Invite them to read or recite with the same inflection.

✔ Perform some of the poems as choral readings—complete with gestures, dance, movement, or drama of all kinds. Let loose! Let your imaginations soar!

✔ Encourage students to write poems of their own. Choose a common theme for the class if you like: insects, trees, flowers, the outdoors, school, people, or whatever. Create sketches or paintings to accompany what you create. If you have an art teacher to guide your work (or if you teach art yourself), you may wish to imitate Florian's watercolor technique.

✔ Notice Florian's fanciful presentation of text—with the poem on salmon and swordfish, for example. If students like this, they may wish to try using the text to reflect the topic, as Florian does.

✔ Talk about the paintings as you share the poems. How would your students describe this writer's artistic voice? Does it match his writing voice?

Grimes, Nikki. 2002. *A Pocketful of Poems*. New York: Houghton Mifflin Books.

Summary

A charming, creative collection of haiku poetry (seventeen syllables), brimming with personality, full of the spontaneity for which Grimes is famous. Best of all, each poem is inspired by just one important word in the poet's life—what could be simpler? *Fun* to read aloud.

Writing Connections

✔ Explain what haiku poetry is: a poem with seventeen syllables that explores just one idea. As you read some poems aloud, ask students to clap hands at each syllable till they start to get the feeling for what a syllable is. Read slowly and clap with them to help them get the idea. This also helps them build a sense of rhythm. (Ask one student to count the syllables as you go—should be seventeen!)

✔ Brainstorm a list of "important words" for your students. Explain that this could be a collection in which to build poems.

✔ Ask students to take just one of those words and create a haiku poem. The object is seventeen syllables, but if your students have trouble with this, don't worry! The ability to count syllables will improve with time. Meanwhile, focus on the main priority: to create a short poem on one important subject.

Marshall, James. 1972. *George and Martha*. Boston: Houghton Mifflin Company.

Summary

Like all the "George and Martha" books (see also *George and Martha Encore*, 1974), this one is an excellent example of voice. George and Martha clearly care for each other deeply, but they have their share of disagreements and small troubles to overcome. They love teasing each other in a kind and friendly way—but with a touch of humor. Use the book to illustrate the effective use of dialogue—a major component of strong sentence fluency.

> *Becoming a writer can also profoundly change your life as a reader. One reads with a deeper appreciation and concentration, knowing now how hard writing is, especially how hard it is to make it look effortless. You begin to read with a writer's eyes. You focus in a new way.*
>
> **—Anne Lamott**
> *Bird by Bird* (1995, p. 233)

Writing Connections

✔ Ask students to try writing a small sample of dialogue, using *George and Martha* as a model.

✔ Ask students to act out one of the "George and Martha" stories. Encourage students to make the most of the dialogue, speaking with lots of expressiveness and letting their faces show their feelings.

✔ If you feel students are ready, ask them to create a new story, putting George and Martha in a different situation: for instance, arguing over which movie to see, deciding what to buy at the grocery store, deciding whose turn it is to drive or to cook, shopping together for something—say, a couch or a pet.

Prelutsky, Jack. 2005. *Read a Rhyme, Write a Rhyme*. New York: Alfred A. Knopf.

Summary

You and your students will enjoy this rich and varied collection of read-aloud poetry by Prelutsky and other poets, all thematically organized. As a bonus, Prelutsky packs this book with "poemstarts": starter poems on specific topics, with suggested rhyming words students can use (if they wish) to extend the writing.

Writing Connections

✔ Listen to the poems. Ask students to read aloud, or even act some out. Many of these samples lend themselves to come-alive poetry.

✔ Choose favorites. Give awards: for example, for the most "recitable" poem, the poem with the best rhyme, the most memorable poem, the most visual poem, or the best poem for a come-alive performance.

✔ Try extending some of Prelutsky's poemstarts. Then, invent some poemstarts of your own, and trade with a "poetry buddy."

Walker, Alice. 2006. *There Is a Flower at the Tip of My Nose Smelling Me.* New York: HarperCollins Publishers.

Summary

Walker herself describes this book as a sort of thank-you note to the world, a thank you for allowing her to experience the beauty and the sensory richness of life. The text is simple, based on the humblest of experiences: smelling a flower, looking at the sky, walking down the road. But the originality of her concept coupled with surreal beauty of Stefano Vitale's illustrations takes those experiences to another level altogether.

I better understand now that reading aloud to children is teaching and that how I read and the talk surrounding that reading has a direct influence on children's growth as readers and writers. Daily read-aloud time cannot be shortchanged for it helps children understand the fundamental purpose of the written word.

—Carol Avery

And with a Light Touch (2002, p. 5)

Writing Connections

✔ After sharing the book and illustrations, talk with your students about this different way of seeing and experiencing the world. What do they think about the idea of a flower *smelling the person*, or a drop of water on the tip of the tongue *tasting the person?* Why does Walker write about things in this way?

✔ Talk about the different senses, and some of your students' favorite or most vivid experiences connected to each sense.

✔ Use some of your sensory details to create both illustrations and writing—using either Walker's intriguing twist on the usual perception or a more direct approach. Talk about why senses are so important in writing.

Books for Teaching CONVENTIONS and PRESENTATION

Cleary, Brian P. 2000. *Hairy, Scary, Ordinary: What Is an Adjective?* Minneapolis, MN: Millbrook Press.

Summary

Who knew a book about parts of speech could be this much fun? In this frolicsome compilation, we learn dozens of adjectives—and the essence of what an adjective is—through Cleary's poetic presentation and Jenya Prosmitsky's expressive illustrations (in which cats play a predominant role).

Writing Connections

✔ Share the book more than once. Add favorite adjectives to word walls or personal dictionaries.

✔ Explore the notion of "adjective." Just what is a modifier, anyway? What does it add to the writing?

✔ Model the revision of a piece of writing that is adjective-free. Ask students to help you add a few adjectives that will make your own writing "hairy," "scary," and anything but "ordinary."

✔ Invite students to use favorite adjectives in any descriptive piece of writing. Examples: Describe a favorite food, the habits of an animal, the behavior of a friend or sibling, the weather on a good or not-so-good day, the experience of getting a haircut.

Lum, Kate. 1998. *What! Cried Granny.* New York: Penguin Putnam Books for Young Readers.

Summary

Patrick is having his first sleep-over at Granny's house, and he's missing a few things: a comfy bed, a feather pillow, a teddy bear to hug. Not to worry; Granny is extraordinarily resourceful—and quick. But is she quick enough to answer all Patrick's requests before dawn? Though this is not a book about conventions per se, author Kate Lum is conventionally creative (with punctuation, capitals, repeated letters, and ellipses) in bringing Granny's voice to life.

Writing Connections

✔ As you share the book, notice how Lum punctuates sentences and employs other conventional devices to help the reader "hear" Granny's voice. Ask students to imitate the voice as they think the writer meant it to be read.

✔ Create samples of writing in which a character speaks. Invite students to use full capitals, mixed punctuation (question mark plus exclamation point), underling, or other devices to help readers understand *how* to read the text.

✔ Model the punctuation of dialogue between two characters. Ask students to help you decide how it should be read and whether full capitals or other conventions are called for.

Pulver, Robin. 2006. *Nouns and Verbs Have a Field Day.* New York: Holiday House.

Summary

The nouns and verbs in Mr. Wright's class feel very exclusive—at first. Nouns want to pair up with other nouns, verbs with verbs. But wait—nothing very exciting is happening. When they look out the window to see the students playing happily, the light dawns: Nouns and verbs have more fun when they work together to form sentences. Let the field day begin!

Writing Connections

✔ It's easy to get the basic idea of this book with one reading: nouns and verbs need to go together. There's much more going on here, though, and to really understand nuances of what a pronoun or proper noun is, you may wish to share the book more than once.

✔ Talk about nouns as naming words, verbs as "happening" words. Act out some verbs. Label some objects in the class with their corresponding nouns. Add words to personal dictionaries.

✔ Model the creation of sentences and ask students to help you identify nouns and verbs. Talk about why they need to work together (It won't be a sentence otherwise!). Exception: verbs can work alone in command sentences—*Get up! Move! Look! Listen! Sing!*

✔ Have fun with the quiz on the last page of the book.

✔ Ask students to look for nouns and verbs in their own writing, and to draw them as characters, using Lynn Rowe Reed's illustrations as models. Notice how different the bodies of the nouns and verbs look as Reed has drawn them. Why is that? What is she trying to show?

Pulver, Robin. 2003. *Punctuation Takes a Vacation.* New York: Holiday House.

Summary

What if punctuation marks got tired of their various duties and just took off on vacation? How would we write? This is the situation in Mr. Wright's class, where the punctuation marks grow tired of being erased, replaced, corrected, or ignored—and decide to take a little time off. Suddenly, writing becomes quite the challenge.

Writing Connections

✔ As you share the book (possibly more than once), invite students to identify the punctuation marks they recognize. Talk about the various "jobs" these punctuation marks do in our writing.

✔ At one point, the vacationing punctuation marks write postcards back to Mr. Wright's class. Have fun guessing who the postcards might be from. Then, ask students to write notes or postcards in character as marks of punctuation. See if you and your students can guess who the cards/notes are from.

✔ Model the punctuation of text that is punctuation-free. Ask students to coach you on which marks to use where.

✔ Invite students to punctuate some unpunctuated text on their own—working with a partner. Hint: This is much easier if you read aloud!

Willems, Mo. 2004. *Knuffle Bunny*. New York: Hyperion Books for Children.

Summary

Trixie, who doesn't speak words yet, is on an errand with Daddy when something awful happens: Knuffle Bunny becomes lost! How will Trixie make her needs known? Emmy Award–winning writer (for *Sesame Street*) Mo Willems uses both conventions and illustrations inventively to help Trixie find her voice.

Writing Connections

✔ Ask students to keep an eye on Trixie as you share this book—possibly more than once. How is she feeling as the story unfolds? How do we know?

✔ Because Trixie isn't actually speaking in the "conventional" sense yet, Willems invents some words for her to say. How does he come up with these words?

✔ Invite students to write a story in which a baby or toddler "speaks." Can they find ways to show speech other than with words? Is it possible to do the same with animals? Inanimate objects, such as a truck?

✔ In this book, Willems imposes ink sketches on top of digital photos to create a special effect. Your students may enjoy doing something like this, beginning with a photo of home or school and imposing a personal drawing (cut out from the page) on top. These special effects pictures will make an impressive display.

LOCATION, LOCATION, LOCATION

I am lucky to work across the street from one of the world's great bookstores, Paulina Springs (www.paulinasprings.com). The owner, Brad, welcomes customers by name. He and his assistants actually read the books on their shelves and can always direct you, it seems, to just the right book. The music is always playing and the lighting is soft. *Reading feels good* is the message.

As I sat there one day, looking through a stack of books I had assembled and trying to select the "keepers" (You can't buy them all—I know because I've tried), in came a slightly younger shopper (she was three) with her dad. Her eyes lit up as she looked at the book covers, and she touched them reverently as if they held magic. I said hello to her and her dad asked her if she wanted to say hi. "No," she said. "Not today." Sara's mind was elsewhere. She pulled a book from the shelf for Dad to read, and he plunked himself right

> *If we don't laugh, gasp, block our ears, sigh, vomit, giggle, curl our toes, empathize, sympathize, feel pain, weep, or shiver during the reading of a picture book, then surely the writer has wasted our time, our money, and our precious, precious trees.*
>
> **—Mem Fox**
>
> *Radical Reflections* (1993, p. 149)

down on the carpet; clearly, this was a routine for them. He read book after book, letting Sara turn the pages, so she could pace it. He asked her questions about the pictures and she responded: "How does the boy look in this picture?" "Sad."

After three or four books, I thought Sara would be ready for something else, but she was just warming up. Dad said, "OK, it's time for you to read to me—so I get to choose the book." He did. He picked *Olivia* by Ian Falconer. Sara read this time (she knew it pretty well), and Dad turned the pages. She asked him questions, just as he had done with her: "Do you think Olivia is happy? What is Olivia doing in this picture?" He answered them all, just as she had answered his. At the end, she asked him if he liked the book, and he said it was one of his favorites.

When it was time to go, Dad said, "I hate leaving the bookstore. Let's decide when we're coming back."

"Tomorrow?"

"Good! I was hoping you'd say that. Let's get a snack—reading makes me hungry."

Me, too. And I bet Sara will always think of reading as something that lifts your spirit and makes you feel good, as well.

CHAPTER 7 IN A NUTSHELL

- Reading aloud is among the most important things we do in teaching writing, because it offers invaluable models.
- Reading aloud IS teaching writing, even if no writing activity follows the reading.
- Reading *as writers* helps us to be better teachers of writing.
- We can—and should—select books for specific features; however, a book chosen to illustrate powerful word choice, for example, may be equally wonderful for fluency or voice or ideas.
- It is not necessary to use the specific books listed here, or anywhere, to teach writing traits. Use any books you wish to guide your young writers to a deeper understanding of ideas, organization, voice, fluency, and other key concepts that define writing.
- Love what you read. Read with passion. The most important lesson you teach is the love of books.

STUDY GROUP: INTERACTIVE QUESTIONS AND ACTIVITIES

1. **Activity and discussion.** Think of your favorite read-aloud books. Do any appear this short list? Make three additions. Write a short summary review of each and share them with colleagues in your study group. Which traits do your favorite books reflect most strongly? List them here:

    Book 1 _____ Strength _____
    Book 2 _____ Strength _____
    Book 3 _____ Strength _____

2. **Activity.** Think of one or two writing connections you *could* make with each of your favorite books. Write these out and share them with your colleagues also.

3. **Activity.** Choose one book from your list and present it to your study group. Read the book aloud (just as you would with students), ask any questions you would ask of your students, and make any writing connections you would make with your students. Use your colleagues'

feedback to refine this reading-writing activity before presenting it to students.

4. **Activity.** How expressive and animated are you when you read aloud? Rate yourself as a reader:

___ Outrageously expressive—over the top, really!

___ Quite expressive, with a flair for drama where it's needed.

___ Timid, really—I don't put enough oomph into it.

Try to think why you've rated yourself as you have. Do you think you are putting enough expression into the reading to bring out the voice? The fluency? Choose a selection to read aloud for your colleagues. Ask for their response. Does it match your own evaluation?

5. **Activity and discussion.** It is possible to assemble hundreds of quotations to support the importance of the reading-writing connection. It's virtually undisputed! But can you think of a way it is *personally* important to you—as a writer, a reader, or both? Write about this briefly. Then, find one quotation (or more) to support your point of view. Share this with your colleagues.

6. **Activity.** In *Books, Lessons, Ideas for Teaching the Six Traits* (Spandel, 2001), I review numerous additional books that can be used to teach traits. Check a copy of this book for additional options—and add some of your own to the list.

SOURCES CITED

Avery, Carol. 2002. *And with a Light Touch.* Portsmouth, NH: Heinemann.

Fox, Mem. 1993. *Radical Reflections.* New York: Harcourt, Brace & Company.

Freeman, Marcia. 1998. *Teaching the Youngest Writers: A Practical Guide.* Gainesville, FL: Maupin House.

Graves, Donald H. 1984. *Writing: Teachers and Children at Work.* Portsmouth, NH: Heinemann.

Johnson, Bea. 1999. *Never Too Early to Write: Adventures in the K-1 Writing Workshop.* Gainesville, FL: Maupin House.

Lamott, Anne. 1995. *Bird by Bird.* New York: Doubleday.

Ray, Katie Wood. 2002. *What You Know by Heart.* Portsmouth, NH: Heinemann.

Ray, Katie Wood with Lisa B. Cleaveland. 2004. *About the Authors: Writing Workshop with Our Youngest Writers.* Portsmouth, NH: Heinemann.

Routman, Regie. 2000. *Conversations: Strategies for Teaching, Learning, and Evaluating.* Portsmouth, NH: Heinemann.

Spandel, Vicki. 2001. *Books, Lessons, Ideas for Teaching the Six Traits* (primary/elementary edition). Wilmington, MA: Great Source Education Group, Inc.

Assessing Young Writers

Assessment must promote learning, not just measure it. When learners are well served, assessment becomes a learning experience that supports and improves instruction. The learners are not just the students but also the teachers, who learn something about their students.

—Regie Routman
Conversations (2001, p. 559)

If children can't talk easily about texts, they will have a hard time being critical readers of their own or anyone else's writing.

—Lucy Calkins
The Art of Teaching Writing (1994, p. 326)

Kindergartners, you know, are often just handed a pencil the minute they walk in the door. We're so worried about getting something to hang on the wall. It's not all about product. We should think about process.

—Minnie Hutchison
Teacher, Thurgood Marshall School, Newark, Delaware

Maximum anxiety does not lead to maximum learning. Rather, confidence in one's self as a learner leads to student success and school effectiveness.

—Richard Stiggins
Student-Involved Classroom Assessment (2001, p. 3)

Assessment is not about making judgments—not really. It's about discovery and learning. In this case, it is about learning what it means to write well and what writing well looks like for us and for our students. As Barry Lane points out in the foreword, the word *assessment* comes from the Latin word *assidere*, which means "to sit beside." Good assessment should be a companion to learning, not a threat, but a help—to the teacher *and* to the student. It should be a way of answering, "How am I doing?" It should provide an opportunity for students to demonstrate all that they *can* do.

The best assessor a *beginning* writer can have is a coach who not only *sits* beside but also *works* alongside the learner, showing the writing process in action, pointing out what that learner is doing especially well (especially things the learner might not otherwise notice), and asking questions that encourage a beginning writer to make good choices and to move forward. A good coach models—continuously. Along with suggestions, he or she finds something to support and celebrate in every performance because even on the worst of days we learn something that can take us to the next level.

The best assessor an *experienced* learner can have is him- or herself. We do not teach children to assess their own work just so that the Monday grade will not come as a surprise. We teach them so that they can review what they have done, take pride in their achievements, revise with purpose, and improve on their efforts next time around—with or without an instructor as a guide. Good assessment pushes the learner toward independence, always.

THREE LEVELS OF ASSESSMENT

Assessment of young writers generally occurs at three levels: large-scale, classroom, and personal.

Large-Scale, Formal Assessment

Large-scale assessment happens at district or state level usually; occasionally, though, individual schools do their own assessments across grade levels. In large-scale writing assessment, more than one rater reads each paper, and if the two readers do not agree, it may go to a third reader for resolution. The readers are usually, but not always, teachers. When papers are sent to a test company for professional evaluation, the readers may include trained teachers, student teachers, journalists, writers, editors, or other persons with a strong language arts background. At this level, students may be assessed analytically, on key components of performance (the kind of assessment described in this book), or holistically, with a single score summing up overall performance. Holistic assessment provides a broad-brushstroke point of view, whereas analytical assessment provides more of a performance profile, helping students and educators identify strengths and problems in students' writing. Scores may be used for reviewing or modifying curriculum, judging how well students meet established standards, or placing/promoting students.

Classroom Assessment

Classroom assessment differs from large-scale assessment in a number of ways, the most striking being that it has the potential to look at performance over time and to consider a body of work versus a single performance. Individual performances may be assessed, it's true, but the summative assessment for a grading period generally takes several performances into account, along with other factors, such as growth. It seems almost a cliché to say that multiple assessments tell a truer story than any single assessment can hope

Figure 8.1

Sample report card.

SAMPLE REPORT CARD			
	GRADING PERIOD		
Writing Process Uses writing process			
Writes narrative piece			
Writes informational piece			
Keeps personal portfolio			
Shares/publishes			
Writing Traits Ideas			
Organization			
Voice			
Word Choice			
Fluency			
Conventions			

to tell: "One test cannot give an accurate picture of what [a] child knows, how the child is doing, and what the child needs to learn next" (Routman, 2001, p. 561). It is like the difference between a snapshot and a full-blown video. (In all fairness, single-test scores *can* provide important information, provided the test is carefully and thoughtfully constructed; they simply do not provide *all* the information.)

In addition to looking at a body of work, classroom assessment usually mixes spontaneous and "best possible" performances, sometimes looking at what students do in their daily work and sometimes focusing on long-term, multiday projects, publishing projects, and so on. Because it is teacher directed, classroom assessment is based on the observations and perceptions of someone who knows and works with each student, so it is by nature more personal. This often means that it is more insightful than large-scale assessment, but it does introduce an increased potential for some types of bias. Bias occurs when a grade is based on something other than performance itself—such as a child's general classroom behavior, quality of work in previous classes, or how a particular performance compares with the child's usual efforts (e.g., "John is really having an off-day").

Large-scale assessment is certainly not bias-free, of course; such factors as neatness, handwriting, selection of topic, general tone of the writing, and many others (even crossouts, size of margins, or ink color!) can influence scores unduly—and unfairly. Nevertheless, in large-scale assessment, readers rarely know the writer personally and so have no preset expectations regarding performance or general attitude or ability, and this does give them a small edge in overcoming many common causes of reader bias.

Classroom assessment (and grades, for that matter) can be based on any or all of the following: performance on individual writing samples (possibly across modes), growth over time, participation in the writing process, skill in revising or editing text, and the student "story" told by a portfolio. An increasing number of district report cards now incorporate the six traits or an amended version thereof. (See Figure 8.1 for a sample of how such a report card might look).

Personal Assessment

Students who keep portfolios, who are taught to use rubrics, and who are taught to make reading-writing connections can also become skilled assessors of their own work. They learn to "look within." The result is not a score or grade but a personal reflection that may be written and may become part of a portfolio. Personal assessment—especially with practice—also becomes the most fundamental and trustworthy basis for revision, as well as for improvement in future writing.

IMPORTANCE = IMPACT

Of these three forms of assessment, the third is most significant, yet it receives (usually) the least attention. After all, personal assessment generally has no grades or paperwork attached to it. Results are all in the students' heads—or sometimes recorded in written reflections. It is significant *not* because it is data-based with elaborate statistics to illustrate growth and *not* because it makes headlines (which it never, ever does) but because it has the most potential to truly influence how students think, write, revise, and edit—and how they will do so throughout their lives. Unless student self-assessment is firmly entrenched as a major goal of our writing curriculum, all other assessments will pale both in importance and in impact. This is so because *only* self-assessment gives students an internal compass to guide their development as writers. They must know whether their work is good not because we tell them or a state test tells them but because they can judge their performance for themselves.

Next in importance, of course, is classroom assessment. Unlike most large-scale assessments, classroom assessment can take into account *both* process and product and can look at students' performance over time and across various forms of writing—informational writing, narratives, personal essays, reflections, and so on. The teacher who is a writer him- or herself is acutely aware of a student's participation in and comfort with the process of writing and is able to pose important questions such as these: Does the student

✔ Have strategies (conversing, sketching, listing) to draw on for prewriting?
✔ Try new things?
✔ Borrow ideas from others?

> *The most important things to know about writing cannot be represented by numbers.*
>
> **—Vicki Spandel**
> *The 9 Rights of Every Writer*
> (2005, p. 110)

Figure 8.2

"Dear New York." Jared (2)

Jared

Deer New York i've herd
wot hapin I hop the
police finds them. I hope
all the engerd git biter. I hope
all the bad peopel fined a
beter heart. I hope people bil
d the bildings back agen.

✔ Borrow print from the environment?

✔ Come up with personally important topics (see Jared's spontaneous piece, Figure 8.2 and Kawai's definition of love, Figure 8.3)?

✔ Show a willingness to try new forms of writing?

✔ Enjoy writing?

✔ Extend individual pieces through use of detail?

✔ Imitate favorite books, poems, or other pieces?

✔ Love reading?

✔ Choose books for him- or herself?

✔ Listen with expectation and appreciation to both professional writing and the writing of peers?

✔ See him- or herself as a writer and reader?

Such questions are vital to creating an accurate portrait of who a student really is as a writer, but they are far beyond the scope of what large-scale assessment can measure. This does not mean that large-scale assessment

> *Student writers have a right to assessment that is not just about numbers, but also includes room for a smile, a laugh, a sigh, applause, and the honest and passionate response that all writers hunger to hear.*
>
> **—Vicki Spandel**
> *The 9 Rights of Every Writer*
> (2005, p. 111)

Figure 8.3

Kawai's definition of love

Name kawai   Date ____

Love means...

caring about people that die.

does not provide important information; it simply means that we should be realistic about its capabilities and limitations. Our reaction to large-scale assessment scores in recent years has grown into a virtual frenzy, sometimes out of all proportion to the substance and completeness of the information this kind of testing can possibly provide. It is like responding to newspaper headlines without bothering to read the stories behind them. Classroom assessment tells a bigger story; it fills in the details—in part because we know the writer behind the words and also because we witness tiny nuances of change and risk up close. Personal assessment, in the hands of an experienced student writer, helps complete the tale.

In the past decade, increasing numbers of teachers have asked whether, given its inherent limitations, large-scale assessment is appropriate for primary students. There is no simple answer to this question (although opinions abound). Let's explore some of the issues at stake.

LARGE-SCALE ASSESSMENT: IS IT RIGHT FOR PRIMARY STUDENTS?

Used properly, large-scale assessment (which typically focuses on just one performance by each student) can give valuable information on how students *as a group* are performing in an area such as writing, and can offer *one indicator of performance* for an individual student who is tested.

Such data are useful in determining whether a school or district ought to devote more time to writing instruction or in identifying the general kinds of problems (or strengths) student writers are having. It can also be *helpful* in determining whether individual students need additional instruction, though, of course (as noted earlier), it is a "single-dip approach" and so necessarily provides *indicators* as opposed to definitive, satisfying, complete answers. Regie Routman notes that "Combined with other assessments, formal, standardized measures are appropriate for accountability, monitoring, selection, and placement *as long as* [emphasis in original] they are supplemented with other assessments." She also notes the importance of specific feedback, stating that the language of any criteria used "must be clear and jargon free" (2001, p. 560). I would add that both prompts and rubrics must be grade-level-appropriate and prompts must be reasonably appealing in order to elicit anything resembling a typical response. Many times, especially with assessments of younger students, this is far from the case.

"I Don't Get It."

Often, primary students do not understand writing prompts, and this seemingly simple problem can greatly influence both how the student writes and how his or her paper is scored. Many things can get in the way of comprehending a prompt: reading skill, knowledge of or familiarity with the topic, and misunderstanding of a particular word or phrase—to name just a few. Sometimes students simply have no experience with the situation that is the focus of the prompt (e.g., "Explain how to care for a pet"), or they may find the topic so vague that they simply cannot tell what is being asked (e.g., "Describe a time you were surprised").

In a classroom, misunderstanding (or disinterest) is less likely to create a problem because the teacher can explain the prompt, come up with a different prompt altogether, or (best of all) give students freedom to come up with their own personally important topics. Students in a large-scale writing context, by contrast, generally are expected to interpret a prompt for themselves, and to respond to that prompt, and that prompt *only*. This means not only understanding what the prompt literally says but also knowing what *kind* of writing is called for—a story, an essay, a description, and so forth. Making such distinctions is a challenge even for older students (sometimes even for adults). It is next to impossible for many young students, even when the teacher reads the prompt aloud. There may be unfamiliar words, or just the way the prompt is written can create confusion—for example, "Describe what happened." *Describe* suggests that the prompt writer is looking for a descriptive piece, but the words *what happened* suggest a story. Prompt writers seldom take time to write to their own prompts (assigning is always easier than writing yourself), and so they seldom discover how confusing their own directions are.

A student who misunderstands such directions may write a description instead of a story or may give up trying to figure out a poorly written prompt and simply write on a different topic altogether. Such responses often lead to lower scores (scores, by the way, that reflect more the student's ability to follow directions or interpret someone *else's* fuzzy writing than the student's writing ability per se). They may even lead to outright dismissal of the paper. Poorly worded prompts plague writers of *all* ages and abilities, but clearly, primary writers are the most susceptible because of their lack of experience in reading, writing, and responding to prompts.

"I Didn't Have Enough Time!"

Few primary students are accustomed to being handed a sheet of paper and timed in their writing. Writing in a classroom is a little warmer and friendlier.

There's a warm-up period during which students draw or listen to a story or brainstorm with classmates. Sometimes they have a chance to converse with a partner. Sometimes they write in response to a project or an event that occurs right in the classroom—a visiting baby or pet, for instance. Usually, there is an opportunity to ask questions, and the teacher may roam the room during writing to offer helpful tips or answer more questions. Many teachers post word banks or checklists from which students can draw.

None of these things is likely to be part of large-scale assessment. Some primary students take this difference in stride; others find it traumatic. Some are even reduced to tears because, after all, it *is* a test, and you don't have to be very old to learn that school is a place where you are expected to succeed. Were this not the case, surely you wouldn't be tested so rigorously or so often.

"I Can't Write This Much."

What about those students who are not yet fluent writers—fluent in the sense of generating *lots* of text? For them, writing assessment can spell panic. Even adults who do not write skillfully or frequently get shaky when handed a blank piece of paper, especially if someone else is going to review what they put on it. (Maybe you feel this way yourself.) Some students simply freeze and turn in a blank page. Others strategize to find ways of filling the page at all costs—writing extra big or repeating familiar words endlessly or filling most of the page with a picture. Such strategies also translate into lower writing scores—or no scores at all. What's more, anxiety itself affects performance, inhibiting some young writers who normally enjoy writing. Young writers who might otherwise delight us with their originality and voice become so afraid of incorporating *any* errors into the text that they write drivel—ridiculously simple sentences with three- and four-letter words that they feel confident they can spell. Ironically, some reviewers are actually pleased with these results, especially if they are relatively error-free. This is unfortunate because it reinforces in students' minds the restrictive and misguided notion that good writing is *correct* writing—and little more.

Correctness is a worthy goal, but it is not enough—not even close. You can have the shiniest shoes in the world, but if they are all you are wearing, it is unlikely that you will be viewed as well dressed. To make a reader shout, clap, laugh out loud, gasp in surprise, tear up with nostalgia, or reach to turn the page—now *those* are goals worth the effort of writing. We must not settle for less—or teach our students to settle for less. We want our students to experience the thrill of writing something, *sometime* that moves a reader—don't we? We steal this opportunity from our student writers when we use assessment to terrify them or when we do not respect personally important topics as sufficiently worthy.

> *American students are the most tested students in the world, and it doesn't look like that distinction is going to change any time soon. Our testing mania is ironic, because if testing were the means to higher achievement, we'd be the top-achieving country. Since we live in a culture where testing is highly valued, we need to be proactive and vocal in being sure that the tests being used are good ones.*
>
> **—Regie Routman**
> *Conversations* (2001, p. 590)

> *In the minds of some people, writing is one thing, but thinking is another. If they define writing as spelling . . . then they might have a case. But who would accept such a definition? Writing is the production of meaning. Writing is thinking.*
>
> **—George Hillocks, Jr.**
> In National Writing Project and Nagin, *Because Writing Matters* (2003, p. 98)

In Summary

Large-scale assessment is an expedient method of gathering "writing at a glance" information from writers who are old enough and experienced enough to deal with the logistics. This generally occurs around midyear of third grade or later. At this point, students are generating sufficient text that the challenge of filling half a page to a page with writing is no longer intimidating. They may have had some practice in the classroom reading and responding orally to various prompts—trying them on for size, if you will. A wise teacher provides this kind of practice. It is a lifeline for students who will be tested. Students may also have had some practice writing quickly, under a prescribed time limit. They are beginning to put conventions into perspective, as tools for showcasing ideas and voice, not an end in themselves. Further, writing to a prompt feels far more comfortable once you have done it a few times, and it becomes easier to judge how long it will really take you to plan and write a paragraph. This does take practice. If we asked many prompt writers to actually write in response to their own prompts, it is unlikely that they could guess the actual time it would take with any accuracy, and many would complain when time was up.

Despite (and in some ways, because of) its efficiencies, large-scale assessment is not ideally suited to the needs of most primary students. It is clearly very much at odds with the kind of writing most young writers are accustomed to doing within the classroom, and the demands are simply beyond the reach of many students—not all, but many. In addition, many of the rubrics customarily used to assess older students (see the appendix for an example) are simply not suited to the assessment of younger writers. They are developmentally at a much higher level, demanding skills beginning writers have not yet acquired and—*more important*—ignoring many of those things (e.g., left-to-right orientation, sentence sense, spacing between words, use of letter strings to form a first complete sentence) that primary students have mastered so brilliantly but for which they receive no credit because *it is not in the rubric.*

Figure 8.4

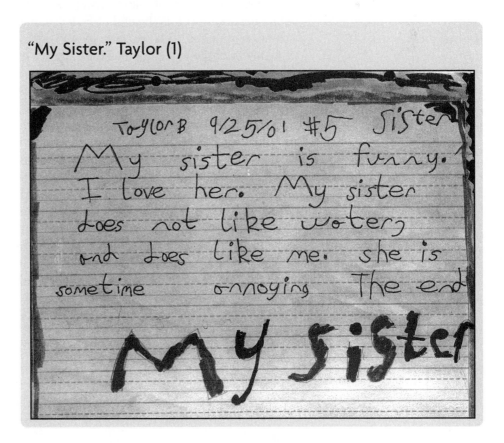

"My Sister." Taylor (1)

To this let me add that we are still, I believe, in the early stages of designing first-rate rubrics with which to assess very young writers, and we need a good deal more field testing at the classroom level before we should dare to embark on a high-stakes assessment venture with primary students. We need to know, with far more certainty than we now do, that we are looking for the right things in our students' work and that we are capable of spotting them. I am not persuaded that large-scale raters of primary-level work see beyond conventions to the detail or voice or even fluency (in letter strings, for instance) that hides within first writing efforts. Nor am I persuaded that artistic expression receives its just due in our assessment of meaning. Such things are far more likely to be addressed well at the classroom level.

Assessment of very young students is also tricky because many of them write very little or write in ways that we cannot comprehend speedily and often lack (or will not take) time to interpret. Or to put it another way, we are not sure what we are looking at. If we wait until students develop a certain level of fluency and comfort with writing (for most students, around late grade 3 or early grade 4 or its equivalent in English-language learners), we are more likely to gain meaningful results from our large-scale assessments. It is not so much that young students have suddenly learned how to write. Very young students may not have mastered conventional text, but they *do write*. They *do* create meaning. It is we, the assessors, who improve in our ability to review performance accurately as students grow older and more capable of creating the sort of text with which *we feel comfortable*.

In Figure 8.5, kindergartener Jacque creates a wide-eyed and fairly detailed self-portrait that seems to say, "It's me, world! I'm here!" In an ironic twist, the student in Figure 8.6 looks wistfully, somewhat regretfully at the coming of summer because "It is the end." She is leaving the teacher to whom she has become so attached. This writer's clear struggle to spell challenging words belies the power of the voice that lies beneath. It's a voice to which we should pay attention, because *this child is a writer*.

Here's the thing: In the bad old days, when conventions reigned supreme, we looked mostly for spelling and punctuation errors. Admittedly, this is a pathetically limited approach to assessing writing if we buy into the belief that writing is the verbal expression of thought. But it has one overriding, huge advantage so appealing that some people cling to it even now: It is easy. When we got elaborate and began to talk about development of ideas, organization, incorporation and support of a thesis, use of transitions, expression of personal voice, and fluent sentence construction, we didn't just raise the bar for students. We raised it for ourselves as well. We agreed to become very, *very* good assessors. When we commit to an assessment as inherently complex as judging performance in writing, a pledge goes with it: "If you meet these standards I have set for you, I will know it. If you express clear ideas, I will understand them. If you organize your writing well, I will follow where you lead. If you write with voice, I will hear you."

If we are to assess primary writers accurately and equitably, it is *ourselves* we must teach first—and we are not there yet. In the context of a *classroom*, we have a fighting chance. We see the children and hear them. We speak to them and observe their responses. We see many samples of writing, not just one. We know what is typical and what is ex-

> *Because of the time needed to assess the samples, and because teachers do not receive the samples back, prompt-driven assessments have little value as tools for instructional improvement for individual students—this is still best achieved by ongoing assessment of student writing in the classroom.*
>
> **—Tommy Thomason and Carol York**
> *Write on Target* (2000, p. 75)

Figure 8.5

Self-Portrait. Jacque (K)

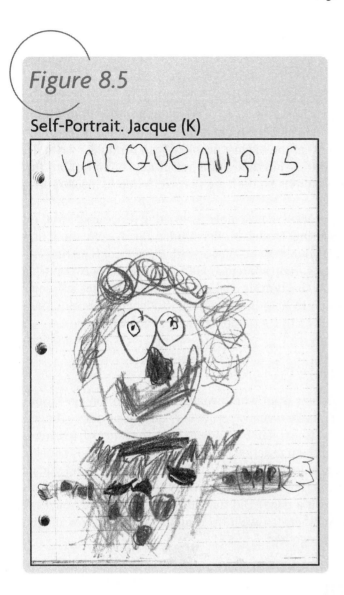

Figure 8.6

"It Is the End" (K).

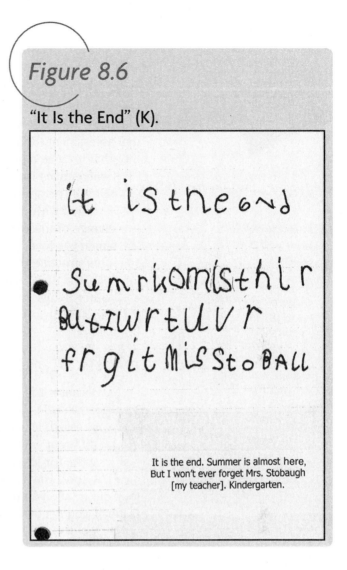

It is the end. Summer is almost here,
But I won't ever forget Mrs. Stobaugh
[my teacher]. Kindergarten.

ceptional. We know what is born of understanding and what is more likely to be fortuitous. And we see change and growth.

My Recommendations

Let's keep large-scale assessment at grade 3 and higher. Assess beginning writers at the classroom level. Continue to improve our writing continuums for young writers based on what we teach ourselves about primary writing. Keep looking. Keep learning. Make students partners in the assessment process, not just targets for our critique. Teach them writers' language and model, through our own work and the writings of others, what we want to see. Recognize their successes, and let them know what they do well. Above all, do not cave into the temptation to make curriculum and teaching strategies "match the test." Rather, continue the conversation about good testing practice so that our assessment methods truly reflect and honor what it is we wish to teach—namely, writing as thinking.

> *Formulaic writing encourages vacuous thinking and freedom from personal investment. In short, it undermines the very soul of what we seek to accomplish through writing instruction.*
>
> —Vicki Spandel
> *The 9 Rights of Every Writer*
> (2005, p. 125)

TEACH FROM YOUR HEART

Teach writing the best way you know how. Do not fall into the trap of thinking that you must abandon the best part of your curriculum in order to teach formulaic writing that will be of no help to students in any situation outside of formal assessment. Remember that the biggest problem with formulaic writing is not that it creates poor writing (dull though the result may often be) but that it encourages formulaic thinking—thinking that lacks depth, insight, originality, or perspective.

Stick with writing process. Allow time for writing. Encourage free exchange of ideas and sharing. Model. Model. Model. Read—and show how much you love it. It fills your students' heads with ideas—content, that is—plus strategies for writing. Help students make connections between what you (or they) read and the writing you all do. The following are some other things you can do to help increase your students' chances of success in any on-demand writing situation, now or in the future.

> *Formula approaches are most useful in boosting the scores of non-fluent writers, whose work may jump a score point. . . . But the same cookie-cutter approach will also prevent those scores from going higher because the writing samples are obviously poured from the same mold. You certainly won't find the formulas in the "real world" of good writing.*
>
> **—Tommy Thomason and Carol York**
> *Write on Target* (2000, p. 67)

Increase Students' Comfort

Because it is so different from what usually happens in the classroom, large-scale testing makes many students uncomfortable. Indeed, stressed. It is helpful to explain to students that this kind of writing *is* different and to give them practice in trying it out. "How does it feel to write for just a certain length of time? Let's try it and see" (and you do it, too). Have students time themselves when the stakes are low: "How long did it take you to fill half a page? Did that surprise you? Could you write faster if you needed to? Another day we'll try it and see. This is how much I wrote." And so on. Practice together.

Have a "Prompt Day"

> *If states really want student writing to improve, they need to insure that teachers have adequate time to teach writing well. Effective teaching means planning for instruction and responding to student writing.*
>
> **—George Hillocks, Jr.**
> *The Testing Trap* (2002, p. 205)

Share a few prompts with students and talk about what kind of writing you would do in response to each prompt. You do not have to *do* the writing—just talk about it. Talk about whether a prompt is asking for a story or for information. Talk about the very first thing you would write (the first sentence is always the hardest). Talk about whether a picture should be included (sometimes, sometimes not). Talk about how long a response needs to be—or *can* be. In some large-scale assessments, responses shorter than four sentences are unlikely to receive scores, so "Four or more" is a good rule of thumb for writers in grades 1 and 2 until they reach a level of fluency where longer pieces are much easier to generate. Teach them some coping skills, such as letter-line strategy, including the first letter of a word followed by a blank for words they simply do not know: for example, s_____ (for *soccer*). This allows them to get text on the page. If time permits, they can return to these "simplified" words and fill in the blanks, if possible. If not, at least they have written more copy than they likely would have had they allowed themselves to be blocked by spelling.

Practice Individual Prewriting

Some students get the wheels turning by talking. Usually, in large-scale assessments, they will need to fall back on some other form of prewriting because talking may not be allowed. You can suggest drawing, webbing, or making a list. Model these forms of prewriting, and make sure that students practice them.

Put Things in Perspective

I know—the stakes *are* high. The media stand ever-ready to pounce on the slightest hint of poor performance (never mind that their own commentators make numerous grammatical errors and their print makes a scrupulous editor's red pen quiver). Districts are held accountable and may lose funding or teachers. Their reputations for "poor performance" can affect real estate prices as parents scramble to find the schools that will magically make writers and readers of their children. These are serious consequences indeed, especially when so much still needs to be done to make state testing a fair and clear measure of student performance.

We must remain clear-headed through the stress, however, even though at times that feels next to impossible. Primary students, after all, cannot take on responsibility for declining real estate values or withheld funding. They must focus on what a child can focus on: *How am I doing today with this piece of paper and this pencil in my hand? Does anyone believe in me?*

Believe. Write with your children. Read to them. Help them feel that writing is a joyful thing to do, not a stressful chore to be done for the approval of a state or a stranger the child cannot picture. Give them practice reading prompts and responding to them—then discussing what was difficult to understand. Participate too so that you can share your perspective. Then, when the day of testing comes, have confidence. Your confidence will be contagious.

And tell your students this: A large-scale writing assessment is important because it provides information—like having your temperature taken by the doctor. It does not tell *everything* about you. No single writing test can tell whether you are a good writer. How you write on another day or on another topic may be different. Relax. Write as if you love it. Write as if you were writing a special note to your best friend in the whole world. And remember—there will be more tests and more opportunities.

IMPROVING TESTS

Large-scale assessment is an easy target because it creates so much stress. It can, however, under the best of circumstances, provide one important indicator of success. In addition, large-scale assessment draws attention to writing (or to any content area being assessed) in a way almost nothing else can do. It is doubtful that so many districts would have committed so passionately to the task of teaching students to write if assessments did not exist.

> *Teachers need to take what they know about teaching reading and use it to help students learn to read these tests. Teachers can help put tests in perspective by reading stories like Miriam Cohen's* First Grade Takes a Test *and by discussing with students what tests can do and what they can't.*
>
> **—Kathleen Strickland and James Strickland**
> *Making Assessment Elementary*
> (2000, p. 121)

> *Every time I thought I was smart enough to write, WHAM, I'd get smacked across the side of the head. And the more I whaled on myself, the dumber I felt, and the more it paralyzed me. I hadn't written the first word, but I hadn't given up hope.*
>
> **—Jack Gantos**
> *Jack's Black Book* (1998, p. 5)

> Too often, in on-demand writing, we do not honor design or thinking or voice as much as we should because these things can almost never be assessed in a rapid, assessment-at-a-glance fashion.
>
> **—Vicki Spandel**
> _In Defense of Rubrics (2006, p. 21)_

The question always arises, of course, "Is it good to teach to the test?" Really, this is the wrong question. Our question should be, "If we teach students to be strong writers, will they do well on the performance test we're giving them?" The answer _should be yes._ When students do not achieve high scores, we almost always look to the curriculum—or to the teachers and students. That may not be where the answer lies at all. If we are allowing time for students to write, if we are reading to them extensively and from a wide range of sources, if we are inviting them to become evaluators, if we are sharing our expectations openly (through rubrics and other means), if we are teaching them writers' language, and if we are responding to their writing with unbridled enthusiasm and marked insight, then we are doing what needs to be done. And if the scores are still low, we must look elsewhere.

We must look to the test itself. Are we measuring _important writing skills_—or ability to follow directions? Are the prompts clear? Are they interesting? Could we write on them _ourselves_ and do well? As well as we expect our students to do? Do we train those who assess our students well and teach them to look for what is significant (e.g., thoughtful creation of meaning)? Our tests can get better. And when (if) they do, large-scale assessment scores will reflect more clearly whether students can write.

Continually Reviewing Performance Standards

Setting standards for performance encourages us to set high expectations for our students, and it encourages conversations about what student writers should be achieving. At the same time, many educators agree that we have a long way to go in setting standards that truly promote academic improvement. In her analysis of current standards, Regie Routman notes that some critics find standards inequitable, "punishing many schools and students by holding them accountable for higher standards while failing to support them" (2001, p. 586). In addition, she notes, standards may be hard for some teachers to interpret or to teach from, and many consider them insufficiently rigorous, focusing too heavily on specific content, especially isolated facts, rather than on "the knowledge and understanding that is important in each discipline" (2001, p. 586).

Teacher and researcher George Hillocks, Jr., agrees with this, concluding from his extensive research on state writing assessments that writing standards in general are too low—for political reasons: "When the standards are low, it is easier to boast of more and more students reaching the same low standard" (2002, p. 204). Ironically, standards that do demand complex thinking may not be backed by classroom curriculum that supports inquiry or in-depth understanding. Marc Tucker and Judy Codding (1998) suggest that what is needed is greater clarity in the standards themselves, coupled with a closer match between expectations and curriculum. In fact, they recommend using samples of actual student work to make expectations clear not only to educators but also to students themselves: "Any student should be able to look at a performance standard and say, 'I understand now. I can do that'" (1998, p. 56).

Should we have performance standards for writing? Yes. We should continually review and improve them, however—even as we have with our rubrics that describe student performance. Assessment specialist Richard Stiggins suggests that "we should never regard performance criteria as 'finished.' Rather, always see them as works in progress" (2001, p. 207).

All good assessment, regardless of level, begins with a vision of success. What does it mean to be successful—in a particular classroom, a particular state, a particular writing situation? Until this is crystal clear, so clear that students can express it in their own words, we have not defined our target well enough. As Richard Stiggins reminds us, "The quality of any assessment depends first and foremost on how clearly and appropriately we define the achievement target we are assessing. . . . If your job is to teach students to become better writers, you had better start with a highly refined vision of what good writing looks like" (2001, p. 19).

One caution: Beware of any test and standards reforms that come marching at you under the banner "Back to Basics." So-called "basics" most often refer to conventions: notably, spelling and punctuation. These are important elements of good writing, to be sure, but they are far from *basic*. That is a gross and potentially costly misperception. Basic writing is thinking and organizing information to ensure understanding, writing to and for a thoughtfully defined audience in a voice compelling enough to ensure the message will be heard. Strong conventions support such writing basics in important ways—but we must never, in our minds or in our assessment practice, allow them to take center stage, for doing so puts both writing assessment and instruction at risk.

In a recent issue of *Newsweek*, the admissions dean at Pomona College clearly defined what colleges are looking for in applicants, and the criteria specified nothing about conventional correctness:

> Admissions officers, even at the most selective institutions, really aren't looking for perfection in 17- and 18-year-olds. . . . We are looking for people whose egos won't get in the way of learning, students whose investment in ideas and words tells us—in the context of their records—that they are aware of a world beyond their own homes, schools, grades and scores. A picture, they say, is worth a thousand words. To us, an essay that reveals a student's unaltered voice is worth much, much more.
>
> —Bruce Poch
> *Newsweek* (2006, p. 52)

RUBRICS AND CONTINUUMS: CREATING A VISION OF SUCCESS

Rubrics (performance descriptors with numbers) and continuums (no numbers) make expectations public and visible. They take the mystery away—and they require us to become more honest, open, and consistent in our assessment. I believe in rubrics because in developing them, we teach ourselves important truths about any content area (writing, reading, math, or whatever)—and what we learn for ourselves guides our teaching forever after. So whether you use the rubrics or continuums in this book is less important by far than whether you use rubrics period. Have guidelines. Design them yourself if you wish. However, do not fool yourself that you know what you

> *Would you ever invite someone to dinner and not provide them with directions? We were inviting children to the learning buffet and telling them that if they could find their way, they were welcome to join us. But if they didn't happen to have the skills necessary to find their way, then—too bad for them. They were out of luck.*
>
> **—Donna Flood**
> In Spandel, *In Defense of Rubrics*
> (2006, p. 20)

expect if you have not put it into writing. If you can't write it, you don't know it—not yet.

In developing their original six-trait rubrics, the Beaverton teachers carefully studied thousands of samples of student writing, *grades 3 through 12. No primary samples were included* because the Beaverton School District (which developed that first model) had no intention of assessing primary students on a large-scale basis. Therefore, to use those original rubrics with primary students is risky, inappropriate, and unlikely to yield valid results. A few primary students, admittedly, are quite ready for assessment at that higher level, but such performance levels are not typical. Therefore, a classroom teacher can selectively apply advanced rubrics with students who are ready, easing other students into trait-based writing process with the more appropriate primary continuums—and eventually moving on to a higher level of difficulty.

Let me be very clear that it is *not* my intention that the primary-level continuums in this book become a basis for large-scale assessment. Much of the student work presented here is the result of students' original thinking combined with time to explore, draw, talk, write, revisit, and confer with the teacher (or another trusted writing coach). It is unreasonable to expect that most of these writing samples would be reproduced under conditions of rigid time constraints and imposed prompts (some of which are not interpretable by the children whose performance is being measured). Further, the writing that *does* emerge under such conditions is often not representative of what students are capable of in typical classroom circumstances.

The primary continuums shared in this book are intended *for classroom use* and for tracking students' progress across time. While they show progression in writing ability, please notice that they focus, very deliberately, on what students *can* do—not on what they *cannot* do. It is easy to think of a thousand writing skills most kindergarten students have not yet mastered. The trick is to identify those things young writers *are* doing—and to capture them in print so that we will not forget them. I suggest using the continuums from this chapter in several ways:

✔ As part of a portfolio, attaching the continuums to specific samples of writing incrementally through the year, to record students' progress.
✔ In parent conferences to help identify in an organized and explicit way the skills a young writer has attained or is working toward.
✔ As a reminder so that in our comments to student writers we can be not only encouraging but also precise about the skills and accomplishments we see. That way, we teach students to see these things in their writing, too.

In the appendix, you will find a copy of the original six-trait rubrics used as the basis for *Creating Writers* (Spandel, 2005). Those originals were developed for use by children in third grade (about February of that year) on up and *are not intended for use with primary students.* However, there are exceptions; if you have students whose writing is *consistently* at the "Experienced Writer" level on the primary continuums, across traits and across various samples of writing, they are most likely ready for assessment on the original, more advanced rubrics that appear in the appendix.

FEATURES OF THE 6-TRAIT PRIMARY CONTINUUMS

1. Inclusion of Art

Like most writing rubrics, our original six-trait rubric does not deal with picture writing or even with the use of art as a form of prewriting. This feature has been added to the primary continuums—for some significant reasons.

For many students (not only those at the primary level), picture writing is an essential form of expression. They need art to communicate. It does not just make the writing pretty. It *is* the writing. Much of the detail and most of the voice within early writing appears in art form (see Figure 8.7). To ignore this is like assessing Picasso's art by asking him to write an essay about his intention.

As Bob Steele notes, "Children use graphic units (schemata) much as we use vocabulary, and the thought processes that go into drawing—raw materials organized into meaningful and expressive forms—are syntactical in nature." He also comments that children "intuitively use the medium most likely to

Figure 8.7 "My very worst boo-boo" (text and picture, 1).

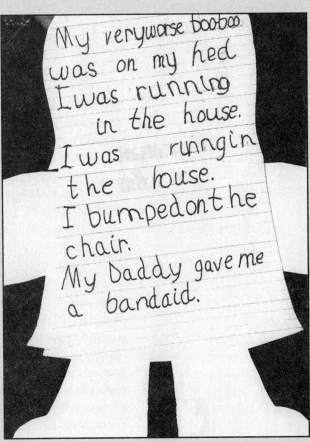

My veryworse booboo was on my hed I was running in the house. I was runngin the house. I bumpedonthe chair. My Daddy gave me a bandaid.

satisfy their [communication] needs: words for practical communication, drawings for expressing more subtle and complex thoughts" (1998, p. 7). In short, when we overlook drawing (or other art forms) in children's work, we may be missing the deepest and most important part of their thinking. Art is "the unrecognized language, and language is the way children make sense of their world and, in doing so, develop their minds" (Steele, 1998, p. 7).

2. Focus on Descriptors, Not Numbers

The primary continuums included in this book (see Figures 8.8 to 8.13) do not have numbers because I feel that the descriptors are more informative and more useful. I encourage educators to use them primarily *within the classroom*, preferably in the context of a writing collection, folder, or portfolio (a body of work), attaching them to three, four, or more selected samples of work created at various times throughout the year.

For each trait, the range of skills runs from Beginner, a writer who is just starting to make marks on paper, and recognizing the importance of print, through Experienced Writer, a writer who is in control of many writing elements, creating full paragraphs and, to an extent managing his or her own writing process. The Borrower is a writer who is really taking notice of environmental print and using it to enrich and expand his or her text. The Experimenter continues to borrow, but goes beyond what is available, launching into greater independence, daring to try, to guess, to invent when no helpful text is readily available. The Meaning Maker has achieved a level at which text is generally interpretable by a reader with no assistance from the writer. Further, the Meaning Maker's text is expanded and developed, rich with detail, stretched into multiple sentences, and filled with new words and complex meanings. Along this continuum, students gain skills not only in writing per se, but in listening and interpreting text, in revising, and in hearing ideas, organizational structures, voice, strong word choice, and fluency in literature shared aloud. A student who is *consistently* at the Experienced Writer level, across traits and across performances, is ready for assessment on the 6-trait rubric that appears in the appendix. As you use these continuums, keep in mind that they focus on the positive, on what writers *can* do. Therefore, they are ideally suited to use with portfolios, or any assessment system that focuses on growth.

3. Inclusion of Behaviors

Some of the indicators within the continuums are behavioral (such as editing one's own text or listening for voice or detail). Thus, the continuum is much easier to use if you are assessing your own students in the classroom than if you are looking at writing by anonymous writers. Behavior is significant because (to use one simple example) it is more important for Meghan to know how to correct her spelling using a spell checker than for her to know how to spell a few words correctly; the first skill will serve her well in all situations. At the same time, much of each continuum relates specifically to what you will see in the writing, so classroom observation of behavior is helpful, but not essential to using these continuums.

Figure 8.8 Primary Continuum for Ideas

Ideas

Beginner
- ☐ Makes marks on paper.
- ☐ "Reads" own writing, invents meaning.
- ☐ Dictates a clear message/story.
- ☐ Uses art to convey message/story.
- ☐ Recognizes that print has meaning/significance.
- ☐ Hears detail in stories read aloud.

Borrower
- ☐ Uses "words" and pictures to express ideas.
- ☐ Uses imitative/borrowed print to create signs, lists, rules, notes, etc. (not always interpretable without help).
- ☐ Chooses own topics sometimes.
- ☐ Notices detail in read-aloud text and in art from picture books.

Experimenter
- ☐ Uses text/art to create interpretable messages.
- ☐ Expresses clear main message/idea in one or more sentences.
- ☐ Can "reread" text shortly after writing it.
- ☐ Creates decodable lists, labels, notes, statements, short summaries, all-about or how-to pieces and/or poems.
- ☐ Can talk about main ideas and details based on picture book text/art.
- ☐ Likes to choose own topics.

Meaning Maker
- ☐ Creates clear message via text or text plus art.
- ☐ Expresses complex, extended thoughts.
- ☐ Uses multiple sentences to add detail.
- ☐ Connects images/text to main idea.
- ☐ Creates images that show detail: eyes, expressive faces, fingers and toes, leaves and grass, etc.
- ☐ Creates writing that is fully decodable by independent reader.
- ☐ Can "reread" text after several days.
- ☐ Adds stories to repertoire.
- ☐ Can interpret or retell message from picture book.
- ☐ Frequently chooses own topics.

Experienced Writer
- ☐ Creates a clear, detailed message though text/art.
- ☐ Uses multiple sentences to enrich ideas or extend story.
- ☐ Incorporates significant detail to enhance meaning.
- ☐ Creates writing that explains, gives directions, tells a story, expresses an opinion, describes.
- ☐ Creates informational and narrative text; may write persuasive paragraphs or poems.
- ☐ Can summarize own text.
- ☐ Can recognize and comment on detail or main message in text of others.
- ☐ Chooses personally important topics.
- ☐ Can revise own text by adding or expanding detail.

Figure 8.9 Primary Continuum for Organization

Organization

Beginner

- ☐ Fills space randomly.
- ☐ Can dictate sequential story or how-to piece.
- ☐ Can point to illustrations that go with text.
- ☐ Can "hear" beginnings/ endings in stories read aloud.

Borrower

- ☐ Can create art and text that go together.
- ☐ Creates layout with purpose/balance
- ☐ Uses two or more drawings to express story or message that has extended meaning and continuity.
- ☐ Recognizes titles as beginning points.
- ☐ Recognizes THE END as a signal of closure.

Experimenter

- ☐ Creates text/art with balanced look.
- ☐ Consistently creates image and text that complement each other.
- ☐ Can arrange or create sequence of drawings to convey a story or extended message.
- ☐ Writes more than one sentence on the same topic.
- ☐ May use title or THE END to signify beginning/ending.
- ☐ Stays focused on message.
- ☐ Creates labels/lists.
- ☐ Can organize recipes, all-about and how-to pieces, directions, and simple stories.
- ☐ Can predict what will happen next in text of others.
- ☐ Creates balanced, pleasing layout.

Meaning Maker

- ☐ Writes multiple sentences or images that suggest development/ sequencing.
- ☐ Sometimes uses art to express sequence of events.
- ☐ Uses connecting words: *first, next, then, once, after, and, but, or, so, because.*
- ☐ Uses identifiable beginning and ending sentences.
- ☐ Creates organized lists, stories, descriptions, or recipes.
- ☐ Can make predictions based on text of others.

Experienced Writer

- ☐ Connects text/art to main message.
- ☐ Uses thoughtful titles.
- ☐ Writes a true lead (usually, the opening sentence).
- ☐ Provides closure (usually with final sentence).
- ☐ Follows logical order/ sequence.
- ☐ Creates easy-to-follow text.
- ☐ Connects ideas.
- ☐ Uses elaborate transitions: *After a while, The next day, Because of this, The first thing, Finally.*
- ☐ Creates organized stories, summaries, how-to pieces, short essays, and other forms.
- ☐ Can use variety of organizational patterns: e.g., step by step, chronological, comparison, problem-solution, main idea and detail.
- ☐ Can revise own text for order, lead, ending.

Figure 8.10 Primary Continuum for Voice

Voice

Beginner

- ☐ Creates bold lines.
- ☐ Uses color.
- ☐ Expresses voice in dictation.
- ☐ Responds to voice in text read aloud.

Borrower

- ☐ Incorporates voice into art through color, images, facial features, etc.
- ☐ Uses exclamation points/underlining to show emphasis.
- ☐ Uses BIG LETTERS to show importance, strong feelings.
- ☐ Shows preference for text/art with voice.
- ☐ Borrows strong "voice" words, e.g., LOVE.

Experimenter

- ☐ Uses expressive language.
- ☐ Often incorporates definite tone/flavor.
- ☐ Creates expressive art.
- ☐ Creates tone that reflects feelings.
- ☐ Puts moments of voice throughout text.
- ☐ Recognizes voice in text of others, can describe personal response: e.g., "I liked it," "It was funny."

Meaning Maker

- ☐ Creates some text recognizable as "this child's piece."
- ☐ Writes/draws with personal style.
- ☐ Creates individual text, art.
- ☐ Elicits emotional response in reader.
- ☐ May use conventional devices (exclamation points, underlining) to enhance voice.
- ☐ Shows beginning awareness of audience: use of *you*, conversational tone, direct questions: *Do you like cats?*
- ☐ Shows preference for certain types of voice in read-aloud pieces.
- ☐ Often comments on voice in others' text/art: e.g., "That has voice," or "I want to hear that again."

Experienced Writer

- ☐ Creates lively, engaging, personal text/art.
- ☐ Creates writing that is FUN to read aloud.
- ☐ Is able to sustain voice.
- ☐ Provokes strong reader response.
- ☐ Uses voice to influence meaning.
- ☐ "Speaks" to audience.
- ☐ Creates voice that is easy to describe: *joyful, funny, moody, sarcastic, fearful, angry, wistful.*
- ☐ Shows growing awareness of own voice and is beginning to control quality and strength of voice.
- ☐ Can rate extent of voice in others' text/art.
- ☐ Can revise own text to strengthen voice.

Figure 8.11 Primary Continuum for Word Choice

Word Choice

Beginner

☐ Scribbles.

☐ Creates letter "shapes."

☐ Uses favorite words in dictation.

☐ Responds positively to text with strong word choice.

Borrower

☐ Borrows recognizable letter shapes from environment.

☐ Borrows simple words.

☐ Labels pictures.

☐ Creates letter strings that contain one- or two-letter words: *lk* (like), *dg* (dog), *hs* (house), *m* (my).

☐ Chooses favorite words from read-aloud text.

☐ Repeats "comfort" (familiar) words in own text.

☐ Guesses at word meanings from read-aloud text.

Experimenter

☐ Writes easy-to-read letters/numbers.

☐ Writes words with consonant sounds and some vowels.

☐ Uses titles.

☐ Writes decodable words/sentences.

☐ Uses many simple, familiar words.

☐ Uses sight words with ease.

☐ Has personal bank of favorite words.

☐ Attempts new or unfamiliar words in personal text.

☐ Adds new words to personal dictionary.

☐ Identifies favorite words from read-aloud text.

Meaning Maker

☐ Writes easy-to-read words.

☐ Writes with variety—dares to try new, less familiar words.

☐ Loves descriptive words and phrases.

☐ Uses some strong verbs.

☐ Uses words to create images or add clarity, detail.

☐ Stretches for the "right word."

☐ Keeps growing personal dictionary of meaningful words.

☐ Selects some "just right" words to express meaning.

☐ Usually avoids repetition.

☐ Uses language that creates imagery or sensory impressions.

☐ Favors literature with strong word choice.

Experienced Writer

☐ Uses vivid, expressive language.

☐ Writes with vocabulary that may extend well beyond spelling ability.

☐ Sometimes uses striking unexpected phrases: *"I felt like a once contented and proud swan who lost its feathers."*

☐ Uses many strong verbs.

☐ Keeps extensive personal dictionary.

☐ Repeats words mainly for emphasis/effect.

☐ Can recognize and describe strong word choice in text of others.

☐ Can revise own text to add descriptors.

☐ Can revise own text to strengthen verbs.

Figure 8.12   Primary Continuum for Sentence Fluency

Sentence Fluency

Beginner

- ☐ Dictates one sentence (or more).
- ☐ Enjoys poetry, rhythmic language.
- ☐ Enjoys music with a beat.
- ☐ Enjoys marching, dancing, clapping to rhythmic beat.

Borrower

- ☐ Creates letter strings that suggest sentences: *nohtipdin.*
- ☐ Writes text with a "sentence look" that may not be translatable.
- ☐ Dictates multiple sentences.
- ☐ Can hear rhythm, rhyme, and variety in read-aloud text.
- ☐ Can hear patterns—and may try imitating them.
- ☐ Can memorize simple poems for group recitation.

Experimenter

- ☐ Writes letter strings that form readable sentences: *I lik skl.* (I like school.) *I HA DOG.* (I have a dog.)
- ☐ Writes more than one sentence.
- ☐ Usually writes sentences that complete a thought.
- ☐ Attempts longer sentences.
- ☐ Dictates a whole story or essay.
- ☐ Favors patterns: *I can pla. I can rid my bik. I can red.* (I can play. I can ride my bike. I can read.)
- ☐ Likes to repeat text read aloud with inflection.
- ☐ Likes to memorize and recite simple poetry.

Meaning Maker

- ☐ Creates easy-to-read text.
- ☐ Consistently writes multiple sentences.
- ☐ Writes complete sentences-but may use fragments for effect.
- ☐ Writes longer (complex or compound) sentences.
- ☐ Begins to show variety in sentence lengths, patterns, beginnings.
- ☐ May experiment with poetry—rhyming or free verse.
- ☐ May experiment with dialogue.
- ☐ Reads aloud with inflection.
- ☐ Favors text with complex or varied sentence patterns.

Experienced Writer

- ☐ Can write two short paragraphs or more.
- ☐ Consistently writes complete sentences.
- ☐ Creates text that sounds fluent read aloud.
- ☐ Uses fragments for effect: *Wow! Crunch! A lot of snow!*
- ☐ Creates text that is easy to read with expression.
- ☐ Experiments with poetry/dialogue.
- ☐ Can read own/others' text aloud with inflection.
- ☐ Can recognize and comment on fluency in others' text.
- ☐ Can combine sentences.
- ☐ Can revise by changing word order.
- ☐ Can revise by varying sentence beginnings.

Figure 8.13 Primary Continuum for Conventions

Conventions

Beginner

☐ May create left to right imitative text.

☐ Can point to conventions in print.

☐ Plays with letter or number shapes.

☐ May "write" first letter (or more) of own name.

☐ May spell own name orally.

☐ Knows what letters are, what writing is.

☐ Draws to convey meaning.

☐ Attempts "words" of personal significance.

Borrower

☐ Imitates print: letters, "cursive flow (*ꝏ*)," punctuation marks.

☐ Writes own name.

☐ Writes one to several sight words.

☐ Loves to copy environmental print.

☐ Creates letters that face the right way.

☐ Can name/describe several punctuation marks: e.g., period, comma, question mark.

☐ May use periods or other punctuation marks randomly in own text.

☐ Asks about conventions.

☐ Usually writes left to right.

☐ Usually writes top to bottom on page.

☐ Can write on a line.

☐ Uses capitals.

Experimenter

☐ Uses capitals and lower case (often correctly).

☐ Uses periods, question marks, commas, and exclamation points (often correctly).

☐ Puts spaces between words.

☐ Spells many sight words.

☐ Creates readable, phonetic versions of harder words.

☐ "Plays" with more difficult conventions: dashes, ellipses, quotations marks.

☐ Can name/describe numerous conventions.

☐ Shows concern for correctness in own text.

☐ Writes left to right.

☐ Writes top to bottom.

☐ Is beginning to "wrap" text (down and left) to form the next line.

Meaning Maker

☐ Uses capitals and lower case with fair consistency.

☐ Uses periods, commas, exclamation points, question marks correctly.

☐ Sometimes uses paragraphs.

☐ Correctly spells ever-growing range of sight words and some challenging words.

☐ Uses some difficult conventions correctly: e.g., quotation marks, ellipses, dashes, parentheses.

☐ Makes corrections in own text.

☐ Writes left to right, notices margins.

☐ Writes top to bottom.

☐ Wraps text easily.

☐ Places title or illustrations thoughtfully on page.

Experienced Writer

☐ Uses wide range of conventions skillfully and accurately.

☐ Creates easy-to-read text with few or no distracting errors.

☐ Uses paragraphs, often in the right places.

☐ Spells most sight words and many challenging words correctly.

☐ Uses conventions to reinforce voice/meaning.

☐ Writes left to right, top to bottom; wraps text, and respects margins.

☐ Is careful with layout and formatting.

☐ Can edit own text for end punctuation, subject-verb agreement, capitalization, spelling of high frequency words.

☐ Can edit simple text of others.

☐ Knows simple copy editor's symbols.

4. Performance Over Time

Please note the blanks for checkmarks to the left of each performance indicator. You can use these to check any skill or observed behavior. There is no expectation that a child's writing will fall *fully* into one of the five performance levels described here—for example, "Beginner," "Borrower," "Experimenter," and so on. It is much more likely that a child will be quite high on the scale in some areas (perhaps ideas and voice) and not so high in others (perhaps conventions or fluency). Further, the levels are only approximations and cannot be more. Most writers will reflect some characteristics of one level and some of another. The purpose of the level descriptors is not to label children but to provide a convenient way of charting growth.

CLASSROOM ASSESSMENT: KEEPING IT SIMPLE

Not everything a child writes needs to be formally assessed. Sometimes a checkmark or a simple comment ("You did it!") is all that is needed. You certainly do not need to put yourself (or your students) through the task of assessing each piece of writing on each trait. You will all go crazy if you try. Your first step to recovery will be to cut down on the amount of writing you do, and that benefits no one. Instead, make a plan something like this:

✔ Assess a large portion of students' writing somewhat *informally*, using personal comments or a simple star (or other mark) to show completion of the task. You do not need a rubric or continuum for this.

✔ Teach *yourself* the traits so that you can spot them in your students' work.

✔ Use trait-related language to make your comments substantive and specific: "What remarkable word choice! Your voice is very clear in this piece!" and so on. If you know the traits, such comments will come easily to you.

- ✔ Help your student writers to identify strengths in their own work by showing them what to look for and by sharing literature that sharpens their listening skills.
- ✔ Encourage students to keep a file (call it a folder, collection, or portfolio) of written work and to select some pieces for inclusion throughout the year. Make sure that they are dated so that when you compare them, you can see growth.
- ✔ On three or four of those pieces, do a formal assessment using some or all of the six-trait continuums for primary students. As you review each piece, check each of the indicators that seems to apply. Attach the continuums to the sample and include it in the student's portfolio/writing collection.
- ✔ During parent conferences, invite parents to review their child's work and to look at the indicators you have marked. As the year goes on, invite parents to make comparisons and to see how many new skills their child has acquired. Using continuums for this kind of comparison allows you to be specific instead of simply saying, "Notice how much Aisha has improved."
- ✔ If you can make time, have an end-of-year conference with each of your young writers, reviewing one or more pieces of writing in light of the traits. You do not need to laboriously comment on every single skill the child is demonstrating, but pick out four or five outstanding accomplishments, and let the child know what he or she is doing well as a writer.
- ✔ Encourage students to create personal reflections commenting on their own views of themselves as writers. This reflection can take the form of a drawing, text, dictation, recording—or some combination of these.
- ✔ Present writing collections to children as important keepsakes, and encourage them to add future writings to those collections.
- ✔ Modify the continuums from this book as you identify potential strengths not yet noted.

THE DREADED GRADES!

No one I talk to—*ever*—likes grades. Everyone has the same comment: "I hate grades myself, but we have to have them because the _____ [fill in the blank to suit yourself—parents, administrators, students, school board members, businesspeople, employers, colleges, teachers at the next level] insist on them, so we have no choice." No choice? Well, this is not precisely correct. What we lack is a better alternative—for now.

Rubrics and continuums are a partial answer (and if done well, they provide infinitely more information than grades), but they only work if everyone uses them, understands them, and believes in them. Grades have an almost universal appeal (even among people who profess to hate them) because they are simple, deceptively so. They seem to tell so much—like fortune cookies. They are mysterious—and powerful.

In actuality, grades are overrated as authentic indicators of performance and frequently overvalued both by those who receive them and by those who hand them out. The danger lies in attaching *so* much weight to grades that we literally allow them to define who we are—as writers, learners, teachers, and people. It takes a strong person to overcome this sort of labeling. As Strickland and Strickland remind us, "Grades don't define people in the real world outside of school. We could list several famous school failures who became successes—Einstein, Lincoln, Rockefeller. . . . We all know 'regular' people who are bright and overcame the odds, achieving more than their grades would predict. Unfortunately, not all [students] overcome such odds. Many believe what grades tell them and adjust their lives accordingly, giving up on themselves and their dreams" (2000, p. 125).

Despite their limitations and risks, though, grades carry with them the illusion of accuracy and thus are likely to be around for a while. Therefore, we must ask ourselves on what basis we should assign grades. No one can make this choice for you, but here are some suggestions you may find helpful for primary writers. Let me add that my recommendations would be decidedly different for older students. College-level writing is mostly about performance; primary-level writing is largely about participation, exploration, and growth. So the basis for grading must be different also, in my view.

Without suggesting percentages (i.e., 50 percent of the grade should be based on this or that), here are some factors to keep in mind in assigning grades:

- ✔ Actual performance
- ✔ Completion of work
- ✔ Participation in writing process
- ✔ Growth as a writer
- ✔ Willingness to branch out
- ✔ Coaching

1. Actual Performance

Kindergartners write from the first day but may not (at first) create text (or pictures) that can be interpreted independently without the assistance of the writer. The early kindergarten writer may "read" his or her text immediately following completion but is often not able to do so a short time later. Nevertheless, even these very young writers have full understanding that marks on paper have meaning and significance. Many can create individual letters and connect some letters to sounds, yet much of the writing is likely to be random. Many can write their own names, names of family members or friends, and a few words of personal significance. They are likely to rely heavily on art to convey meaning. By the end of the kindergarten year, many are creating letter strings, moving into more phonemic spelling and including some sight words, and generating quite a lot of print that is meaningful to others.

First graders typically write numerous letters and some sight words. Many use letter-string sentences and, by the end of the year, may incorporate spacing and make enough letter-sound connections to spell or "create" most of the words they need to communicate. Most can write their names and words of personal significance: *mom, dog, cat, house, love, friend, school.* Spelling (except on simple sight words) may not be conventionally correct, but it is often phonetically close enough to allow most readers to make sense of the text without the writer's help. Many writers can read their work after writing, even when some time has passed. Some, however, cannot—or will place a slightly different spin on it. A close text-picture connection is common, and many first graders still rely heavily on art to create meaning. They are beginning to develop a sense

Figure 8.14 Holiday pictures. Taylor (1)

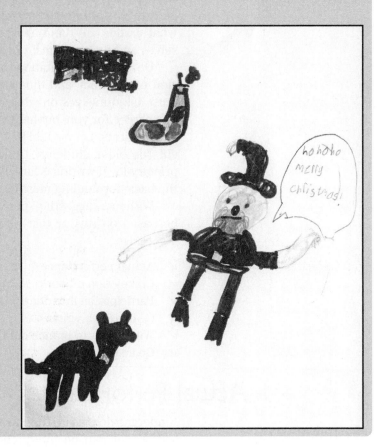

of topic (as message) and of sequence. A few are attuned to their own personal voice—and most are highly attuned to voice in the work of others. Writing is expanding in terms of both actual length and depth of detail. First graders who write single sentences early in the year may well be writing multiple sentences and short paragraphs by year's end. Drawings or paintings are marked by increased attention to detail as well.

Second graders are moving toward independence, creating multiple sentences, and by the end of the year, full paragraphs (sometimes several paragraphs). They are gaining an increasing sense of topic or main idea, as well as an understanding of how details expand a main idea. They are beginning to make choices about how to write rather than writing "first thoughts." They choose words deliberately and have favorite words or phrases. They also like to choose topics. Most of their spelling is correct on familiar words and sight words or phonetically close enough to make for fairly easy reading. Some are stretching constantly (especially with encouragement through reading) to include more difficult words. They still rely on pictures to express meaning, but their text is expanding in both length and complexity. Many are experimenting with dialogue and with poetry. Some have pronounced voice and write with a

Figure 8.15

"If I Were a Flower." Ellie (2)

If I Were A Flower

I was scared when I first bloomed. There were no other flowers. I can see a little bit of sky but all around me is snow. The snow was glittering like a diamond. It was very quiet. I was starting to feel sad and lonely because there are no other flowers and no friend or people to take care of me. Then I hear some thing. I do not know what it is. I look up and see someone who was moving the snow off of me. "Good Morning, Spring!"

highly individual style. Attention to audience is increasing. Awareness of conventions is growing rapidly, and many are experimenting with an ever-growing range of punctuation marks.

Third graders write stand-alone text; that is, the writer does not need to interpret for the reader. Most can easily return to a previously written text and read it aloud. Many write multiple paragraphs. If it has been encouraged, personal voice may be quite strong. Vocabulary often runs well ahead of spelling skills unless spelling is overemphasized, and so expressiveness has grown markedly. Third graders also have a strong sense of topic and a deepened understanding of detail. Text is less repetitive, more informative. Expository writing may still be the favorite form for some, although many now have a sense of story (from text read aloud) and can create stories with beginnings, development of plot, and endings. Poetry is also a favorite form, especially among students with a strong sense of fluency or well-developed vocabulary. Many enjoy free verse. Simple spelling and punctuation are well under control for many, and some experiment with sophisticated conventions: dashes, ellipses, parentheses, semicolons, and so on. Confident third grade writers will attempt spelling of difficult words and will not let spelling block expression. Some are experimenting with revision also.

2. Completion of Work

At primary level, just completing the work—participating—is important. You may wish to base a certain percentage of the grade on the fact that a student simply writes, regardless of what that writing looks like.

3. Participation in Writing Process

Participation is something you can only assess through careful observation and only over time. Overall, you are looking for such things as prewriting (through conversation, drawing, listing, thinking, reading/listening), sharing writing, offering or receiving suggestions, participating in a conference (with you or a peer), revising (even if it is just adding one detail to a drawing or putting in one new word), editing (even if it is only adding a forgotten name or date to a paper), or participating in group-writing activities. Listening is a form of participation, too. Children are not all noisy, and reflective learners need to be rewarded along with the talkers.

Figure 8.16

"Splash" by Kate (3)

> **Splash!**
> Look! People shout.
> I look into the blue water
> and see a glistening tail.
> Look!
> The dolphin leaps back out
> then into the water . . .
> Splash!
> I look at the beautiful
> silver smoothness of her skin.
> Look!
> Look!
> Look!

Author's note: I changed the last three lines from *Splash! Splash! Splash!* to *Look! Look! Look!* Because I liked the sound better and because I wanted the reader to *Look!*

4. Growth as a Writer

This will be simple to measure if you keep writing folders/portfolios. It will be very difficult if you do not. Do *not* rely on your memory, no matter how well you think you know your students and their work. You need multiple samples, dated, and you need to look at them *with continuums in front of you*. When you identify specific differences, you have documented growth, and at this level, when growth is the fundamental goal we want for our students, we certainly should allow it to influence our grading. Be careful, though! Do not base the whole grade on *how much* growth you see. For some students, the rate of growth will be phenomenal, whereas for others, little victories must make us rejoice. For some students, a little step forward (e.g., putting spaces between words) *is* big.

5. Willingness to Branch Out

In the real world of writers, risk taking is usually rewarded. Safe, functional, voice-free writing may win a polite nod of approval, but it will not get you published (except, perhaps, in government reports, where voiceless writing, like dead seaweed on the beach, is so common that no one thinks about it). It is never too early to teach this important lesson. Risk taking—in the sense of trying something new—takes many forms. A student may be experimenting with a different kind of writing (poetry or directions or a brochure or news article), trying out new words, or new kinds of punctuation, using multiple drawings to illustrate a story or expository piece, writing a first letter, tackling a difficult or sensitive topic, or whatever. To some extent, this experimentation is reflected in the continuums, but if you feel that they do not go far enough, give more credit.

6. Coaching

A good coach does not have to be an expert writer. Above all, a good coach only needs to be a good listener and an enthusiastic responder. If you routinely pair students for writing activities, you make it easy for them to fulfill this role, and you provide another means for them to gain writing skills even when they are not actually writing themselves.

In Summary

My preference is to focus heavily on participation and growth for young writers versus performance per se. Performance changes so rapidly and so much at this age that it is mercurial. We need to pay attention to it, but not so much for the purpose of grading as to help students see what they are doing *well*. With primary writers, your comments count more than grades.

WHAT YOU CAN DO

1. **Make *sure* that you have a very clear vision** of success for your classroom. If you were a student writer in your own class, would you know *exactly* what you had to do to be successful? Could you express it in your own

words? Can your students do so? If they can't, you haven't made the vision clear yet. Start right there.

2. **Use rubrics, continuums, and checklists** to share your vision of success and to keep your own assessment consistent. Start with those in this book, but if they do not cover everything you value or if you need to reword something, by all means make the necessary changes. Rubrics are tools, not holy writ. Revise. A word of caution, though: A rubric with vague language is like mindless advice: "Be cool," "Stay out of trouble," "Take care." It says nothing. Make sure that your rubric or continuum says something. Picture a student reading (or hearing) your rubric and saying, "Oh, I get it." Picture a parent doing the same.

3. **Share your vision** of success with parents and with children. Use common language to talk about writing performance so that everyone knows what the target is.

4. **Make your writing curriculum clearly and indisputably connected** to everything you assess so that your students have every chance to perform successfully. Do not assess what you do not teach.

5. **Check for significance.** Is everything you assess truly valuable? In other words, are you targeting significant skills, such as including details or organizing information, versus more superficial qualities, such as centering a title on the page or making margins wide enough?

6. **Become very familiar with the performance standards** for writing (and other content areas, of course) in your state. Look for the links to the six traits described in this book. You will find some because, as I point out in every workshop, the traits are just descriptors of basic good writing, nothing more. Do not be misguided by shifting terminology: *wording* is still word choice, *style* is often a mix of voice and fluency, *mechanics* are conventions, *design and structure* are organization, and so on. Do not expect precise parallels, but look for connections. They will give you confidence that your trait-based instruction is standards-based, too.

7. **Do not assess *everything*** your students write. It is not necessary or productive. In fact, it is a misuse of rubrics, in my view. Rubrics offer guidance. Once they are internalized, your students will think—always—of voice, detail, leads, and the rest. You do not need to reinforce this writer's way of thinking with a constant barrage of scores.

8. **Remember that a rubric,** in the sense of a guide, really has three parts:
   ✔ The written rubric that defines performance
   ✔ Models of writing (including your own) that show what performance looks like at those levels
   ✔ Your own teacher judgment and experience, the filter through which criteria are interpreted wisely and appropriately

9. **Practice assessing your students' work.** Practice until you feel confident that you are hearing moments of voice and fluency that you might have overlooked before. Practice until you know with *certainty* that you can offer the kinds of comments that will let your students know what they have done well and what they need to work on.

10. **Make self-assessment the goal** of your writing program, thereby making students partners in the assessment process. Do not expect to get there in a week or even a month. But do expect that by the end of their time with you, your students will be able to look at a piece of their own work and say something like, "I really put a lot of voice into this."

11. **Keep portfolios/folders/collections of writing**. Call them what you will. Keep them as small and manageable as you need to. But do keep samples of performance from throughout the year so that you can see where the journey began and how far the writer has come.

12. **Keep your expectations high**. As Mem Fox says, "If you don't have the highest expectations, how do you know you're not underestimating what your students can do? If you don't reach for the stars, you might be killing potential" (1993, p. 165). At the same time, though—

13. **Allow students to screw up now and then.** A welcoming, nurturing, successful classroom demands risk, persistence, and belief—not perfection. I once knew a principal who would allow no work to be hung on the walls until it was conventionally perfect. (He did not mention voice or ideas, though.) Odd as it seems to some people, demanding perfection can squelch success because it stifles effort, and rewards sameness. When students live and write in an environment that encourages growth, they dare to stretch—and to risk failure. Eventually, those who dare take off and soar.

14. **Voice your view.** Be heard. Write to or visit your state department of education, your district administrators, your school board, or legislature. Discuss ways of assessing students well and equitably. Bring samples of writing with you. Express what you value. Ask them to state clearly what it is they are looking for—and to offer their own samples of what that should look like.

15. **Provide practice.** Most of the time, the classroom focus should be on helping students become lifelong writers and readers. But so long as state testing is a reality (and for most of us, this might as well be forever), we need to offer students a lifeline. It is OK to explain that this is *a special situation*. "Writing for the test" is a genre unto itself. And because large-scale assessment is kind of a hurry-up process, you need to think and work fast. This is why you have to practice. Let your students know that you want them to feel ready so that the day of the test will be more comfortable.

> *Students always rise to meet our expectations, you know.*
>
> **—Penny Clare**
> *Second Grade Teacher*
> *Write Traits Trainer*

Figure 8.17

Katie's Flowers (K).

16. **Be part of a writing community.** Participate. Let students hear, read, and assess your work, too. Hear, read, and assess the work of other writers outside your classroom as well. Assessment never falls so heavy as when it falls only on you (the student). Let your students know that all writers are assessed, one way or another, whether by a state test or by a publishing house. It is part of the process. It does not feel so scary when you are not alone.

17. **Think beyond conventions.** Don't be afraid to display your students' work under a banner that reads "A Celebration of Our Voices" or "Listen to Our Fluency." Like Katie (Figure 8.17), let the flowers bloom.

 # CHAPTER 8 IN A NUTSHELL

- Assessment is not about making judgments; it is about discovery and learning. In the case of writing assessment, we assess to discover who our students are and to learn what makes writing work so that we can teach more effectively.
- Assessment occurs on three levels: large-scale, classroom, and personal (self-assessment). Of these three, large-scale assessment receives the most attention, but personal assessment has the most impact when it comes to shaping writers.

- Large-scale assessment has definite limitations and poses a number of risks for use with primary students. It is important for us to question whether the results we receive from such assessments yield an accurate picture of primary students' performance.
- At the same time, large-scale writing assessment, when well constructed, can provide useful information about older writers, those with sufficient fluency and comfort with writing to create extended, meaningful, detailed text under time constraints.

- In cases where large-scale assessment is a given, we can offer students lifelines: teaching for lifelong learning, diminishing stress as much as possible, having a "prompt day" for practice, encouraging personal forms of prewriting, practicing timed writing.

- Like large-scale assessment, use of performance standards offers some real benefits when applied carefully and reviewed often. Standards keep us focused on what we hope our students will achieve and also encourage discussion about writing.

- Student performance in writing (or any area) is highly dependent on a clear vision of success. Rubrics and continuums help support such a vision. They cause us to be consistent and honest about our expectations.

- Rubrics, continuums, and checklists are all a little different. A *rubric* is a numbered scale that defines performance along multiple levels (usually from four to six). It is designed for scoring. A *continuum* is a verbal scale that describes growth from beginning to strong levels, showing how writers (or performers of any sort) gain skill with time and experience. A *checklist* is not a measure of performance at all. It is a list of reminders, a summary of what is important with respect to a particular feature of performance, and is ideal for personal use in revision.

- The primary-level continuums included in this book are intended for classroom use and have several features specific to primary writing: inclusion of art, focus on descriptors rather than numbers, inclusion of behaviors (not just products), and focus on performance over time.

- Assessment looks a little different in each classroom, but some key indicators can help determine whether assessment is working as it should; for example, much of students' work is assessed informally (completion versus a grade), trait language (writers' language) is used by both teacher and students, and assessment is based on a body of work and includes consideration of growth over time.

- Grades can be misleading and can be overvalued as indicators of performance. Unlike criteria on a rubric, they are seldom backed by language that defines meaning. Grades used as rewards encourage students to work for the grade, not for the joy of performing well.

- Given that grades are often a required part of the educational process, we must carefully consider what to base them on. Possibilities include actual performance, completion of work, participation in the writing process, growth as a writer, a willingness to try new things, and a willingness to serve as a writing coach for others.

STUDY GROUP: INTERACTIVE QUESTIONS AND ACTIVITIES

1. **Activity and discussion.** Compare the primary continuums in this chapter with the rubrics developed for use with older students (grades 3 and up) that appear in the appendix of this book. What similarities do you see? Make a list. What differences do you see? Make a list. Discuss what your lists show.

2. **Activity and discussion.** Now, think about how you would determine which (continuums or rubrics) to use for a given student or group of students. What specific factors would influence your decision? Make a list. Certainly grade level is one of the factors. Could there be instances, however, in which the continuums would be more appropriate for students at grade 3 and even beyond? Could there be instances in which the advanced rubrics might be appropriate for use with students in, say, grade 2 or even grade 1? Discuss this.

3. **Discussion.** In what specific ways could continuums or rubrics be misused or misapplied—with an inappropriate target group of students, for example. Write about this or discuss it as a group.

4. **Activity.** Ask each member of your group to select a separate student sample from this book or (preferably) from your own classrooms. Make a case for using the primary continuums or the advanced rubrics in assessing *this particular child's work.* Be prepared to present the writing sample and your reasoning to your study group.

5. **Activity.** Though rubrics, continuums, and checklists are interconnected, each is slightly different. Define each of these assessment tools in writing. Share and discuss definitions with your group.

6. **Activity and discussion.** Whether you are currently teaching or preparing to teach, do you have a clear vision of success for your classroom with respect to writing performance? Write out your vision—as a paragraph, bulleted list, or whatever. If possible, include student samples to illustrate aspects of performance you would look for in your students' work. Be prepared to discuss your vision of success with group members.

7. **Activity and discussion.** If you are currently teaching, rate yourself on how well your students understand your vision of success:

___ Extremely well. They could express it in their own words.

___ Somewhat. They have a general idea what I am looking for.

___ Not well. Grades are a surprise. They often do not know what I expect.

Discuss your ratings with those of other group members. If either of the second two options describes your classroom, discuss specific steps you could take to make your vision more clear to students.

8. **Discussion.** Is your vision of success clear to parents as well? If not, what steps could you take to improve this situation?

9. **Activity and discussion.** Based on your experience in working with primary writers, what are the most important elements to consider in assessing their work? As a group, make a list; then, compare your list with the continuums presented in this chapter. Are the elements you identified well represented? If not, what revisions could you make so that the continuums would better apply to the students you serve? (Be cautious in revising, though, to base your revisions on careful review of *actual student performance.*)

10. **Discussion.** This chapter recommends keeping folders or portfolios of student work so that assessment can be based on a body of work rather than on individual samples of performance. What are the advantages of this practice? What are the roadblocks? How can they be overcome?

11. **Activity and discussion.** What specific practices (prompts versus personal topic selection, time allowed for writing, match with writing process, methods of assessment, etc.) are typical of writing assessment in your classroom or school? Make a list. What practices are typical of writing assessment at your district or state level? Make a list. What similarities or differences do you see? What practices from each could make the other more effective?

12. **Discussion.** This chapter makes an argument that large-scale assessment may not be appropriate for primary students. Do you agree or disagree? Commit your thoughts to paper and/or hold a discussion of this issue with your colleagues. What particular concerns emerge? Are there ways of making large-scale assessment more effective, accurate, and useful—or less threatening to primary students?

13. **Activity and discussion.** On what do you base grades (on writing) in your own classroom? Check all that apply, and try to assign a percentage (or weight) to each factor:

___ Student performance in writing ___ % (of total grade)

___ Participation in writing process ___ %

___ Completion of work, regardless of quality ___ %

___ Improvement over time ___ %

___ Enthusiasm and attitude about writing ___ %

___ Other _____ ___ %

Compare your list with the lists of your colleagues and discuss the benefits or disadvantages of weighting things as you do. Should both process and product be considered in grading students' work? Why or why not?

14. **Activity and discussion.** Assessment specialist Rick Stiggins emphasizes (in *Student-Involved Classroom Assessment*) that stress can dramatically influence student performance. Has this ever happened to you? Create a journal entry about this and/or share your "stress story" with colleagues. Then, as a group, make a list of specific things you can do to minimize students' stress both (1) within your classroom, and (2) in relation to any large-scale assessment with which they may be involved.

15. **Activity and discussion.** It is now a given that large-scale assessments and their results will, to a degree, influence classroom practice. To what extent is this true for you?

___ It has great influence on what and how I teach.

___ It has some influence; however, I continue to teach what I feel is important.

___ It has little or no influence on my teaching.

Compare your response with those of your colleagues. What are the benefits of allowing large-scale assessment to influence teaching practice? What are the risks?

SOURCES CITED

Brodie, Deborah, ed. 1997. *Writing Changes Everything.* New York: St. Martin's Press.

Calkins, Lucy McCormick. 1994. *The Art of Teaching Writing*, rev ed. Portsmouth, NH: Heinemann.

Clare, Penny. Personal interview with second grade teacher and Write Traits Trainer. Lee, NH, October 29, 2006.

Fox, Mem. 1993. *Radical Reflections.* New York: Harcourt Brace.

Gantos, Jack. 1998. _Jack's Black Book._ New York: Farrar, Straus and Giroux.

Hillocks, George, Jr. 2002. _The Testing Trap: How State Writing Assessments Control Learning._ New York: Teachers College Press.

Hutchison, Minnie. Personal interview with a teacher at the Thurgood Marshall School. Newark, DE, April 23, 2002.

National Writing Project and Carl Nagin. 2003. _Because Writing Matters: Improving Student Writing in Our Schools._ San Francisco: John Wiley & Sons, Inc.

Olshansky, Beth. 2006. _Picturing Writing: Fostering Literacy Through Art_ and _Image-Making Within the Writing Process._ Durham: University of New Hampshire. Website: www.picturingwriting.org.

Poch, Bruce. 2006. "Don't Be Bland." _Newsweek_ (August 21–28). August 21, 2006.

Routman, Regie. 2001. _Conversations._ Portsmouth, NH: Heinemann.

Spandel, Vicki. 2005. _Creating Writers Through Six-Trait Writing Assessment and Instruction._ Boston: Allyn & Bacon.

Spandel, Vicki. 2005. _The 9 Rights of Every Writer._ Portsmouth, NH: Heinemann.

Spandel, Vicki. September 2006. "In Defense of Rubrics." _English Journal_, Vol. 96, No. 1.

Steele, Bob. 1998. _Draw Me a Story._ Winnipeg, Manitoba, Canada: Peguis Publishers.

Stiggins, Richard J. 2001. _Student-Involved Classroom Assessment_, 3d edition. Upper Saddle River, NJ: Merrill/Prentice Hall.

Strickland, Kathleen, and James Strickland. 2000. _Making Assessment Elementary._ Portsmouth, NH: Heinemann.

Thomason, Tommy, and Carol York. 2000. _Write on Target: Preparing Young Writers to Succeed on State Writing Achievement Tests._ Norwood, MA: Christopher-Gordon Publishers.

Tucker, Marc, and Judy B. Codding. 1998. "Commentary: Raising Our Standards for the Standards Movement." _Education Week_ (February 18): 56.

Figure 8.15 (sample of student work) from this chapter was inspired by the work of Beth Olshansky: www.picturewriting.org

Making Magic

The golden rule of writing is to write what you care about.

—Jerry Spinelli
As quoted in Laura Benson, "A Writer's Bill of Rights" (2002, p. 17)

If you don't have clear expectations, how can your students know what to aim for? If you don't have the highest expectations, how do you know you're not underestimating what your students can do? If you don't reach for the stars, you might be killing potential.

—Mem Fox
Radical Reflections (1993, p. 165)

Writing is predominantly learned rather than taught.

—Janet Emig
In Tommy Thomason and Carol York, *Write on Target* (2000, p. 1)

Children will remember only a fraction of what they learn in your classroom. However, when you empower them to express their views through writing, they continually will seek out new knowledge and have the tools for lifelong learning.

—Melissa Forney
Dynamite Writing Ideas (1996, p. 6)

HOW DO YOU SEE IT?

hat would a successful writing classroom look like—in your vision of things? Would the room be very neat and orderly—or a little chaotic? Would it be quiet or a bit on the noisy side? What would you be doing? Sitting at a desk, roaming the room, modeling at the overhead or chalk board, curling up in a corner reading aloud to students gathered around you on the floor—or all these things at different times? Would students be at individual desks, in groups, or at tables? Picture your walls. What's on them? Picture your bookshelves or book racks. Do you have a few books? A lot? Is there artwork on display? Does student work mingle with the work of professionals—or do you keep them distinct? If I walked in spontaneously one day, what would I hear? Music? Your voice? A tape of an author reading? Students talking? One student sharing writing?

There are no right answers to these questions, of course. Teachers work in a wide variety of ways, and the magic of teaching is a highly personal thing. One thing is for certain, though: The magic comes from within, from who you are. This is why I begin this chapter by asking you to visualize the environment within which you teach because it is an extension of yourself. The way you arrange your room, where you put your desk (if you have one), how you group students, how you schedule activities, whether your teaching is meticulously planned or pretty spontaneous or a mix of the two—it is all *you*. In *Teaching the Youngest Writers*, Marcia Freeman (1998, p. xvii) talks about some of the things she looks for: among them—an "environment conducive to writing," writer's workshop at a regular time each day so that children expect it, teachers and students (even the youngest) using "writer's vocabulary," targeted lessons designed to teach specific skills, an evaluation process owned and understood by teachers and students, a place to keep portfolios, and parent involvement.

This is a pretty good list. To this I would add just some small things I have noticed in those classrooms in which it seems to be working—by which I mean children are writing and loving it, and children are sensing and seeing their own growth as writers. The first is that student writers' work is celebrated and honored either through portfolios or through displays of some kind. Those displays might include less-than-perfect work; they feature art, voice, ideas—the more personal side of writing. Second, the room is filled with books. Maybe I care about this so much because when I was a young writer, our classrooms held mostly basals, dictionaries, and encyclopedias— and a book you'd read for fun was a treasure.

There is one more thing to keep in mind as you put your own vision for success together: A nurturing writing environment always encourages risk. As Linda Crafton says, "Playing it safe is a dead end when it comes to language and learning" (in Thomason and York, 2000, p. 3). If your students do not feel safe trying new topics and new forms of writing and writing in a way no one else has before, they can still plod along at a functional level. But nothing truly exciting will happen. Comfort with risk has a side benefit, too: "Students whose workshop environment has made them comfortable with risk-taking and comfortable with writing and unafraid of failure have a definite advantage when they sit down to respond to the state's writing prompt" (Thomason and York, 2000, p. 3). Confidence is half the battle.

It's always helpful, I think, to see what other successful teachers of writing are doing to make magic happen in their classrooms. It is impossible, of course, to capture everything in a book. But in these few vignettes I will try to give you a glimpse of successful teaching in some different and highly original forms.

IN JULIE'S CLASSROOM

Julie Towne teaches kindergarten at Jurupa Vista Elementary School, part of the Colton Joint Unified School District, Fontana, California. Her room is set up to promote interaction between teacher and students (with a community meeting area in front) as well as among students (with desks combined into groups of four to six). A writing table holds markers, envelopes, and several types and sizes of paper. The library area holds baskets of books and pillows to make reading inviting. The walls are covered with student-generated work: writing, art, graphs. Only the calendar and alphabet charts are commercially produced materials.

Writing is a way of life for Julie's students, and she works hard to make both audience and purpose consistently clear: "We write interactively about whatever science, social studies, or math subject we are studying. For example, we write expository text about rocks and rabbits, we write a variety of information about our class-generated graphs, we write our rules, we write about the presidents. We also rewrite *The Gingerbread Man* to practice sequencing events. My students have an expectation that we will write *many times* during the day—for many different reasons. And all the writing is re-read, which connects reading and writing right from Day 1."

Julie emphasizes the integration of writing and art, reading aloud from a wide body of literature, sharing simple forms of revision—and use of the six-trait model. She bases a favorite lesson for teaching ideas on an idea inspired by teacher-writer Ralph Fletcher: "The teacher draws a simple picture—such as a tree with a single branch—then discusses with students some ways of giving the picture more detail. While the teacher takes suggestions from the class and adds details to the drawing, she is talking (thinking aloud) about ways the added details in the art help her develop ideas for her writing."

In addition, Julie likes to demonstrate the importance of good organization. "We use characters and settings from familiar stories like *The Three Bears* or *The Gingerbread Man*," she explains. "But instead of starting at the beginning, we may start in the middle—or make the beginning the end. They catch on pretty quickly, and understand that a story needs organization that makes sense." With this lesson, as with the one on details, students are not always writing, but they are talking, conferring, coaching the teacher—and thinking. Julie adds that teaching the traits has improved the quality of her students' writing—largely through her practice of reading aloud frequently from books she loves: "We use so many books as the starting point for discussing what good writing sounds like. I strongly believe it will also help my students in the future because writing terminology like *voice* or *word choice* will be familiar to them."

It is only necessary to observe Julie for a few minutes to know how passionate she is about reading and writing—and how much confidence she has in her student writers. She acknowledges that kindergarten is different, and that one must love it to do it well because K students know the difference. "My students are four and five years old, meaning that they have only lived for a very short time, and were literally crawling and barely speaking a short time ago. They often have miniscule attention spans, and some have little or no oral language because no one has conversed much with them. But I truly have high expectations. The old saying 'You get what you expect' is especially true in education. I want people to understand what I know about Kindergarten: They can *all write* from the first day of school."

IN ARLENE'S CLASSROOM

Arlene Moore, a veteran K–1 teacher from Lincoln Elementary in Mt. Vernon, Washington, tells every child that he or she is a writer right from the first day. Some children do not believe it—at first. Arlene shows them how to make simple writing-like marks on paper and asks them to imitate her. She invites them to write any letters or numbers they know, and she also asks them to create pictures. Many are surprised that this is accepted as a form of writing. But, as Arlene says, "I am interested to see what they *can* do. We build confidence first."

> *This is where we begin—with the belief that all children can write.*
>
> **—Arlene Moore**
>
> In Spandel, *Creating Writers*
> (2005, p. 266)

Like virtually all teachers, Arlene gets some students who do not want to write. As one young writer told her, "I can't write, and I won't." Arlene squatted close to the ground, very near, and whispered, "In this class, everyone writes. We all write. Me, too." His eyes widened. His excitement at having a teacher who would also write eclipsed his own fears, and from that day, he did write. Not much at first, but he wrote.

Arlene writes almost daily with her students, and she asks for their help as coaches. They suggest words, details, beginnings and endings, and titles. As she reads her writing, she listens for their suggestions. During this kind of activity, she is the one making the marks on paper, but they are doing much of the thinking. This prepares them for the personal writing they do, which for many is a word or two, a letter string, or a single sentence. But in their minds, through Arlene's voice and her pen, they compose volumes. Gradually, the words and the sentences on their papers grow, too.

Figure 9.1

"Dog" (K).

The magic in Arlene is easy to spot. She truly loves, *lives* in fact, to hear what her students will write next. She is unfailingly energetic and enthusiastic about their writing. She listens with her whole body, her whole face, her whole being. She responds with her body language, her voice, her expression, and her comments. Her students write because they have an audience who never tires of their writing and who finds wonder in their words, their expressiveness, their willingness to try. Moreover, she is one of them. She is a writer.

Arlene is an ardent believer in teaching trait language to even the youngest students, who, she maintains, pick it up "much faster than we do ourselves." She loves to tell the story of one of her six-year-old students who was listening to her mother read and, totally caught up in the book, turned to her mother and said, "Do you *hear* the voice? Don't you *love* the voice in this book?" No worksheet in the world can take a child to this level of understanding.

Figure 9.2

"Friends" (K).

IN PENNY'S CLASSROOM

Penny Clare is a veteran second grade teacher and writing consultant who effectively, gracefully blends art with writing to maximize students' creativity and expressiveness. The magic in Penny's instructional style comes from her ingenious ability to use art both as a strategy for stimulating thinking and as a complement to writing—an extension of students' writing, really. Penny has been a student of Beth Olshansky, developer of *Picturing Writing: Fostering Literacy Through Art* and *Image-Making Within the Writing Process* at the University of New Hampshire (in Durham). Beth's influence is evident in Penny's approach to writing, which relies on art as a stimulus for thought, and a means of linking thought to language. As Penny's students draw, they begin to visualize, and through that visualization, they expand their sense of meaning and the details that might not otherwise have appeared in their text. As they write, they think of more ways to enrich the art. And so it goes, each form feeding the other.

When she speaks of the importance of students' engaging in art, Penny becomes quite passionate, noting that art is not always given the credibility and respect of text-based writing: "[So many] teachers are not doing [original writing] with their children as much and are doing more prompts. Kids need art to preplan, organize, elicit details, sequence, allow plot to build and unfold, develop confidence, and . . . well, I could go on and on!"

In one of Penny's lessons on Africa (her approach to teaching is consistently thematic), students read and hear about life on the Serengeti Plains and

> *To be a teacher of writing, first and foremost, write. Engage in the journey you ask your students to take every day*
>
> **—Laura Benson,** (2002, p. 24).

Figure 9.3

"Yesterday We Went Tide Pooling." Brian (2)

Brian.

Yesterday we went tide pooling. I cot a crab. when I pickt it up it scuteld on my hand. I fuawnd a shrimp. I trided to catch it but it swam away. After that we had lunch. Then we went to the touch tank. I picked up a sea urchen.

Figure 9.4   "On the Gentle Coast of Africa." Kevin (2)

On the gentle coast of Africa all is quiet. Nothing but the drifting waves is heard. The sun is rising. It looks like a piece of gold is lifting above the turquoise sea. Crabs scurry from their tiny holes.

use their facts and the mental images those readings conjure up to begin drawing. "They begin to understand and picture what animals in that biome look like—prey and predator—and a story between two animals at a waterhole emerges. Based on facts, the child fictionalizes characters and does a storyboard. Not a word has been written, but the story is planned, researched, and bursting to come out!" Art, Penny maintains, results in excitement—students "bursting" to write and to tell stories. "This, I believe, is how social studies and science can be taught well." Writing reinforces understanding of content areas (see Figures 9.3, 9.4, and 9.5); it is the foundation for thinking and making sense of the content. It also gives young writers information to inform their writing. As Melissa Forney notes, "Written communication is the key to self expression and the platform for knowledge. If you teach good writing skills first, those skills will benefit kids in every content area. Teachers who tack writing on last are robbing kids of their most valuable tool" (1996, p. 6).

As Julie, Arlene, and Penny (along with many other teachers) have discovered, all-about and other informational papers, especially those based on personal experience, are easier for many young students to write than are stories. The notion that storytelling is simple is a myth. To create a true plot with characters who face problems or adventures and come out on top (or not) is

Figure 9.5

"On the rockey beche." Kevin (2)

Kevin

On the rockey beche littel smails go uq the salty rocks safe from the crashing waves the crabs skpede undr the rocks looking fore mussels to munch on the sea weed glides in to the tide pod a wave crashed on a rock it lft a small tide pod and a crab it shootted out at lite speed and hid under a rock a bote pasis littel fish moov in the tide pool it gets croudid in the tide pool it beegns to tern into high tide

exceedingly difficult, and unless the story is based on a real-life event, the writing often dissolves into madcap fantasy or a simple listing of events.

Sometimes, when a student is allowed to write "About My Cat" (see Figure 9.6) rather than forcing information into a *story* of the cat, the writing tends to be more fluid, more authentic, and more detailed. Marcia Freeman suggests that most children "love to tell what they know. . . . Their natural mode of writing is informational expository: *I love my dog; This is me; I saw a fish*. What they communicate is information that is important to them" (1998, p. x). She goes on to point out that personal informational writing (based on reading, conversation, and firsthand experience) is the "emergent writer's first and natural mode" and "the easiest and best place to begin

Figure 9.6

> ### "I have a cat." By David (3)
>
> I have a cat. It is realy cute I think. She is really hairy. She sheds all over the couch. That is why I uashuly sit on the other couch. My cat is a girl. Well it is really the familys cat. She is really lazy. She justs moapes around the house like she is a queen. Are cat is really picky. She only eats some sort of food. She wines alout because she wants to go out side or som thing. In the winter it is really bad. She wants to go out side then she wants to come back in because she dosint want to go in the snow. When I am takeing a bath she come in on th side of the tub and I drip water off of my finger and she licks it up. Sometimes she drinks out of the dogs water bowl. The dog chases the cat all around the house. Oh in case your wondering our cats name is Misty. So, the dog uasly trys to pounce on the cat. My cat jumps on a chair so the dog doesint get her. Misty is a lazy cat. In the summer she chases mice and try's to catch birds. One time she was gone for 7 days. We were worried. Are grandfathe searched for her but he coudint find her. One day she came back. We were so glad to see her. She was holding a mouse in her mouth. I bet she did more than that though. That cat wounders me.

writing instruction" (1998, p. 94). This is a concrete form of informational writing, quite unlike a more abstract mode, such as persuasive writing, in which the writer must foresee consequences of particular paths of action and compare this path to that. Such writing demands sophisticated predictions, evaluations, and inferences for which primary students may not be ready (Piaget, in Freeman, 1998, p. 94).

Marcia Freeman also makes the point that it is important to call informational writing (or any writing) by its correct name (1998, p. 95). You can simply call it an informational piece or your piece, your writing, your paper. Do not, however, refer to informational pieces as "stories"—for example, "Bring your story to the author's chair"—unless, of course, the piece *is* a story. This is confusing to students, who often refer to their own writing, regardless of mode, as "my story." Later, this global definition of all writing as stories can prove hard to unteach and can cause student writers to try organizing everything chronologically. It can also make it difficult for many to look at a piece of writing and to state whether it is informational, persuasive, or narrative in form. As one student told me, "If it has the word 'I' in it, it's a story—that's how you know." In fact, stories tell what happened; expository writing gives information. Pronouns have nothing to do with it. Dylan (Figure 9.7) responds to a very confusing prompt (inviting both narrative and description) with a mostly descriptive piece. It is not a story. It is, however, a detailed, visual, and vivid description.

Figure 9.7

"My Favorite Gift." Dylan (2)

> **Writing Prompt**
>
> Think of the best gift you ever received. Tell about receiving that gift. Be sure to include enough detail in your writing so that your reader will understand why the gift was special to you.

My favorite gift I ever got is my teddy bear named Berry. I have had Berry for 6 years. Berry reminds me of when I was a baby. He looks a little funny but I still love him. The color of his fur is brown. I got him from my mom and dad. I put him under the covers of my bed because I have two brothers that might steal him. I also put him in my closet. Sometimes I wrap him around my neck. Berry is very soft and cute. I think Berry is the best bear in the world.

IN LOIS'S CLASSROOM

When I first met Lois Burdett (author of the *Shakespeare Can Be Fun* series), I was struck by the apparent modesty of someone so undeniably talented. Lois has rewritten several of William Shakespeare's plays in rhyming couplets and teaches them to her grade 2–3 class; they act out the plays and write in character about the situations in which they find themselves (see the "Sources Cited" at the end of this chapter for references). Lois's students read and write throughout the day. Lois reads from Shakespeare (her rhyming couplet version, or sometimes the original), from picture books, the newspaper, and letters she receives. When she reads aloud, Lois asks students to listen attentively: "When you read to me, *I* will listen," she promises, "so I ask that *you* listen to me now."

Students write in every subject area. They might list steps for math problem solving or completing a science experiment or jot down "The most important thing I just learned." They write poetry and letters (to visitors, parents, people in the community). They write in character as people within Shakespeare's plays, and write and draw in response to their study of Shakespeare (see Figure 9.8).

Lois routinely asks students to share their work aloud. When one student found this difficult, Lois asked if he might share just with himself in a whispered voice in a quiet corner. He agreed, and then, eventually, could whisper to just one trusted friend from class—then two. Within a month, he was reading in a subdued but normal voice to a small group of three. Lois also writes and shares her writing, modeling what she asks of her students.

Figure 9.8

Response to Shakespeare by Anika and Elly

Shakespeare is like a big piece of chocolate cake. Once you've started, you wish you could go on and on forever, in a nonstopping dream.
Anika
8 yrs. old

During one-to-one conferences, Lois is not afraid to offer specific suggestions on everything from adding detail to putting space between words. She calls her suggestions "writers' secrets," which gives them a positive spin; they're not criticisms, they're pearls of wisdom. "Would you like me to share a writer's secret?" she will ask, and who could resist? "Did you know," she'll go on (in a hushed voice), "that if you put spaces between your words, everything you write is really easy to read? Want to try?" Next time, the secret might involve adding details, using a stronger verb, putting periods after sentences, using quotation marks. Secret by secret, she creates writers.

As I watched Lois confer with her students, it struck me: She was not asking questions in an auto-pilot fashion: *How old were you when. . . . What is your cat's name. . . .* None of that. She was asking questions to which *she really wanted answers: How did you know your hamster was dead? How did you and your dad decide where to bury the cat?* Heartfelt questions produce heartfelt answers, answers with voice.

The real magic, though, I discovered one day as I was watching Lois's children act out the opening scene from Act 4 of *Macbeth*, in which the witches chant "Double, double, toil and trouble; / Fire burn and caldron bubble." Though three "witches" stirred the brew in a huge caldron Lois had brought to class for purposes of this drama, all 22 of her students were participating. They formed two large circles and were weaving their way round the caldron, one circle clockwise, one counterclockwise. "Put on your ugliest witch faces," Lois directed them. "Be fierce." They did, but of course, being second graders, when they looked at one another, they became hysterical and fell in one heap onto the floor, rolling with laughter. I was laughing myself. I couldn't help it. Lois brought us all to attention: "This scene is not supposed to be funny. Let's remember, Macbeth is about to get a message from the witches that spells doom for him. If you laugh, you'll make the audience laugh—and right now we want them a little frightened and full of anticipation, wondering what is going to happen. And by the way, speak up! That man in the last row of the theater can't even hear you." The "witches" shifted their mood. Their faces were more gruesome than ever, but this time, no one laughed. And when they spoke, their voices were clear and audible. These were actors, and they took their work seriously. Later, they wrote with the same intensity.

The magic is in Lois herself. Her love of words, her passion for theater, her uncanny gift to see each child's strength and bring it out, her belief that her students can do what many people would say second graders can't (second graders performing *Macbeth*?), her patience in finding a way for the child who dares do no more than whisper.

IN JUDY'S CLASSROOM

Books dominate Room 12, Judy Mazur's third grade classroom at Buena Vista Elementary School in Walnut Creek, California: "Physically my classroom is arranged with only two things in mind: books and talk. I have *manymanymany* books—to come out during certain studies, to use in Guided Reading, and to read aloud during minilessons. After all, what better model can I be than a person who loves books? I want Room 12 to be the place James Britton described as 'floating on a sea of talk.' "

Judy also has a goal of creating "an atmosphere of thoughtfulness," in which students continually coach one another, and care deeply about their work. "I want each child to feel safe and comfortable and important and valued because only then can we learn and be joyous in our learning. I want students to be proud of their writing, and to share their work with the confidence that classmates will ask respectful questions and offer caring, thoughtful advice."

She is a self-proclaimed traits fan, and the six traits underlie virtually all of her writing instruction. Her students write in many genres. As Figure 9.9 (*The Game*) shows, poetry is a favorite. Among Judy's most successful trait-based activities is one in which she divides each trait into its salient features. For example, ideas might be divided into (1) main idea, (2) details, and (3) focus—or staying with the topic. "I introduce each feature using a picture book as an example," she explains, "with the feature written on a sentence strip that is added to a pocket chart. That chart defines the trait during our entire study. Initially, I model the feature, using the book, but by the end of the lesson, the kids are giving me examples. I wish you could see my third graders when we share our writing, and one child comments on another's writing referring to the chart we've built together and using the language of the traits."

Judy echoes the wish of many teachers when she says, "I am always hoping to have my students write with more voice!" Her strategies: "I use picture books, other published work, and student work as examples. One of my favorite activities was inspired by an earlier edition of *Creating Young Writers*—we compare an encyclopedia entry on basketball to a newspaper article about an actual game. The kids get the point immediately. And later, when I bring in the picture book *Hoops*, they are thrilled with their ability to identify the voice in that writing and connect it to their own."

Like all teachers, Judy continues to face some challenges in teaching writing. Her students are good editors, she confesses—and can handle revision for one trait at a time—but sometimes have difficulty just looking at a piece, with no hints or directions, and determining how it could be improved, especially if the writing is their own! And while Judy professes that she "NEVER [has] students who don't want to write," she also admits that sometimes they have trouble deciding what to write about. "I think it is my job," she says, "to help them see the possibilities. I do this in two ways—a long study of the trait of ideas, and individual conferences—all year—in which I help kids see their lives and thoughts as *writeworthy*."

Her approach must be working. Recently, two former students who had moved out of state came to visit. Their mother had e-mailed

Figure 9.9

"The Game." Conor (3)

ahead saying that what her sons "wanted most" to do on their visit to California was attend Writing Workshop in Ms. Mazur's class. They not only attended, but wrote with the class and shared their pieces. They told Judy, "We just don't have this experience at home." Got to be doing something right, Judy!

MAKING YOUR OWN MAGIC

The magic lies within you, too. As Tommy Thomason tells us, "Some teachers are forever attending seminars and reading books and looking for the secret to writing well and loving it. If they could learn to write better, they reason, they would become writers. The secret keeps eluding them, because it isn't found in seminars or books. Even books about writing. Even this book" (1993, p. 5). I love Tommy's words because they remind us that the real magic does not lie in strategies or steps but within ourselves.

In the end, the greatest gift you can give to your young writers is *you:* Your willingness to "use yourself" as a good actor does when you read—to read with passion and total involvement. Your willingness to write—well or not so well—and to share not only your writing but also the process you are going through to create it, and your revision or even your hopelessness when the words will not come. Your ability to create a classroom community in which it is OK to fail sometimes as long as you never give up, where writing and reading are always encouraged and risk is applauded even when it does not go hand in hand with perfection. Your ability to listen, really listen, with your ears, eyes, whole body, and mind to every student writer who dares to share his or her work. Your energy when you are almost too tired to move, your continual expression of enthusiasm for your students' work so that they will know that they are not playing to an empty house.

> The only job I do, the only promise I make, the sole objective that I have is to guarantee safety.
>
> **—Nancy Slonim Aronie**
> *Writing from the Heart* (1998, p. 122)

The traits give you a language for encouraging your students to think and to speak like writers. In the end, though, the traits are only what you make of them. If you are timid in your teaching, you cannot expect much to happen, no matter how many trait charts you post in your room. I observed a second grade teacher one day who wore the most elegant clothes of anyone in her school. Her hair was neatly coifed, and her makeup was impeccable. She stood tall and straight, with rigid and proper posture, every vertebra in line, feet neatly spaced, hands quiet, and voice muted and refined, reading without overtones or expression, turning the pages with silent precision. I couldn't tell you what the book was. The hum of her soft voice was so hypnotic that she might have been reading a bus schedule and I would not have known. Behind her was a poster on voice, neatly pinned to the wall, framed in colored paper, all the margins even. When she closed the book, she asked the students to define voice, and they did, carefully reciting each bulleted phrase from the poster. "The book we just read," she told them, "was an example of voice." They didn't question this. But I wondered—still wonder—if they equate voice with a low hum, a vaguely sleepy feeling, or flat-out monotony.

Do not be timid. To teach voice, write and speak with voice. Read as if your life depended on it. Laugh, cry, respond. Use the words you want to hear from your students. Be fluent. Share your ideas, and speak and write with detail. When you return home at night, you'll feel good—until you look in the mirror. Your hair will be mussed, you may be missing a button or two, your clothes will be wrinkled, your shoes may be untied (or you may have lost one along the way). You may have lost other personal possessions as well (an earring, your favorite pen, loose change, keys, your lunch, your calendar), and it is likely that the only things you have for sure are a headache, tired legs, a favorite book, and the student papers to which you are clinging tightly. Laugh. Rejoice. This day has been a success. You are teaching with voice—which is to say, with your whole self. You are making magic.

CHAPTER 9 IN A NUTSHELL

- Our classrooms are extensions of ourselves—and reflect the kind of personal "magic" we put into our teaching.
- Each teacher has a slightly different take on what contributes to the magic—safety, sharing, books, liveliness,

opportunities to try what's new, art and music, or whatever.
- As important as the traits are, they are only a tool. In the end, the real magic comes from you—and from the students who teach you.

STUDY GROUP: INTERACTIVE QUESTIONS AND ACTIVITIES

1. **Activity.** Think of a teacher who made magic for you, primary level through college. Who was this person? Write him or her a letter, even if you do not send it. Tell that teacher what he or she did to make the classroom come alive.

2. **Activity and discussion.** What is your vision of a successful classroom? Describe it by making a list of key features. They could be physical features, curriculum components, or qualities of the classroom environment. Share your vision with your colleagues.

3. **Activity and discussion.** In the final chapter of *Radical Reflections*, Mem Fox lists her "Concluding Ideals." These are pledges she would make to herself in order to be the "excellent and effective" teacher she wants to be. What would your personal list of "ideals" look like? Get a copy of Mem's list (1993, pp. 162ff) and read it for inspiration, but do not feel compelled to see yourself in the same way. Make your list as individual as you can; then share your ideals with those of your colleagues.

4. **Activity and discussion.** The "magic" that happens in any classroom often comes as much from the teacher's personal touch as from any strategies or techniques he or she uses. What personal qualities do you bring to your

teaching that can strengthen your students' reading and writing skills? List them. Which of these do you believe most strongly distinguishes your classroom from that of other teachers? Invite one colleague to observe you in your classroom; see if they have additions for your list that you didn't think of (almost certainly they will!).

5. **Activity and discussion.** Magical moments can be hard to capture—but try anyway. Think of a favorite spot in your classroom, a favorite time of day, or a favorite activity. Take a photograph—or draw a sketch. Then create a personal reflection in prose or poetry to go with the moment. Add it to a journal or share it with colleagues—or both.

6. **Activity and discussion.** Plan a poster-making project with your class (or your study group). Remember that traits are best owned by any writer when the writer translates them into his or her own words. You do not need to do all the traits (unless you choose to do so). Pick one or two to begin with, and encourage student writers to express their own thoughts about that trait. Just collect for a time—then choose a few favorites to create a bulleted list. Plan to display or otherwise share the posters you create.

SOURCES CITED

Aronie, Nancy Slonim. 1998. *Writing from the Heart: Tapping the Power of Your Inner Voice*. New York: Hyperion.

Benson, Laura. "A Writer's Bill of Rights." *Colorado Reading Council Journal* 13 (Spring 2002): 17–25.

Burdett, Lois. *Shakespeare Can Be Fun* (series including *Macbeth, Twelfth Night, Romeo and Juliet, The Tempest, Hamlet,* and others). Willowdale, Ontario, Canada: Firefly Books (copyright dates vary according to edition). Website: lburdett@ shakespearecanbefun.com

Forney, Melissa. 1996. *Dynamite Writing Ideas.* Gainesville, FL: Maupin House.

Fox, Mem. 1993. *Radical Reflections.* San Diego, CA: Harcourt Brace.

Freeman, Marcia S. 1998. *Teaching the Youngest Writers.* Gainesville, FL: Maupin House.

Hutchison, Minnie. Personal interview with a teacher at Thurgood Marshall Elementary School. April 23, 2002.

Lane, Barry. 1993. *After THE END.* Portsmouth, NH: Heinemann.

Olshansky, Beth. 2006. *Picturing Writing: Fostering Literacy Through Art* and *Image-Making Within the Writing Process.* Durham, NH: University of New Hampshire. Website: www.picturingwriting.org*

Shakespeare, William. 1998. *Macbeth.* New York: Penguin (first folio edition of the play, 1623).

Spandel, Vicki. 2005. *Creating Writers Through Six-Trait Assessment and Instruction,* 4th ed. Boston: Allyn & Bacon.

Thomason, Tommy. 1993. *More than a Writing Teacher: How to Become a Teacher Who Writes.* Commerce, TX: Bridge Press.

Thomason, Tommy, and Carol York. 2000. *Write on Target: Preparing Young Writers to Succeed on State Writing Achievement Tests.* Norwood, MA: Christopher-Gordon Publishers.

Figures 9.3, 9.4, and 9.5 from this chapter were inspired by the work of Beth Olshansky: www.picturewriting.org

Teacher Six-Point Writing Guide

Ideas

6
- ☐ Clear, focused, compelling—holds reader's attention
- ☐ Striking insight, impressive knowledge of topic
- ☐ Takes reader on a journey of understanding
- ☐ Clear main idea and significant, intriguing details

5
- ☐ Clear and focused
- ☐ Reflects in-depth knowledge of topic
- ☐ Authentic, convincing info from experience/research
- ☐ Clear main idea well supported by details

4
- ☐ Clear and focused more often than not
- ☐ Writer knows topic well enough to write in broad terms
- ☐ Some new info, some common knowledge
- ☐ Main idea can be easily inferred, quality details outweigh generalities

3
- ☐ Clear, focused moments overshadowed by undeveloped, rambling text
- ☐ Writer needs greater knowledge of topic—gaps apparent
- ☐ Mostly common knowledge and best guesses
- ☐ Generalities outweigh quality details

2
- ☐ Writer lacks clear vision—still defining topic
- ☐ Writer struggles with insufficient knowledge—writing is strained
- ☐ Broad unsupported observations, invented details
- ☐ Filler dominates—main idea wanders in and out of focus

1
- ☐ Very foggy—no "land in sight" yet
- ☐ Apparent lack of knowledge or discomfort with topic
- ☐ Hastily assembled notes, random thoughts
- ☐ Bits of info wander in search of a main idea

Organization

6
- ☐ Thoughtful structure guides reader through text like a bright beacon
- ☐ Provocative opening—enlightening, satisfying conclusion
- ☐ Smooth, well-crafted transitions give whole piece cohesion
- ☐ Structure enhances reader's understanding/enjoyment

5
- ☐ Purposeful organization draws attention to key ideas
- ☐ Strong lead—conclusion that provides closure
- ☐ Thoughtful transitions clearly connect ideas
- ☐ Structure helps reader track/process ideas

4
- ☐ Organization works in harmony with ideas
- ☐ Functional lead and conclusion
- ☐ Transitions often suggest connections
- ☐ Structure helpful, but often predictable

3
- ☐ Reader must be attentive—organization loose, or out of synch with ideas
- ☐ Lead and/or conclusion need work
- ☐ Transitions sometimes missing or formulaic
- ☐ Structure relies too much on formula—or necessitates re-reading

2
- ☐ Hard to follow, even with effort
- ☐ Lead and/or conclusion missing or formulaic, minimally helpful
- ☐ Transitions unclear or missing
- ☐ Reader feels lost or feels need to reorder information

1
- ☐ Lights out—path is dark
- ☐ Starts right in (no lead)—just stops (no conclusion)
- ☐ Transitions missing—or points *actually aren't connected*
- ☐ Disjointed collection of thoughts, observations

Voice

6
- ☐ As individual as fingerprints
- ☐ Reader can't wait to share it aloud
- ☐ Uses voice as tool to enhance meaning
- ☐ Passionate, vibrant, electric, compelling

5
- ☐ Original—definitely distinctive
- ☐ A good "read aloud" candidate
- ☐ Voice appealing and well-suited to topic/audience
- ☐ Spontaneous, lively, expressive, enthusiastic

4
- ☐ Sparks of individuality
- ☐ Reader might share a line or two
- ☐ Voice fades at times—but writer still present in the writing
- ☐ Pleasant, sincere, emerging, earnest

3
- ☐ Voice emerges sporadically
- ☐ A "share-aloud" moment—possibly
- ☐ Voice often distant, not always directed to audience
- ☐ Quiet, subdued, restrained, inconsistent

2
- ☐ Writer seems to be in hiding
- ☐ A *hint* of voice—text not ready for sharing
- ☐ Voice faint—OR, not right for audience, purpose
- ☐ Distant, encyclopedic—OR inappropriate for context

1
- ☐ No sense of person behind words—is anyone *home?*
- ☐ Reader feels no invitation to share text aloud
- ☐ No apparent engagement with topic, concern for audience
- ☐ Voice . . . just . . . missing . . .

Word Choice

6
- ☐ Everyday language used in original ways
- ☐ Engaging, hard to put down
- ☐ Every word carries its own weight
- ☐ Powerful, striking verbs, unique phrasing, words to savor
- ☐ Words invoke sensory impressions, create vivid images

5
- ☐ Natural language used well
- ☐ Memorable, noteworthy
- ☐ Concise
- ☐ Strong verbs, clear, appealing phrasing
- ☐ Words appeal to senses, create clear images

4
- ☐ Functional, clear language used correctly
- ☐ Easy to understand
- ☐ Reasonably concise
- ☐ Some strong verbs
- ☐ Strong moments outweigh clichés, over-written or vague text

3
- ☐ Generally clear but imprecise language—"first thoughts"
- ☐ Reader must hunt for a word or phrase to highlight
- ☐ Strong verbs in short supply—modifiers *may be* overworked
- ☐ Overwritten, wordy, or vague text outweighs strong moments

2
- ☐ Tired language, incorrect usage, and/or thesaurus overload
- ☐ Vague, wordy, or obscure—hard to decipher
- ☐ Where are the *verbs?* Where are the *sensory details?*
- ☐ Strong moments rare or missing

1
- ☐ Words chosen at random—something to fill the page
- ☐ Apparent struggle to get words on paper
- ☐ Message buried, language not functional, reader feels bewildered

Sentence Fluency

6
- ☐ Easy to read with inflection that brings out voice
- ☐ Dances along like a lively script
- ☐ Impressive variety in style, length
- ☐ Fragments effective, dialogue authentic/dramatic/performable

5
- ☐ Can be read with expression
- ☐ Easy going rhythm, flow, cadence
- ☐ Noticeable variety in style, length
- ☐ Fragments add emphasis, dialogue authentic

4
- ☐ Natural phrasing—easy to read
- ☐ Rhythmic flow dominates—a few awkward moments
- ☐ Some variety in style, length
- ☐ Fragments not a problem, dialogue natural

3
- ☐ Mechanical but readable
- ☐ Gangly, tangly, never-ending or chop-chop-choppy text
- ☐ Occasional variety in style, length
- ☐ Fragments (if used) do not work, dialogue (if used) a little stiff

2
- ☐ You can read it if you're patient—and you rehearse
- ☐ Run-ons, choppy sentences, non-sentences, other problems
- ☐ Minimal variety in style, length
- ☐ Fragments (if used) are oversights, dialogue (if used) hard to read with expression

1
- ☐ Hard to read, even with effort
- ☐ Missing words, awkward moments, irregular structure
- ☐ Hard to tell where sentences begin
- ☐ Fragments (if used) impair readability, dialogue (if used) does not sound authentic

Conventions

6
- ☐ Only the pickiest editors will spot errors
- ☐ Thoroughly edited—conventions enhance meaning, voice
- ☐ Control over wide range of conventions
- ☐ Enticing layout *(optional)*
- ☐ Virtually ready to publish

5
- ☐ Minor errors that are easily overlooked
- ☐ Edited—conventions support meaning, voice
- ☐ Skill in using numerous conventions
- ☐ Pleasing layout *(optional)*
- ☐ Ready to publish with light touch-ups

4
- ☐ Noticeable errors—message still clear
- ☐ Edited for general readability
- ☐ Control over basics (e.g., caps, end punctuation)
- ☐ Acceptable layout *(optional)*
- ☐ Good once-over needed prior to publication

3
- ☐ Noticeable, distracting errors—may slow reading, affect message
- ☐ Erratic editing—many things missed
- ☐ Problems even with basic conventions
- ☐ More attention to layout needed *(optional)*
- ☐ Thorough, careful editing needed prior to publication

2
- ☐ Frequent, distracting errors make reading slow
- ☐ Minimal editing—if any
- ☐ Numerous errors even on basics
- ☐ Limited attention to layout *(optional)*
- ☐ Line-by-line editing needed prior to publication

1
- ☐ Serious, frequent errors make reading/decoding a real effort
- ☐ Lack of editing leaves even patient readers struggling
- ☐ Errors on basics obscure meaning, put up road blocks
- ☐ No apparent attention to layout *(optional)*
- ☐ Word-by-word editing needed prior to publication